Guide to Madagascar

HAINTENY

The *dingadingana* has borne fruit without coming into leaf,
the *hazotokana* has borne fruit without coming into flower,
and the fishing has been uncertain this year.
Why have these changes occurred, my elder brother?
- Have you forgotten, perhaps, the sayings of our ancestors?
Consider, children, the conditions here on earth:
the trees grow, but not unceasingly,
for if they grew unceasingly, they would reach the sky.
Not only this,
but there is a time for their growing,
a time for their becoming old,
and a time for their breaking.
So it is, too, for man: there is a time for youth,
a time for old age,
a time for good,
a time for evil,
and a time for death.

Guide to
Madagascar

4th edition

Hilary Bradt

BRADT PUBLICATIONS
THE GLOBE PEQUOT PRESS

First edition published in 1988 by Bradt Publications. This edition published by Bradt Publications, 41 Nortoft Road, Chalfont St Peter, Bucks SL9 0LA, England and The Globe Pequot Press, Inc, 6 Business Park Rd, PO Box 833, Old Saybrook, Connecticut 06475-0833, USA.

British Library Cataloguing in Publication data
A catalogue record for this book is available from the British Library
ISBN 1 898323 03 8

Library of Congress Cataloging in Publication data
A catalogue record for this book is available from the Library of Congress
ISBN 1-56440-530-3

The author and publishers have made every effort to ensure the accuracy of the information in this book at the time of going to press. However, they cannot accept any responsibility for any loss, injury or inconvenience resulting from the use of information contained in this guide.

Maps by Hans van Well
Photographs and drawings by Hilary Bradt unless otherwise stated
Cover photos: Front – *Oeonia brauniana* orchid, crowned lemurs, shield bug (Johan Hermans). Back – street kid, Antananarivo (Hilary Bradt)
Typeset from the author's disc by Patti Taylor, London NW10 1JR
Printed and bound in Great Britain by
The Guernsey Press Co. Ltd, Guernsey, Channel Islands

ACKNOWLEDGEMENTS

This guide has evolved from readers' experiences and letters and I owe them a debt of gratitude that can never be repaid. So many people have spent time and effort compiling new information, writing about their experiences, and keeping me up to date with happenings in obscure parts of Madagascar. Some correspondents deserve a special mention: Chris Ballance, who sent 21 pages of evocative and amusing description, parts of which are quoted in the text (including *The Magic Show*), John Kupiec of Rhode Island who travelled most adventurously and provided unique information on seldom-visited parts of the country, and Bishop Brock whose journey by mountain bike gave me insights into this mode of travel. Hilana Steyn inspired me with her enthusiasm despite being shipwrecked (and hosted a wonderful visit to Jersey Zoo), Basia Filzek wrote a long, informative letter from Tanzania, Catherine Price compiled detailed and particularly useful information, as did Derry Edwards. Philip Thomas provided thoughtful comments on the traveller's impact on local communities, and letters from Henk Beentje of Kew Gardens were always a pleasure to read for his amazing adventures while in quest of new species of palm.

I am particularly grateful to readers who wrote in length in English, despite this not being their first language: Herman Snippe and Jolyn Geels (Netherlands) filled an entire exercise book with information, and Marten Mosch gave me lots of hard-to-find facts on the Ambanja area and his travels by 'taxi-brush'. However, the winner of the Best Reader competition (no, it doesn't exist, but perhaps it should) is Luc Selleslagh of Belgium who sent 37 long pages of information, opinion and anecdote, in almost perfect English, and only stopped because he ran out of paper!

Everyone who takes the trouble to write to me, or to meet me in Madagascar, is special. There is never a letter which does not add to my knowledge and understanding of the country. Some of the names below are well-known experts on Madagascar, others are ordinary travellers – and just as valued. Heartfelt thanks to all of you: Leone Badenhorst, Laura Benson, Mervyn Brown, Apolline Bucaille, Stephen Cartledge, Renato Cianfarani, Helen Crowley, Jean-Marie de la Beaujardière, Robin Harris & Glynis Jackson, David Haring, Clare Hawkins, Nick Garbutt, Dean Gibson, Werner Joswig, Philip Jones, Allyson Joye, Judy & Rob MacFarlaine, Jonathan Miller, Raoul Mulder, Solveig Nepstad, Mark Ottaway, Rick Partridge, Nirina Rabarison, Duncan Scobie, Peter Smith, D & G Simpson, Gavin and Val Thomson, Seraphine Tierney, Frederic Viaux, Sheila Watson, Emma Webb, Garth Wellman & Willem Coetzer, Patricia Wright, Linda & Victor Yerrill. My apologies if I have missed anyone out.

Finally there are the three faxers who let me know when things change: Alan Hickling of Antananarivo, Monique Rodriguez of Cortez Travel and Derek Schuurman of Madagaskar Adventures. Derek has been responsible for a sharp rise in my expenditure on fax paper – and a sharp rise in my knowledge of the far reaches of Madagascar. His enthusiasm keeps me going during those long nights at the word processor and he deserves an extra special thank you.

Extracts from *Hainteny* are reproduced by kind permission of the publishers: Associated University Press, London and Toronto.

To everyone: *Misaotra!*

THE AUTHOR

Hilary Bradt has visited Madagascar about fifteen times since her first trip in 1976. She is a tour leader for American, South African and British companies, and lectures, broadcasts and writes on the joys and perils of travelling in Madagascar and other countries.

CONTRIBUTORS

Ian Anderson (*The Music of Madagascar* is the editor of the magazine *Folk Roots* and a regular broadcaster on the subject of folk music.

Richard Byrne (*Nocturnal lemurs*) is a primatologist lecturing at St Andrews University.

Sally Crook (*The Sarimanok expedition*) was the only woman on an 8-crew outrigger canoe which sailed from Indonesia to Madagascar.

Joanna Durbin (*Local people* and *Angonoka project*) works for the WWF and the Jersey Wildlife Preservation Trust in Madagascar.

Ed Fletcher (*Baobabs*) is a specialist in bonsai trees and is probably the only person growing baobabs in Great Britain.

Johan and Clare Hermans (photographs, *Orchids* and *Vanilla*) are award-winning orchid growers with a special interest in Madagascar.

John Jones (photographs) is a professional travel photographer and author of several travel and photographic books.

Gordon and Merlin Munday (*Flora*) are a retired physicist/medical practitioner team with a strong interest in botany.

Jane Wilson (*Health*) is a medical doctor with a degree in biology. She has researched and practised medicine in several tropical countries, writes about travellers' health for *Wanderlust* magazine, and is currently writing a book on this subject.

BRADT PUBLICATIONS

Publishers of specialist guide books to unusual parts of the world, along with hiking/trekking and rail guides, Bradt aims to have the most up-to-date and comprehensive selection of guides to the places other books don't reach, and to give the reader a deeper appreciation and understanding of the landscape, wildlife, and local cultures seen along the way.

TABLE OF CONTENTS

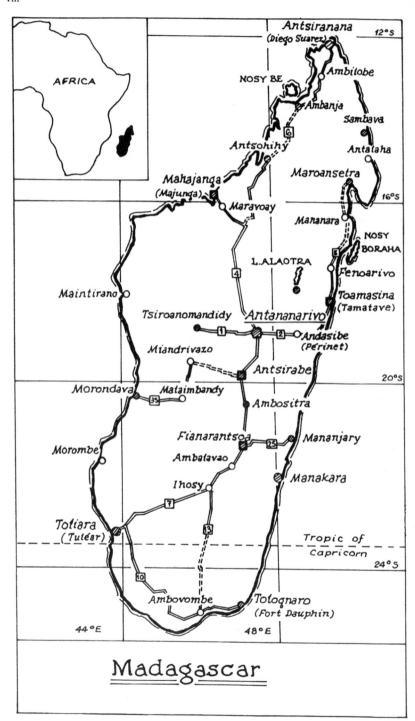

Madagascar

Chapter 1

The Country

PERSPECTIVES ON MADAGASCAR

'[Madagascar is] the chiefest paradise this day upon earth.'

Richard Boothby, 1630

'I could not but endeavour to dissuade others from undergoing the miseries that will follow the persons of such as adventure themselves for Madagascar ... from which place, God divert the residence and adventures of all good men.'

Powle Waldegrave, 1649

As it was in the 17th century, so it is today. Some people love Madagascar, others hate it. If this book helps to dissuade some from making an expensive trip that could leave them bitter and disappointed, I will have done a good job. If I recruit some more Madophiles I shall be happy.

My love affair with Madagascar has lasted 18 years and, like any lover, I tend to be blind to its imperfections and too ready to leap to its defence. I am therefore fortunate to receive so much feedback from travellers both new and experienced, wide-eyed or blasé, to help me appreciate why Madagascar is not for everyone. This is not a holiday island, it is not even a tourist island in that it lacks tangible tourist sights and events. As one disappointed traveller put it: 'I need to be hit in the face with garish temples, outrageous costumes, bizarre practices. I agree toying with Grandad's bones is pretty bizarre but what chance has a tourist like me of seeing a *famadihana*?'

The mid-1990s finds Madagascar in a difficult position. It has a new government which is anxious to encourage tourism and a large number of potential visitors have seen television programmes about the island's natural history or are looking for a new holiday destination. Yet this is one of the poorest countries in the world, climbing out of a period of economic crisis due to the strikes that brought down the previous government, and coping with the aftermath of the worst cyclone for 27 years. It has more pressing things on its mind than keeping tourists happy. And the Malagasy culture is based on respect for the past rather than anticipation of the future.

Despite all this, why does Madagascar continue to work for me? Well, these are a few of my favourite things:

The natural history. I have seen spectacular wildlife in many parts of the world, but nothing to equal the surprises of Madagascar's small-scale marvels, such as the uroplatus, the spiny tenrec, the spiders with their golden webs, the weird and wonderful beetles. Nor have I seen any mammals more endearing than lemurs. For the anthropomorphic, gooey brigade they are winners!

The snorkelling. There are not a great number of good snorkelling places, but the underwater world around Nosy Tanikely (off Nosy Be) is so wonderful I have difficulty not gasping with delight and drowning. The area around Toliara is equally blessed.

The beauty of the Malagasy people. I remember sitting in a bus and gazing at the faces around me as though I was in an art gallery. I never get tired of their infinite variety. That it is combined with smiles and courtesy is an added delight.

The scenery. Always varied, often beautiful; from the air there's the tragic drama of the great red fissures in the overgrazed hillsides like terracotta fingers clawing the soft green landscape, and the emerald green rectangles of rice paddies stacked like tiles up the mountain slopes. From the ground, the granite crags and domes that dominate the road to the south dramatically contrast with the small red-earth villages.

The food. Even the tiniest village or the humblest *hotely* is capable of producing an astounding meal. Even travellers on rock-bottom budgets write to me misty-eyed about some of the meals they ate.

Serendipity. Madagascar's size and former isolationist government has kept it free from many western influences. Wander away from the main tourist places in any town and you are likely to stumble across a market, a street fair, a group of musicians, or a gathering that brings home what we have lost in our culture: the ability to be joyful despite poverty, and a sense of wonder.

Now for the negative aspects, which irritate or depress all visitors, and are the last straw for some:

The towns. Excluding some of those in the highlands, there are few attractive Malagasy towns. All are shabby and some are in an advanced state of decay.

The poverty. Over 1,500 people in Antananarivo live exclusively off rubbish tips and there are many child beggars. Despite the ever-present laughter, seeing such deprivation is profoundly saddening to many visitors. Poverty has led to a rise in street crime against tourists.

Transport. Flights are often delayed or cancelled and other public transport is more crowded and less reliable than in other comparable countries. However fast the roads are improved they deteriorate with equal speed, so the situation is unlikely to change in the short-term.

Let's turn to other travellers for some final words. Some love it...

'I could probably go on for a hundred more pages. In Madagascar each day something special happened to me; these on their own would have made the trip memorable but together they have left me permanently touched by all things Malagasy and constantly daydreaming about the trip. As one person told me: "You can't come to Madagascar just once, you will be back some day."'

'I wish I had the time and the ability to put down on paper exactly what I felt about Madagascar, about how it somehow got under my skin.'

'It was a truly memorable holiday. I don't think a person can be indifferent to Madagascar. It delights and offends, grabs and holds on. We are already planning our next trip.'

'[Nosy Mangabe] was fantastic! We saw so much on this small island that we stayed for three whole days instead of just one. And we will return!'

'Tana is a beautiful place. The light is marvellous, particularly in the late afternoon.'

... and some are not so keen:

'We met people who had successfully travelled around in South America and Central Africa but, like ourselves, they had never encountered such nightmarish problems as we did in Madagascar. The authorities and the tourism infrastructure are totally, but totally, incompetent.'

'Yes, we saw some unusual birds but as for the forest, it was a disappointment... it looks just like our own bushveld... and as for Périnet, well our own Knysna forests are better.'

'Tana and shit are synonymous... I want to tear out the page where you describe this dung-heap as one of the world's most beautiful capitals...'

'My advice is to see Madagascar before the Malagasy finish with it.'

Most independent travellers, however, reflect Stephen Cartledge, who wrote:

'We have travelled quite extensively in Africa and Asia but never quite encountered the problems we had in Madagascar. Emotions can fluctuate between elation at some of the fantastic scenery (at, for example, Isalo) to exasperation at the transport difficulties in getting there. You sometimes want to pick up the country and shake it, demanding that it gets its act together! But for all that, we have found the charm and openness of the Malagasy people, the wonder of the scenery and National Parks, the delights of the small towns in the south simply wonderful. When you leave Madagascar, you leave a country that has touched you with its many problems but one that has also left indelible and lasting memories. Go with an open mind, with plenty of patience and a strong sense of humour. Then you will appreciate Madagascar for what it really is: a remarkable country!'

SOME MALAGASY PROVERBS

Tantely tapa-bata ka ny foko no entiko mameno azy.
This is only half a pot of honey but my heart fills it up.

Aza manontany basy amin' ny Angilisy.
Don't talk to the English about guns.

Mahavoa roa toy ny dakam-boriky.
Hit two things at once like the kick of a donkey.

Tsy midera vady tsy herintaona.
Don't praise your wife before a year.

Ny omby singorana amin' ny tandrony, ary ny olona kosa amin' ny vavany.
Oxen are trapped by their horns and men by their words.

Tondro tokana tsy mahazo hao.
You can't catch a louse with one finger.

Ny alina mitondra fisainana.
The night brings wisdom.

Aza manao herim-boantay.
If you are just a dung beetle don't try to move mountains.

Aza midera harena, fa niter-day.
Do not boast about your wealth if you are a father.

Ny teny toy ny fonosana, ka izay mamono no mamaha.
Words are like a parcel: if you tie lots of knots you will have to undo them.

FACTS AND FIGURES

Location

Madagascar, also known as the Malagasy Republic ('Malagasy' is the correct adjective, not 'Madagascan'), lies some 250 miles (400 kilometres) off the east coast of Africa, south of the equator. It is separated from Africa by the Mozambique channel and is crossed by the Tropic of Capricorn near the southern town of Toliara (Tuléar).

Size

The world's fourth largest island (after Greenland, New Guinea and Borneo), Madagascar is 1,000 miles (1,580 kilometres) long by 350 miles (570 kilometres) at its widest point. Madagascar has an area of 227,760 square miles (590,000 square kilometres), 2½ times the size of Great Britain and a little smaller than Texas.

Topography

A chain of mountains runs like a spine down the east-centre of the island descending sharply to the Indian Ocean, leaving only a narrow coastal plain. These eastern mountain slopes bear the remains of the dense rain forest which once covered all of the eastern section of the island. The western plain is wider and the climate drier, supporting forests of deciduous trees and acres of savanna grassland. Madagascar's highest mountain is Maromokofro (9,450ft - 2,876m), in the north of the island. In the south is the 'spiny forest' also known as the 'spiny desert'.

History

First sighted by Europeans (the Portuguese) in 1500, but there were Arab settlements from about the 9th century. The name Madagascar comes from Marco Polo, who described (from other travellers' imaginative accounts) a land where a giant bird, the Roc, picked up elephants with ease. United under one monarch from the early 19th century, a time of British influence through the London Missionary Society. Became a French colony in 1896 and gained independence in 1960.

Government

From 1975 to the late 1980s the country followed its own brand of Christian-Marxism under President Didier Ratsiraka, though the latter years of the decade saw the emergence of a market-based economy and a multi-party democracy. Ratsiraka was forced to step down in 1991 following nation-wide strikes and demonstrations. President Albert Zafy was elected in 1992 and legislative elections took place in 1993. The Prime Minister is Francisque Ravony.

Population

The people of Madagascar, the Malagasy, are of Afro-Indonesian origin, divided into 18 'tribes' or clans. Other races include Indian/Pakistani, Chinese and European. The population numbers approximately 12 million, half of which are under the age of 15. By the year 2015 the population is expected to have doubled.

Language

The first language is Malagasy, which belongs to the Malayo-Polynesian family of languages. French is widely spoken in towns, and is the language of business. Some English is spoken in the capital and major tourist areas.

Place names

Since independence the Colonial names of some towns have been changed. Many foreigners – and people who deal with foreigners – still use the easier-to-pronounce old names, however. I normally use the Malagasy names (except where there is exceptional resistance to the change) but with the other name in parenthesis so as to avoid confusion: Tolagnaro (Fort Dauphin), Toliara (Tuléar), Andasibe (Périnet), Nosy Boraha (Île Ste Marie), Antsiranana (Diego Suarez), Mahajanga (Majunga). Antananarivo (Tananarive) is often shortened to Tana.

Time

Greenwich Mean Time plus three hours.

Religion

Christianity is the dominant organised religion, with the Catholic church slightly stronger than other denominations. Islam and Hinduism are also practised, mainly by the Asian community, but to the majority of Malagasy their own unique form of ancestor worship is the most important influence in their lives.

Economy

Madagascar withdrew from the French Franc Zone in 1973 and set up its own central bank. After a promising recovery at the end of the 1980s, it suffered badly as a result of the political upheavals of the early 1990s and the foreign debt is currently $770,000,000. Major exports are vanilla, coffee, meat and fish. In the World Bank statistics of 1994, assessing poverty by Gross National Product per head of population, Madagascar came 183rd out of 203 countries.

Literacy

The literacy rate is approximately 40%. 5,000 literacy centres have been established.

Currency

The Malagasy franc (Franc Malgache, fmg). From May 1994 the Franc is floating against hard currencies so these rates are approximate only: £1 = 4,400fmg, $US1 = 3,000fmg, 1FF = 540fmg, 1DM = 1,770fmg.

Climate

A tropical climate with rain falling in the hottest season − coinciding with the northern hemisphere winter. The amount of rainfall varies greatly by region, averaging 140ins (355cm) annually in the wettest area, but only on an average of 51 days of the year (12ins or 30cm) in the arid south-west. It is hot and humid in low-lying areas. Temperatures can drop to freezing in Antananarivo (4,100ft/1,250m) and close to freezing in the extreme south during the coldest month of June.

Flora and fauna

A naturalist's paradise, most of the island's plants and animals are unique to Madagascar and new species and even new genera are being found by each scientific team that goes out there. 80% of the native plants are endemic, all of the mammals (excluding those introduced by man), half of the birds, and well over 90% of the reptiles. The incredible number of unique species is due to the island's early separation from the mainland some 165 million years ago, and to the relatively recent arrival of man (around 2,000 years ago).

HISTORY

Note: A more detailed regional history is given at the beginning of each chapter in Part 2.

The first Europeans
The first Europeans to sight Madagascar were the Portuguese in 1500, although there is evidence of earlier Arab settlements on the coast. There were unsuccessful attempts to establish French and British settlements during the next couple of centuries; these failed due to disease and hostile local people. Hence a remarkably homogeneous and united country was able to develop under its own rulers.

By the early 1700s, the island had become a haven for pirates and slave-traders, who both traded with and fought the local kings who ruled the clans of the east and west coast.

The rise of the Merina Kingdom
The powerful Merina Kingdom was forged by Andrianampoinimerina (be thankful that this was a shortened version of his full name: Andrianampoinimerinandriantsimitoviaminandriampanjaka!). In 1794 he succeeded in conquering and uniting the various highland tribes, helped considerably by the purchase of guns from Britain. In many ways the Merina kingdom at this time parallelled that of the Inca empire in Peru: Andrianampoinimerina was considered to have almost divine powers and his obedient subjects were well provided for; each was given enough land for his family's rice needs, with some left over to pay a rice tribute to the king, and community projects such as the building of irrigation canals were imposed through forced labour (though with bonuses for the most productive worker). The burning of forests was forbidden.

Conquest was always foremost in the monarch's mind, however, and it was his son, King Radama I who fulfilled his father's command to 'Take the sea as frontier to your kingdom'. This king had a friendly relationship with the European powers, particularly Britain, and in 1817 and 1820 Britain signed treaties recognising Madagascar as an independent state.

The London Missionary Society
To further strengthen ties between the two countries, the British Governor of Mauritius, which had recently been siezed from the French, encouraged King Radama I to invite the London Missionary Society to send teachers. In 1818 a small group of Welsh missionaries arrived in Tamatave (now Toamasina). David Jones and Thomas Bevan brought their wives and children, but within a few weeks only Jones remained alive; the others had all died of fever. Jones retreated to Mauritius, but returned to Madagascar in 1820 to devote the rest of his life to its people, along with equally dedicated missionary teachers and artisans. The British influence was

established and a written language introduced for the first time (apart from some ancient arabic texts) using the roman alphabet.

'The wicked queen' and her successors

Radama's widow and successor, Queen Ranavalona I, was determined to rid the land of Christianity and European influence, and reigned long enough (33 years) largely to achieve her aim. These were repressive times for Malagasy as well as foreigners. One way of dealing with people suspected of witchcraft or other evil practices was the 'Ordeal by Tangena'. First the accused was given a large meal of rice, then the *Tangena* nut (a strong emetic) followed by three pieces of chicken skin. If all three pieces were vomited up, the person was deemed innocent; if not, he or she was guilty and put to death.

It was during Queen Ranavalona's reign that an extraordinary Frenchman arrived in Madagascar: Jean Laborde, who, building on the work of the British missionaries, introduced the island to many aspects of Western technology. He remained in the queen's favour until 1857 – much longer than the other Europeans (see Box on page 142).

The queen drove the missionaries out of Madagascar and many Malagasy Christians were martyred. However, the missionaries and European influence returned in greater strength after the Queen's death and in 1869 Christianity became the official religion of the Merina kingdom.

After Queen Ranavalona I came King Radama II, a peace-loving and pro-European monarch, who was assassinated after a two-year reign in 1863. There is a widely-held belief, however, that he survived strangulation with a silk cord (it was taboo to shed royal blood) and lived in hiding in the north-west for many years.

After the death of Radama II, Queen Rasoherina came to the throne, but the monarchy was now in decline and power shifted to the prime minister who shrewdly married the queen. He was overthrown by a brother, Rainilaiarivony, who continued the tradition by marrying three successive queens and exercising all the power. During this period, 1863 - 1896, the monarchs (in title only) were Queen Rasoherina, Queen Ranavalona II and lastly Queen Ranavalona III.

The French conquest

Even during the period of British influence the French maintained a long-standing claim to Madagascar and in 1883 they attacked and occupied the main ports. The Franco-Malagasy War lasted thirty months, and was concluded by a harsh treaty giving France a form of protectorate over Madagascar. Prime Minister Rainilaiarivony, hoping for British support, managed to evade full acceptance of the protectorate but the British government signed away its interest in the Convention of Zanzibar in 1890. The French finally imposed their rule by invasion in 1895. For a year the country was a full protectorate and in 1896 Madagascar became a French colony. A year later Queen Ranavalona III was exiled to Algeria and the monarchy abolished.

The first French Governor-General of Madagascar, Joseph Simon Gallieni, was an able and relatively benign administrator. He set out to break the power of the Merina aristocracy and remove the British influence by banning the teaching of English. French became the official language.

British military training and the two world wars

Britain has played an important part in the military history of Madagascar. During the wars which preceded colonisation British mercenaries trained the Malagasy army to fight the French. The First World War saw 46,000 Malagasy recruited for the allies and over 2,000 killed. In 1942, when Madagascar was under the control of the Vichy French, the British invaded Madagascar to forestall the possibility of the Japanese Navy making use of the great harbour of Diego Suarez. Prior to that, in 1941, Hitler considered the forced deportation of European Jews to Madagascar.

In 1943 Madagascar was handed back to France under a Free French Government. An uprising by the Malagasy against the French in 1947 was bloodily repressed (some 80,000 are said to have been killed) but the spirit of independence lived on and in 1960 the country achieved full independence.

The first 30 years of independence

The first president, Philibert Tsiranana, was pro-French but in 1972 he stepped down in the face of increasing unrest and student demonstrations against French neo-colonialism. An interim government headed by General Ramanantsoa ended France's special position and introduced a more nationalistic foreign and economic policy.

In 1975, after a period of turmoil, a military directorate handed power to a naval officer, Didier Ratsiraka, who had served as Foreign Minister under Ramanantsoa. Ratsiraka established the Second Republic, changing the country's name from the Malagasy Republic to The Democratic Republic of Madagascar. He introduced his own brand of 'Christian-Marxism' and his manifesto, set out in a 'little red book', was approved by referendum. Socialist policies such as the nationalisation of banks followed. Within a few years the economy had collapsed and has remained in severe difficulties ever since. Ratsiraka was nevertheless twice re-elected, though there were claims of ballot rigging and intimidation.

The 1990s

In 1991 a pro-democracy coalition called the Forces Vivres, in which the churches played an important part, organised a remarkable series of strikes and daily demonstrations calling for Ratsiraka's resignation. In August an estimated 500,000 demonstrators marched on the President's Palace. Though unarmed and orderly, they were fired on by the presidential guards and an estimated 100 demonstrators died. This episode further weakened Ratsiraka and at the end of the year he was compelled to relinquish executive power and agree to a referendum which approved a new constitution and fresh elections.

A transitional administration was formed with Professor Albert Zafy, who was Minister of Social Services under Ramanantsoa, at its head and a coalition government with Ratsiraka's nominee Guy Razanamasy as Prime Minister. Elections took place in 1992/93 and were won by Albert Zafy. His Prime Minister is now Francisque Ravony, a lawyer. The Third Republic, born in 1993, has embraced the principles of multi-party democracy and a free-market economy, and wide-spread changes in local government are being discussed.

Further reading
For a complete history of Madagascar read *A History of Madagascar* by Mervyn Brown (see *Bibliography*).

ROBERT DRURY

The most intriguing insight into 18th century Madagascar was provided by Robert Drury, who was shipwrecked off the island in 1701 and spent over 16 years there, much of the time as a slave to the Antandroy or Sakalava chiefs.

Drury was only 15 when his boat foundered off the southern tip of Madagascar (he had been permitted by his father to go to India with trade goods). The shipwreck survivors were treated well by the local king but kept prisoners for reasons of status. After a few days they made a bid for freedom by seizing the king as a hostage and marching east. They were followed by hundreds of warriors who watched for any relaxation in the guard, they were without water for three days as they crossed the burning hot desert, and just as they came in sight of the river Mandrare (having released the hostages) they were attacked and many were speared to death.

For ten years Drury was a slave of the Antandroy royal family. He worked with cattle and eventually was appointed royal butcher, the task of slaughtering a cow for ritual purposes being supposedly that of someone of royal blood — and lighter skin. Drury was a useful substitute. He also acquired a wife.

Wars with the neighbouring Mahafaly gave him the opportunity to escape north across the desert to St Augustine Bay, some 250 miles away. Here he hoped to find a ship to England, but his luck turned and he again became a slave, this time to the Sakalava. When a ship did come in, his master refused to consider selling him to the captain, and Drury's desperate effort to get word to the ship through a message written on a leaf came to nothing when the messenger lost the leaf and substituted another less meaningful one. Two more years of relative freedom followed, and he finally got away in 1717, nearly 17 years after his shipwreck.

Ever quick to put his experience to good use, he later returned to Madagascar as a slave trader!

CLIMATE

Madagascar has a tropical climate divided into rainy and dry seasons. South-west trade winds drop their moisture on the eastern mountain slopes and blow hot and dry in the west. North-west 'monsoon' air currents bring heavy rain in summer, decreasing southward so that the rainfall in Tolagnaro is half that of Toamasina. There are also considerable variations of temperature dictated by altitude and latitude. On the summer solstice of December 22 the sun is directly over the Tropic of Capricorn, and the weather is very warm. Conversely, June is the coolest month.

Average midday temperatures in the dry season are 77°F (25°C) in the highlands and 86°F (30°C) on the coast. These statistics are misleading, however, since in June the night-time temperature can drop to freezing in the highlands and close to freezing in the south, and the hot season is usually tempered by cool breezes on the coast.

The east of Madagascar frequently suffers from cyclones during February and March and these may hit other areas, particularly in the north but also the west. A savage cyclone – or rather series of cyclones – struck in February 1994 leaving about 300 dead and some 500,000 people homeless. Cyclone Geralda tore a 500-mile swathe across the island from close to Toamansina up to Antananarivo.

The chart and map that follow give easy reference to the driest and wettest months and regions.

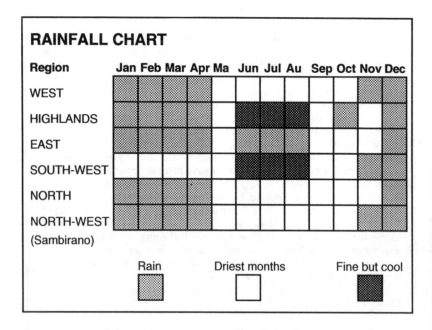

RAINFALL CHART

Region	Jan	Feb	Mar	Apr	Ma	Jun	Jul	Au	Sep	Oct	Nov	Dec
WEST												
HIGHLANDS												
EAST												
SOUTH-WEST												
NORTH												
NORTH-WEST (Sambirano)												

Rain   Driest months   Fine but cool

Climatic regions

West

Rainfall decreases from north to south.
Variation in day/night winter temperatures
increases from north to south.
Average number of dry months: 7 or 8.
Highest average annual rainfall within zone
(major town): Majunga, 152cm.
Lowest: Tulear, 36cm.

Central

Temperatures and rainfall
influenced by altitude. Day/
night temperatures in
Antananarivo vary 14°C. A
few days of rain in October are
known as *pluie des mangues* or
'mango rains' when that fruit is
ripening. The main rainy
season starts end of November.
Average number of dry
months: 7
Highest average annual rainfall
within zone (major town):
Antsirabe, 140cm.
Lowest recorded temperature:
-8°C in Antsirabe

East

In the north and central areas there are no months (or weeks) entirely without
rain, but drier, more settled weather prevails in the south.
Reasonably dry months: May, September, October, November.
Possible months: April, December, January.
Impossible months (torrential rain and cyclones): February, March.
Highest annual rainfall (major town): Maroantsetra 410cm.
Lowest: Fort Dauphin, 152cm.

Southwest

The driest part of Madagascar. The extreme west may receive only 5cm of rain in
a year, with precipitation increasing to around 34cm in the east.

North

This could be included with the East zone were it not for the dry climate of the
Diego Suarez region, which receives only 92cm per year, during a long and fairly
reliable dry season.

North-west (Sambirano)

Dominated by the Massif of Tsaratanana, with Maromokofro the highest mountain,
this region includes the island of Nosy Be and has a micro-climate with frequent
heavy rain alternating with clear skies. Nosy Be gets an average rainfall of 203 cm
a year on 175 days.

THE SARIMANOK EXPEDITION

By Sally Crook

The Sarimanok is a 60 foot double outrigger canoe constructed on the initiative and under the direction of Bob Hobman, a New Zealander, on the Philippine island of Tawi Tawi in the Sulu Sea, near to Borneo.

His intention was to construct a vessel of the kind that would have been used by the ancient Island South-east Asians (linguistically closest to the people of modern Borneo) for their migrations to Madagascar, and to sail it directly across the Indian Ocean rather than following the coasts of India, Arabia and Africa. This safer coastal route is the one championed by most historians. Hobman, impressed by the courage and sailing prowess of modern day Indonesians, wanted to show that a traditional vessel made entirely of wood and bamboo, held together by rattan bindings with no contribution from metal nails, and propelled by wind in palm-weave sails, could weather the open ocean for long enough to reach Madagascar without other landfalls.

The food type, preservation techniques and cooking methods were also to be like those of 2,500 years ago – the era in which he believes the migrations took place, though most consider the first millenium AD a more likely period – and the navigation was to be by readings of the positions of sun and stars.

The 'shakedown' voyage in 1984 from the Philippines to Bali was not performed with all the traditional elements, and an outboard motor had to be used to push against the wind. The voyage was eventful, however, with several stops on the coast of Sulawesi, Borneo and Java for repairs. Then one of the crew, Chico Hansen, died of hepatitis shortly after the port town of Surabaya, Java, was reached. The loss was devastating to the crew, but preparations and improvements to the boat design continued the next year, and on 3rd June 1985 the Sarimanok, now without motor, radio or sextant, set off across the Indian Ocean to be driven to Madagascar by the south-east trade winds.

Apart from a stop on the Cocos (Keeling) Islands to let off a sick member of the crew (which comprised eight men and one woman), the navigator, Bill McGrath, guided the vessel through high seas and unseasonal frequent rain directly to Diego Suarez on the northern tip of Madagascar. (An Argos satellite tracking device confirmed the accuracy of his calculation of the boat's position throughout the voyage to the tracking station in Toulouse, though the information was not accessible to the Sarimanok crew.)

Lack of help to land the unwieldy vessel resulted in the boat sailing on to Mayotte, the French island off the Comores where it was towed ashore. The Sarimanok finally landed at Nosy Be on 5th September 1985 to a warm welcome from the local people who were proud that their history had been relived by this seven week crossing of the Indian Ocean, and that the possibility that their revered ancestors had taken this more difficult and dangerous route had been vindicated.

Sally's account of her voyage was published in 1990 under the title Distant Shores *(see Bibliography).*

Chapter 2

The People

THE MALAGASY PEOPLE TODAY

Origins

Archaeologists believe that the first people arrived in Madagascar from Indonesia/Malaya about 2000 years ago. A journey in a reconstructed boat of those times (see page opposite) has proved that the direct crossing of the Indian Ocean – 6,400 kilometres – was possible, but most experts agree that it is much more likely that the immigrants came in their outrigger canoes via Southern India and East Africa, where they established small Indonesian colonies. The strong African element in the coastal populations probably derived from later migrations from these colonies since their language is also essentially Malayo-Polynesian with only slightly more Bantu-Swahili words than elsewhere in the island. The Merina people of the highlands retain remarkably Indonesian characteristics and may have arrived as recently as 500 - 600 years ago.

Later arrivals, mainly on the east coast, from Arabia and elsewhere in the Indian Ocean were also absorbed into the Malagasy-speaking population while leaving their mark in certain local customs clearly derived from Islam. The two-continent origin of the Malagasy is easily observed, from the highland tribes who most resemble Indonesians, to the African type characterised by the Bara or Makoa in the south. In between are the elements of both races which make the Malagasy so varied and attractive in appearance. Thus there is racial diversity but cultural uniformity.

Beliefs and customs

The Afro-Asian origin of the Malagasy has produced a people with complicated and fascinating customs. Despite the various tribes or clans the country shares a common language and belief in the power of dead ancestors (*razana*). This cult of the dead, far from being a morbid preoccupation, is a celebration of life since the dead ancestors are considered to be potent forces that continue to share in family life. If they are remembered by the living, the Malagasy believe, they thrive in the spirit world and can be relied on to look after their descendants in a host of different ways. These ancestors wield enormous power, their 'wishes' dictating the behaviour of the family or community. Their property is respected, so great-grandfather's field may not be sold or changed to a different crop. Calamities are usually blamed on the anger of *razana*, and a zebu bull may be sacrificed in appeasement. Huge herds of zebu cattle are kept as a 'bank' of potential sacrificial offerings.

The Malagasy believe in one god, *Andriamanitra* (which, interestingly, is also one of their words for silk, the material of shrouds) and creator (*Zanahary*). This probably accounts for their ready acceptance of Christianity which is not at odds with their traditional beliefs – the concept of resurrection is not so far from their veneration of ancestors.

Belief in tradition, in the accumulated wisdom of the ancestors, has shaped the Malagasy culture. Respect for their elders and courtesy to all fellow-humans is part of the tradition. But so is resistance to change.

Fady

The dictates of the razana are obeyed in a complicated network of *fady* or taboos. These vary from family to family and community to community, and even from person to person. Perhaps the eating of pork is *fady*, or the killing of lemurs (most useful for conservation!). In Imerina it is *fady* to hand an egg directly to another person – it must first be put on the ground. Many villages have a *fady* against working in the rice-fields on Tuesdays and Thursdays, or consider it *fady* to dig a grave with a spade that does not have a loose handle since it is dangerous to have too firm a connection between the living and the dead. Other examples of regional *fady* are given in the *Ethnic groups* section, and there is a fascinating book on the subject (see *Bibliography*).

Vintana

Along with *fady* goes an even more complex sense of destiny called *vintana*. Broadly speaking, *vintana* is to do with time – hours of the day, days of the week, etc, and *fady* involves actions or behaviour. Each day has its own *vintana* which makes it good or bad for certain festivals or activities (and helps explain why it often seems so difficult to get things done in Madagascar!). Sunday is God's day; work undertaken will succeed. Monday is a hard day, not a good day for work although projects undertaken (such as building a house) will last; Tuesday is an easy day – too easy for death so no burials take place – but all right for *famadihana* (exhumation) and light work; Wednesday is usually the day for funerals or *famadihana*; Thursday is suitable for weddings and is generally a 'good' day; Friday, *zoma*, is a 'fat' day, set aside for enjoyment but is also the best day for funerals; Saturday, a 'noble' day, suitable for weddings but also for purification.

As an added complication, each day has its own colour. For example Monday is a black day. A black chicken may need to be sacrificed to avoid calamity, dark-coloured food should not be eaten, and people may avoid black objects.

Tody and Tsiny

There is a third force shaping Malagasy morality. In addition to *fady* and *vintana*, there is *tody* and its partner *tsiny*. *Tody* is somewhat similar to the Hindu/Buddhist *kharma*. The word means 'return' or 'retribution' and indicates that for any action there is a reaction. *Tsiny* means 'fault', usually a breach of the rules laid down by the ancestors.

Healers, sorcerers and soothsayers

The Malagasy have a deep knowledge of herbal medicine and all markets display a variety of healing plants and artifacts. In rural places these piles of herbs will be presided over by the *ombiasy* or divine healer. The name derives from *olona-be-hasina* meaning 'person of much virtue' and their power is considered good. They do not just dispense medicinal herbs but evoke the power of the ancestors to help effect a cure. In some areas they are also soothsayers.

Mpamonka are witch doctors with an intimate knowledge of poison and *mpisikidy* are sorcerers who use amulets, stones, and beads (*ody*) for their cures.

Perhaps the most significant person in the lives of rural people is the *mpanandro*, an astrologer or soothsayer who has an intimate understanding of the *vintana* and is thus a highly respected and sometimes feared member of a village. It is he who decrees the most auspicious day and time for family celebrations or major activities such as *famadihana* (see below) or laying the foundations of a new house. He may also be at hand during a *tromba*, a trance-like state, to act as a medium for the ancestors.

After death

Burial, second burial, and 'bone turning' is the focus of Malagasy beliefs and culture. To the Malagasy, death is the most important part of life, when a person abandons his mortal form to become a much more powerful and significant ancestor. Since a tomb is for ever whilst a house is only a temporary dwelling, it follows that tombs should be more solidly constructed than houses. Burial practices differ among the various tribes but whatever method is used, all clans consider the fresh or decomposing body polluted, and must purify themselves with water after contact with it or its possessions. Objects laid on a tomb are there because they are polluted, and in some cases the house of the deceased is burnt down to prevent contamination.

The different tribes vary in the way they show respect for the dead. The southern tribes carve commemorative wooden stelae, often depicting important scenes from the life of the deceased and the tombs themselves are more elaborate and better built than any house in the area. A

HAINTENY

References in this book to the Merina have hithero been focused on their military abilities, but this tribe has a rich and complex spiritual life. Perhaps the shortest route to the soul of any society is through its poetry, and we are fortunate that there is now a book of the traditional Malagasy poetry, *Hainteny*. Broadly speaking, *hainteny* are poems about love: love between parent and child, between man and woman, the love of nature, the appreciation of good versus evil, the acceptance of death. Through the sensitive translations of Leonard Fox, the spiritual and emotional life of the Merina is made available to the reader who cannot fail to be impressed by these remarkable people. As Leonard Fox says: 'On the most basic level, *hainteny* give us an incomparable insight into a society characterised by exceptional refinement and subtlety, deep appreciation of beauty, delight in sensual enjoyment, and profound respect for the spiritual realities of life'.

There are examples of *hainteny* below, and others are scattered throughout this book.

What is the matter, Raivonjaza,
That you remain silent?
Have you been paid or hired and your mouth tied,
That you do not speak with us, who are your parents?
~ I have not been paid or hired
and my mouth has not been tied,
but I am going home to my husband
and am leaving my parents,
my child, and my friends,
so I am distressed,
speaking little.
Here is my child, dear Mother and Father,
If he is stubborn, be strict, but do not beat him;
and if you hit him, do not use a stick.
And do not act as though you do not see him
when he is under your eyes, saying:
"Has this child eaten?"
Do not give him too much,
Do not give him the remains of a meal,
and do not give him what is half-cooked.
for I will be far and will long for him.

Destiny is a chameleon at the top of a tree:
a child simply whistles and it changes colour.
The lake did not want to create mud,
but if the water is stirred, it appears.
There are many trees,
but it is the sugar cane that is sweet.
There are many grasshoppers,
but it is the *ambolo* that has beautiful colours.
There are many people,
but it is in you that my spirit reposes.

prodigious number of zebus will be killed for a rich man's funeral; 50 is not unusual.

In the highlands, among the Merina and Betsileo, exhumation or *famadihana* (pronounced 'famadeean') takes place. The 'turning of the bones' ceremony is a time of great rejoicing, when the remains of a dead relative are wrapped in a fresh shroud (*lamba mena*) and sometimes paraded round the village before being returned to the family tomb. The corpse is treated as though it were alive: spoken to, shown new developments in the town and involved in the feasting.

The occasion for *famadihana* may be because an ancestor died elsewhere and his remains are being returned to the family tomb, or maybe he died shortly after another relative so was buried in a temporary grave (the tomb must not be opened for two years), or the *razana* decreed it was time for an outing, perhaps in a dream. A *famadihana* is a great economic burden on the family concerned. It can cost 4 million francs (the average wage is 50 thousand francs per month).

By law, a *famadihana* may only take place during the dry months (June to September). During this time tourists may get the opportunity to witness one. Some families consider it an honour to have a foreigner present. If you see a *famadihana* taking place during your travels you may ask the village leader, *Président du Fokontany*, if you can be there. The President will ask the head of the family. Almost certainly you will be made welcome and should reciprocate by joining in with the dancing and feasting with the thoroughly inebriated family and guests. It would be impolite to take photographs without involving yourself in some way. This is, after all, a very personal family occasion.

Famadihana is not just the custom of rural or more traditional Malagasy. Jane Wilson was lucky enough to be invited to one on the outskirts of Antananarivo by a sophisticated and devoutly Christian family. She describes it below:

When we arrived it looked as though the party had already been going on for some hours. We were given a drink and told to wait in the courtyard for the exhumation. There was a lot of activity in and around the tomb, and soon a group of six men came out carrying our hostess's great uncle. His bones, dusty and dry, were now contained in a polythene bag, the old *lamba mena* having disintegrated long ago. They brought him to a special shelter, wrapped him in a vastly expensive, beautifully embroidered new white *lamba mena* (mena means red, but the burial shroud is not always red) and laid him in the midst of the guests. Above his body hung a photograph of the man in his youth: with a waxed moustache and in the straw boater and fashionable clothes of the 1920s. The bones of his wife joined him on the little sheltered table and so did those of another relative.

As a Catholic girls school choir began to sing, I studied the incongruous scene. There were around 200 guests, the men in their Sunday best and the women with their long, straight hair plaited into the traditional oval bun. They wore smart European clothes with fine embroidered lambas draped around their shoulders. A priest said some prayers and preached a short sermon before the Protestant girls choir took over, their faces glowing with pleasure as they harmonised.

After the priest and choristers had dispersed our host showed us a room entirely filled with the butchered carcasses of perhaps 30 zebu cattle – there was going to be quite a feast! The bands were setting up their guitars and drums on the temporary stage and soon the room was throbbing with the sounds of rock music and everyone was disco dancing.

Then I noticed that several more bodies were surreptitiously being taken out, quickly whisked around the tomb the required seven times (which makes it harder for death to re-emerge) and returned to their resting places. What was going on? The explanation was that the government taxes these famadihana parties according to the number of bodies turned. Our hosts were officially turning three ancestors and pulling a tax fiddle on the others. Or were they just pulling my leg!'

The beliefs and customs of Madagascar may seem too complicated for the short-term visitor to take in, but we are aware of them at a deeper level. As Leonard Fox, author of *Hainteny* says: 'Although the traditional Malagasy life appears to be bounded by a myriad restrictions and what at first sight seems to be a sort of resigned fatalism, this is actually not the case. By obeying the rules of *fady*, an individual learns self-restraint and keeps the precepts of his ancestors; by acknowledging the forces of *vintana* and their flux, he also acknowledges the existence of cosmic laws that are beyond the power of man to change, regardless of his endowment with free will; in accepting the principle of *tody*, he accepts responsibility for all his acts and their ultimate consequences...

'Whoever has witnessed the silent radiance of those who come to pray... at the house of Andrianampoinimerina in Ambohimanga and has experienced the nobility, modesty and unobsequious courtesy, and balanced wholeness of the poorest Merina who has remained faithful to his heritage can have no doubt as to the deep integrative value of the Malagasy spiritual tradition.'

Malagasy society

The Malagasy have a strong sense of community which influences their way of life. Just as the ancestors are laid in a communal tomb, so their descendants share a communal way of life, and even children are almost considered common property within their extended family. Children are seldom disciplined but learn by example from the many members of their extended families.

Malagasy society is a structured hierarchy with two fundamental rules: respect for the other person and knowing one's place. Within a village, the community is based on the traditional *fokonolona*. This concept was introduced by King Andrianampoinimerina when these councils of village elders were given responsibility for, among other things, law and order and the collection of taxes. Day to day decisions are still made by the *fokonolona*.

Part of the Malagasy culture is the art of oratory, *kabary*. Originally *kabary* were the huge meetings where King Andrianampoinimerina proclaimed his plans, but the word has now evolved to mean the elaborate form of speech used to inspire and control the crowds at such gatherings. Even rural leaders can speak for hours, using highly ornate language and many proverbs; a necessary skill in a society that reached a high degree of sophistication without a written language.

Rural Malagasy houses generally have only one room and the furniture is composed of mats, *tsihy*, often beautifully woven. These are used for sitting and sleeping, and sometimes food is served on them. There are often *fady* attached to *tsihy*. For example you should not step over a mat, particularly one on which meals are eaten.

ETHNIC GROUPS

This section is mainly taken from A Glance at Madagascar *by kind permission of the author.*

The Malagasy form one nation with one basic culture and language (though with many dialects), but there are eighteen different 'tribes' or clans officially recognised by the government. This division is based more upon old kingdoms than upon ethnic grouping. These tribes are listed individually below.

Antaifasy (People-of-the-sands)
Living in the south-east around Farafangana they cultivate rice, and fish in the lakes and rivers. Divided into three clans each with its own 'king' they generally have stricter moral codes than other tribes. They have large collective burial houses known as *kibory*, built of wood or stone and generally hidden in the forest away from the village.

Antaimoro (People-of-the-coast)
These are among the most recent arrivals and live in the south-east around Vohipeno and Manakara. They guard Islam tradition and Arab influence and still use a form of Arab writing known as *sorabe*. They use verses of the Koran as amulets.

Antaisaka
Centred south of Farafangana on the south-east coast but now fairly widely spread throughout the island, they are an off-shoot of the Sakalava tribe. They cultivate coffee, bananas and rice — but only the women harvest the rice. There are strong marriage taboos amongst them. Often the houses may have a second door on the east side which is only used for taking out a corpse. They use the *kibory*, communal burial house, the corpse usually being dried out for two or three years before finally being put there.

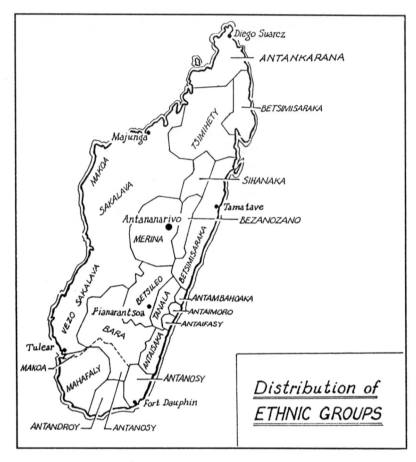

Distribution of ETHNIC GROUPS

Antankarana (Those-of-the-rocks)

Living in the north around Diego-Suarez they are fishers or cattle raisers whose rulers came from the Sakalava dynasty. Their houses are usually raised on stilts. Numerous *fady* exist amongst them governing relations between the sexes in the family; for example a girl may not wash her brother's clothes. The legs of a fowl are the father's portion, whereas amongst the Merina, for instance, they are given to the children.

Antambahoaka (Those-of-the-people)

The smallest tribe, of the same origin as the Antaimoro and living around Mananjary on the south-east coast. They have some Arab traits and amulets are used. They bury in a *kibory*. Group circumcision ceremonies are carried out every seven years.

Antandroy (People-of-the-thorns)

Traditionally nomadic, they live in the arid south around Ambovombe. A dark-skinned people, they wear little clothing and are said to be frank and open, easily roused to either joy or anger. Their women occupy an inferior position. The villages are often surrounded by a hedge of cactus plants. They do not eat much rice but subsist mostly on millet, maize and cassava. They believe in the *kokolampo*, a spirit of either good or bad influence. Their tombs are similar to those of the Mahafaly tribe. Sometimes it is *fady* among them for a child to say his father's name, or to refer by name to parts of his father's body. Thus he may say *ny fandiany* (the-what-he-moves-with) for his feet, and *ny amboniny* (the-top-of-him) for his head.

Antanosy (People-of-the-island)
The island is a small one in the Fanjahira river. They live in the south-east principally around Taolagnaro. Their social structure is based on clans with a 'king' holding great authority over each clan. There are strict *fady* governing relationships in the family. For example, a brother may not sit on or step over his sister's mat. As with many other tribes there are numerous *fady* regarding pregnancy: a pregnant woman should not sit in the doorway of the house; she should not eat brains; she should not converse with men; people who have no children should not stay in her house overnight. Other *fady* are that relatives should not eat meat at a funeral and the diggers opening a tomb should not wear clothes. When digging holes for the corner posts of a new house it may be *fady* to stand up so the job must be performed sitting down.

Bara
Originally in the south-west near Toliara, these nomadic cattle raisers now live in the south-central area around Ihosy and Betroka. Their name has no special meaning but it is reputed to derive from an African (Bantu) word. They may be polygamous and women occupy an inferior position in their society. They attach importance to the *fatidra* or 'blood pact'. Cattle stealing is regarded as proof of manhood and courage, without which a man cannot expect to get a wife. They are dancers and sculptors, a unique feature of their carved wooden figures being eyelashes of real hair set into the wood. They believe in the *helo*, a spirit that manifests itself at the foot of trees. In the past a whole village would move after somebody dies owing to the fear of ghosts. They use caves in the mountains for burial. It is the custom to shave the head on the death of a near relative.

Betsileo (The-many-invincibles)
They are centred in the south of the *Hauts Plateaux* around Fianarantsoa but about 150,000 of them also live in the Betsiboka region. They are energetic and expert rice-producers, their irrigated, terraced rice-fields being a feature of the landscape. *Famadihana* was introduced to their culture by the Merina at the time of Queen Ranavalona I. It is *fady* for the husband of a pregnant woman to wear a lamba thrown over his shoulder. It may be *fady* for the family to eat until the father is present or for anyone to pick up his fork until the most honourable person present has started to eat.

Betsimisaraka (The-many-inseparables)
They are the second largest tribe and live on the east coast in the Toamasina - Antalaha region. Their culture has been influenced by Europeans, particularly pirates. They cultivate rice and work on vanilla plantations. Their clothes are sometimes made from locally woven raffia. Originally their society included numerous local chiefs but they are not now important. The *tangalamena* is the local official for religious rites and customs. The Betsimisaraka have many superstitious

beliefs: *angatra*, ghosts, *zazavavy an-drano*, mermaids, and *kalamoro*, little wild men of the woods, about 25 inches high with long flowing hair, who like to slip into houses and steal rice from the cooking pot. In the north coffins are generally placed under a shelter, in the south in tombs. It may be *fady* for a brother to shake hands with his sister, or for a young man to wear shoes while his father is still living.

Bezanozano (Many-small-plaits)

The name refers to the way in which they do their hair. They were probably one of the first tribes to become established in Madagascar, and live in an area between the Betsimisaraka lowlands and the Merina highlands. Like the Merina, they practise *famadihana*. As with most of the coastal tribes their funeral celebrations involve the consumption of considerable quantities of *toaka*, rum.

Mahafaly (Those-who-make-taboos or Those-who-make-happy)

The etymology of the word is sometimes disputed but the former meaning is generally regarded as being correct. They probably arrived around the 12th century, and live in the south-west desert area around Ampanihy and Ejeda. They are farmers, with maize, sorgho and sweet potatoes as their chief crops; cattle rearing occupies a secondary place. They kept their independence under their own local chiefs until the French occupation and still keep the bones of some of their old chiefs — this is the *jiny* cult. Their villages usually have a sacrificial post, the *hazo manga*, on the east of the village where sacrifices are made. Some of the blood is generally put on the foreheads of the people attending.

The tombs of the Mahafaly attract a great deal of interest. They are big rectangular constructions of uncut stone rising some three feet above the ground and decorated with *aloalo* and the horns of the cattle slain at the funeral feast. The tomb of the Mahafaly king Tsiampody has the horns of 700 zebu on it. The *aloalo* are sculpted wooden posts set upright on the tomb, often depicting scenes from the person's life. The burial customs include waiting for the decomposition of the body before it is placed in the tomb. It is the practice for a person to be given a new name after death — generally beginning with 'Andria'.

The divorce rate is very high and it is not at all uncommon for a man to divorce and remarry six or seven times. It is very often *fady* for children to sleep in the same house as their parents. Their *rombo* (very similar to the *tromba* of the Sakalava) is the practice of contacting various spirits for healing purposes. Amongst the spirits believed in are the *raza* who are not real ancestors and in some cases are even supposed to include *vazaha* (white foreigners), and the *vorom-be* which is the spirit of a big bird.

Makoa/Mikea

Originally spread along the north-west region, many have moved south to the area of the Onilahy river and between Morombe and Toliara. They live in the forest, rather than by the sea, and are descended from African slaves. Racially they rememble Africans and are said to be the most primitive tribe in Madagascar.

Merina (People-of-the-Highlands)

They live on the *Hauts Plateaux*, the most developed area of the country, the capital being 95% Merina. They are of Malayo-Polynesian origin and vary in colour from ivory to very dark, with straight hair. They used to be divided into three castes: the

The children of Madagascar (bottom photograph by Steven Garren)

Mud-fishing in the Anjozorobe (Highlands) area. (John R. Jones)

Famadihana ("turning of the bones"). (John R. Jones)

Masikoro tomb painting near Toliara. Every picture tells a story!

Zebu

Zebu cow and herder. (John R. Jones)

Portable road warning. (John R. Jones)

Aloalo, Mahafaly country. (John R. Jones)

Andriana (nobles), the *Hova* (free-men) and the *Andevo* (serfs), but legally these divisions no longer exist. Most Merina houses are built of brick or mud; some are two storey buildings with slender pillars, where the people live mostly upstairs. Most villages of any size have a church – probably two, Catholic and Protestant. There is much irrigated rice cultivation, and the Merina were the first tribe to have any skill in architecture and metallurgy. The *famadihana* is essentially a Merina custom.

Sakalava (People-of-the-long-valleys)
They live in the west between Tulear and Majunga and are dark skinned with Polynesian features and short curly hair. They were at one time the largest and most powerful tribe, though disunited, and were ruled by their own kings and queens. Certain royal relics remain – sometimes being kept in the north-east corner of a house. The Sakalava are cattle raisers, and riches are reckoned by the number of cattle owned. There is a record of human sacrifice amongst them up to the year 1850 at some special occasion such as the death of a king. The *tromba* (trance state) is quite common. It is *fady* for pregnant women to eat fish or to sit in a doorway. Women hold a more important place amongst them than in most other tribes.

Sihanaka (People-of-the-swamps)
Their home is the north-east of the old kingdom of Imerina around Lake Alaotra and they have much in common with the Merina. They are fishers, rice growers and poultry raisers. Swamps have been drained to make vast rice-fields cultivated with modern machinery and methods. They have a special rotation of *fady* days.

Tanala (People-of-the-forest)
These are traditionally forest-dwellers, living inland from Manakara, and are rice and coffee growers. Their houses are usually built on stilts. They were the most recent tribe to arrive – about 250 years ago. The Tanala are divided into two groups: the Ikongo in the south and the Menabe in the north. The Ikongo are an independent people and never submitted to Merina domination, in contrast to the Menabe. Burial customs include keeping the corpse for up to a month. Coffins are made from large trees to which sacrifices are sometimes made when they are cut down. The Ikongo usually bury their dead in the forest and may mark a tree to show the spot.

Tsimihety (Those-who-do-not-cut-their-hair)
The refusal to cut their hair (to show mourning on the death of a Sakalava king) was to demonstrate their independence. They are an energetic and vigorous people in the north-central area and are spreading west. The oldest maternal uncle occupies an important position.

These are the 18 officially recognised tribes. Other groups include:

Vezo
These fishing people are not generally recognised as a separate tribe but as a clan of the Sakalava. They live on the coast in the region of Morondava in the west to Faux Cap in the south. They use little out-rigger canoes hollowed out from tree trunks and fitted with one outrigger pole and a small rectangular sail. In these frail but stable craft they go far out to sea. The Vezo are also noted for their tombs, which are graves dug into the ground surrounded by wooden palisades, the main

posts of which are crowned by wooden carved figures of the most erotic kind. No effort is made to keep them in repair as it is only when the palisades finally fall into decay and ruin that the soul of the dead is fully released.

Zafimaniry

A clan of about 15,000 distributed in about 100 villages in the forests between the Betsileo and Tanala areas south-east of Ambositra. They are known for their wood carvings and sculpture, and are descended from people from the *Hauts Plateaux* who established themselves there early in the 19th century. The Zafimaniry are thus interesting to historians as they continue the forms of housing and decoration of past centuries. Their houses, which are made from vegetable fibres and wood with bamboo walls and roofs, have no nails and can be taken down and moved from one village to another.

St Marians

The population of Île Ste Marie (Nosy Boraha) is mixed. Although Indonesian in origin there has been influence from both Arabs and European pirates of different nationalities.

In the last few years there have been several anthropological books published in English about the people of Madagascar. See *Bibliography*.

The tribes may differ but a Malagasy proverb shows their feeling of unity: *Ny olombelona toy ny molo-bilany, ka iray mihodidina ihany*; 'Men are like the lip of the cooking pot which forms just one circle.'

THE VAZIMBA

Vazimba is the name given to the earliest inhabitants of Madagascar, especially in the centre, who were displaced or absorbed by later immigrants. Once thought to be pre-Indonesian aboriginals from Africa, it is now generally accepted that they were survivors of the earliest Malayo-Polynesian immigrants who were pushed inland by later arrivals.

Vazimba come into both legends and history of the Malagasy. Vazimba tombs are now places of pilgrimage where sacrifaces are made for favours and cures. It is *fady* to step over such a tomb. Vazimba are also thought to haunt certain springs and rocks, and offerings may be made here. They are the ancestral guardians of the soil.

LANGUAGE

The Indonesian origin of the Malagasy people shows strongly in their language which is spoken, with regional variations of dialect, throughout the island. (Words for domestic animals, however, are derived from Kiswahili, indicating that the early settlers, sensibly enough, did not bring animals with them in their outrigger canoes.) Malagasy is a remarkably rich language, full of images, metaphors and proverbs. Literal translations of Malagasy words and phrases are often very poetic. 'Dusk' is *Maizimbava vilany*, 'Darken the mouth of the cooking pot'; two or three in the morning is *Misafo helika ny kary*, 'When the wild cat washes itself'. The richness of the language means that there are few English words that can be translated to a single word in Malagasy, and vice versa. An example given by Leonard Fox in his book *Hainteny* is *miala mandry*; *miala* means 'go out/go away' and *mandry* means 'lie down/go to sleep'. Together, however, they mean 'to spend the night away from home, and yet be back in the early morning as if never having been away'! No wonder there is no practical Malagasy/English dictionary for travellers!

There is, however, an excellent casette and accompanying phrase book which will enable you to learn the rudiments of the language without becoming overwhelmed by its complexities: *Malagasy Basics* by Rasoanaivo Hanitrarivo. The author is better known as Hanitra Anderson, the leader of Tarika, the internationally known group of Malagasy musicians. *Malagasy Basics* is available from Bradt Publications or from FMS in London (tel: 081 348 6297).

Learning, or even using, the Malagasy language may seem a challenging prospect to the first time visitor. Place names may be 15 characters long (because they usually have a literal meaning, such as Ranomafana: Hot water), with erratic syllables stress. However, as a courtesy to the Malagasy people you should learn a few Malagasy words and phrases rather than trying to communicate in the language of their former colonial rulers.

Some basic rules
Pronunciation
The Malagasy alphabet is made up of 21 letters. C, Q, U, W, and X are omitted. Individual letters are pronounced as follow:

a: as in Father
e: as in the a in Late
g: as in Get
h: almost silent
i: as ee in Seen
j: pronounced dz
o: oo as in Too

s: usually midway between sh and s but varies according to region
z: as in Zoo.

Combinations of letters needing different pronunciations are:

ai: like y in My
ao: like ow in Cow
eo: pronounced ay-oo

When k or g are preceded by i or y this vowel is also sounded *after* the consonant. For example *Alika* (dog) is pronounced Aleekya, and *Ary koa* (and also) is pronounced Ahreekewa.

Stressed syllables

Some syllables are stressed, others almost eliminated. This causes great problems with visitors trying to pronounce place names, and unfortunately – like English – the basic rules are frequently broken. Generally, the stress is on the penultimate syllable except in words ending in na, ka, and tra when it is generally on the last syllable but two. Words ending in e stress that vowel. Occasionally a word with the same spelling changes its meaning according to the stressed syllable, but in this case it is written with an accent. For example, Tanana means Hand, and Tanána means Town.

When a word ends in a vowel, this final syllable is pronounced so lightly it is often just a stressed last consonant. For instance the Sifaka lemur is pronounced 'She-fak'. Words derived from English, like *Hotely* and *Banky* are pronounced much the same as in English.

Getting started

The easiest way to begin to get a grip on Malagasy is to build on your knowledge of place names (you *have* to learn how to pronounce these in order to get around) and to this end I have given the phonetic pronunciation in the text. As previously noted, most place names mean something so you only have to learn these meanings and – hey presto – you have the elements of the language! Here are some bits of place names:

An-, Am-, I-: at, the place where
Arivo: thousand
Be: big, plenty of
Fotsy, -potsy: white
Kely: small
Kily: tamarind
Mafana: hot
Maha: which causes
Mainti: black

Maintso: green
Manga: blue
Maro: many
Nosy: island
Rano, -drano: water
Tany, tani-: land
Vato, -bato: stone
Vohitra, vohi-, bohi-: hill

Vocabulary

ENGLISH	MALAGASY	PHONETIC PRONUNCIATION

Social phrases

Stressed letters or phrases are underlined.

Hello	*Manao ahoana*	*Mano own*
Hello (north & east coast)	*Mbola tsara*	*M'boola tsara*
What news?	*Inona no vaovao?*	*Inan vowvow?*
No news	*Tsy misy*	*Tsimeess*

These three easy to learn phrases of ritualised greetings establish contact with people you pass on the road or meet in their village. For extra courtesy (important in Madagascar) add *tompoko* (pronounced 'toomp'k') at the end of each phrase.

Simple phrases for 'conversation' include:

What's your name?	*Iza no anaranao?*	*Eeza nanaranow?*
My name is	*Ny anarako*	*Ny anarako*
Goodbye	*Veloma*	*Veloom*
See you again	*Mandra pihaona*	*Mandra pioon*
I don't understand	*Tsy azoko*	*Tsi azook*
Very good	*Tsara tokoa*	*Tsara t'koo*
Bad	*Ratsy*	*Rats*
Please/Excuse me	*Aza fady*	*Azafad*
Thank you	*Misaotra*	*Misowtr*
Pardon me (ie may I pass)	*Ombay lalana*	*m'buy lalan*
Let's go	*Andao andeha*	*Andow anday*
Crazy	*Adaladala*	*Adaladal*
Long life! (Cheers!)	*Ho ela velona!*	*Wellavell!*

If you are pestered by beggars try:

I have nothing (there is none)	*Tsy misy*	*tsimiss*
Go away!	*Mandehana!*	*Man day han*

Note: the words for yes (*eny*) and no (*tsia*) are hardly ever used in conversation. The Malagasy tend to say 'yoh' for yes and 'ah' for no, along with appropriate gestures.

Market phrases

How much?	*Ohatrinona?*	*Ohtreen?*
Too expensive!	*Lafo be!*	*Laff be!*
No way!	*Tsy lasa!*	*Tsee lass!*

Basic needs

Where is...?	*Aiza...?*	*Ize...?*
Is is far?	*Lavitra ve izany?*	*Lavtra vayzan?*
Is there any...?	*Misy ve...?*	*Mees ve...?*
I want...	*Mila ... aho*	*Meel ... a*
I'm looking for...	*Mitady ... aho*	*M'tadi ... a*
Is there a place to sleep	*Misy toerana hatoriana ve?*	*Mees too ayran atureen vay?*
Is it ready?	*Vita ve?*	*Veeta vay?*
I would like to buy some food	*Te hividy sakafo aho*	*Tayveed sakaff*
I'm hungry	*Noana aho*	*Noonah*
I'm thirsty	*Mangetaheta aho*	*Mangataytah*
I'm tired	*Vizaka aho*	*Veesacar*
Please help me!	*Mba ampio aho!*	*Bampeewha!*

Useful words

Village	*Vohitra*	*Voo-itra*
House	*Trano*	*tran*
Food/meal	*Hanina/sakafo*	*An/sakaff*
Water	*Rano*	*Rahn*
Rice	*Vary*	*Var*
Eggs	*Atody*	*Atood*
Chicken	*Akoho*	*Aku*
Bread	*Mofo*	*Moof*
Milk	*Ronono*	*Roonoon*
Road	*Lalana*	*Lalan*
Town	*Tanana*	*Tanan*
River (large)	*Ony*	*Oon*
River (small)	*Riaka*	*Reek*
Ox/cow	*Omby/omby vavy*	*Oomby/omb varve*
Child/baby	*Ankizy/zaza kely*	*Ankeeze/zaza kail*
Man/woman	*Lehilahy/vehivavy*	*Layla/vayvarve*

'The mercies of God [be bestowed on] this people, whose simplicity hath herein made them more happy than our too dear- bought knowledge hath advantaged us'.   Walter Hamond, 1640

Chapter 3

Natural History

INTRODUCTION

For most people it is the flora and fauna that draws them to Madagascar. This is 'nature's laboratory', where evolution took a different route.

The reason so many unique species evolved in Madagascar goes back to the dawn of history. It is thought that in the early Cretaceous era a huge land mass known as Gondwanaland began to break up and form the present continents of Africa and Madagascar, Asia, South America and Australasia. The phenomenon of continental drift explains why some Malagasy plants and animals are found in South America and Asia but not Africa. The boa constrictor, for instance, occurs only in South America and Madagascar and the urania moth and six plant families are also limited to these two places.

Madagascar broke away from Africa as much as 165 million years ago, during the time of the dinosaurs. It is thought to have reached its present position about 120 million years ago. No one knows what reptiles and other early forms of life were the original inhabitants but mammals had yet to evolve, so the lemurs, tenrecs and other unique families most probably arrived on rafts of vegetation. Not many made it – there are now only 108 mammal species in Madagascar.

Once established there was little need for evolutionary change since there were no large carnivores to threaten their existence and the thickly forested island provided food without competition. Thus the term 'living fossil' is appropriate here.

Man arrived some 2,000 years ago. Only 1,000 years later nearly two dozen species of fauna were extinct. 14 of these were lemurs, some the size of gorillas, hanging from the trees like sloths or browsing on the forest floor. There were dwarf hippos, tortoises larger than any known today, and the *aepyornis* or elephant bird, which stood ten feet high. Man was probably responsible for the extinction of these animals through hunting and destruction of habitat.

Madagascar has an amazing percentage of unique species: it is said that of the 200,000 living things so far identified there, 150,000 are found

GONDWANALAND AND THE FIT OF THE SOUTHERN CONTINENTS

The rukh (roc), as visualised by an artist in 1595.

nowhere else. Of the world's 400 flowering plant families, 200 grow only here. There are eight species of baobab (as against one in Africa), and as for palms... In the last edition I wrote that there were 135 palm species. Now, after the Palms of Madagascar Project (organised by the Royal Botanic Gardens at Kew and funded by McDonald's Hamburgers) we can add three new genera and 70 new species! This is the astonishing thing about Madagascar. Any scientific expedition that goes out there finds scores of new species and many discover a new genus. So the following statistics: 450 species of frog, 235 reptiles and so on will already be out of date. In short, whatever species you are observing in Madagascar, you are unlikely to have seen it elsewhere.

GEOLOGY

The main geological features of Madagascar are a precambrian crystalline basement (eastern two thirds of the island) overlaid with laterite, a sedimentary region in the south and west (Jurassic, Cretaceous, and Tertiary) and volcanic outcrops. The Ankaratra mountains near Antananarivo are of volcanic origin. There are no active volcanoes but in the highlands there are many hot springs, craters and ashcones.

Millions of years of weathering have produced the smooth granite mountains of the southern highlands, the eroded sandstone shapes of Isalo, in the south-west, and the extraordinary spikes of the *tsingy* or limestone karst.

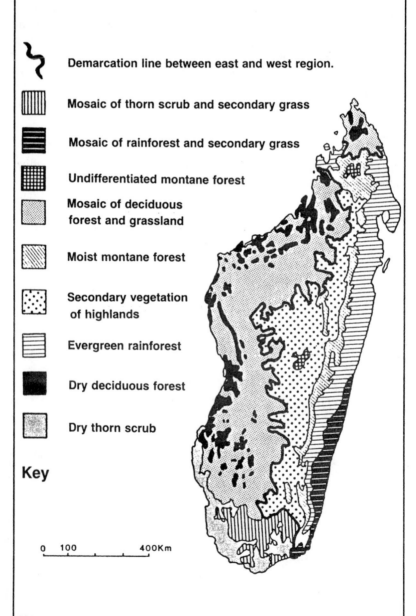

TYPES OF VEGETATION

Demarcation line between east and west region.

Mosaic of thorn scrub and secondary grass

Mosaic of rainforest and secondary grass

Undifferentiated montane forest

Mosaic of deciduous forest and grassland

Moist montane forest

Secondary vegetation of highlands

Evergreen rainforest

Dry deciduous forest

Dry thorn scrub

Key

0   100   400Km

A great variety of precious and semi-precious gemstones are found in Madagascar, including several types of tourmaline, amethyst, citrine, rhodonite, celestine, amazonite, Labradorite (moonstone), iolite, kornerupine, sphene, spinel, chryosoberyl, rose quartz, milky quartz, and grossular garnets (known as cinnamon stone in Madagascar). There is a rare, dark blue variety of aquamarine (beryl) and the finest Morganite in the world comes from Madagascar. The largest crystal ever found was in Madagascar: a beryl measuring 18 metres long and 3.5 metres in diameter; it weighed about 380 tons.

This enormous diversity of beautiful minerals may be found in the markets and shops of Madagascar in the form of colourful Solitaire sets and similar souvenirs. There are tours available specialising in minerals and gemstones; well worth considering if you are a rock-hound.

FLORA

A glance at the statistics will warm a botanist's heart: Madagascar has around 10,000 species (estimates vary from some 7,000 to 12,000 but with so many still to be classified, the larger figure seems more realistic) whilst Great Britain has 1,750. The large number of species is due to the dramatically different climate zones, and around 80% of the flora is found nowhere else in the world. Unlike the fauna, however, which looks unique even to the unscientific eye, a large proportion of Madagascar's vegetation appears familiar to the non-botanist. Having worked out a successful blueprint in other parts of the world, Nature has come up with the same basic design to fit the different environments: water-retaining plants for arid zones and tall trees with buttress roots for the rainforest.

Descriptions of regional flora are given in respective chapters, particularly Chapter 8 *The South*. The account below is extracted from a more detailed survey of Madagascar's flora, kindly written by Gordon and Merlin Munday. You may order a full copy from Bradt Publications.

Flora: an overview

You may be surprised to discover that you already know a few Madagascar plants – many house or florist's plants come from Madagascar. These include 'crown of thorns' (*Euphorbia millii*), with its bright red flowers and sharp spines, 'flaming Katy' (*Kalanchoe blossfeldiana*) with brilliant red and long lasting flowers, 'panda plant' (*Kalanchoe tomentosa*), 'Madagascar dragon tree' (*Dracaena marginata*), 'Madagascar jasmine' (*Stephanotis floribunda*) – the bridal bouquet with waxy, white, heavily scented flowers, the 'polka dot' plant (*Hypoestis phyllostachya*), and 'velvet leaf' (*Kalanchoe beharensis*). Then there is the poinciana (*Poinciana regia*) or flamboyant and the pointsettia (*Pointsettia madagascariensis*).

Few of Madagascar's many unique species have been given English names, but one Malagasy plant name has made its way into English: raffia. The palm *Raphia pedunculata* grows in swampy ground to the east and has been a mainstay for craft workers and gardeners all over the world.

Estimates of the number of species of flora in Madagascar range from 7,370 to 12,000, making it one one of the richest botanical areas in the world. Of about 400 flowering plant families worldwide almost 200 are known to occur in Madagascar. There are eight endemic families and 18% of the genera and nearly 80% of the species are also endemic.

Evidence suggests that primitive flowering plants (Angiosperms) originated in the western part of Gondwanaland, probably in the early Cretaceous period, and that subsequently they spread north while diversifying, leading to the establishment of flora in the two large supercontinents. Africa has many genera in common with Madagascar, but individual species are quite distinct. For example, of the 300 African aloe species, not one is identical to the 60 found in Madagascar, and the 'succulent' euphorbias are here more woody than succulent. Africa has only a few hundred species of orchid, whilst Madagascar claims around a thousand. Nevertheless, many plants such as the African violet (*Viola abyssinica*) and *Cardamine africana* are widely distributed and identical in both places. Mangroves, as one would expect of water disseminated plants, are all identical with those found on the East African coast, whereas Madagascar's endemic palms – 16 genera – almost all show affinities with those of Asia and South America.

SCIENTIFIC CLASSIFICATION

Since many animals and plants in Madagascar have yet to be given English names, I have made much use of the Latin, or scientific name. For those not familiar with these and the associated terminology, here is a brief guide:

Having been separated into broad **classes** like mammals (mammalia), angiosperms (angiospermae) – flowering plants – etc, animals and plants are narrowed down into an **order**, such as Primates or Monocotyledons. The next division is **family**: Lemur (*Lemuridae*) and Orchid (*Orchidaceae*) continue the examples above. These are the general names that everyone knows, and you are quite safe to say 'in the lemur family' or 'a type of orchid'. There are also sub-families, such as the 'true lemurs' and 'the indri sub-family' which includes sifakas. Then come **genera** (**genus** in singular) followed by **species**, and the Latin names here will be less familiar-sounding. It is these two names that are combined in the scientific name precisely to identify the animal or plant. So *Lemur catta* and *Angraecum sesquipedale* will be recognisable whatever the nationality of the person you are talking to. We call them ring-tailed lemur and comet orchid, the French say maki and orchidée comète. With a scientific name up your sleeve there is no confusion.

ORCHIDS IN MADAGASCAR

by Johan and Clare Hermans
illustrated by Cherry-Anne Lavrih

Like so many other living things on the Island, the orchids of Madagascar are extremely varied and most are endemic. Well over 800 different species have been recorded so far and pressure on their habitats may cause many to expire before ever being found. The orchids have adapted to every possible habitat, including the spiny forest and the cool highland mountain ranges.

Compared with the tropical cloud forests of South and Central America, orchids are not very easily found in Madagascar; Good habitat sites are scarce, and even there plants will not be plentiful, also many are small if not insignificant. The main flowering season is during January, February and March, just when the climate is less benevolent to visitors. However something will be flowering most times of the year and their scarcity will enhance the delight of finding an intricate, fragrant *Angraecum* orchid in its natural environment.

Plant taxonomists have not made it easy to learn the different orchid names: *Angraecum, Aeranthes* and *Aerangis* are all too easily confused in the big mass of white, star shaped flowers found in Madagascar. The following may help to unravel some of the initial confusion.

The eastern coastal area

A great number of truly exciting orchids can be seen in this area, it is the habitat of large *Angraecums, Eulophiellas* and *Cymbidiellas*. Most orchids here are epiphytes – they live on tree branches or stems with their roots anchoring the plants and although they scramble over their host, collecting moisture and nutrients, they are not parasites.

Angraecum eburneum is frequently seen in flower from September to May. The thick leathery leaves form a half metre wide fan shape, the flower stems reach above the leaves carrying a number of large greenish white fragrant flowers. Our first close encounter with a Malagasy orchid was a gigantic flowering plant of *eburneum* planted in front of our bungalow at Hotel Soanambo on Nosy Boraha (Ile St. Marie). Aeroflot jet-lag promptly vanished.

The Comet Orchid, ***Angraecum sesquipedale***, is one of the most striking, it flowers from June to November; the plants are similar to *eburneum* but slightly more compact. Individual flowers can be almost 26cm. across and over 30cm. long, including its long nectary spur at the

Angraecum

back of the flower. The spur is characteristic for the *Angraecoid* orchids. The flower was described by Charles Darwin at the end of the 19th century when he predicted that there would be a moth with a very long tongue that could reach down to the nectar at the bottom of the spur. This idea was ridiculed by his contemporaries but in 1903 a moth with a proboscis of over 30cm. was found in Madagascar!

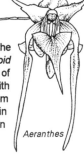

Aeranthes

Aeranthes plants look similar to *Angraecum*. Their spider-like greenish flowers are suspended from a long thin stem, gently nodding in the seabreeze. Most *Aeranthes* flower in January - February.

Eulophiella roempleriana (L'Orchidée Rose) is now extremely rare. One of the few remaining, gigantic almost two metre high plants can be seen on Île aux Nattes (Nosy Natto) a small Island off Île Ste Marie, where one of the local entrepreneurs will show you the site for a small fee. The large, deep pink flowers normally appear from October onwards.

Cymbidiella orchids are also very striking, they generally flower from October to January; *Cymbidiella pardalina* with its huge crimson lip, cohabits with a stag-horn fern; *Cymbidiella falcigera*, with large black spotted yellow flowers, prefers the exclusive company of the raffia palm.

Cymbidiella

The highlands

The Highlands of Madagascar with their cooler and more seasonal climate are inhabited by numerous terrestrial orchids, growing in soil or leaf litter; underground tubers produce deciduous leaves and flower stems.

Cynorkis is a semi-epiphyte growing in moist shady places; the squat plants carrying bright pinkish-purple flowers on the roadside by the Ranomafana reserve are a fine representative of the genus. The flowers are not to be confused with a *Strepto-carpus* growing on the same dripping rocks. Epiphytic orchids like *Angraecum* and *Aeranthes* are also common in the Highlands.

Jumellea

Aerangis plants are instantly recognisable by their shiny, dark green foliage. The flowers superficially resemble those of *Angraecum* but they are often much smaller, carried on elegant racemes. The plants are commonly seen in the wet shade of the rain forest reserves of Perinet and Ranomafana.

Aerangis

Jumellea are again similar but have a more narrow, folded back single flower on thin stems.

Bulbophyllum orchids are easily missed by the untrained eye; their rounded, plump pseudo-bulbs are often seen on moss covered trees, they are always worthwhile investigating; small gem like blooms may be nestled amongst the foliage.

Oeonia with its huge white lip and two red dots in its throat can sometimes be seen rambling amongst the undergrowth.

The apparently bare higher peaks of the *hauts-plateaux*, like Ibity near Antsirabe, also contain a very specialised community of orchids; the thick leaved, sun-loving *Angraecoid* and *Bulbophyllum* species share the rock faces with succulents.

One of the best and easiest places to see orchids, such as *Angraecum*, *Cymbidiella* and *Phaius*, is in hotel and private gardens but one must be aware that these domesticated collections may contain the odd foreign interloper; orchids from the Orient and South America are grown for their aesthetic value, the flowers being often bigger and brighter than the native plants.

Bulbophyllum

Phaius

It is very important to stress that on no account should plants be collected or bought from street traders; the orchids are unlikely to survive and export is also restricted. The customs officers at Ivato have no trouble detecting plants.

It is only possible to give a taste of the subject in these few pages, more information on the native orchids of Madagascar can be obtained from more specialised literature.

Further reading

Flore de Madagascar. Henri Humbert, Editor. Tanarive Imprimerie Officielle, Madagascar, 1941. 49e. Famille. – Orchidees by H. Perrier de La Bathie. Now very difficult to obtain and incomplete.

An Introduction to the Cultivated Angraecoid Orchids of Madagascar.
Fred. E. Hillerman & Arthur W. Holst. Timber Press, Oregon: 1986. 302 p. 95 line drawings, 36 colour plates, maps. Large tome on a small selection of Malagasy plants

The Orchid Review. Johan & Clare Hermans. RHS. 1994-95. Various articles.

Malagasy Orchids, an annotated Bibliography. J. & C. Hermans. Privately published, 1994. For the seriously addicted (available from Bradt Publications).

Regional flora and vegetation and where to see it

The island's vegetation falls naturally into two regions: East and West (see map). These are further divided into Domains, giving a broad classification in terms of geography, climate and vegetation.

EASTERN REGION

This coincides with the climatic eastern region but includes the Sambirano Domain and Nosy Be. The Central Domain is also included; this is the backbone of the region with erosion creating deep gullies, or *lavaka*. Heavy storms carry away the soil — thin clay over friable sedimentary layers — made vulnerable by tree clearance. Vegetation of the region is classified as evergreen forest, mosaic of rainforest and secondary grass, moist montane forest, secondary vegetation of the highlands, and montane bushland and scrub.

Evergreen forest Occurs below 800m. The rainfall is generally over 2,000mm and in some places up to 3,500mm. The vegetation is stratified in canopies, the competition for light resulting in no undergrowth. Many trees have buttress roots or stilt-like aerial roots. Epiphytes, including orchids and ferns, are abundant.

The Madagascar rainforest is distinct from corresponding forests in Africa in having a higher species diversity, a lower main canopy and an absence of large emergent trees. Tree density is also three times greater than comparable rainforests in other continents. Families that form part of the upper canopy include Euphorbiaceae (nearly all with the milky latex sap), Sapindaceae (woody lianas), Rubiaceaae (including wild coffee), Ebenaceae, including the genus Diospyros (with 97 species, one of which is the true ebony), and palms.

Tourist-accessible evergreen forest can be seen in Lokobe (Nosy Be), Masoala Peninsula and Nosy Mangabe.

Île Ste Marie is botanically rewarding. Here you can see the spectacular comet orchid, *Angraecum sesquipedale*. The tubular nectary of this creamy-white flower is 38cm (15ins) long. When Charles Darwin was shown the orchid he predicted that a hawkmoth with a 15 inch tongue must exist in Madagascar to fertilise it. Sure enough: the moth is named *praedicta*, and the flower sometimes called Darwin's Orchid. Features of the coastal landscape on the island are large Barringtonia trees on the shoreline, with 'bishop's hat' fruits, and coconut palms leaning into the sea which disseminates their fruit.

Mosaic of rainforest and secondary grass An outstanding example of a successful indigenous secondary forest tree is the traveller's palm or traveller's tree (*Ravenala madagascariensis*) the symbol of Madagascar and the logo of Air Madagascar. It gets its name from the relief it affords a thirsty traveller: water is stored in the base of its leaves and can be released with a panga blow. The fan arrangement of the leaves is extremely decorative. The Ravenala is, in fact, not a palm but is related to the *Strelitzia* or bird of paradise flower. It often occurs in combination with Pandanus (screw pine), which is somewhat like a palm, and Typhonodorum, which grows in or by water and has huge spinach-like leaves.

Other indigenous vegetation does less well in competition with introduced grasses, ferns and shrubs which take over after fire. Indigenous forest species able to colonise the edges of cut forests include some useful to man such as *Canarium*, a valuable all-purpose wood and a source of essential oils, Croton, from which drugs are derived, and two guavas, *Psiadia altissima* and *Haronga madagascariensis* which is also the source of a valuable drug, Harunganin, used for stomach disorders.

This type of vegetation (unfortunately) can be seen anywhere near inhabited places by the east coast, where the landscape is degraded as a result of fire, and dominated by grass. There are few trees.

Moist montane forest Generally occurs between 800m and 1,300m but can go as high as 2,000m if the conditions are right. The canopy is about 5m lower than the lowland forest, and there is more undergrowth, including some temperate genera such as *Labiatae* and *Impatiens*. There are abundant epiphytes, ferns and mosses, and large lianas and bamboo. As the altitude increases, so the height of the canopy decreases, letting in more light and permitting the growth of epiphytes and shrubby, herbaceous undergrowth with an abundance of moss. Leaves become tougher, with a thicker cuticle to help retain water.

Trees at this altitude include *Dalbergia*, rosewood, and *Weinmannia*, a useful light timber; species of palm and tree fern grow in lower areas.

The most accessible example of medium altitude moist montane forest is Périnet. The upland variety can best be seen in Montagne d'Ambre National Park, and high altitude moist montane forest is best shown on the lower slopes of the Marojejy massif.

Highland vegetation (the Central Domain) The forest that formerly covered the *Hauts Plateaux* has been replaced by grassland. This is relieved by granite outcrops which harbour succulents. These hills are called 'Inselbergs'. Pachypodium occur in this environment, with, among others, aloes and euphorbia.

The most rewarding accessible area is probably the Ibity range of mountains near Antsirabe.

High altitude montane forest Beginning at 1,300m and extending to 2,300m, the vegetation here is shaped by lower, more varied temperatures, wind, sun and rain. The forest resembles tall scrub with small, tough leaves. Moss and lichens clothe branches and cover the ground up to 30cm, and provide anchorage for epiphytic ferns and orchids. Ericaceous species predominate in the undergrowth.

The massif of Marojejy provides the best example, along with the botanical reserve of Ambohitantely.

Tapia forest This is the local name for the dominant species *Uapaca bojeri*, a tree with a thick, crevassed bark which is fire resistant. The forest is on the western slopes of the central highlands, with a drier climate than Eastern Domains. The impenetrable vegetation appears similar to Mediterranean cork oak forests. There are few epiphytes or ground mosses.

Isalo National Park has tapia groves and also various succulents on its sandstone outcrops.

Montane bushland and thicket Characterised by a single stratum, up to six metres, of impenetrable branching evergreen woody plants growing above 2,000m, and interesting for trees belonging to the daisy family (*Compositae*).

None of Madagascar's high mountains is easily accessible. Probably Andringitra offers the best possibility.

THE WESTERN REGION

Dry deciduous forest The flora is extensive and varied but of lower density and less rich than in the moister eastern forests. Deciduous trees grow to a height of 12 to 15m with some emergent trees up to 25m. There are abundant lianas, and shrubby undergrowth, but no ferns, palms or mosses covering the forest floor, and few orchids.

Dry deciduous forest grows on clay or sandy soil. The latter includes the luxuriant gallery forests along rivers where tamarind trees predominate. Away from water, it is the baobabs that take precedence. A third environment, calcareous plateaux, produces a lower forest canopy with fewer lianas and evergreens. Trees and shrubs with swollen trunks or stems (*pachycauly*) are much in evidence.

The Forestry Station of Ampijoroa is an easily accessible area of dry deciduous forest. Harder to reach, but rewarding when you get there, are the reserves of Ankarana and Tsingy de Bemaraha, which has a dense combination of dry forest, savanna, and plants specially adapted to the pinnacles, or calcareous karst (*tsingy*).

Deciduous thicket ('spiny forest') Madagascar's most strikingly different landscape comes into this category, where Didiereaceae, an endemic family, are associated with tree Euphorbias. There are some evergreens here, probably because of sea mists bathing the plants. Heavy morning dews are a boon to the local people who collect the precious water with 'dew ladles'. Thickets vary in height from three to six metres, and with their thorns are impenetrable. Emergent trees are mostly baobab.

Didiereaceae show some resemblance to the Boojum cactus (Fouquieriaceae) of the south-west USA and Mexico. There are four genera, exclusive to the west and south of Madagascar: *Alluaudia* (six species), *Alluaudiopsis* (two species), *Didierea* (two species), and *Decaryia* (one species). Examples of the tree euphorbia of the thicket are *E. stenoclada* (thorny, the latex used for caulking pirogues), *E. enterophora* (thornless, up to 20 metres), and *E. plagiantha*, also thornless, and characterised by peeling yellowish-brown bark.

Very conspicuous are the 'barrel' and 'bottle' trees with their massive trunks adapted for water storage. *Adansonia*, *Moringa*, and *Pachypodium* are the genera.

Leaf succulents are well represented, with several species of tall (three to four metre) aloes. The shrivelled redundant leaves wrap the stem and give some resistance to fire. Look also for the genus *Kalanchoe*. One of the most interesting species, *K. beauverdii* (two to three metres long) forms buds around the leaf margins, each of which then becomes a tiny daughter plant, thus giving it great survival powers.

These are only a few examples of from well over a thousand species belonging to genera of widely different plant families, which nevertheless show much resemblance to one another in their methods of circumventing drought. After rain, leaves and flowers form fast and in some species the flowers even form before rain, thus giving maximum time for fruit formation and dispersal before the next drought.

The best place to view the spiny forest is near Toliara along the Tolagnaro - Ambovombe road, and in Berenty reserve. Berenty is also an excellent example of gallery forest.

Secondary grassland After the excitement of the spiny forest this is inevitably a let down, but inescapable as about 80% of the western region is covered with secondary or wooded grassland, burnt yearly. Two species of palm, *Medemia nobilis* and *Borassus madagascariensis* (both riverside species) have settled in this habitat.

Mangrove This is an environment of shrubs or small trees growing in muddy lagoons, river deltas, bays or shores, their roots washed by salt or brackish water. Mangroves are found mainly on the west coast and are characterised by stilt-like roots, some of which emerge above the water to take in oxygen. Some have another advantage because their seeds germinate in the fruit while remaining on the tree (viviparity), the fruit then drops into the mud with its plantlet well on the way to independence. There are three families (nine species) in Madagascar. In the Toliara region the contrast of spiny vegetation inland and a bright green band of mangroves is particularly striking. Mangroves are economically important to the people for various aspects of fish or shellfish farming. The wood is hard and very dense but not very durable, and is used for poles and planks and also firewood. The bark is good for tanning leather.

Apart from the Toliara region, there is a population of *Avicennia marina* in the Betsiboka estuary and Nosy Be has the same species in a much smaller area.

THE BAOBAB

By Ed Fletcher

Baobabs occur in Africa and Madagascar: one species in Africa and eight in Madagascar (including the African species). Many myths and much folklore have been created about baobabs; it is commonly being called the upside-down-tree, the legend being that the devil plucked up the baobab, thrust its branches into the earth and left its roots in the air. It has been described as 'A Caliban of a tree, a grizzled distorted old goblin with a girth of a giant, the hide of a rhinoceros, twiggy fingers clutching at empty air'.

Baobabs can reach an age of several thousand years. Age calculations have been carried out on mature baobabs using a formula of rate of growth, size and growing conditions in areas of low rainfall; some baobabs could be over 5,000 years old, which has caused theological arguments centred around the Great Flood destroying all animal and plant life. Michel Adanson, the botanist who first recorded the baobab in 1743, angered David Livingstone by his calculations of the age of some African specimens.

One of the most contentious issues surrounding the baobab is its classification as a tree. It could by definition be classed as a succulent, being able to store water in its trunk unlike other trees, temperate or tropical.

In Madagascar one of the common names for the baobab is the Bottle Tree. These are planted near the tombs of the Mahafaly tribe.

The baobab has many traditional uses: bark fibre is used to make rope, baskets, snares, fibre cloth, musical instrument strings, and waterproof hats (one characteristic of the baobab, which other trees do not possess, is that stripping the bark will not kill the tree: the bark will regenerate). Wood pulp makes strong coarse paper, floats, trays and platters. The fresh leaves provide a vegetable similar to spinach and a beverage. Seeds are a source of food high in protein and oil content. The empty seed husks are used for various utensils, and the pulp makes a refreshing drink high in vitamin C.

Listed below are the species of baobab native to Madagascar:

Adansonia grandidieri This is the largest. The trunk is cylindrical and very fat, with reddish bark. The flower is completely white and blossoms in March. The Sakalava regard the fruit as a valuable source of food, harvesting the fruit and edible seeds which produce a valuable fatty substance. The sheer vertical trunks are scaled by means of wooden spikes driven into the bark. The local name given is *Reniala*.

This baobab is rare, localised in the southern part of the Menabe area in the western region, particularly around Morondava.

Adansonia madagascariensis One of the most beautiful of all the baobab species, its trunk generally has little swelling, being cylindrical or tapering from the base to the branches, ranging from 10-35 metres in height. The local names include *Za*, *Zabe*, *Renida*, and *Bozy* depending on the size and appearance of the tree and between the different tribes. The flower is red, and generally blossoms at the start of the rainy season in November. The fruit is ready for harvesting in the dry season. It has a wide distribution, being common on the western coast of Antsiranan (north) and Cap Sainte Marie (south), around the Ambongo-Boina area and around Manombo to the north of Toliara.

Adansonia za It varies in appearance. The trunk tapers from the base to the top, or is cylindrical and can be confused with *A. Grandidieri*. The height varies between 10-39 metres. The local names are *Za, Ringy* and *Boringy*. The flower is yellow tinged with red. It grows in regions where the climate is harsh, with little rainfall, in parts of Ambongo-Boina and Sambirano in the west and north-west. This baobab is becoming rare since it is used to feed zebu in times of drought; after felling, the bark is peeled off to enable the cattle to feed on the water-saturated fibre.

Adansonia fony It is of variable appearance, generally standing around 4-10 metres. The trunk can be swollen in various shapes, tapering from the base to the branches, or swollen in the middle, or cigar-shaped and constricted at the top. A truly remarkable tree. The local names are *Za, Ringy, Zamena, Boringy*. The flowers are yellowish, and blossom according to the rainfall which is irregular in the dry areas in which this species grows: the rocky regions in the southern park of Menabe, around Morondava, Mt Ambohibitsika (basin of Mangoky), Marofandilia forest in the north of Morondava and the sandhills between Fiherena and Manombo.

Adansonia suarezensis This species has a smooth trunk, usually tapered from the base, swelling at the branches. The height varies from 20-30 metres. The local names are not known. The flowers are large and deep red.

Adansonia perrieri Only discovered in 1960, in the region of Diego-Suarez (Antsiranana) on the plateau of Ankarana, it has a yellow flower. There is very little other information.

Adansonia alba It has a swollen trunk, tapering gradually from the base to the top. The height varies from 10-15 metres. The local names are unknown. The flower is white, and the species is found to the north of Bezofo in dense wood and at an altitude of about 500 metres in an area where baobabs generally do not exist.

Adansonia digitata This species is the one found on mainland Africa where it has a wide distribution. It has a large trunk up to 15 metres in diameter and can contain up to 30,000 gallons of water. The many local names include: *Sefo, Bontona* or *Vontona* ('swollen one'), *Reniala* ('Father or Mother of the forest'). The flower is white and large. It is often found in the central square of Sakalava villages, particularly the ports in the Ambongo-Boina area of the western region (there is a famous one in Mahajanga).

'Some day, when I am old and worn and there is nothing new to see, I shall go back to the palm-fringed lagoons, the sun- drenched, rolling moors, the pink villages, and the purple peaks of Madagascar'.
E A Powell, Beyond the Utmost Purple Rim, 1925

FAUNA

Mammals

There are five orders of land mammals in the island: Primates (lemurs), Insectivora (tenrecs and shrews), Chiroptera (bats), Carnivora (carnivores) and Rodentia (rodents). Of these it is the three families of **lemur** that get the most attention so it is worth describing them in some detail.

Once upon a time there were lemur-type animals all over the world, including North America. Known as prosimians, these creatures had evolved from the ancestral primate, father of all primates including ourselves. They had some monkey-like characteristics but retained the foxy face of their insectivorous forebears, the long nose being needed for a highly developed sense of smell. Lemurs have changed little since the Eocene period 58 - 36 million years ago. Other descendants of the ancestral primate evolved into monkeys; faced with competition from other mammals these developed a greater intelligence and better eyesight. Their sense of smell became less important so their noses lost their physical prominence.

Lemurs are the only surviving prosimians in the world apart from the bushbabies, pottos and angwantibos of Africa and the lorises of Asia. From their faces it's hard to believe they are our relatives, but quoting from *Defenders of Wildlife* magazine (April 1975) 'One needn't be a scientist to look at a lemur's hand ... and feel the thrill of recognition across a gap of 60 million years'.

There are 30 species of lemur, with three newcomers. For scientists to discover a new species of primate is extremely rare. That this should happen three times in so many years is extraordinary, and demonstrates the vital importance of preserving habitats which no doubt harbour thousands of unclassified living things. The newcomers are the golden bamboo lemur, *Hapalemur aureus*, of Ranomafana (see page 158) the golden-crowned sifaka, *Propithecus tattersalli*, found in 1988 in Antsiranana province, and the endearingly named hairy- eared dwarf lemur, *Allocebus trichotis*, which was thought to be extinct but reappeared near Mananara in 1989 to be identified by the indefatigable Bernard Meier who discovered the golden bamboo lemur.

Primatologists have recently divided the *Lemur* genus into two: *Lemur* and *Eulemur*. The latter include the various subspecies of brown lemur, *Eulemur fulvus*, the black lemur, *Eulemur macaco*, the mongoose lemur, *Eulemur mongoz* and the crowned lemur *Eulemur coronatus*.

Nearly half of all lemur species (14) are diurnal so easily seen. Dedicated lemur-watchers can look for nocturnal animals with the help of a headlamp (see page 48). The diurnal lemurs that are common in certain nature reserves are described in those sections: ring-tails and sifakas in *Berenty*, indri in *Andasibe* and black lemurs in *Nosy Be* but there are some generalities which are interesting. Diurnal lemurs live in troops where the females are dominant (which is rare in primates, where males are usually larger) and they sunbathe in the morning to raise the body temperature. Lemurs have slow metabolism, and need a bit of help from the sun for their daily quota of energy. Female dominance may be necessary because lemur young are dependent on their mother's milk for a long time so extra nutrition is needed for lactation.

The strangest lemur is the aye-aye. It took a while for scientists to decide that the aye-aye *is* a type of lemur – for years it was classified as a squirrel – and it has a family of its own, *Daubentonia madagascariensis*. The aye-aye seems to have been assembled from the leftover parts of a variety of animals. It has the teeth of a rodent (they never stop growing), the ears of a bat, the tail of a fox, and the hands of no living creature since the middle finger is like that of a skeleton. It's this finger which so intrigues scientists as it shows the aye-aye's adaptation to its environment. In Madagascar it fills the ecological niche left empty by the absence of woodpeckers. The aye-aye evolved to use its skeletal finger to winkle grubs from under the bark of tree. It has added the skill (shown by the Chinese when using chopsticks to eat soup) of flicking coconut milk into its mouth. Coconuts are now a favoured item of diet. The aye-aye's fingers are unique among lemurs in another way – it has claws not fingernails (except on the big toe). It is now known that the aye-aye is the only animal which can detect its dinner by tapping on the wood to find a cavity. Its enormous ears enable it to detect the presence of a cavity and even whether this is occupied by a nice fat grub. There is nothing random about its search.

Another anatomical feature of the aye-aye that sets it apart from other primates is that it has inguinal mammary glands. In other words, its teats are between its back legs.

This fascinating animal was long considered to be on the verge of extinction, but recently there have been encouraging signs that it is more widespread than previously supposed. Although destruction of habitat is the chief threat to its survival, it is also at risk because of its supposedly evil powers. Rural people believe the aye-aye to be the heralder of death. If one is seen near a settlement it must be killed, and even then the only salvation may be to burn down the village. The aye-aye is protected on the island reserve of Nosy Mangabe to which it was introduced in 1966, and in Mananara, and it has been sighted in Ankarana, Ranomafana and Andasibe. Being strictly nocturnal, aye-ayes can only be watched with the help of a torch (flashlight) so for a prolonged session with this amazing animal treat yourself a visit to Jersey Zoo where the purpose-built 'night-into-day' aye-aye house allows you to watch behaviour to your heart's content.

Almost as strange as the aye-aye are the 33 species of **tenrec**. These insectivores are considered by some zoologists to be the most primitive of all mammals, and the most prolific. A female may give birth to 32 young! Many tenrec species have prickles and resemble miniature European hedgehogs, and the little striped tenrec (*Hemicentetes*) has rows of specialised spines which it can vibrate and strike together, producing a

IDENTIFYING NOCTURNAL LEMURS

By R W Byrne

Seeing nocturnal lemurs isn't hard at all. They are far less shy than the often-hunted diurnal species and let you walk right underneath them in the trees, and their eyes have a silvery tapetum behind the retina which reflects the light, so 'eyeshine' is easily picked out with a torch. To see eyeshine, the axis of the torchlight has to be close to your own eyes so a strong headtorch is best. Then you can see a smallish, brown lemur... but what is it? Most illustrations are pretty confusing, but it's not difficult to work out what genus it is. Notice if it sits upright, or along branches like a squirrel; whether the face is flattened or pointed; any markings or colour contrasts; the size; the tail. Then, assuming it's smaller than a brown lemur and brown or grey, use this key:

1. (a)   Face flattened, owl-like; body usually held upright, see 2.
   (b)   Face pointed, body usually held horizontally, see 3.
   (c)   Face blunt but not flat; body usually held horizontally; big, thick tail; short legs. Chiefly diurnal, no prominent dark marks (eg on face), no white marks = **Hapalemur**. *H. griseus*: rabbit sized, eating bamboo, greyish. *H. simus*: much bigger size of brown lemur, greyish, nearly extinct. *H. aureus*: much bigger, size of brown lemur, orange-brown, rare.

2. (a)   Tail invisible or curled up in front of body; pale underside or hind limbs show no stripe on thigh; ears tiny; yellowish and reddish colour. Sluggish, strictly nocturnal = **Avahi** (*A. Laniger*).
   (b)   Tail quite easily seen; animal smaller (size of rabbit or less); no clear contrasts in colour, ears small or tiny. Nocturnal, may sleep in visible position, especially Nosy Be = **Lepilemur**. (The best way of telling the seven species apart is by range.)

3. (a)   Tiny, rapid running and leaping in branches; tail thin. Nocturnal = **Microcebus** (mouse lemur. Either *M. murinus* or *M. rufus* – very hard to separate, range different).
   (a)   Medium small, contrasting pale underparts; black 'spectacles' and black ears and nose; long thick tail. Nocturnal = **Cheirogaleus** (dwarf lemur). *C. medius*: relatively small but tail very fat, greyish. *C. major*: relatively large, tail untapered and not flattened, brownish.

This key doesn't include *Microcebus coquereli*, which is very local and I suspect would look like a big edition of *M. rufus* and act like one, nor *Allocebus trichotis* which hasn't been seen for years, nor *Phaner furcifer* which is conspicuously marked and anyway very localised.

If what you've seen still doesn't fit, could it be a 'diurnal' lemur like brown lemur, which forages much of the night? And if it's hefty, has big bat-like ears, a bushy tail and coarse grey fur... you hit the jackpot, it's an aye-aye !

sound (inaudible to humans) which is used to call the young when they scatter to feed. Not all tenrecs have prickles. Some are furry, resembling mice or shrews. Spines seem to be the favoured form of defence, however, and even the furry species often have a few prickles hidden in the fur. Tenrecs are commonly eaten by the Malagasy, especially the largest species, known as the tail-less tenrec, which is the size of a rabbit. There is also an aquatic tenrec which is hunted in the fast-flowing rivers of the eastern rainforest.

Some species of tenrec aestivate (go into a torpor) during the dry season when food is scarce.

Of the 28 **bat** species in Madagascar nine are endemic (evidently they could fly across the Mozambique Channel). Very few studies have been done on them. The most visible are the fruit bats or flying foxes (*Pteropus rufus*), an endemic species closely related to those of Asia.

The eight species of Malagasy carnivore all belong to the family **Viverridae**, and are related to the mongoose, civet and genet of Africa. The largest is the puma-like **fossa** (*fosa* in Malagasy). The fossa's scientific name is *Cryptoprocta ferox* and although rarely seen it is not uncommon. The fossa is an expert tree climber, and the only serious predator (apart from hawks) of lemurs. It has sandy-brown fur, a long body, short strong jaws, retractable claws, a long tail, and is about the size of a spaniel. The name 'fossa' brings confusion with the smaller nocturnal *Fossa fossana* or fanalouc, also known as striped civet.

Of the 'mongooses' the most frequently seen is *Galidia elegans* (Madagascar ring-tailed mongoose) which is chestnut brown with a striped tail. It frequents the east and northern rain forest. There are several differences between it and true mongooses: *Galidia* has webbed feet, retractable claws, and teats between its back legs.

None of the **rodents** is the same as ours (although mice and rats have been introduced). There are 17 species, of which the rabbit-sized giant jumping rat is the most interesting — and charming: it leaps like a wallaby in the forests north of Morondava.

'The breast-leaper... It is a small animal which attaches itself to the bark of trees and being of a greenish hue is not easily perceived; there it remains with its throat open to receive the flies, spiders and other insects that approach it, which it devours. This animal is described as having attached to the back, tail, legs, neck, and the extremity of the chin, little paws or hooks like those at the end of a bat's wing with which it adheres to whatever it attaches itself in such a manner as if it were really glued. If a native happens to approach the tree where it hangs, it instantly leaps upon his naked breast, and sticks so firmly that in order to remove it, they are obliged, with a razor, to cut away the skin also'.
Samuel Copland, History of the Island of Madagascar, 1822

Frogs and reptiles

Madagascar is particularly rich in this group of fauna – there are over several hundred species of **frog** (the only amphibians here, there are no toads, newts or salamanders) most of which are treefrogs. New species are regularly added to the list.

Reptiles number some 300 species. Of the many types of lizard in Madagascar, the iguanids are interesting since other members of this family are not found in Africa but in South America: they were probably inhabitants of Gondwanaland. There are two genera in Madagascar, *Chalaradon* and *Oplurus*. The lizards that most interest tourists (and film-makers) are the **chameleons** (see page 60). The world's smallest and largest chameleon species are found in Madagascar.

The real masters of the art of camouflage are the **fringed geckos** (also called leaf-tailed lizard) of the *Uroplatus genus*. These reptiles blend so perfectly into the bark of the trees on which they spend the day, that when I pointed one out on Nosy Mangabe (particularly rewarding for *Uroplatus*) my companions failed to see it until I had encouraged it to gape in self defence. Not only does the lizard's skin perfectly match the bark, but its sides are fringed so no shadow appears on the tree; even its eye is flecked like bark. It is truly almost invisible.

None of Madagascar's 60 species of land **snake** is venomous; or to be accurate, since they are all back-fanged they cannot inflict a venomous bite (there are, in fact, six genera of poisonous snakes). The most commonly seen snake is the boa constrictor, which, like the iguanids, are otherwise only found in South America. Two species are easily seen, the land boa, *Acrantophis madagascariensis*, and the 'tree boa' (which doesn't spend much time up trees) *Sanzinia madagascariensis*. It is interesting that despite the harmlessness of the island's snakes, the local population still hold them in fear and myths abound. It is thought, for instance, that the long, slim *fandrefiala* can spear a zebu by dropping down from a tree, tail first. They say this devilish creature measures its aim by dropping a couple of leaves first. The Malagasy name for the tree boa is *Kapilangidro*, 'lemur's plate'. They say that this snake will coil itself into a bowl to tempt lemurs to approach for a drink. There is also the 'lazy boa' story: in the forest you will often come across large holes with the rim surrounded by the detritus brought out by ants. This often includes bits of snake skin. A slim boa, so the story goes, enters the hole where it lives a life of luxury being tended and fed by ants. It grows so fat it cannot escape. When it dies the ants get their reward – a fat and juicy snake!

There are several species of **tortoise** but 80% of these reptiles are thought to have been killed off by introduced animals. The radiated and plough-share tortoise (*Angonoka*) are the most attractive and also in danger of extinction. A successful breeding programme for the latter has been established in Ampijoroa which is also successfully breeding the very rare flat-tailed tortoise.

Invertebrates

Loosely categorised as 'creepy-crawlies' by many visitors, the insects, spiders, and other arthropods provide enthusiasts with endless surprises and delights. There are extraordinary flatworms, eight-inch long millipedes, golf-ball sized pill-bugs, bizarre stick insects and mantids disguised as leaves, huge hissing cockroaches, brilliantly-coloured giant grasshoppers, little hopping larvae dressed in imitation feathers, beetles and spiders of all shapes and colours and, of course, butterflies.

Madagascar has around 300 species of butterfly and moth, of which over half are endemic. Since Madagascar became separated from Africa before the evolution of butterflies, the forefathers of these Malagasy species probably flew – or were blown – over from East Africa. Many species have their counterpart in Africa. However, there is a swallowtail, *Atrophaneura antenor*, whose nearest relative is in India, and the Urania moth *Chrysiridea madagascariensis* is very similar to the one found in South America.

The most spectacular moth is the comet (*Argema mittrei*), one of the largest in the world, with a beautiful silver cocoon. They are still relatively common and a captive breeding programme in Mandraka provides the mounted specimens for the tourist trade.

Birds

Compared with mainland Africa Madagascar is poor in birds, and even the forests can seem eerily silent as a traveller in 1942 noted: 'Had it not been for the fact that my porters kept up an incessant chatter, telling each other stories and folk tales...I should have been struck by the uncanny stillness of the forest, the apparent absence of animal life and the scarcity of birds.'

There are 258 species, of which 198 are resident and 107 endemic (with a further 35 shared with the Comoro Islands and Aldabra). Endemic families comprise mesites (similar to rails), ground-rollers, cuckoo-rollers, asitys, vangas and couas. The latter are a striking group (10 species) which, with their long broad tails, resemble the African touraco. The vanga family (14 species) is also conspicuous and interesting in that it mirrors Darwin's finches in the Galapagos Islands, having evolved a variety of different bills to help it deal most efficiently with the food available (mostly insects) in the different habitats.

There are 11 endemic species of birds of prey, and ornithologists have recently been excited by the discovery that the Madagascar serpent eagle is not extinct, as previously thought, but hunts beneath the canopy of the rainforest so is seldom seen. The Masoala Peninsula and Morojejy are its known habitats. In sad contrast is the Alaotra little grebe, which apparently became extinct in 1993, and the Madagascar pochard, also from Lake Alaotra, which is on the brink of extinction.

Madagascar has no vultures, perhaps because of the absence of large native animals to provide carrion.

BIRDING IN MADAGASCAR

By Derek Schuurman

Birding is becoming very popular in Madagascar, and with good reason: there are 108 endemics on the island and another 35 shared with the Comoros and Aldabra. It's a case of quality, rather than quantity, as none of these is numerous and the species diversity in Madagascar is quite low.

To see a reasonable selection of the Malagasy endemics, one should plan a trip encompassing visits to at least one site in each of the three prime habitats: the eastern rainforests, the western deciduous forests and the southern semi-arid spiny bush. Each of these floristic/climatic zones boasts its own endemics. Below are the best sites.

Eastern rainforests

Andasibe/Périnet   For those who have very little time, this is ideal being near to Antananarivo. Specials in the reserve include blue and red-fronted couas; velvet and sunbird asitys. Of the vangas there are Chabert's, blue, nuthatch, red-tailed and white-headed. You may also find the Madagascar flufftail.

Ranomafana   Much the same as Périnet but some rarer species include the pitta-like, short-legged and rufous-headed ground-rollers, the Pollen's vanga, forest rock-thrush, brown mesite, Crossley's babbler, white-throated and yellow-browed oxylabes, brown and grey emutails, and the grey-crowned and dusky greenbuls.

Masoala Peninsula   This is for hard-core birders who wish to see the region's specials: the red-breasted coua, scaly ground-roller; helmet and Bernier's vangas. The elusive brown mesite is there too, as is Henst's goshawk, Madagascar pratincole and the very rare red-tailed newtonia. Birds common in the eastern rainforests are seen here such as the nelicourvi weaver, red forest fody, blue and green pigeons.

Western deciduous dry forests

Ampijoroa Forestry Station   The birding is exceptional here: red-capped, Coquerel's and crested couas; Chabert's, sicklebill and hook-billed vangas, as well as rufous, blue and the very rare Van Dam's vanga. The elusive Schlegel's asity is present. The white-breasted mesite is common here and Madagascar fish eagles frequent the lake area; raptor enthusiasts may find the rare banded kestrel.

Ankarana Special Reserve   Much the same as Ampijoroa, including the Madagascar pygmy kingfisher, the crested ibis and the banded kestrel. But there are no asity or Van Dam's vangas.

Southern semi-arid spiny bush and dry gallery forest

Berenty and Amboasary-Sud   There is rewarding birding here; specials of the region include the giant coua, the white- browed owl, and the littoral rock-thrush.

Spiny forests near Ifaty   This is the place to search for the three specials of the south: the long-tailed ground-roller, the subdesert mesite and the Lafresnaye's vanga. Also found are the running and verreaux's coua.

Zombitsi Forest   The only locality for the Appert's greenbul. Other species include the giant coua, Frances's sparrow-hawk and the Madagascar partridge. At nearby Isalo National Park is found Benson's rock-thrush.

CONSERVATION
An age-old problem
When people first settled in Madagascar, the culture they brought with them depended on rice and zebu cattle. Rice was the staple diet and zebu the spiritual staple, the link with the ancestors. Rice and zebu cannot be raised in dense forest, so the trees were felled and the undergrowth burned.

Two hundred or so years ago King Andrianampoinimerina punished those of his subjects who wilfully deforested areas. The practice continued, however. 100 years later, in 1883, the missionary James Sibree commented: 'Again we noticed the destruction of the forest and the wanton waste of trees.' The first efforts at legal protection came as long ago as 1927 when ten reserves were set aside by the French colonial government, which also tried to put a stop to the burning. Successive governments have tried − and failed − to halt this devastation.

Since independence in 1960, Madagascar's population has doubled and the remaining forest has been reduced by half. Only about 15% of the original cover remains and an estimated 2,000 square kilometres is destroyed annually. By the year 2015 the population is expected to have doubled again. Yet at the current 12.2 million, the population density averages only 21 people per square kilometre; in Great Britain it is 228. The pressure on the forests is because most of Madagascar is sterile grassland and bare, eroded laterite. Here, forests are not destroyed by timber companies (although there have been some culprits) but by impoverished peasants clearing the land by the traditional method of *tavy*, slash and burn, and cutting trees for fuel or to make charcoal. There is still some 'wanton destruction'; burning has been illegal for so long, defying this law has become a means of defying authority.

The race against time
Madagascar has more endangered species of mammal than any other country in the world. The authorities are not unaware of this environmental crisis: as long ago as 1970 the Director of Scientific Research made this comment in a speech during an international symposium on conservation, 'The people in this room know that Malagasy nature is a world heritage. We are not sure that others realise that it is *our* heritage.' Resentment at having outsiders make decisions on the future of their heritage without proper consultation with the Malagasy was one of the reasons there was little effective conservation in the 1970s and early 1980s. This was a time when Madagascar was demonstrating its independence from western influences.

Things changed in 1985, when Madagascar hosted a major international conference on conservation for development. The Ministry of Animal Production, Waters and Forests (MPAEF), which administered the

LOCAL PEOPLE AND PROTECTED AREAS

By Joanna Durbin

The first protected areas were created in Madagascar in 1927. They were ten strict nature reserves which aimed to protect representative ecosystems and access was usually strictly limited to authorised scientific research. Since then a series of special reserves, also for wildlife protection and scientific research, and four national parks, the only category where benefits to the general public such as recreation and education are included in the aims, have been added.

Consideration for the requirements of local communities varied but was minimal for the initial planning and management of the majority of these reserves. Many of the protected areas are now suffering from acute pressure from local exploitation as resources outside the reserves have been depleted, the local people perceive no benefit in maintaining the reserve and the authorities do not have the resources to police the area.

Similar problems have been encountered throughout the world where protected areas have been considered as wildlife sanctuaries that must be protected from any direct human influence. It is increasingly recognised that such reserves cannot be managed as biological islands but must be integrated within a broader ecological and human framework. It is now understood that protected areas can play a role in rural development as part of multiple land-use strategies which encourage environmental stability and the sustainable use of resources.

In recent years the Malagasy government, with help from the World Wide Fund for Nature and other organisations, has initiated some integrated conservation and development projects. These are based around some of the original protected areas, three new national parks and a biosphere reserve. Initiatives include tree planting schemes to ensure the availability of construction and fire wood to avoid destructive extraction of wood from the reserves. Efforts are being made to improve agricultural techniques, for example by improving irrigation of rice paddies, with the aim of eliminating the deforestation of new zones of intact forest for agriculture. Some projects involve the introduction of new economic schemes, for example helping villagers to grow new types of vegetables for sale. Local employment opportunities are being created, for example as tourist guides and conservation agents. Programmes of education and awareness for the local population help to explain the relevance of conservation and how the protected area project can be used to help focus attention on the needs of people living in the vicinity. The aim is to reduce pressure on the protected areas by providing alternative resources and to increase the benefits the reserve provides to local people.

A complete solution cannot be expected in a few years; these projects need long term commitment and secure international funding, but there is a new air of optimism.

'All these people are sufficiently civil and courteous, not having the brutality of other black nations. They are clever and elegant'.
Sieur De Bois, 1669

protected areas, went into partnership with the World Wide Fund for Nature. Their plan was to evaluate all protected areas in the country, now numbering 37 (2% of the country) and in their strategy for the future to provide people living near the reserves with economically viable alternatives. They have largely achieved their aims. All the protected areas have been evaluated and recommendations for their management made. They are now the responsibility of the National Association for Management of Protected Areas (Association Nationale pour la Gestion des Aires Protégées, ANGAP) which was established under the auspices of the Environmental Action Plan (EAP), sponsored by the World Bank. Among their successes are a three year Debt for Nature swap negotiated by the WWF with the Central Bank of Madagascar.

The WWF funds a number of projects in Madagascar. Other outside agencies involved in conservation are the World Bank, USAID (US Agency for International Development), The Swiss Corporation, UNDP (United Nations Development Programme) and UNESCO.

The stated aims of the WWF and other conservation agencies working in Madagascar are to: 'Ensure the conservation of Malagasy biodiversity and ecological processes by stopping, and eventually reversing, the accelerating environmental degradation, and by helping to build a future in which humans live in harmony with nature.'

During the Earth Summit in Rio in 1992, Madagascar expressed its commitment to international conservation, and signed both the Biodiversity and Climate Change conventions.

How you can help
- Support the organisations listed at the end of this chapter.
- Don't interrupt the work of scientist in the reserves.
- Do not encourage the illegal trade in endangered species by admiring or paying to photograph pet animals.
- Pay the full park/reserve fee with a good grace. The money is used for conservation.
- Help local people by paying the standard fee for guides and using local services.

THE NATIONAL PARKS AND RESERVES

Categories
There are six categories of protected area, of which the first three have been established to protect natural ecosystems or threatened species:
1. Réserves Naturelles Intégrales (Strict Nature Reserves).
2. Parcs Nationaux (National Parks).
3. Réserves Spéciales (Special Reserves).
4. Réserves de Chasse (Hunting Reserves).

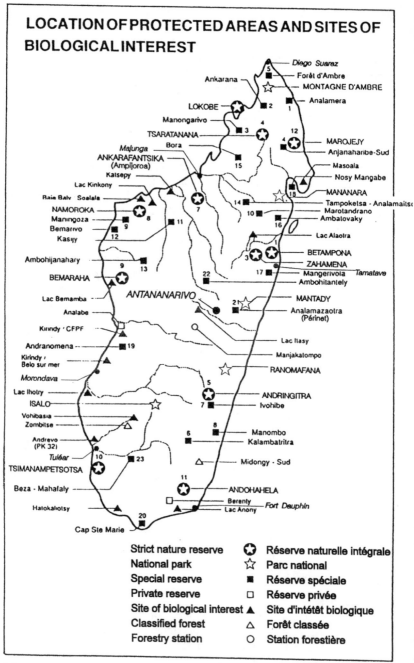

LOCATION OF PROTECTED AREAS AND SITES OF BIOLOGICAL INTEREST

Diego Suarez
Ankarana
Forêt d'Ambre
MONTAGNE D'AMBRE
Analamera
LOKOBE
Manongarivo
TSARATANANA
Bora
Majunga
MAROJEJY
ANKARAFANTSIKA
(Ampijoroa)
Anjanaharibe-Sud
Katsepy
Masoala
Lac Kinkony
Nosy Mangabe
Baia Balv   Soalala
MANANARA
NAMOROKA
Tampoketsa - Analamaitso
Maningoza
Marotandrano
Bemarivo
Ambatovaky
Kasijy
Lac Alaotra
Ambohijanahary
BETAMPONA
ZAHAMENA
BEMARAHA
Mangerivola   Tamatave
Ambohitantely
Lac Bemamba
ANTANANARIVO
Analabe
MANTADY
Kirindy / CFPF
Analamazaotra
(Périnet)
Andranomena
Lac Itasy
Kirindy /
Belo sur mer
Manjakatompo
Morondava
RANOMAFANA
Lac Ihotry
ISALO
ANDRINGITRA
Vohibasia
Ivohibe
Zombitse
Manombo
Andrevo
Kalambatritra
(PK 32)
Tuléar
TSIMANAMPETSOTSA
Midongy - Sud
Beza - Mahafaly
ANDOHAHELA
Hatokaliotsy
Berenty
Fort Dauphin
Lac Anony
Cap Ste Marie

Strict nature reserve	★	Réserve naturelle intégrale
National park	☆	Parc national
Special reserve	■	Réserve spéciale
Private reserve	□	Réserve privée
Site of biological interest	▲	Site d'intétêt biologique
Classified forest	△	Forêt classée
Forestry station	O	Station forestière

Map reproduced from *Madagascar: Revue de la conservation et des aires protégées* by kind permission of the WWF, Switzerland.

5. Forêts Classées (Classified Forests).
6. Perimètres de Reboisement et de Restauration (Reafforestation Zones).

1. There are 11 reserves in this category, four of which are described in this book: Tsingy de Bemaraha, Andringitra, Andohahela, Marojejy, and Lokobe.

These reserves protect representative ecosystems, and are open only to authorised scientific research.

2. As in other countries, National Parks protect ecosystems and areas of natural beauty, and are open to the public (with permits). There are now five National Parks: Ranomafana, Montagne d'Ambre, and Isalo are the best known. Mananara, Mantadia, and a marine park are the new ones.

3. There are 23 Special Reserves, of which Ankarana, Périnet-Analamazaotra, Cap Ste Marie, Beza-Mahafaly, Andranomena, and Nosy Mangabe are described. These reserves are for the protection of ecosystems or threatened species. Not all are supervised. Access may be limited to authorised scientific research.

4. Four lakes (including Kinkony and Ihotry) are duck hunting preserves.

5 and 6. The 158 Classified Forests and 77 Reafforestation areas conserve forests and watersheds using accepted forestry principles.

There are also some private reserves, the most famous of which is Berenty. Permits are not required, the cost of admission being decided by the owner.

Ecotourism

Ecotourism is part of the WWF's development plan for certain parks and reserves. Some reserves with hitherto restricted access are being opened up or reclassified as National Parks. Planned facilities are the creation of access roads, nature trails, accommodation, education and visitor centres.

In 1993 ANGAP, in conjunction with the Ecotourism Society (of America), sponsored an ecotourism seminar. In 1994 the Prime Minister made the following statement: 'We intend to include ecotourism in our policy, that is to say, conservation of the fauna, flora and local culture in a protected zone and the creation of national parks and reserves open to tourists.'

Permits

Permits to visit the reserves and national parks cost foreigners 20,000fmg per person per reserve. The money is used for conservation so each visitor is playing his or her part. From time to time visitors have succumbed to the tempation of trying to bribe their way into parks or reserves. Please do not cheat the wildlife of its financial support in this way, nor put the warden at risk of losing his job. Permits are taken seriously by the authorities. In 1993 two German herpetologists, suspected of illegally collecting reptiles in one of the reserves, were shot by the police.

Some permits are available at the park/reserve entrance (be sure to get a receipt) but for others you should go to the ANGAP office in Antananarivo (see Chapter 7). This is a welcoming and informative place so worth a visit whatever your plans.

Hiring guides

There has been much confusion on the subject of guides and their fees, with an unstructured system of tips causing anger and resentment in guides and tourists alike. ANGAP are now trying to standardise the fees that are paid to their guides in the national parks and reserves. This is the 1993 rate: short excursion: 5,000fmg; half day: 10,000fmg; full day: 15,000fmg. With the current price instability, however, you should check the latest rates with ANGAP.

To encourage the emergence of merit rather than greed, it would be sensible to encourage the guides to keep a book of recommendation in which tourists can praise a job well done (or the contrary). If the guide has been exceptional, by all means add a tip or present to the fee, but do not feel that it is obligatory.

CONSERVATION ORGANISATIONS

Madagascar needs all the financial help it can get. If you can spare some money to help save the wildlife the following agencies will welcome donations:

World Wide Fund for Nature (UK)
Panda House, Weyside Park, Godalming, Surrey GU7 IXR.

Jersey Wildlife Preservation Trust
Les Augres Manor, Jersey, Channel Islands, Great Britain.

Conservation International (USA)
1015 18th St NW, Washington DC, 20003, USA.

'There are some birds the size of a large turkeycock which have the head made like a cat and the rest of the body like a griffin; these birds hide themselves in the thick woods, and when anyone passes under the tree where they are they let themselves fall so heavily on the head of the passengers that they stun them, and in the moment they pierce their heads with their talons, then they eat them'. Sieur de Bois, 1669

CORAL

Only the upper two centimetres or so of a lump of coral is alive. The reefs around Madagascar are composed of the skeletons of dead coral, and the black 'rocks' found on the Malagasy shores are mostly old coral.

Coral spawns once a year in October during full moon. The larvae are like tiny jellyfish and are so numerous they make the sea look milky. These larvae collect in same-species groups and settle in one place. Coral also reproduces by budding, and this is how coral grows; it is a slow process and coral is easily damaged.

All over the world coral is threatened. Although the anchors of tourist boats and careless divers' feet will kill it, in Madagascar the silt-laden rivers are likely to be the main cause of the disappearance of once plentiful coral. Some rivers carry six milligrams of soil per litre of water, and all this ends up in the sea. Coral feeds on minute particles of organic matter and inert substances like silt 'clog up the works'. Human contamination is also a factor. As visitors soon find out, beaches are latrines and coral cannot survive if the water becomes over-enriched with organic matter; seaweed flourishes and smothers the coral. Near villages coral is further damaged during the search for edible sea creatures or for shells to sell to tourists.

COMMERSON

Joseph Philibert Commerson has provided the best-known quote on Madagascar:

'C'est à Madagascar que je puis annoncer aux naturalistes qu'est la véritable terre promise pour eux. C'est là que la nature semble s'être retirée dans un sanctuaire particulier pour y travailler sur d'autres modèles que ceux auxquels elle s'est asservie ailleurs. Les formes les plus insolites et les plus merveilleuses s'y rencontrent à chaque pas.'

Of Madagascar I can announce to naturalists that it is truly their promised land. Nature seems to have retreated there into a private sanctuary to work on other models from those she has created elsewhere. There one meets the most strange and marvellous forms.

Commerson was a doctor who travelled with Bougainville on a world expedition in 1766, arriving at Mauritius in 1768. He studied the natural history of that island, then in 1770 journeyed on to Madagascar where he stayed for three or four months in the Fort Dauphin region. His famous description of 'nature's sanctuary' was in a 1771 letter to his old tutor in Paris.

CHAMELEONS

Everybody thinks they know one thing about chameleons: that they change colour to match their background. Wrong! You only have to observe the striking *Chamaeleo parsonii*, commonly seen at Périnet, staying stubbornly green while transferred from boy's hand to tree trunk to leafy branch to see that this is a myth. Many chameleons are cryptically coloured to match their preferred resting place (there are branch-coloured chameleons, for instance, and leaf-coloured ones) and some species make a half-hearted effort to respond to a change of background, but their abilities are mainly reserved for expressing emotion. An anxious chameleon will darken and grow stripes (this is the most common response to being picked up by a chameleon-doting tourist) and an angry chameleon, faced with a territorial intruder, will change his colours dramatically. The most impressive displays, however, are reserved for sexual encounters. Chameleons say it with colours. Enthusiastic males explode into a riot of spots, stripes, and contrasting colours, whilst the female usually responds by donning a black cloak of disapproval. Only on the rare occasions that she is feeling receptive will she present a brighter appearance.

Chameleons use body language more than colour to deter enemies. If you spot a chameleon on a branch you will note that his first reaction to being seen is to put the branch between you and him and flatten his body laterally so that he is barely visible. If you try to catch him, he will blow himself up, expand his throat, raise his helmet (if he has one) and hiss. His next action will be either to bite, jump, or try to run away. Fortunately they must be the slowest of all lizards, are easily caught, and pose for the camera with gloomy resignation (who can resist an animal that has a constantly down-turned mouth like a Victorian headmistress?). This slowness is another aspect of the chameleon's defence: when he walks, he moves like a leaf in the wind. This is fine when the danger is an animal predator, but there are few more anguish-making sights in Madagascar than to watch a chameleon creeping across the road, swaying backwards and forwards, while a taxi-brousse bears down on him. In a tree, his best protection is to keep completely still. He can do this by having feet shaped like pliers and a prehensile tail so he can effortlessly grasp a branch, and eyes shaped like gun-turrets which can swivel 180 degrees independently of each other, enabling him to view the world from front and back without moving his head. This is the chameleon's true camouflage.

The lungs of a chameleon branch throughout the body. This enables the animal to blow itself up to look more threatening, to 'bounce' when falling from a height, and to swim without risk of drowning.

There are two genera of chameleon in Madagascar. At the last count there were 34 species of chameleon and 20 species of brookesia, a very small and extremely well-camouflaged creature that lives mainly in the leaf-litter of the rainforest. Unlike *Chamaeleo* its short tail is not prehensile. In chameleons there is often a striking colour difference between males and females. Many males have horns (occasionally used for fighting) or other nasal protruberances. Where the two sexes are the same you can recognise the male by the bulge of the scrotal sac beneath the tail, and a spur on the hind feet. It is interesting to know how the chameleon achieves its colour change. It has a transparent epidermis, then three layers of cells – the top ones are yellow and red, the middle layer reflect blue light and white light, and the bottom layer is comprised of black pigment cells with tentacles or fingers that can protrude up through the other layers. The cells are under control of the autonomic nervous system, expanding and contracting according to a range of stimuli. Change of colour occurs when one layer is more stimulated than others, and patterning when one group of cells receives maximum stimulation.

In the early 17th century there was the firm conviction that chameleons subsisted without food. A German author, describing Madagascar in 1609, describes the chameleon living 'entirely on air and dew' and Shakespeare refers several times to the chameleon's supposed diet: 'The chameleon ... can feed on air' (*Two Gentlemen of Verona*) and 'of the chameleon's dish: I eat the air promise-crammed' (*Hamlet*). Possibly at that time no-one had witnessed the tongue flash out at 4/100s of a second to trap an insect. A chameleon's tongue has been likened to a bottle fitted over a billiard cue and connected to it by an elastic tube. If you thrust the cue forward the bottle would fly off to the length of the elastic, then retract more slowly. The billiard cue is the hyoid spike, over which the tongue fits, and the projectile is the hyoid bone. The process is aided by powerful circular muscles. The diagram below shows how this is achieved.

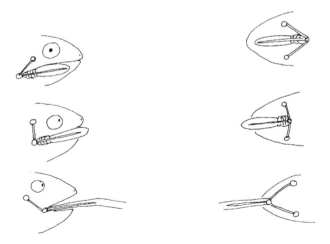

The name apparently comes from Greek: *chamai leon*, dwarf lion. I suppose a hissing, open-mouthed reptile *could* remind one of a lion, but to most visitors to Madagascar they are one of the most appealing and bizzare of the 'strange and marvellous forms' on show.

Chapter 4

Planning and preparations

WHEN TO GO

Read the section on climate in Chapter 1 before deciding when to travel. Broadly speaking, the dry months are in the winter between April and September, but rainfall varies enormously in different areas. The months to avoid are August and December, during the Christmas holidays, when popular places are crowded, and February and March (the cyclone season) when it will rain. However, the off-peak season can be rewarding, with cheaper international airfares and accommodation and fewer other tourists. Botanists will want to go in February when the orchids are in flower, and herpetologists will also prefer the spring/summer because the chameleons are in their flamboyant breeding colours. September is nice, but very windy in the south. My favourite months are October and November, when the weather is fine but not too hot, the jacarandas are in flower, the lemurs have babies, and lychees are sold from the road side.

RED TAPE

Visas

A visa is required by everyone (except citizens of Malawi and Lesotho) and is normally issued for a stay of 30 or 90 days and valid for travel within six months of the date of issue. Applications from some professions, such as journalists, may have to be referred to Head Office before a visa will be granted. Business visitors need a letter of recommendation. Visa prices vary from country to country.

Long-term visas are usually available for stays of more than 90 days, but need authorisation from Antananarivo so can take about two months to process.

Forms must usually be completed in quintuplicate but most embassies have a photocopier. You will need four or five photos. You may be asked to show evidence of a return ticket; a letter from the travel agent dealing with your flights is sufficient.

Embassy and consulate addresses

Australia
Consulate. Floor 7, 19 Pitt St, Sydney, NSW 2000. Tel: 252 3770. Hours 9.00 to 12.00, 14.00 to 15.00. Visas are issued within 48 hours and cost $25. The consul-general, Frederic Barnes, is very helpful.

Austria
Consulate. Pötzleindorferstr. 94-96, A-1184 Wien. Tel: 47 41 92 & 47 12 73.

Belgium
Embassy. 276 Ave de Tervueren, 1150 Bruxelles. Tel: 770 1726 & 770 1774.

Canada
Embassy. 282 Somerset W. St, Ottawa, Ontario K27 0J6. Tel: (613) 563 2506. Honorary Consulate. 853 Rue Sagurnay, Brossard, Quebec, J4X IM6. Tel: (514) 422 9991, ext. 311.

Honorary Consulate. 335 Watson Ave., Oakville B.P. L6J 3V5 Toronto. Tel: (416) 845 8914.

France
Embassy. 4 Ave Raphael, 75016 Paris. Tel: 145 04 62 11. Visas take three days and cost 70FF.

Germany
Consulate. Rolandstrasse 48, (Postfach 188) 5300 Bonn 2. Tel: 0228 331057.

Great Britain
Honorary Consulate. 16 Lanark Mansions, Pennard Rd, London W12 8DT. Tel: 081 746 0133. Fax: 081 746 0134. Hours 09.30 - 13.00. Visas supplied immediately or by post; very helpful. £35 (single entry) tourist visa. £50 business visa.

Italy
Embassy. Via Riccardo Zandonai 84/A, Roma. Tel: 327 7797 & 327 5183.

Kenya
Visas (inexpensive) are obtainable from Air Madagascar on the second floor of the Nairobi Hilton (PO Box 41723). Tel: 25286/26494. Allow 24 hours.

Mauritius
Embassy. Ave Queen Mary, Port Louis. Tel: 6 50 15 & 6 50 16.

La Réunion
Consulate. 73 Rue Juliette Dodu, 97461 Saint Denis. Tel: 21 05 21/21 65 58. Visas cost the same as in France.

South Africa
At the time of writing there is no Madagascar representative in South Africa. A seven-day visa is obtained on arrival in Antananarivo for all nationalities departing from Johannesburg. This must then be extended in Madagascar.

Spain
Honorary Consulate; Avda Diagonal 432, 08037 Barcelona. Tel: 416 0936.

Switzerland
Birkenstr. 5, 6000 Lucerne. Tel: 01 211 2721. Also Kappelgasse 14, CH-8022 Zürich. Tel: 01 211 2324.

United States
Embassy. 2374 Massachusetts Ave NW, Washington DC 20008. Tel: (202) 265 5525. Visas also available from the Permanent Mission of Madagascar to the United Nations, 801 Second Ave, Room 404, New York, NY 10017. Tel: (212) 986 9491.

Honorary Consulate. 123 South Broad St, Philadelphia, PA 19109. Tel: (215) 893 3067.

Honorary Consulate. 229 Piedmont Ave, Berkeley, CA 94720. Tel: (510) 643 8301 or toll-free (800) 856 2721. 'Annex': 410 East St, Vienna, VA 22180. Tel: (703) 319 0731. Mr de la Beaujardière gives far more than just a visa: advice, enthusiasm, and an excellent information leaflet.

Visas in the US cost $22.50 for a one-entry visa, $44.15 for two entries.

Extending your visa
A two month visa extension is usually easy to obtain. As early in your trip as possible go to the Ministry of the Interior, five minutes from the Hilton Hotel in Antananarivo. For your *prolongation* you will need: three photos, a photocopy of your currency declaration, a typewritten declaration (best done at home) of why you want to stay longer, your passport, your return ticket, and 10,400fmg. Every provincial town has an immigration office, or at least a *Commissariat de Police*, so in theory you can extend your visa anywhere but some places are much more cooperative than others.

Currency restrictions and other requirements
Since March 1994 visitors have been required to spend at least 2,000FF (£235/US$350) during their stay. You may not bring in any Malagasy currency, nor can you exchange it back into hard currency at the end of your trip. Currency declaration forms have been replaced by a form for recording all exchange transactions including credit card payments.
  These requirements do not apply to children under 12 years, foreigners with a work permit, business visitors with proof of an invitation from a local company, and tourists on organised visits providing they have vouchers from a foreign tour operator or a certificate from a Malagasy travel agency.
  A yellow fever vaccination certificate is required if you are coming from a fever area (eg Africa).

GETTING THERE

From Europe

The cheapest way of getting to Madagascar from Britain is with **Aeroflot** who fly via Moscow on Sundays (returning Tuesdays). Despite all that is happening in Russia these flights still seem to be fairly reliable. Since the price is nearly £300 less than that of Air France/Air Madagascar it is the ideal option for budget travellers and besides, Aeroflot puts you in the right frame of mind for Madagascar — anything can happen!

Rick Partridge writes: 'Aeroflot is in danger of becoming an attractive proposition! They are beginning to get the hang of customer relations. Their in-flight catering was quite acceptable too apart from the bullet-hard bread rolls. Fired from guns, these could be Russia's alternative to the nuclear deterrent.' You are advised to bring toilet paper and snacks to tide you over in Moscow, and something to drink as an alternative to the very sweet soft drinks beloved by the Russians.

Don't try to book direct through Aeroflot, but use one of their agents in London such as Wexas (see below), Sam Travel (tel: 071 636 2521 or 071 434 9561), or World Travel and Tours (tel: 081 673 4434).

On all airlines serving Madagascar there are low season and high season rates. Low season is from January to the end of June, and mid September to mid December.

Alternatives to Aeroflot are the much more comfortable and gourmet **Air Madagascar** and **Air France**. The two airlines are linked, food and comfort being much the same on each, although Air Madagascar is currently offering lower fares. Both leave from Paris CDG (section 2a).

Flights leave four times a week and schedules are reviewed twice a year. Those listed here are valid until October 1994. This year they are all going via Nairobi (goodbye Jeddah and Djibouti!). Air Madagascar goes on Wednesdays via Frankfurt, and Saturdays via Zürich. Air France leaves on Mondays, stopping en route in Moroni (Comoros), and on Thursdays. All these flights are overnight, taking approximately 14 hours. Madagascar is three hours ahead of GMT.

Until 1994 Air Madagascar had no representative in the UK and Air France took the lion's share of bookings. Now Aviareps is handling Air Madagascar and bookings and information are easily obtained. For reservations/information phone 0283 523958. Selected travel agents will be able to sell reduced-price Air Mad tickets; Globe Post Travel Services (tel: 071 587 0303) is one. Air France tickets are best bought from Wexas International (071 581 8761) or Trailfinders (071 938 3366). Wexas also does Aeroflot.

Flight arrangements may also be made through a new travel consultancy, Discover Madagascar, which is run by Seraphine Tierney. This very helpful and knowledgable Malagasy woman can arrange flights and give advice on travel arrangements. Phone (weekday afternoons) for an appointment: 081 747 4659.

British (and other European) travellers may want to make their travel arrangements in **France**. The visa price is much less than in London and they should be helpful over the *Madagascar à Liberté* offer detailed in Chapter 6 since they provided the information. The Paris office is at 29, Rue des Boulets, Paris 75011. Tel: 43 79 74 74. Fax: 43 79 30 33. There are also Air Madagascar offices in Zürich, **Switzerland**: c/o ATASH Sa, 34, Neumuhlequai, 8006 Zürich, Tel: 01 362 72 40, and Munich, **Germany**: Herzog-Rudolf-Strasse 3, 8000 München 22, Tel: 089 2318 0113.

From other Indian Ocean islands

You may be able to pick up a cheap flight from Paris to **La Réunion** from where there are almost daily flights to Antananarivo, and also to Toamasina (Tamatave) on the east coast. Air Mauritius flies between **Mauritius** and Antananarivo three times a week, and finally there are several flights from the Comoro Islands.

From Africa

From **Kenya** there are several flights per week (Air Madagascar and Air France) from Nairobi. (Air Mauritius used to fly between Nairobi and Antananarivo, but not in 1994.) With so many cheap flights from London to Nairobi, this is a good option – if you can stand the departure time of 02.50 Thursday morning and 06.00 Sunday morning, and the danger of the planes being overbooked since they are coming from Europe. In 1993 a reader bought a ticket, valid for a year, that took him Nairobi - Moroni - Antananarivo - Réunion - Mauritius - Nairobi for less than US$1000 so it is worth making enquiries. The current Nairobi - Antananarivo fare is US$367.

Flights now go twice a week from **South Africa**. Air Madagascar flies from Johannesburg on Sundays, and the highly-praised Air Austral goes on Thursdays (both flights leave Madagascar the previous day). The flight takes four hours and costs R2820 (£520).

South Africans are lucky; they have Madagaskar Adventures to make all their arrangements. They are particularly strong on specialised natural history tours, and their knowledge of the country and understanding of its hassles are second to none in Africa. Madagaskar Adventures, 21 Ivy Rd, Norwood, 2192. Tel: (011) 728 7384; Fax: 728 2419.

From the USA

Madagascar is about as far from California as it is possible to be. Indeed, San Francisco and the southern town of Toliara *are* as far apart as it is possible to be. Understandably, therefore, the normal fare from the USA is expensive. However, as in South Africa, there is a specialist tour operator who combines reasonably-priced flights on Air France and Air

Madagascar with individualised land arrangements and a great knowledge of, and love for, Madagascar: Monique Rodriguez, Cortez Travel Services, 124 Lomas Santa Fe Dr, Solano Beach, CA 92075. Tel: 619 755 5136 or (toll free) 800 854 1029, Fax: 619 481 7474.

The General Sales Agent for Air Madagascar can be reached toll free on 800 821 3388, Fax: 619 792 5280.

From Australia

Air Madagascar has an office in the same building as the Sydney Consulate. There are no direct flights; you have a choice of going via Mauritius (the shortest route) or via Johannesburg. Also possible is via Singapore and Mauritius, but this is the longest.

Arrrival in Antananarivo

See Chapter 7 for the rather complicated arrivals and departure procedure.

WHAT TO BRING

Luggage

A sturdy duffel bag or backpack with internal frame is more practical than a suitcase. Backpackers should consider buying a rucksack with a zipped compartment to enclose the straps when using them on airlines. Bring a light folding nylon bag for taking purchases home, and the largest permissible bag to take as hand baggage on the plane. Pack this with everything you need for the first four or so days, especially if travelling by Aeroflot. Then, if they lose your luggage, you won't be too inconvenienced.

Clothes

Before deciding what clothes to pack, take a look at the climate chart of page 12. There is quite a difference between summer and winter temperatures, particularly in the highlands and south where it is distinctly *cold* at night between May and September. A fibre-pile jacket or a body-warmer (down vest) is useful in addition to a sweater. At any time of the year it will be hot during the day in low-lying areas, and very hot between October and March. Layers of clothing − T-shirt, sweatshirt, light sweater − are warm and versatile, and take less room than a heavy sweater. For trousers I am a devotee of Rohan Bags (30, Maryland Rd, Tongwell, Milton Keynes, Bucks MK15 8HN. Tel: 0908 216655). They are lightweight, dry overnight whatever the humidity, and have an inside zipped pocket for security. At any time of year you will need a light showerproof jacket, and during the wet season, or if spending time in the rain forest, appropriate rain gear and perhaps a small umbrella. A light cotton jacket is always useful for breezy evenings by the coast. Don't forget a hat.

Good outdoor clothing and other travel supplies can be bought in England from the excellent YHA shops; phone 0784 458625 for the address of your nearest branch.

The most versatile footwear are trainers (running shoes) and sandals. 'Sports sandals' which strap securely to the feet yet are waterproof (Merrell make a good selection) are better than flip-flops. Hiking boots may be needed in places like Ankarana but are not necessary for the main tourist circuits.

Give some thought to beachwear if you enjoy snorkelling. You may need an old pair of sneakers (or similar) to protect your feet from sea urchins, and a T-shirt and shorts to wear while in the water. The underwater world is so absorbing it is very easy to get badly sunburnt, especially on the shoulders and back of thighs.

Toiletries

In the early 1980s you could not even buy soap in Madagascar. Then, with the lifting of import restrictions, all sorts of luxury goods appeared in the shops. In 1994, in an attempt to save on foreign currency, the government once again banned the import of some luxury items. Bring everything you need, especially insect repellent, sun-screen, skin creams, and so on. You should also bring a roll of toilet paper. The paper provided by most hotels is the sort favoured by the rural French – more like tree-bark than anything you want to bring in repeated contact with your bottom. This is awkward for those planning a long stay; one traveller, pointing out that you can't bring enough toilet paper to last the trip, recommends wetting the local stuff to make it less abrasive – and cooler. If you normally blow your nose on loo paper you'd better bring a handkerchief.

Women should bring enough tampons to last the trip. The brands without an applicator take up less luggage space. Men (and women) should bring condoms if there is any chance of a sexual encounter.

Some toilet articles have several uses: dental floss is excellent for repairs as well as for teeth, and a nail brush gets clothes clean as well.

Don't take up valuable space with a bath towel – a hand towel is perfectly adequate.

Women (and men) should leave all jewellery at home. Apart from the high risk of theft, such items of value have to be declared on arrival and may even be weighed to make sure you don't sneakily sell a link or two of your gold chain!

Protection against mosquitoes

With malaria on the increase, it is vital to be properly protected. There are a lot of products on the market, one of the most useful being Buzz-Bands (made by Traveller International Products). These slip over the wrists and ankles (mosquitoes' favourite area) and really do the job. For hotel rooms, pyrethrum coils which burn slowly through the night and repel insects with their smoke are available all over Madagascar. The brand name is Big-Tox. They really do work.

If you expect to be using C category hotels, or sleeping outside it is sensible to have a mosquito net, and a self- standing one at that since there is rarely anywhere to hang the other sort. The best ones I know are made by Long Road, USA whose Indoor Travel Tent is sturdy enough to use outdoors and has a built-in groundsheet giving protection from bed bugs and fleas as well as mosquitoes (but meaning that you must use your own sleeping bag inside it). Mosquito nets are available in the UK through MASTA and other specialist suppliers.

Rough travel equipment

Basic camping gear gives you the freedom to travel adventurously and can add a considerable degree of comfort to overland journeys.

The most important item is your backpack: this should have an internal frame and plenty of pockets. Protect it from oil, dirt, and the effluent of young or furry/feathered passengers with a canvas sack or similar adapted covering. If this can be locked, so much the better.

In winter a light sleeping bag will keep you warm in cheap hotels with inadequate bedding, and on night stops on − or off − 'buses'. A sheet sleeping bag plus a light blanket or space blanket is ideal for the summer

months (October to May) and when the hotel linen is missing or dirty.

An air-mattress or pillow pads your bum on hard seats as well as your hips when sleeping out. One of those horseshoe-shaped travel pillows lets you sleep sitting up (which you'll need to do on taxi-brousses).

A lightweight tent allows you to strike out on your own and stay in nature reserves, on deserted beaches and so forth. It will need to have a separate rain fly and be well-ventilated. A bivi-sac or the Long Road Travel Tent is sufficient.

Most people forgo a stove in order to cut down on weight, but if you will be camping extensively bring a stove that burns petrol (gasoline) or paraffin (kerosene). Meths (*alcohol à bruler*) is usually available as well. There are always fresh vegetables for sale in the smallest village so bring some stock cubes to make vegetable stew.

Bring your own mug and spoon (and carry them with you always). That way you can enjoy roadside coffee without the risk of a cup rinsed in filthy water, and market yoghurt without someone else's germs on the spoon.

Don't forget a water-bottle. The sort that has a belt attached – or can be attached to a belt – is ideal.

An excellent selection of travel goods are available from some of the immunisation centres such as Trailfinders and British Airways; see Chapter 5 for addresses.

Photography

Ordinary print film is available in Madagascar, but may disappear during the period of import restrictions so it is safer to bring plenty. It can be competently developed at the photo shop near the Colbert. Slide film is hard to find; all you need should be brought with you – and you need twice as much as you think.

You will not need a telephoto lens for the lemurs of Berenty and Nosy Komba (wide-angle is more useful for these bold animals) but you'll want a long lens plus very fast film (400 asa) for most forest creatures. For landscapes 64 or 100 asa is ideal. A macro lens is wonderful for all the weird insects and reptiles. Don't overburden yourself with camera equipment – there's no substitute for the eye/brain combination!

Miscellaneous

Some random tips: bring a transparent pouch (the sort you carry maps in) to hang round your neck at the airport to cope with all those papers and documents. Bring a roll of the wide, brown type of Sellotape; it can be used for taping up anything. A rubber wedge will secure your hotel door at night, and a combination lock is useful in a variety of ways (see Chapter 5 *Safety*). I hesitate to write this, but last year I found my Walkman a godsend during uncomfortable nights. My image may be improved when you know that I was lulled to sleep listening to the musical sounds of the Malagasy language from *Malagasy Basics* (see Chapter 2).

Checklist

Small torch (flashlight) with spare batteries and bulb, or headlamp (for nocturnal animal hunts), travel alarm clock (or alarm wristwatch), penknife, sewing kit, scissors, tweezers, safety pins, sellotape (Scotchtape), felt-tipped pen, ballpoint pens, a small notebook, a large notebook for diary and letters home, plastic bags (all sizes, sturdy; Zip-loc are particularly useful), universal plug for baths and sinks, elastic clothes line or cord and pegs, concentrated detergent (available in tubes in camping stores) and biodegradable soap for camping, ear plugs (a godsend in noisy hotels and taxi-brousses), insect repellent, sunscreen, lipsalve, spare glasses or contact lenses, sun glasses, medical and dental kit (see *Health*), dental floss, a water container, water purifying tablets or other sterilising agent. Compact binoculars, camera and film, books, miniature cards, Scrabble/pocket chess set.

If you are travelling independently, you should also bring an adequate knowledge of French and a willingness to learn some Malagasy. A phrase book and/or dictionary is useful.

Goods for presents, sale or trade

This is a difficult area. In the past tourists have handed out presents to children and created the tiresome little beggars you will encounter in the popular areas (if you don't now know the French for pen or sweets, you soon will). They have also handed T-shirts to adults with similar consequences. There are, however, plenty of occasions when a gift is appropriate, although as Will Pepper points out 'On a number of occasions people said this souvenir of Ireland is all well and good but I would prefer cash'. Giving money as a 'present' is entirely acceptable (see Chapter 6) so in rural areas it's best to pay cash and refrain from introducing a new consumer awareness.

There are items you should bring which will increase your interaction with the people: postcards of your country, picture books, paper and a knowledge of origami, string and a knowledge of cat's cradles. Simple conjuring tricks go down a treat. Photos of your family will be pored over gratifyingly or, if you haven't got a family, the Royal Family will do. If you're unfortunate enough to come from a country that doesn't have a Royal Family, film stars are a good substitute — particularly the muscle-bound type, preferably scowling. Any colour picture is an attraction; I've been told that the photos in this book drew about 50 viewers at one time! Frisbees and balls all add to the fun. However, to call yourself a real traveller you should be capable of being entertaining without the use of props.

In urban areas or with the more sophisticated Malagasy people, presents are a very good way of showing your appreciation for kindness or extra good service. Goods can also be used instead of cash for hotel rooms, transport, etc. Will Pepper says: 'Trade samples of perfume (small bottles) were such a hit with women and husbands that I got free accommodation and meals on two occasions. Music cassettes were a huge hit with taxi-brousse drivers, and also mean that you can listen to good quality music on long trips.' It's worth bringing some duty-free cigarettes, however much you disapprove of the habit. Clothes, especially trendy T-shirts, are often requested by those with an appetite for the 'western' look, and you will always find a home for trainers (running shoes).

If you want to contribute something a little more intellectually satisfying, here is a suggestion from Dr Philip Jones, who travelled in Madagascar on behalf of the charity Money for Madagascar. 'I was asked several times for an English Grammar, so any such books would be valued gifts. If visitors take a French-English dictionary, why not leave it in Madagascar?' Linda and Victor Yerrill, who visited a school, point out the shortage of books. 'One school in Tana has three books in its English library — paperbacks of dubious literary quality which had been left behind in a visiting businessman's hotel room! If everyone who visited the country could leave two or three books behind to be given to schools, it would be a great help.' The book situation should be alleviated, however, by the gift from the British government of 300 English books for each of 82 *lycées* across the country.

MONEY

How much money to take is covered in Chapter 6, but give some thought to *how* to take it.

Bring your money in US dollar or pound sterling travellers cheques. Money may only be changed at 'accredited establishments' — banks, some hotels, and some travel agents. It is useful to bring some cash — French francs, dollars or sterling banknotes are equally good — for those occasions when you want to change a small amount of money or haven't got your passport with you.

Some of the large hotels accept credit cards, but there are some notable exceptions, such as the Dauphin in Taolagnaro. However, credit cards may be used to draw cash (see Chapters 6 and 7) so it is well worth bringing one. The French for Visa card is *Carte Bleue*.

'One of the great evils arising from [slavery] is the dignifying of idleness as belonging to freedom, and the degrading of labour by making it the badge of slavery'.
Rev W. Ellis, The Martyr Church, 1869

WAYS AND MEANS

Madagascar... Are you sure?

With the right planning almost everyone can enjoy Madagascar. It will not be a cheap holiday, however, so if you have serious doubts about your ability to adapt to its ways you would do better not to go.

Having decided that you have the enthusiasm and flexibility to make your trip a success consider the options below.

What sort of traveller are you?

Deciding what's best for your budget and inclinations is as important as planning where to go in this huge island. Consider which of the following options suits you best.

Group departure

This is the easiest option for the person with only limited time available, and who is happy to leave the arrangements to someone else. Group travel is usually a lot of fun, ideal for single people who do not wish to travel alone, and if you choose the tour company and itinerary carefully you will see a great deal of the country, gain an understanding of its complicated culture and unique wildlife, and generally have a great time without the need to make decisions.

Many tour operators in Britain and America do set departures to Madagascar; some of them have advertised in this book.

One tour operator that should be mentioned because it's different is **Earthwatch**. This non-profit organisation involves paying volunteers in scientific projects. Among other things in Madagascar you can work with Dr Alison Jolly on lemur research. Addresses: Belsyne Court, 57 Woodstock Rd, Oxford OX2 6HU, England, tel: 0865 311600 and 680 Mt Auburn St, PO Box 403, Watertown, MA 02272-9104, USA.

Tailor-made tours

This is the ideal option for a couple or small group who are not restricted financially. It is also the best choice for people with special interests or strong ideas, and who like things to go as smoothly as possible. You will be the decision-maker and will choose where you want to go, but the logistics will be taken care of. Although a good travel agent can make these arrangements, you are strongly recommended to use a specialist such as Cortez Travel in the USA or Madagaskar Adventures in South Africa, or their associates in Britain, Reef and Rainforest Tours.

Some sample tours: fishing, diving, trekking, river journeys, sailing, mineralogy, speleology, bird-watching, herpetology, botany (which can be further split into orchids and succulents), and entomology.

If you have a fax machine and are willing to persevere with Madagascar's erratic telecommunications, you can save money by dealing

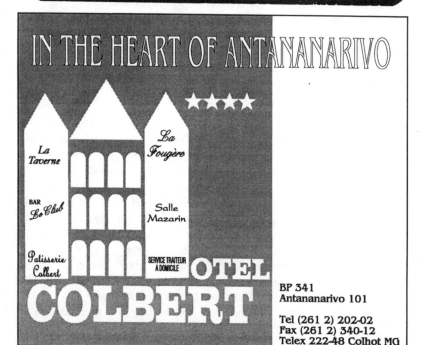

directly with a tour operator in Madagascar. The best ones are listed later in this chapter.

Independent travel

Independent travellers usually have a rough idea of where they want to go and how they will travel, but are open to changes of plan dictated by local conditions, whim and serendipity. Independent travellers are not necessarily budget travellers: those that can afford to fly to major towns, then rent a vehicle and driver, can eliminate a large amount of hassle and see everything they set out to see — providing they set a realistic programme for themselves. What they miss out on is contact with the local people, and some of the smells, sounds and otherness of Madagascar.

The majority of independent travellers (and users of this book) go by public transport and stay in B or C category hotels. They are exposed to all Madagascar's joys and frustrations and most seem to love it, even if all agree that they have never travelled in a country that is so difficult to get around in. The key here is not to try too much. When it can take an entire day for your taxi-brousse to decide to leave, and all night and much of the following day for it to achieve a 300km journey, you need both time and a very stiff upper lip.

The seriously adventurous

Madagascar must be one of the very few countries left in the world where large areas are not yet detailed in a guide book. I have deliberately kept it that way, occasionally leaving out a traveller's description of the fantastic road he (or she) cycled down or the village he walked into. For the seriously adventurous, a study of the standard 1:2,000,000 map of Madagascar reveals some mouth-watering possibilities, and a look at the detailed 1:500,000 maps confirms the opportunities for people who are willing to walk or cycle. In my very thick Readers' Letters file I have some wonderful accounts from travellers Luc Selleslagh, John Kupiek and Bishop Brock who did just that. Not everyone is courageous enough to step into the unknown like this, but in fact it's one of the safest ways to travel: the Malagasy that you meet will, once they have got over the shock of seeing you, invariably be welcoming and hospitable. The risk of crime is very low. It's how I first saw Madagascar and why I fell in love with the place.

Tour operators in Madagascar

There are many tour operators in Madagascar. This is by no means a complete list, just a selection of those that I can recommend. The Maison du Tourisme de Madagascar in Antananarivo puts out a comprehensive list.

Madagascar Airtours. Hilton Hotel, Antananarivo. BP 3874. Tel: 341 92. Fax: 343 70. Telex: 222 32 AIR MAD MG. The most experienced agency, with offices in most major towns, they can organise a wide variety of specialist tours including natural history, ornithology, speleology, trekking, mineralogy, river trips, sailing, etc.

SETAM. Ave 26 de Juin, Antananarivo. Tel: 272 49. Fax: 2347 02. Extremely helpful and efficient. Excellent English spoken. Highly recommended.

Sambava Voyages. BP 1605, Antananarivo. Tel: 305 70. Telex: 22461 MARCAM MG. A highly competent company with its head office in Sambava on the east coast. Recommended for tours in eastern Madagascar.

Transcontinents. 10 Ave de l'Indépendance, Antananarivo. BP 541. Tel: 223 98. Telex 22259 ZODIAC.

Voyages Bourdon. 15 Rue P. Lumumba, Antananarivo. Tel: 296 96. Telex 22557 YOYDON MG.

Rova Travel Tours. 35 Rue Refotaka. BP 5179. Tel: 276 67. Fax 276 89. A new company which offers tailor-made and special interest tours.

Tropica Touring. 41 Lalana Ratsimilaho. BP 465. Tel: 222 30 or 276 80. Fax: 349 01.

Highlights and itinerary suggestions

One of the hardest decisions facing the first-time visitor to a country as diverse as Madagascar is where to go. Even a month is not long enough to see everything so itineraries must be planned according to interests and the degree of comfort wanted. Here are some suggestions for tours lasting three to four weeks.

Reliability and comfort

The following places provide as much luxury as is possible in Madagascar, and a good overview of its attractions: Antananarivo, Antsirabe, Toliara (Tuléar), Taolagnaro (Fort Dauphin) and Berenty, Nosy Be. The stretch between Antananarivo and Antsirabe should be done by taxi or private car, and the rest by plane.

Nature reserves in moderate comfort

These are accessible by good road (if cyclone damage has been repaired) and have good to moderate accommodation: Andasibe (Périnet), Ampijoroa (as a day trip from Mahajunga), Montagne d'Ambre (as a day trip from Antsiranana (Diego Suarez)), Berenty, Ivoloina (near Toamasina).

The best reserves, comfort immaterial

See page 56 (map of protected areas) or the index to find descriptions of these reserves: Andasibe (Périnet), Ampijoroa (camping), Montagne d'Ambre (camping), Ankaranana (camping), Ranomafana, Nosy Mangabe and the Masoala Peninsula, Beza Mahafaly (camping), Kirindy and/or Tsingy de Bemaraha (camping).

Birding

See page 52 for full details, but these places cover all the different habitats: Ampijoroa (and along the road from Mahajunga), Ranomafana, Masoala Peninsula, Forest of Ambohetantely, spiny forest north of Toliara, Zombitse forest.

Landscape, people and tombs

For those whose interest lies more in the people and the countryside, a journey overland is recommended. RN7 from Antananarivo to Toliara gives a wonderful overview from rice-paddies in the highlands to the lovely town of Ambalavao and its magnificent granite mountains, and the small villages between Ihosy and Toliara. It also gives you a chance to see Isalo National Park. The journey is best done in a private vehicle so you can stop and look; there are good hotels at the main towns. Take a side trip from Toliara to see the Mahafaly tombs.

A more adventurous alternative (but still on a good road) is by train or bus to Toamasina then north by public transport to Soanierana-Ivongo and by boat to Nosy Boraha (Île Ste Marie). Another east coast journey is from Fianarantsoa to Manakara by train, then south to Farafangana. Probably the most challenging west coast trip is to Morondava by road then overland to Toliara.

LEECHES

Few classes of invertebrates elicit more disgust than leeches. Perhaps some facts about these well-adapted animals will give them more appeal.

Leeches, as you might guess, are related to worms and, like them, are hermaphrodite. Terrestial leeches such as those found in Madagascar are small (1-2cm long) and find their warm-blooded prey by vibrations and odour. Suckers at each end enable the leech to move around in a series of loops and to attach itself to a leaf, or to your skin, by its posterior while seeking or sucking its meal with the front end. It has sharp jaws and can quickly – and painlessly – bite through the skin and start feeding. When it has filled its digestive tract with blood the leech drops off and digests its meal – a process that can take several months since leeches have pouches all along their gut to hold as much blood as possible. The salivary glands manufacture an anticoagulant which prevents the blood clotting during the meal or period of digestion. This is why leech wounds bleed so spectacularly.

Chapter 5

Health and safety

HEALTH

The health section is written by Dr Jane Wilson, who led two expeditions to Ankarana. She has studied bilharzia in western Madagascar and tropical hygiene in Indonesia and Pakistan.

Before you go
Malaria prevention

About 2,000 travellers a year return to Britain with malaria: ten or a dozen subsequently die of it. This is the most common serious tropical disease that affects international travellers and it is reckless to ignore the risk of contracting it. You should start taking malaria prophylaxis tablets one week before leaving for Madagascar and for six weeks after returning home.

At the time of writing two chloroquine (Nivaquine) weekly and two proguanil (Paludrine) daily were recommended. Up to date advice is available from the Malaria Reference Laboratory in London, Tel: 0891 600 350 for a recording of where malaria is a problem and what tablets to take, or 0891 600 274 for advice on avoiding bites.

Malaria tablets are best taken with or soon after food (or milk or a couple of biscuits) when they are least likely to cause the side effect of nausea which troubles some people. It is safe to take Chloroquine during pregnancy and breast feeding. Proguanil is also safe in pregnancy, but you should then take Folic Acid – a vitamin supplement – with it. Fansidar is *not* a safe drug to take as prophylaxis but if you are travelling far from reliable medical facilities you could carry three Fansidar tablets for emergency treatment of malaria. Take plenty of insect repellent (DEET-based are best), long sleeved shirts, long trousers and consider carrying a mosquito net.

Immunisations

Disease patterns and international health regulations change so it is worth taking special advice. Travel clinics such as those operated by Thomas Cook and British Airways (phone 071 831 5333 for the nearest of the 30 or so BA clinics) offer constantly up-dated health briefs as well as immunisations. It is important that your immunisations for tetanus, polio and typhoid are up to date. A highly effective vaccine against Hepatitis A, Havrix, is recommended for those travelling for several months. Two shots, taken two weeks apart, provide protection for a year. A third shot, taken six months to a year later, gives 10-year immunity.

It is also worth having a Schick Test to check that your childhood immunisation for diphtheria is still protective. An 'ordinary' intramuscular shot against rabies is now available and may be worth arranging if you think you are at risk. The disease is a problem in Madagascar because of semi-feral dogs in many parts of the island.

Remember that 'live' vaccines cannot be given within a fortnight of each other, so plan well ahead. There is a list of vaccination centres at the end of this section.

If you are coming from Africa you will be required to show an up to date International Vaccination Certificate for yellow fever; these are not required for passengers arriving from Europe or the USA.

Teeth
Have a dental check-up before you go. There is now a Dental Emergency Kit on the market (if you can't get it at Boots ask your dentist). Amongst other things it contains emergency fillings.

Insurance
Make sure you have insurance covering the cost of an air ambulance and treatment in La Réunion or Nairobi which offer more sophisticated medical facilities than are available in Madagascar.

In Madagascar
Local medical facilities
The local medical services are excellent considering the constraints imposed by poor communications, lack of drugs and facilities. Malagasy doctors are knowledgeable and well trained and all I met seemed reliable, trustworthy and friendly. Many of the younger doctors speak English.

Water sterilisation
Although the standard advice on water sterilisation in the tropics is to boil it for 20 minutes, merely bringing water to the boil kills nearly all bugs and renders it pretty safe. This means that tea, coffee, *ranovola*, etc bought in *hotelys* are probably the most convenient drinks to take when travelling. If you need a higher level of safety (eg when travelling with an infant) take a thermos flask: almost boiling water kept in this for half an hour or more will be thoroughly sterilised.

By drinking *Eau Vive* or mineral water, you will cut down the risk of water-borne diseases but this is not always available and can be quite expensive. It's often better to purify your own tap water. The most convenient and effective sterilising agent is iodine (preferable to chlorine because it kills amoebic cysts) which is available in liquid or tablet form. To make treated water more palatable bring packets of powdered drink. An alternative is a water filter such as the Travel-Well. It gives safe water with no unpleasant flavour, but is too slow for most people's thirst. Another possibility is a plug-in immersion heater so you can boil your water and have a nice hot cuppa (if you bring teabags).

Note that most travellers acquire diarrhoea from inadequately heated, contaminated food, salads, ice, icecream, etc, rather than from disobeying the 'don't drink the water' rule.

Some travellers' diseases
Malaria and insect-borne diseases
Tablets do not give complete protection from malaria although they should make it less serious if it does break through; it is important to protect yourself from being bitten. The mosquitoes which give you malaria usually bite in the evening (from about 5 pm) and throughout the night so at dusk it is wise to dress in long trousers and long sleeved shirts and cover exposed skin with insect repellent. *Anopheles* mosquitoes generally hunt at ankle level and tend to bite the first piece of exposed flesh they encounter so DEET impregnated ankle bands (available from MASTA) are surprisingly effective protection.

Malaria transmission is rare in urban environments, but it does occur around Antananarivo; the altitude here is insufficient to limit the malaria mosquito. Cerebral malaria is a problem and is presumably caught by people bitten by mosquitoes which breed in the paddy fields around the city; malaria mosquitoes can fly five kilometres from their breeding grounds.

At night protect yourself by sleeping under a mosquito net or burning mosquito coils. And be sure to take your malaria tablets meticulously.

Even if you have been taking your malaria prophylaxis carefully there is a slight chance of contracting malaria. You should therefore consult a doctor (mentioning that you have been abroad) if you get a flu-like illness within a year of getting home.

Mosquitoes pass on malaria but also elephantiasis and a variety of unpleasant viral fevers. By avoiding mosquito bites you also avoid these serious diseases as well as those itching lumps which so easily become infected. Once bitten, tiger balm, calamine lotion or calamine-based creams help stop the itching.

The African forms of sleeping sickness do not exist in Madagascar as there is no tsetse vector to spread it. The only known Trypanosome organism (sleeping sickness) which exists in Madagascar affects only chameleons!

Travellers' diarrhoea, etc

Diarrhoea is very common in visitors to Madagascar and you are more likely to suffer from this if you are new to tropical travel. A survey in Antananarivo showed that 100% of home made and 60% of factory made ices and ice creams contained the faecal bacteria which cause travellers' diarrhoea. So if you want to stay healthy avoid ice cream, ice, untreated water, salads, uncooked foods and cooked food that has been hanging around or has been inadequately reheated. Sizzling hot street food is likely to be far safer than food offered in buffets in expensive hotels.

There is a high prevalence of tapeworm in Malagasy cattle so I would recommend eating your steaks well done.

The way to the quickest recovery from travellers' diarrhoea is to stop eating solid food, milk and alcohol and take only clear fluids. Mix a rounded dessert spoon (or 4 teaspoons) of sugar with ¼ teaspoon of salt in a large glass of boiled and cooled water and drink every time you open your bowels − more if you are thirsty. Substituting glucose for sugar will make you feel even better. Young coconut (with a little salt added) is also a good rehydration fluid, as is *ranovola*, marmite or oxo drinks, herbal teas, etc. Hot drinks and iced drinks cause a reflex emptying of the bowel so avoid these whilst the diarrhoea is at its worst.

Once the bowel has ejected the toxic material causing the diarrhoea the symptoms will settle quite quickly and you should be able to start eating again after 24-48 hours. Taking 'blockers' such as Imodium, Arret or Lomotil should stop the diarrhoea but keeps the toxic products inside so you feel lousy longer. However, if you have to go on a long bus journey you may have to resort to these. Should the diarrhoea be associated with passing blood or slime it would be sensible to have a stool check at some stage, but provided you continue to drink clear fluids no harm will come from waiting for advice for a few days.

[Since Dr Wilson wrote this chapter there has been some media coverage of the antibiotic Ciprofloxacin being used very effectively to cure travellers' diarrhoea. The advantage over other antiobiotics is that the dose is a single pill rather than a course of pills. Discuss this with your doctor or travel clinic. The problem, as Jane Wilson points out in a letter, is that a Cyprofloxacin-resistant strain of bug will no doubt emerge, 'which will be a pity since it clobbers *real* nasties − the serious infections which kill people.' This drug must not be given to children or where the fluid intake is inadequate.]

If you are worried or feel very ill seek local medical advice, but as long as you keep well hydrated you should come to no harm and symptoms will usually settle without further treatment. Even bacillary dysentery and cholera(!) will resolve in a week without treatment as long as you drink plenty of rehydration fluids.

Similarly if you pass a worm, this is alarming but treatment can wait and indeed travellers often only carry one and so need no treatment.

Sometimes the gut alternates between mild diarrhoea and constipation. Constipation is made worse by dehydration (a problem in the heat), eggs and bananas. Other fruits will help relieve it.

Some people believe in having a stool check-up when they return home. Personally I would only bother if I had symptoms.

Bilharzia

This is a nasty debilitating disease which is a problem in much of lowland Madagascar. It is caught by swimming or paddling in clean, still or slow moving water (not fast-flowing rivers) where an infected person has defaecated or urinated. The parasite then infects pond snails and then people by penetrating the skin where it causes 'swimmer's itch'. Since it takes at least 10 minutes for the worm to infect you, a quick wade across a river (as long as you dry off quickly) should not put you at risk. It is cured with a single dose of Praziquantel, but the parasites are acquiring resistance to this medicine.

Sexually transmitted diseases

These are common in Madagascar (a doctor in Diego told me 10% of his consultations were for gonorrhoea!), and AIDS is on the increase. If you enjoy nightlife, condoms will make encounters less risky.

Rabies and animal bites

Should you be unfortunate enough to be bitten by any mammal, wild or domesticated, you are at risk from both rabies and tetanus. If you are not immunised against tetanus you must seek medical help speedily. The risk of rabies should also be taken very seriously if you have not been immunised, particularly if you are bitten by a dog.

Once the rabies virus enters the body it migrates slowly along the nerves and the dramatic symptoms of hydrophobia, etc do not appear until the virus has reached the brain. Symptoms will begin after perhaps two weeks if the bites have been to the face, but may be delayed for as much as two years if the bite is on the foot. Once symptoms have appeared, rabies is untreatable and invariably fatal. Before the onset of symptoms, the disease can be prevented by a simple course of injections into the arm spaced over three months (the painful ones into the abdomen have long been superseded). Although it is wise to seek medical help as soon as possible after you are bitten (and bites to the face must be attended to within 10 days) it may not be too late to do so after you get home.

Immunisation against these diseases before you travel is therefore strongly recommended if you are travelling off the beaten track. Even if immunised, it is advisable to seek medical attention if the bite is severe or the wound dirty and deep. A rabies booster is sensible after any suspect bite.

Infection and trivial breaks in the skin

The skin is very prone to infection in hot, moist climates so anything that makes even the slightest break to its surface is likely to allow bacteria to enter and so cause problems. Mosquito bites — especially if you scratch them — are probably the commonest route of infection so apply a cream to reduce the itching. Toothpaste helps if you are stuck for anything better. Keep any wounds, especially oozing wounds, covered so that flies don't snack on them.

Fairly major infections can arise through even a small nick in the skin. Antiseptic creams are not advised since they keep wounds moist and this encourages further infection. A powerful antiseptic which also dries the skin is Potassium permanganate crystals dissolved in water. Another alternative is diluted tincture of iodine (which you should be carrying anyway as a water steriliser). Bathe the wound twice a day, more if you can, by dabbing with cotton wool dipped in the Potassium permanganate or iodine solution.

Bathing in sulphur springs cures mild skin infections.

Sunburn

Light-skinned people burn remarkably quickly near the equator, especially when snorkelling. Wearing a T-shirt, especially one with a collar, protects the back and long shorts can also be worn. Use high protection factor waterproof sunscreen on the back of the neck, calves, and other exposed parts.

The nasty side of nature
Animals

Malagasy land-snakes are back-fanged so are effectively non-venomous. Sea-snakes, although venomous, are easy to see and unaggressive.

Particularly when in the dry forest it is wise to be wary of scorpions and centipedes. Neither is fatal but they are very unpleasant. Scorpions are nocturnal but often come out after rain; they like hiding in small crevices during the day. If you are camping in the desert or the dry forest it is not unusual to find they have crept into the pocket of a rucksack — even if you have taken the sensible precaution of suspending it from a tree. Scorpion stings are very painful for about 24 hours but are not life-threatening. After a sting on the finger I had an excruciatingly painful hand and arm for several days. The pain was only eased with morphine. My finger had no feeling for a month and still has an abnormal nerve supply.

Madagascar has some very unpleasant (15cm) centipedes; large spiders can be dangerous and the black widow occurs in Madagascar as well as an aggressive hairy spider with a nasty bite. Navy digger wasps have an unpleasant sting, but it is only the scorpions which commonly cause problems because they favour hiding in places where one might plunge a hand without looking. If you sleep on the ground, isolate yourself from these creatures with a mat, hammock or tent with sewn-in ground sheet.

Leeches can be a nuisance in the rainforest but they are only revolting, not dangerous. These are best avoided by covering up, tucking trousers into socks and applying insect repellent (even under the socks and on shoes — but beware, DEET dissolves plastics). Once leeches have become attached they should not be forcibly removed. Either wait until they have finished feeding (when they will fall off) or encourage them to let go by applying a lit cigarette or salt. A film canister is a convenient salt container. The wound left by a leech bleeds a great deal and may become infected if not kept clean.

Beware of strolling barefoot on damp, sandy river beds. This is the way to pick up jiggers. These are female sand fleas which resemble maggots and burrow into your toes to feed on your blood while incubating their eggs. Dig them out with a sterilised needle, and disinfect the wound thoroughly to prevent infection.

Plants
Madagascar has quite a few plants which cause skin irritation. The worst one I have encountered is a climbing legume which has pea-pod like fruits which look furry. This 'fur' penetrates the skin as thousands of tiny needles which must be painstakingly extracted with tweezers. Prickly pear fruits have the same defence. Relief from secretions of other irritating plants is obtained by bathing. Sometimes it is best to wash your clothes as well and immersion fully clothed may be the last resort!

Medical kit
Apart from personal medication taken on a regular basis it is unnecessary to weigh yourself down with a comprehensive medical kit as many of your requirements will be met by the pharmacies.

The list below is the absolute maximum an ordinary traveller needs to carry (I always carry less). Expeditions or very adventurous travellers should contact MASTA (*Useful addresses*, next page).

Malaria tablets, lots of plasters (Band-aids) to cover broken skin, infected insect bites, etc, antiseptic (potassium permanganate crystals to dissolve in water are best), small pieces of sterile gauze (Melonin dressing) and sticky plaster, soluble aspirin — good for fevers, aches, and for gargling when you have a sore throat. Lanosil or some kind of soothing cream for sore anus (post diarrhoea), Canestan for thrush and athletes foot, foot powder. Vaseline for cracked heels. A course of Amoxycillin (or Erythromycin if penicillin-allergic) which is good for chest infections, skin infections and cystitis, Cicatrin antibiotic powder for infected bites, etc., antibiotic eye drops, anti-histamine tablets, travel sickness pills, Tiger Balm or calamine lotion for itchy bites, tweezers for extracting splinters, sea-urchin spines, small thorns and coral.

Useful addresses
Britain
Thomas Cook Vaccination Centre, 45 Berkeley Square, London W1 (near Green Park tube station). Tel: 071 499 4000.

British Airways Travel Clinic and Immunisation Service). There are now about 30 BA clinics around Britain. Phone 071 831 5333 for the nearest. The London one is at 156 Regent St, London W1. Tel: 071 439 9584. They also sell travellers' supplies and there's a branch of Stanfords travel book and map shop here.

Trailfinders Immunisation Centre, 194 Kensington High St, London W8 7RG. Tel: 071 938 3999.

Travel Clinic and Vaccination Centre, Hospital for Tropical Diseases. This used to be located at the hospital itself (4 St Pancras Way, London NW1 OPE) but this now only operates on a part time basis, 9.00 - 11.00. The new centre is on the 1st floor, Queens House, 182 Tottenham Court Rd, London W1. Tel: 071 637 9899. They sell many useful things such as dental first aid kits.

An excellent service for travellers is MASTA (Medical Advisory Services for Travellers Abroad). They can provide an individually tailored Personal Health Brief, or a cheaper, standard one. The Personal one gives up to date information on how to stay healthy in Madagascar (or any country you specify) and includes malaria, inoculations, and what to bring. For expeditions they offer a Comprehensive Health Brief. Forms for ordering your Health Brief are available from Boots or other chemists, or ring 071 631 4408. MASTA also sells basic tropical supplies, mosquito anklets and a Medical Equipment Pack with sterile syringes, etc, available by mail from MASTA, Keppel St, London WC1E 7HT.

USA and Canada
North American travellers looking for further health information should phone the Center for Disease Control in Atlanta, Georgia. The hotline here provides information on a range of subjects: malaria, vaccinations, disease outbreaks in specific regions. Tel: (404) 332 4559.

As a postscript, Jane Wilson comments on a study she did in Indonesia. Village mothers were given soap and an explanation of the need for hand-washing after using the toilet and before eating to protect their children from faecally transmitted diarrhoea. The reduction in diarrhoea during the period of study was 89%!

Top left: Uroplatus fimbriatus *(Johan Hermans)*   *Top right:* Parson's chameleon *(Johan Hermans)*

Middle: Phelsuma gecko *(Johan Hermans)*

Mid left: Flatid leaf bug nymphs. The white "feathers" are a waxy secretion (Johan Hermans)

Mid right: Leaf-mimic praying mantis (Phyllocrania illudens)

Bottom left: Giant jumping rat

Bottom right: Mantella *frog (Johan Hermans)*

Lemurs

Top left: red-bellied lemur, Ranomafana

Top right: Verreaux's sifaka, Berenty

Mid right: Hapalemur alaotrensis
(photographed at Jersey Zoo)

Bottom left and right: Aye-aye

Note the long skeletal middle finger probing the gnawed hole in the bamboo (photographed at Jersey Zoo)

Eulophia pulchra, a large terrestial orchid from south and central Madagascar (Johan Hermans)

Taxi-brousse. (John R. Jones)

Readers' comments on health problems

'An ordinary little scratch becomes a big infected wound after three days. Once I couldn't walk for several days after a scratched open mosquito bite became infected. I never had this problem before'. (Luc Selleslagh)

'I always drank the local tap-water and even water from pot-holes in the track, and from rivers and I was never sick'. (Luc Selleslagh)

'My last two month trip to Madagascar was somewhat fraught: despite being inoculated I caught typhoid which left me tramping the forest trails with a continuous but slight fever... On my return trip I managed to get stung by a scorpion on my left middle finger. This nearly gave me a heart attack, since I remembered Jane Wilson's description and that she had quite a hard time of it. So my heart beat like a robotics factory, and I did not know whether this was from the poison or just scaredness! It turned out to be the latter. It hurt like blazes for about five hours – especially since I tried to keep it cool with my hand in the air outside the car window. Later in Tana I discovered you have to keep it warm... Then there were a few hours of prickly feelings (like tasting a 9V battery) and that was the last of it. No scars, no after effects...' (Henk Beetje)

CLOSE ENCOUNTERS OF THE TURD KIND

The surf sparkled in the early morning sun and the sand was firm underfoot as the tourist strode along the beach, revelling in the freedom of miles and miles of eastern coastline. As he approached the picturesque fishing village of bamboo and reed huts he saw people on the beach: the villagers, wrapped in their lambas, were squatting near the water. He approached, curious to see every aspect of their daily lives, and the men greeted him politely. Then he saw what they were doing. Turning away in acute embarrassment and disgust, he headed quickly back to the hotel. His morning's walk was spoiled.

Even the most basic pit toilets are unknown to most rural Malagasy. This lack of concern over one of the west's most taboo bodily functions is rightly disturbing. No rationalisation can diminish the disgust we feel when confronted by a neat pile of human faeces in a rural beauty spot. And disgust turns to anxiety when we consider the role that flies play in spreading disease.

The tourist involved in the beach experience asked a Malagasy why they do not bury their faeces. He was told that this would be *fady* because the dead (ie ancestors) are interred in the earth. Dr Jane Wilson, who studied schistosomiasis and intestinal parasites in western Madagascar, made the following observations in *Journal of Tropical Medicine and Hygiene.* 'It is common to find human faeces within 10 metres of houses. It is *fady* for Sakalavas to use latrines, or to defaecate in the same place as siblings of the opposite sex. There are several well-defined areas for defaecation, and also places where it is *fady* – but usually out of respect for the ancestors rather than for reasons of public health.'

Much as I support the adherence to local customs and traditions, this is one that I hope disappears soon.

SAFETY

Sadly, the widening gap between rich and poor in Madagascar has produced a sharp rise in crime against tourists. Robbery is now a danger in all large towns. It is worst in the capital, Antananarivo, where it is unsafe to walk about at night and a visit to the market (*zoma*) is almost certain to leave you with slit pockets or bags if you are not prepared. It pays to be paranoid, but remember that the vast majority of Malagasy are touchingly honest; often you will have people call you back because you have overpaid them (while still unfamiliar with the money) and every traveller can think of a time when his innocence could have been exploited – and wasn't. In my experience, too, hotel employees are, by and large, trustworthy. So try to keep a sense of proportion. Like health, safety is often a question of common sense. Keep your valuables hidden, keep alert in potentially dangerous situations, and you will be OK. Remember, thieves have to learn their profession so theft is only common where there are plenty of tourists to prey on. In little-visited areas you can relax and enjoy the genuine friendliness of the people.

Violent crime against tourists used to be very rare. Recently, however, there have been some nasty incidences (although even Antananarivo is probably safer than a large American city). If you are outnumbered or the thief is armed, it is sensible to hand over what they want. One traveller reported that he was 'thrown to the ground and relieved of my watch and shoes' in the early evening on Ave de l'Indépendance, Antananarivo. An unpleasant experience. A cheap watch and shoes might have been the best deterrent. 'Name' trainers (running shoes) have the same status here as at home. Don't bring them.

You are far more likely to be robbed by subterfuge. Razor-slashing is very popular (with the thieves) and is particularly irritating since your clothes or bag are ruined, maybe just for the sake of the used tissue that caused the tempting-looking bulge in your pocket. When visiting crowded places avoid bringing a bag (even a day-pack carried in front of your body is vulnerable); bring your money in a money belt under your clothes. If you must have a bag, make sure it is difficult to cut.

Robbery from taxi passengers is on the rise. The thief reaches through the open window and grabs your bag. 'My purse was snatched from my hand while I was *inside* a taxi negotiating the price. The back window of the taxi was open, giving easy access for a thief's arm. Up to that point I'd had no problems in eight weeks of travel.' (A. Jarman).

Having escorted dozens of first-timers through Madagascar, I've learned the mistakes the unprepared can make. The most common is wearing jewellery ('But I always wear this gold chain'), carelessness with money, etc ('I just put my bag down while I tried on that blouse'), and underestimating the value of clothes ('It's not as though it was an expensive T-shirt..').

Following are some guidelines for a thief-free stay:

● Remember that most theft occurs in the street not in hotels, and you are vulnerable on a lonely beach.
● Your luggage should be lockable. Combination locks are more secure than small padlocks.
● Bring a rubber wedge to keep your door closed in cheap hotels in cities. In posh hotels leave your valuables in a security box.
● Leave your valuable-looking jewellery at home. You do not need it in Madagascar. Likewise your fancy watch; buy a cheap one.
● Carry your cash in a money belt or deep pocket. Make these yourself by cutting the bottom off existing pockets and adding an extra bit. Fasten the 'secret' pocket with velcro. Wear loose trousers that have zipped pockets. Keep emergency cash (eg a 100 dollar bill) in a Very Safe Place.
● Divide up travellers cheques so they are not all in one place. Keep a note of the numbers of your travellers cheques, passport, credit cards, plane ticket, insurance, etc in your money belt. Keep a copy in your luggage.
● Keep a photocopy of the first page of your passport and of your Madagascar visa. Guard your currency declaration as carefully as your passport.
● Remember, what the thief would most like to get hold of is money. Do not leave it around (in coat pockets hanging in your room, in your hand while you concentrate on something else, in an accessible pocket while strolling in the street).
● The next best thing after money is clothes. Avoid leaving them on the beach while you go swimming (in tourist areas) and never leave swimsuits or washing to dry outside your room near a public area.
● Bear in mind that it's impossible to run carrying a large piece of luggage. Items hidden at the bottom of your heaviest bag will be safe from a grab and run thief.
● Avoid misunderstandings – genuine or contrived – by agreeing on the price of a service *before* you set out.
● Enjoy yourself. Better to lose a few unimportant things and see the best of Madagascar than to mistrust everyone and ruin your trip.

If you are robbed, go to the police. They will write down all the details then send you to the chief of police for a signature. It takes the best part of a day, but you will need the certificate for your insurance. If you are in a rural area, the local authorities will do a declaration of loss. If you lose your currency declaration form, go to the Direction Generale des Douanes in Tana (near the Colbert) and ask to see an 'inspecteur des douanes'.

Major robberies: what to do
Last year I met a *vazaha* who had lost *all* his valuables when robbed at

knife-point on a beach in Taolagnaro. Fortunately he had his airticket back to Tana where he was in the long-drawn out process of replacing everything. Andrew Matsuda offers this advice.

The two most important things that you need to sort out are a new passport and money. Try to get the paperwork started on the first day back in the capital. Both American and British embassies can make emergency loans ($200 or £200 in local currency) to help you get by. This is a true loan which must be repaid, so be prepared to fill out lots of paperwork. Knowing your bank account number is useful in this instance. Bring extra passport sized photos. I had to buy a new passport at $65.00 which needed two photographs of a size larger than the standard identification photos needed for Madagascar nationals. I recommend Studio Tony. They usually ask that you return the next day for the photographs (as a roll of film needs to be processed) but the people at Studio Tony did it in about five hours. The price was about 7,000fmg. (Studio Tony also has a photocopier, so make a duplicate of the second most important document, the police report). Opticam (photographers) are also recommended.

'This is Madagascar' was the explanation I was given when it turned out that the man with the only key to the safe holding the travellers cheques had gone home after the lunch break. My travellers cheque receipts were with the stolen cheques and through a combination of bad telecommunications, not knowing the full address of the bank where I purchased them, and other setbacks, it took me four days to get an incomplete refund from American Express. When they know which cheques were already used it makes a tremendous difference in the speed and amount of the refund. Without accurate information on this they must guess at the amount of the refund. The American Express refund office is in the rear of the Air Madagascar office in the Hilton Hotel. You will need to give them a copy of the police report. The refunds (larger amounts, anyway) are picked up at the BFV bank near the Peugeot dealer off L. Refotaka.

If necessary your embassy will cable a request for money to someone back home for you. Commit to memory the address and telephone number of this person, since your address book with it written inside probably will have been stolen along with everything else.

The average rural Malagasy bag snatcher is looking for cash and has not yet reached a more sophisticated level of criminal activity by forging signatures on travellers cheques or perpetrating credit card fraud (my missing cheques were unused, as was the credit card). This may be different in Antananarivo, but reporting the lost card back home can wait until the passport and spendable cash problems are sorted out first.

When purchasing your one way air ticket back to Paris, be sure to find out how much it costs before going to the bank if flying on Air France. Air Madagascar has facilities to change money, but Air France does not. With no credit card, Malagasy cash must be used. At the time the fare for a flight the next day was 2,885,500fmg and the conspicuous bulk of this amount of cash made for an exciting 200 yard dash across a crowded central throughfare. Buy your onward tickets (in my case to London) in Paris.

You will need an exit visa if you didn't make a photocopy of your original visa. Get this at the Ministry of the Interior. Be prepared to wait. I got away without a replacement currency documentation form, but I had a letter from the US embassy stating that the original was stolen (don't forget as I did to mention this on the police report).

Although your embassy can give advice on the particulars, here is a short check list that would have saved me three or four days.

1) File a police report (if the currency document was stolen, don't forget to mention this).

2) Decide whether or not to continue your journey.

3) Get to Antananarivo. If this isn't possible, try to get in touch with your embassy for assistance.

4) Contact your embassy for new passport and emergency money.

5) Get new passport photos and photocopies of the police report.

6) File a stolen travellers cheque report (they will need a copy of the police report). Serial numbers of the unused cheques are very useful for the refund claim and an updated record of the used cheques is even better. American Express has offices in other major tourist cities so ask at your hotel if there is a local branch. If you are to fly out of the country in the next day or two, it may be better to both file the report and collect the refund at the next major destination you plan on staying at.

7) Fill out lost ticket form at the respective airline. Airlines don't re-issue lost or stolen tickets, new ones must be purchased. They would like to have the ticket number for the form, so a photocopy would have been handy to have.

8) Pick up the photos and go back to the embassy for a new passport to be issued.

(If you get an early start in Antananarivo you should just about be able to get some emergency money, have your photos taken and developed, have a new passport issued, have the official letter from your embassy stating that your currency document was stolen (if it isn't mentioned in the police report), get the paperwork started on the lost traveller's cheques and air tickets all in a very full day.)

9) When collecting travellers cheques, try to get some small denominations.

10) Get a new currency document if you're planning to continue the trip or, if you want to leave soon, have your embassy write an official letter stating that it was lost. Be warned that without the currency document, they will confiscate any Malagasy cash you declare or they find on you at the airport.

11) Purchase new air tickets.

12) With your new passport, get an exit visa allowing for delays when naming the date. When requesting a new departure date, (especially when you want to leave as soon as possible), try to allow for delays should you still need to buy a ticket (a week should be safe). Better still, try to have your air tickets by this time for a definite date to leave Madagascar for if you overstay the departure date given on the visa, you will have to go back to the visa office and get it changed.

Women travellers

This is the first edition where I have had to warn against occasional unsolicited male attention. Some women travelling alone have reported the same courtesy and lack of hassle that I commented on in the first three editions. Sadly, however, with the increase of tourism comes the increase of men who think they may be onto a good thing. A firm 'no' is usually all you need. Try not to be too offended. Think of the image of western women that the average Malagasy male is shown via the cinema or TV. Anyway, I still treasure the way it was put to me back in 1987 when a small man sidled up to me in Nosy Be and asked 'Have you ever tasted Malagasy man?'

Men travellers

Judging from the letters from some of my most adventurous male readers, being pursued by women happens everywhere (whilst women are usually only pursued by men in tourist spots). One wrote: 'I was constantly fighting off women where ever I went. One night in Fort Dauphin I actually had to run away from someone!' Another was offered the mother of the Président du Fokontany! Saying you're married is considered irrelevant...

'MADAGASCAR: ISLAND OF EXCITEMENT!'

By Henk Beentje

We spent three days in Farafangana, collecting palms in the Manombo Forest [Henk is employed by Kew Gardens]. On leaving we were mobbed by about 200 irate locals who accused my Malagasy companion and me of being *voleurs de sang* and of abducting young maidens. On the advice of my companion we reported to the police, who thought this was quite funny but advised us to leave town all the same. We were escorted out of town by the Chief of Police himself, who was careful to use the side streets. Two days later we were back at Ranomafana. As we got into our Landcruiser we were stopped by three *gendarmes*, one of whom was toting a submachine gun. We were arrested and taken to the *Gendarmerie*. There had been an 'all points bulletin' to arrest two *vazaha* (one Merina, one white) in a red Landcruiser. We were accused of having abducted no fewer than three girls from Farafangana, and to have put them in sacks at the back of the vehicle (this clearly referred to my palm collection, indeed esconced in large sacks). It took us four hours to regain our freedom and I was very glad we had reported to the Farafangana police, because after a request from us they were contacted and could confirm our story. Who said you cannot have adventures anymore in this streamlined world of ours?

HAINTENY

Yes, my friend,
If you bear me a love of full measure,
Then I will bear you a love that overflows.
Love me like a small pearl: Though small, many of them form a necklace.
I will love you like a little crab:
I eat it together with its shell.

HIRA GASY

For a taste of genuine Malagasy folklore, try to attend the traditional entertainment of *hira gasy* which takes place every Sunday in Tana. It used to be held in an arena at Isotry, but now unfortunately happens in different locations. Taxi-drivers may know where: ask for 'hira gasy' (pronounced 'heera gash') and see what happens.

In the British magazine *Folk Roots* Jo Shinner describes *hira gasy*:

'It is a very strange, very exciting affair: a mixture of opera, dance and Speaker's Corner bound together with a sense of competition.

'The performance takes place between two competing troupes of singers and musicians on a central square stage. It's an all day event so the audience packs in early, tea and peanut vendors picking their way through the throng. Audience participation is an integral part — the best troupe is gauged by the crowd's response. Throughout the day performers come into the crowd to receive small coins offered in appreciation.

'The most immediate surprise is the costumes. The men enter wearing 19th Century French, red, military frock coats and the women are clad in evening dress from the same period. Traditional *lamba* are carefully arranged around their shoulders, and the men wear straw Malagasy hats.

'The musicians play French military drums, fanfare trumpets, flutes, violins and clarinets. The effect is bizarre rather than beautiful.'

'The *hira gasy* is in four parts. First there are the introductory speeches or *kabary*. Each troupe elects a speaker who is usually a respected elder. His skill is paramount to a troupe. He begins with a long, ferociously fast, convoluted speech excusing himself and his inadequacy, before the audience, ancestors, his troupe, his mother, God, his oxen, his rice fields and so on — and on! Then follows another speech glorifying God, and then a greeting largely made up of proverbs.

'The *hira gasy* pivots around a tale of everyday life, such as the dire consequences of laziness or excessive drinking, is packed with wit, morals and proverbs and offers advice, criticism and possible solutions.

'The performers align themselves along two sides of the square at a time to address different parts of the audience. They sing in harsh harmony, illustrating their words with fluttering hand movements and expressive gestures, egged on by the uproarious crowd's appreciation.

'Then it is the dancers' turn. The tempo increases and becomes more rhythmic as two young boys take to the floor with a synchronised display of acrobatic dancing that nowadays often takes its influence from karate.'

VIVE LE TAXI-BROUSSE!

'At about 10 o'clock we (two people) went to the taxi-brousse station. "Yes, yes, there is a car. It is here, ready to go". We paid our money. "When will it go?" "When it has nine passengers." "How many has it got now?" "Wait a minute." A long look at notebooks, then a detailed calculation. "Two". "As well as us?" "No, no including you." It finally left at about 7 o'clock.'
Chris Ballance

'To go from Morondava to Tana by taxi-brousse took us over 22 hours, and for most of the way the Peugeot 504 had more than 12 people (17 for several hours). And all our luggage. And one man was taking a huge clothing stall to market. And, of course, the woman who was carrying her plough home with her...'
Chris Ballance

'After several hours we picked up four more people. We couldn't believe it — the driver had to sit on someone's lap!'
Stephen Cartledge

'The taxi-brousse from Tana to Majunga was supposed to leave in the early afternoon. At 4.00pm we left (all ten of us) and went to a furniture stall to buy pineapples — well it makes sense. At 6.00pm we had the first of seven punctures. The driver pushed his tyre two kilometres down the road to get it mended... We drove all night (four punctures) and as the light rose over the countryside we — well, you guessed — had a puncture. Now we had no spare and no airpump. A lorry eventually passed and helped to repair the tyre. At 11.00am we had another puncture... I took my rucksack off the car roof and hitchhiked into Majunga.'
Jonathan Miller

'At last we were under way. I had my knees jammed up against the iron bar at the back of the rows in front where sat a very sick soldier, who spent most of the journey with his head out of the window spewing lurid green bile at passers-by like something from a horror-movie... After about 20 minutes we had to stop at a roadside stall to buy mangoes. Since I was now on the sunny side of the vehicle the temperature of my shirt rose to what, had it been made of polyester, would have been melting point. Our next stop was Antsirabe where we were surrounded by about 50 apple vendors and all and sundry went absolutely beserk. I hadn't seen so many apples since...since we left Ambositra. At about 5.00pm the radio was turned on so we could listen to two men shouting at each other at a volume which would have caused bleeding of the eardrums in Wembley Stadium. When one passenger complained our driver managed to find a few extra decibels. At about 6.00pm it started to get decidedly brisk, and since the ailing squaddie in front of me showed no sign of having rid himself of toxic enzymes I now had to endure an icy blast in my face. Our next stop was for grapes. We now had enough fruit on board to start a wholesale business in Covent Garden, and I was a bit tetchy.'
Robert Stewart

Chapter 6

In Madagascar

TOURISM IN MADAGASCAR: GOVERNMENT POLICY

When prime-minister Ravony announced his government programme to the newly elected members of parliament in August 1993 he singled out tourism as a profitable sector that ought to be one of the country's most important currency earners. He recommended formulating a Tourism Policy requiring the combined efforts of the state and private sector. A Code of Tourism is to be drawn up regulating hotel standards and the management of sites of tourist interest. This is encouraging for upmarket package tourists, but may spell restrictions aimed at low-spending backpackers who have received adverse coverage in the press as 'drug-users'.

MONEY

Cost of travel

At the time of writing (May 1994) this section should be composed of question marks since Madagascar is poised on the brink of Major Changes as the government programme on tourism begins to be implemented. Negotiations are currently under way to impose a 17% tourist tax on tourist facilities/services such as hotels and meals. This is likely to affect package tourists more than budget travellers, but the latter have their own cross to bear: from March 1994 visitors have been required to spend at least 2,000FF (£235/US$350) during their stay. If, on departure, their currency declaration form shows they spent less, they are supposed to have their passports stamped to the effect that they will not be allowed to return to Madagascar. Tourists on pre-paid packages or business people will be given a certificate by their Malagasy tour operator or business associate, exempting them from this requirement.

To counteract all this there was a 50% devaluation in May 1994; the Malagasy Franc is now floating against hard currencies. This has resulted in a price rise of 50% - 90% for services such as car-hire and the better hotels.

Budget travellers staying and eating in *hotelys* with an occasional splurge should be able to travel very cheaply: £25/US$38 per day for a couple used to be about average, so in theory with the devaluation you can cut that to £15/$22. Couples can travel almost as cheaply as singles, since most hotels charge by the room (with double bed).

The easiest way to save money on a day to day basis is to cut down on expensive drinks; bring a water container and sterilising agent.

Note: I give prices in french francs (FF) or US$ (if the service must be paid for in hard currency). Most fmg prices will be at least 50% higher than the pre-devaluation rate given in the text.

Malagasy francs

Madagascar's unit of currency is the *Franc Malgache* (FMG/fmg). With recent inflation one rarely sees the small lower denomination brass coins of 5, 10, and 20 francs, but to confuse you there are also large silver coins which look, at face value, to be for 10 and 20 francs. Closer inspection show that they are *ariary* (one ariary is 5 francs) so they are worth 50 and 100 francs respectively. There are new, smaller ariary coins, and a newly introduced 5,000 ariary banknote which (remember to multiply by 5) is worth 25,000fmg. Many a porter has received a tip of $13 from a harassed new arrival who thought it was $2.50. It must be nice – for the porter.

If this is complicated, pity the poor traveller 100 years ago:

> The French five-franc piece is now the standard of coinage in Madagascar; for small change it is cut up into bits of all sizes. The traveller has to carry a pair of scales about with him, and whenever he makes a purchase the specified quantity of this most inconvenient money is weighed out with the greatest exactness, first on his own scales, and then on those of the suspicious native of whom he is buying.

Learn the colour of your money: 500fmg banknotes are brown, 1,000fmg purple, 5,000fmg blue, 10,000fmg green, and 25,000fmg (the afore-mentioned 5,000 ariary) green and brown. Learn too its value. Just after the May 1994 devaluation the rates of exchange were 4,400fmg to the pound, 3,000fmg to the dollar, 540fmg to the French Franc, and 1,770fmg to the German Mark. With a 'floating' currency these rates are bound to change, however.

Transferring funds

Now that you can draw cash from many BTM banks using your credit card you are less likely to need money transferred from home. If you are staying a long time in Madagascar, however, it's best to make the transfer arrangement beforehand. The best bank for this is Banque Malgache de l'Ocean Indien, Place de l'Indépéndance. Its corresponding bank in the UK is Banque Nationale de Paris, King William St, London.

TRANSPORT

There are three mechanised ways of getting around Madagascar: rail, road and air. To this you can add boat, either with a motor or a sail. Whichever method you use, you'd better learn the meaning of *en panne*; it is engine trouble/break down. During these *en panne* sessions one can't help a certain nostalgia for the pre-mechanised days when Europeans travelled by *filanzana* or palanquin. These litters were carried by four cheerful porters who, by all accounts, were so busy swapping gossip and telling stories, that they sometimes dropped their *vazaha* in a river. The average distance travelled per day was 30 miles — not much slower than a taxi-brousse today! The *filanzana* was used for high officials as recently as the 1940s. To get around town the locals depended on an earlier version of the current rickshaw, or *pousse-pousse*. The *mono-pousse* was a chair slung over a bicycle wheel. One man pulled and another pushed. The more affluent Malagasy possessed a *boeuf-cheval*: a zebu trained to be ridden. (I've seen a photo; the animal looks rather smug in its saddle and bridle.)

Rail

There are only four railway lines in Madagascar, and these have deteriorated in the last few years. Rebel action (in 1992) and landslides caused by cyclone Geralda cut the lines to the coast (but all are expected to be repaired by mid 1994). But even before the cyclone the service on each route was reduced from daily to three times a week and first class carriages were removed. Perhaps the push for tourists will motivate the government to restore them to something like their former splendour. Train travel, even in second class, is usually preferable to taxi-brousse.

The four lines are Antananarivo to Toamasina (Tamatave), Moramanga to Ambatondrazaka, Antananarivo to Antsirabe, and Fianarantsoa to Manakara.

Road

'If I make roads, the white man will only come and take my country. I have two allies — *hazo* [forest] and *tazo* [fever]...' (King Radama I)

Coping with the 'roads' is one of the great travel challenges in Madagascar. It's not that the royal decree has lasted 180 years but a third ally that the king didn't mention — the weather: torrential rain and cyclones destroy roads as fast as they are constructed. But they *are* being repaired and reconstructed, mostly with foreign aid. At the time of writing the roads of Madagascar, especially in the east and the central highlands, are in a dreadful state following the terrible series of cyclones which struck early in 1994. Bear in mind that when I write '...by a good road' that will be a pre-cyclone assessment.

Taxi-brousse, **car-brousse**, and **taxi-be** are all varieties of 'bush taxi' which run between major towns. I doubt if there is any country offering more crowded, less reliable transport. If you think you're a well-seasoned traveller, wait until you try Madagascar! Since publishing one reader's taxi-brousse horror story I have received several indicating how lucky he was to have such a comfortable ride. See page 96.

Taxi-brousses are generally minibuses or Renault vans with seats facing each other so no good view out of the window (a *baché* is a small van with a canvas top). More comfortable are the Peugeot 404s or 504s known as taxi-be (although some people call the 25-seater buses taxi-be) designed to take nine people, but often packed with 14 or more. A car-brousse is any sort of vehicle sturdy enough to cope with bad roads. Being sturdy it is usually excessively uncomfortable. These vehicles are also known as *tata*. The vehicles *are* improving (there is even a new hybrid called **buxi**, a cross between a bus and a taxi) but it is still the exception to find a taxi-brousse in good condition. Breakdowns are frequent. Buses are now being introduced on the most-travelled routes.

Vehicles leave from a *gare routière* on the side of town closest to their destination. You should try to go there a day or two ahead of your planned departure to check times and prices. Whether you should buy a ticket in advance is debatable; probably only sensible if you have a confirmed seat. It is wise to arrive early since seats are usually allocated on a first come first served basis. Expect the vehicle to leave hours later than scheduled and always be prepared (with warm clothing, fruit, water, etc) for a night trip, even if you thought it was leaving in the morning. On short journeys vehicles simply leave as soon as they fill up.

There is no set rate per kilometre; fares are calculated on the roughness of the road and the time the journey takes. They are set by the government and *vazahas* are seldom overcharged. A sample of rates by bus over popular routes: Antananarivo to Toliara/Tuléar, 19,000fmg (£15/US$10); Antananarivo to Tomoasina/Tamatave, 8,000fmg (£3/$US5); Antananarivo to Mahajanga, 13,000fmg (£4.65/US$7). Taxi-brousse rates would be cheaper.

Drivers usually stop to eat and sleep, but they may drive all night. During night stops most passengers stay in the vehicle or sleep on the road outside, but there is often a hotel – of sorts – nearby.

Luc Selleslagh comments: 'As a foreigner you usually end up in the best place (in front) or in the worst place (since the Malagasy know the worst places better than you), depending on the driver. It's really worth checking the vehicle before taking off and also the driver's mentality'.

Be prepared. There is much that a committed overland traveller can do to soften his/her experiences on taxi-brousses – see *What to bring* on page 00. In addition to basic camping equipment, bring a good book, cards, Scrabble, etc, as well as snacks and water, to pass the time during inevitable breakdowns and delays. If you're prepared for the realities, an overland journey can be very enjoyable and gives you a chance to get to know the Malagasy and practise character-building. As one reader says

'When a taxi-brousse driver joins two wires together to start his vehicle one needs a sense of humour — but one arrives'.

Note: Several readers have stressed the need to point out that it is unwise to use taxi-brousses if on a tight schedule: vehicles break down or fail to leave. Unless you have lots of time, alternatives such as hiring a car or joining a tour should be considered. The challenge is even greater if you do not have an adequate command of French. Or even if you have. Stephen Cartledge advises: 'One has to remember that "*Defitivement*" means "Never", and "*Maintenant*" means five hours! Then one is equipped to travel in Madagascar by taxi-brousse'.

Car hire
With public transport so unreliable, more visitors have been renting cars or 4WD vehicles in recent years. You would need to be a competent mechanic to hire a self-drive car in Madagascar, and generally cars come with chauffeurs (providing a local person with a job and you with a guide/interpreter). There are car-hire firms in most large towns. The Maison du Tourisme in Antananarivo has a comprehensive list.

I have personal recommendations for the following in Antananarivo: Locaut, 52 Ave du 26 Juin (BP 8150); tel: 219 81, fax: 248 01. Aventour, 55 Route de Majunga; tel: 317 61, fax 272 99. Eurorent, BP 5282; tel: 297 66, fax: 297 49. They have a desk at Ivato airport. Rahariseta, BP 3779 (located next to Lake Behoririka); tel: 257 70, fax: 224 47.

There is also Avis, 3 Rue P. Lumumba; tel: 340 80, fax: 216 57 (they have an office at the Hilton hotel) and Hertz, but these tend to be more expensive.

Prices currently work out at about £50/US$75 per day, including fuel and driver, around Antananarivo. It is more expensive if you intend to drive on the poor roads away from the capital.

Mountain bicycle
An increasingly popular means of touring Madagascar is by the most reliable transport: mountain bike. Bikes can be hired in Antananarivo, Antsirabe, Tolagnaro (Fort Dauphin), Antsiranana (Diego Suarez) and Nosy Be. Or you can bring your own. You can do a combination of bike and taxi-brousse, or set out to cycle the whole way but don't be overambitious; dirt roads are so rutted you will make slow progress. And you are advised to keep to dirt roads, choosing your route from the 1:500,000 scale maps available in Antananarivo. Although there is little traffic, Malagasy drivers love to race on the tarred roads which makes them dangerous for cyclists, and it seems a shame to miss the opportunity to get away from the tourist routes (although I have had happy letters from travellers who stayed on the main roads — and evidently survived).

Bishop Brock, who toured for 10 weeks by mountain bike writes:

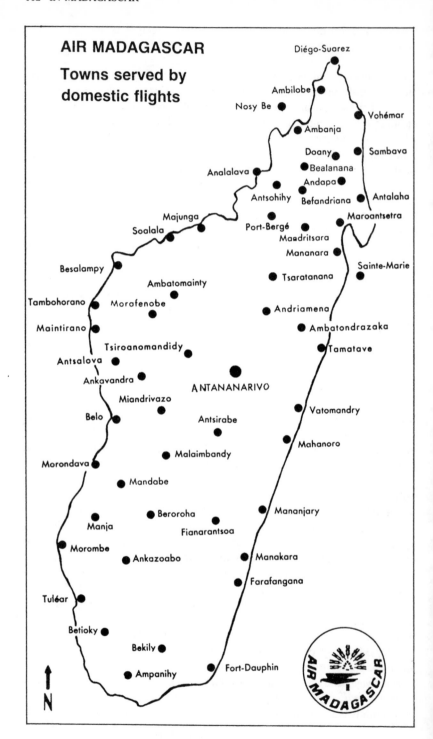

'Madagascar is an excellent country for cycle touring, definitely one of my favourite places in the world, and I've taken my holidays by bicycle for the last 13 years. Route 7 now has a good to excellent surface most of the way and there are lots of opportunities for interesting side trips for avid mountain bikers. The people are very friendly, colourful and polite – although I was often surrounded by crowds it was very rare that anyone would touch my bike without an invitation... Having a bike gave me access to places that otherwise can only be reached on foot. If I had to advise a prospective cyclist with limited time I would say that Fianar to Manakara and Fianar to Sakaraha were the favourite parts of my trip. I should add that it's not a problem to put the bike on a train or taxi-brousse after payment of a small fee.'

Stewart Heather-Clark, of South Africa, also toured by bike, but often carried it on a taxi-brousse, paying the equivalent of one seat for the bicycle which was strapped on the roof (the trip finished when it was swept off by a low branch and irreparably damaged). These are his *What to bring* suggestions: A tent (although you can usually find accommodation), alcohol stove, water purification tablets, a mosquito net, insect repellent, sun screen, a sun-peak, first aid kit. Cycling equipment and spares should include: spare tyre, tubes, spokes, spanners and tools, puncture kit, and – very important – a Teflon-based lubricant that does not attract dust. The sandy, dusty roads play havoc with the gear system.

Safety when cycling

Hitherto there have been no reports of robberies directed at cyclists, but of course you *are* vulnerable. Apart from carrying the minimum of cash and valuables, the best defence is to cycle off the beaten track. Here you will meet only hospitality and curiosity, and will be in no danger – intentional or unintentional – from other road-users.

Air travel

Air Madagascar started its life in 1962 as Madair but understandably changed its name after a few years of jokes. Most people now call it Air Mad. It serves 59 destinations, making it the most efficient way – and for some people the only way – of seeing the country. Foreigners must pay their fares in hard currency. Here are some sample single fares from Antananarivo: Mahajanga 550FF/US$94, Nosy Be 885FF/US$150, Antsiranana (Diego Suarez) 955FF/US$162, Toliara (Tuléar) 885FF/US$150. Short hops cost little and save a lot of discomfort and delay. For example Sambava to Maroantsetra (see Chapter 9) is 218FF/US$37, and Bealanana to Ambanja (see Chapter 11) is 147FF/US$25.

The recent rise in tourism in Madagascar has brought more passengers than Air Mad can cope with, particularly at peak holiday times. Try to book in advance through one of their agents (see Chapter 4). If you are doing your bookings once you arrive, avoid the crush by getting to the Air Mad office when it opens in the morning. Often flights which are said to be fully booked in Antananarivo are found to have seats when you reapply at the town of departure. In any case, you should reconfirm your next flight as soon as you arrive at your destination (at the Air Mad office in town). You can very often get on fully booked flights if you go standby. Paying with cash dollars may find you a seat. There are no numbered seats or refreshments on internal flights.

Air Madagascar discontinued their Air Touristic Pass, which gave unlimited travel for one month, some years ago. It has been replaced by the *Madagascar à Liberté* discount on four flights: four long flights (eg to Antsiranana (Diego Suarez), Nosy Be, or Tolagnaro (Fort Dauphin) and back) cost, in 1994, 1,400FF and four short flights are 900FF. The catch is you must first buy a full-price international ticket on Air Madagascar.

It is useful to know that *Enregistrement Bagages* is the check-in counter and *Livraison Bagages* is luggage arrival.

Schedules are reviewed twice-yearly at the end of March and the end of October, but are subject to change at any time and without notice.

The current airport tax is 33,000fmg for Europe, 25,000fmg regional (Africa, Mauritius etc) and 3,300fmg domestic. See Chapter 7 for arrivals/departure procedure.

Air Madagascar have the following planes: Boeing 747 (jumbo) on the Paris to Antananarivo route, Boeing 737 (flying to the larger cities and Nosy Be), the smaller Hawker Siddeley 748, and the very small and erratic Twin Otter and Piper which serve the smaller towns.

With a shortage of aircraft and pilots, planes are often delayed or cancelled. Almost always there is a perfectly good reason: mechanical problems, bad weather. Sometimes, however, it is better for your blood-pressure not to know why. The group I was accompanying last year were bumped from a Twin Otter despite our reconfirming the seats the previous day. The seats were indeed available, but they had loaded the plane to the maximum permitted weight with freight. Then there was the time when a wealthy Indian businessman demanded successfully to be flown direct to Antananarivo from Tolagnaro (Fort Dauphin) without making the scheduled stop at Toliara...

To give Air Mad their due, on the whole they provide as safe and reliable a service as one can expect in a poor country. Their safety record, in particular, is excellent.

Private charters

For a small group this is a viable option and not as expensive as you may think. TAM (Travaux Aeriens de Madagascar) offer light aircraft for one to seven passengers. Prices range from US$130 per flying hour for a two-seater to US$658 per flying hour for a seven-seater. The cost of fuel must be added: US$38 to US$165 per flying hour. Bigger planes fly faster, so they may not end up more expensive. Some flying time examples for a six-seater Piper: Antananarivo - Ste Marie - Antananarivo, 1 hr 46 mins; Antananarivo - Fort Dauphin - Antananarivo, 5 hrs 20 mins. Remember there is no such thing as a one-way flight – you still have to pay for the pilot to return to Antananarivo. More sensible to pay him to spend the night.

TAM's address is 31 Avenue de l'Indépendance, Antananarivo. Tel: 222 22. They also have an operations office at the Hilton Hotel, tel: 296 91. There are, however, other companies so shop around.

Boat

The Malagasy are traditionally a seafaring people (remember that 6,000km journey from Indonesia) and in the absence of roads, their stable outrigger canoes, *pirogues*, are used to cover quite long distances. Quite a few adventurous travellers use pirogues to cover sections of their journeys. You will read their accounts in the relevant chapters of this guide. Romantic though it may be to sail in an outrigger canoe, it is both uncomfortable and, at times, dangerous.

Ferries and cargo boats travel to the islands. These provide a different version of discomfort.

Transport within cities

There are **taxis** in all cities. Their rates are reasonable – usually a fixed price for the centre of town – and they will usually pick up other passengers. They have no meters, so agree on the price before you get in. Some major cities have Japanese **buses**.

Rickshaws, known as *pousse-pousse* ('push-push' – said to originate from the time they operated in the capital and needed an additional man behind to push up the steep hills), are a Madagascar speciality and provide transport in Antsirabe, Mahajanga, Toamasina and some other coastal towns. Occasionally you see them in Antananarivo, but they are mostly used for transporting goods.

Many western visitors are reluctant to sit in comfort behind a running, ragged, bare-foot man and no-one with a heart can fail to feel compassion for the *pousse-pousse* drivers. However, this is a case of needing to abandon our own cultural hang-ups. These men want work. Most rickshaws are owned by Indians to whom the 'drivers' must pay a daily fee. If they take no passengers they will be out of pocket – and there's precious little *in* their pockets. Bargain hard (before you get in) and make sure you have the exact money. It would be optimistic to expect change. 1,000fmg is generous payment for most medium-length journeys. *Pousse-pousse* drivers love carrying soft-hearted tourists and have become quite cunning in their dealings with *vazahas*. On the other hand, remember how desperately these men need a little luck – and an innocent tourist could make their day!

ACCOMMODATION

Hotels in Madagascar are classified by a national star system – five star being the highest – but in my experience this indicates price, not quality. In this book I have used three categories: A, B and C. Five and four star hotels must usually be paid for in hard currency.

Outside the towns, hotels in the form of a single building are something of a rarity. Accommodation is usually in bungalows which are often constructed of local materials and are quiet, atmospheric and comfortable.

A word about bolsters. Visitors who are not accustomed to the ways of France are disconcerted to find a firm, sheet-covered sausage anchored to the top of the bed. In the better hotels you can usually find a pillow hidden away in a cupboard. Failing that, I make my own pillow with a sweater stuffed into a T-shirt.

Category A

Up to international standard in the large towns and tourist areas, but sometimes large and impersonal and usually foreign- owned. There has been quite a boom in hotel building during the last few years, and there are now some very good Malagasy-owned hotels in this category, so the difference between *A* and *B* has become somewhat blurred. Prices range from 200FF (£23/US$35) to 1,000FF (£116/US$173) double. .

Category B

These are often just as clean and comfortable, though you may occasionally find a gecko in your room. There will be no TV beaming CNN into your bedroom, but you should have a basin and bidet and comfortable beds although bolsters are the norm. The hotels are often family-run and very friendly. The average price is £10/US$15.

Category C

In the previous editions I described these as 'Exhilaratingly dreadful at times' but one reader has written: 'We were rather disappointed by the quality of the Category C hotels... We found almost all the beds comfortable, generally acceptably clean, and not one rat. We felt luxuriously cheated!'. Take heart, Chris, you can still meet rats and cockroaches in abundance as well as other surprising features, but you do have to get well off the beaten track and try the little *hotelys*. Apart from resident fauna the pillows are filled with sisal and the double beds can be quite amazingly uncomfortable with lumpy mattresses sagging like hammocks so that couples are thrown companionably together in the centre. Some hotels have basins in the room, but the toilet is likely to be a stinking hole or – better – out in the bushes. Ask for the WC ('dooble vay say') not *toilette* which means shower or bathroom. In these hotels (and some B ones too) used toilet paper should not be thrown into the pan but into the box provided for it. Not very nice, but preferable to a clogged loo.

Many of the C hotels in this book are clean and excellent value, only earning the C because of their price. Almost always they are run by friendly Malagasy who will rustle up a fantastic meal. In an out-of-the-way place you will pay as little as £1/US$1.50 for the most basic room, although £3 or £4 would be more usual.

Many B and C hotels will do your washing for you at a very reasonable price.

Hotely usually means a restaurant/snack bar rather than accommodation, but it's always worth asking if they have rooms.

Hotel prices

Remember that Madagascar is on the brink of changes which will inevitably affect the FF/fmg price given for hotels. The A and B category are the most likely to be affected. At the time of writing in May 1994 many hotels had raised their published 1994 prices to reflect the expected 17% tax. If the tax doesn't happen they may be cheaper than printed here. The prices given in local currency may well be higher, especially following devaluation. There's nothing much I can do about it. Sorry. *You* however, can do something by sending me prices for the next edition. You'll get a BIG thankyou!

FOOD AND DRINK

Food

Eating well is one of the delights of Madagascar, and even the fussiest tourists are usually happy with the food. International hotels serve international food, usually with a French bias and often do special Malagasy dishes. Lodges and smaller hotels serve local food which is almost always excellent, particularly on the coast where lobster, shell fish and other sea food predominates. Meat lovers will enjoy the zebu steaks, although they are usually tougher than we are used to. Outside the capital, most hotels offer a set menu (*table d'hôte*) to their guests. Where the menu is *à la carte* it is a help to have a French dictionary, preferably one with a food section.

Independent travellers will find Chinese and Indian restaurants in every town; these are almost always good and reasonably priced. *Soupe Chinoise* is available almost everywhere, and is filling and tasty. The Malagasy eat a lot of rice (see Box, page 000) so away from the tourist routes most dishes are accompanied by a sticky mound of the stuff. It's bland and flavourless, but sops up the tasty sauces.

In *hotelys*, often open-sided shacks, the menu may be chalked up on a blackboard:

Henan-omby (or *Hen'omby*) – beef.

Henam-borona (or *Hen'akoho* – chicken.
Henan-kisoa – pork.
Henan-drano (or *Hazan-drano*) – fish.

The menu may add *Mazotoa homana*. This is not a dish, it means *Bon appétit!*.

Along with the meat or fish and inevitable mound of rice (*vary*) comes a bowl of stock. This is spooned over the rice, or drunk as a soup.

Thirst is quenched with *ranovola* obtained by boiling water in the pan in which the rice was cooked. It has a slight flavour of burnt rice, and since it has been boiled for several minutes it is safe to drink.

The national dish in Madagascar is *romazava* (pronounced 'roomazahv'), a meat and vegetable stew, spiced with ginger and containing *brèdes* (pronounced 'bread'), tasty, tongue-tingling greens. Another good local dish is *ravitoto*, shredded manioc leaves with fried pork.

For do-it-yourself meals there is a great variety of fruit and vegetables, even in the smallest market. A selection of fruit is served in most restaurants, along with raw vegetables or *crudités*. From June to August the fruit is mostly limited to citrus and bananas, but from September there are also strawberries, mangoes, lychees, pineapples and loquats. Slices of coconut are sold everywhere, but especially on the coast where coconut milk is a popular and safe drink, and toffee-coconut nibbles are sold on the street, often wrapped in paper from school exercise books.

Madagascar's dairy industry is growing. There are now some good, locally produced cheeses and Malagasy yoghurt is excellent and available in the smallest shops.

Drink

The Malagasy 'Three Horses' beer is wonderful on a hot day. I think it's wonderful on a cold day, too. The price goes up according to the surroundings: twice as much in the Hilton as in a *hotely* and there is always a hefty deposit payable on the bottle.

Madagascar produces its own wine in the Fianarantsoa region, and some is excellent. L'azani Betsileo (*blanc* or *gris*, *reservé*)) is recommended.

A pleasant aperitif is *Maromby* (the name means 'many zebu') and I have been told that *Litchel*, made from lychees, is good. Rum, *toaka gasy*, is very cheap and plentiful, especially in sugar-growing areas such as Nosy Be, and fermented sugar cane juice, *betsabetsa* (east coast) or fermented coconut milk, *trembo* (north), make a change. The best drink cocktail is *punch au coco*, with a coconut milk base, which is a speciality of the coastal areas.

Fresh is an agreeable shandy, and *Tonic* is – you guessed it – tonic water. The good but rather expensive springwater is called *Eau Vive* and, of course, there is Coca-Cola. The locally produced *limonady* sadly bears no resemblance to lemons.

Caffeine-addicts have a problem. The coffee is OK if drunk black, but usually only condensed milk is available. The locally-grown tea is very weak, the best quality being reserved for export. A nice alternative is *citronelle*, lemon-grass tea, which is widely available.

HANDICRAFTS AND WHAT TO BUY

You can buy just about everything in the handicrafts line in Madagascar. Most typical of the country are wood carvings, raffia work (in amazing variety), crocheted and embroidered table-cloths and clothes, semi-precious stones (the solitaire sets are typical and most attractive), leather goods, carved zebu horn, Antaimoro paper (with embedded dried flowers), and so on. The choice is almost limitless, and it can all be seen in the artisans' market, *Marché Artisanal* in Antananarivo.

Other local products which make good presents are vanilla pods (although strictly speaking you are limited to 100 grams), pepper corns, saffron and other spices, and honey.

Do not buy products from endangered species. That includes tortoiseshell, snake skins (now crocodiles are farmed commercially, their skins may be sold legally) and, of course, live or stuffed lemurs and other animals. Also prohibited are endemic plants, fossils (including Aepyornis eggs) and any genuine article of funerary art.

THE MUSIC OF MADAGASCAR: A BRIEF INTRODUCTION
By Ian A. Anderson

The music of Madagascar is like the island itself — owing many things to other parts of the world, but unique.

The Malagasy are very fond of harmony singing, varying from Polynesian style (the Merina) to almost East African on the west coast. Traditional musical instruments include the celebrated *valiha*, a member of the zither family with 21 strings stretched lengthways all around the circumference of a hollow bamboo tube (there's also a box variety called the *marovany*), the *sodina*, an end-blown flute that can work magic in the hands of a master like Rakotofra (find his picture on the 1000 FMG note); the *kabosy*, a small guitar with paired strings and partial frets; the *jejy voatavo* with a gourd resonator and two sets of strings on adjacent sides of the neck; the *lokanga bara*, a 3-string fiddle; and a great variety of percussion instruments.

You'll also find most western instruments, successfully adapted to local music. Visit Ambohimanga, for example, to hear one of several generations of blind accordion players. Catch one of the *hiragasy* troupes and they'll be using ancient brass instruments and clarinets. Visit a nightclub or a larger concert and a modern band such as Jaojoby, Mily Clement or Tianjama will have electric guitars, synthesizers, and kit drums and might play one of the wild Malagasy dance styles such as *salegy*, *balesa*, *watsa watsa* or *sega*. The most famous modern groups playing distinctly Malagasy-rooted popular music have been Mahaleo (virtually the Beatles of Madagascar in the '70s but now only re-forming for special occasions), Rossy, Ricky and, internationally, Tarika Sammy.

Finding live music in Madagascar is a hit-and-miss affair; don't expect the real thing to be laid on for tourists in hotels. Keep an eye open for concert posters, and check out clubs used by local people.

Sadly, although the local cassette market is now fast expanding, recorded music is better purchased in the West, largely on CD which is as yet fairly unknown in Madagascar. The following are particularly recommended from over 40 Malagasy CDs now issued:

Bemiray: *Polyphonies Des Hauts-Plateaux* (Silex Y225209) France 1993

Jaojoby: *Salegy!* (Rogue FMSD 5025) UK 1992

Rossy: *Island of Ghosts* (RealWorld CDRW19) UK 1991

Tarika Sammy: *Balance* (Rogue FMSD 5028) UK 1994 (in USA, Green Linnet GLCD 4011)

Madagascar – Musique Traditionnelle Du Sud-Ouest (Pithys 25.9103.2) France 1991

Madagasikara Two – Current Popular Music (GlobeStyle CDORBD 013) UK 1986

Madagaskar 1 – Music From Antananarivo (Feuer & Eis FUEC 704) Germany 1989

World Beat Vol 7 – Madagascar (Celluloid 69619-2) France 1993

Most of the above recordings are available in London from Stern's African Record Centre, 116 Whitfield Street, London W1P 5RW. Tel: 071-388 5533

To help stamp out the sale of endangered animal products, tourists should make their feelings – and the law – known. If, for instance, you are offered a tortoise or turtle shell, tell the vendor it is *prohibé* and to push the point home you can say it is *fady* for you to buy such a thing.

The luggage weight limit when leaving Madagascar is 20kg (30kg if you are going non-stop to Paris which manages to count as a 'national' flight!). Bear this in mind when doing your shopping.

Permits

Some purchases need, in theory, an export permit, but the rule is seldom enforced with tourists – indeed, looking at the official list which contains every item tourists are likely to buy, it would be impossible to enforce it. If you are taking a lot of minerals, you can get an export permit at the airport providing you have a receipt from the vendor. For other goodies, use your judgement: if you are planning to take home a rosewood wardrobe you'd do well to get the paperwork; if it's a carved bookend, I wouldn't bother.

Export permits for major craft items are obtained from Ministère de la Culture et de la Communication, Antsahavola. Tel: 270 92. You will need to list your purchases and have receipts. Leave the list in the morning and pick up your permits in the afternoon. For animal products such as mounted butterflies apply to room 42 or the 4th floor of the Départment des Eaux et Forêts, Antsahavola. Tel: 240 26.

MISCELLANEOUS

Tipping

During the Marxist era tipping was frowned on and there were too few tourists (who always tip, whatever) to make much difference. These days a service charge is added to most restaurant meals so tipping is not strictly necessary, but waiters in tourist hotels expect it. 5-10% is ample. Before you give a dollar to the doorman for carrying your bag from the taxi to the hotel lobby, bear in mind that a labourer earns that for a half-day's work, and a doctor charges about US$15 for a private consultation. That said, the porters in posh hotels make their disgust very clear if you tip as a local would (about 500fmg).

Electrical equipment

The voltage in Madagascar is 110 or 220 (it varies in different parts of the country). Assume 220 to avoid wrecking your electrical gadget. Outlets (where they exist) take 2-pin round plugs.

Business hours

Most businesses open from 08.00-12.00 and 14.00-18.00. Banks are open 08.00-16.00, and are closed weekends and the afternoon before a holiday.

Communication with home

International telephone calls are hideously expensive. Tell your nearest and dearest that you won't be phoning to say you arrived safely. If you must telephone do it from the post office; hotels add up to 50%.

The mail service is reasonably efficient and letters generally take about two weeks to reach Europe and a little longer to the USA. If you want to receive mail, have your correspondent address the envelope with your initial only, your surname in block capitals, and send it to you c/o Poste Restante in whichever town you will be. It will be held at the main post office. (During the general strike of 1992 mail was not sorted for months. Frantic residents were told by amiable post office workers that for a small fee they were welcome to search for their letters in a pile which nearly reached the roof. Few took up the challenge.)

If you are an Amex member the Amex Client Mail Service allows you to have letters sent to their office in the Hilton Hotel. They keep it for a month.

BP in an address is *Bôite Postale* – the same as PO Box...

PUBLIC HOLIDAYS

January 1 New Year's Day
March 29 Commemoration of 1947 rebellion
Easter Monday (movable)
May 1 (Labour Day)
Ascension Day (movable)
Whit Monday (movable)
June 26 Independence Day
August 15 Feast of the Assumption
November 1 All Saints Day
December 25 Christmas Day
December 30 Republic Day
When these holidays fall on a Thursday, Friday will be tacked onto the weekend.

DID YOU KNOW?

- Earthquakes mean the whales are bathing their children.
- If a woman maintains a bending posture when arranging eggs in a nest, the chickens will have crooked necks.
- If the walls of a house incline towards the south, the wife will be the stronger one; if they incline towards the north it will be the husband.
- Burning a knot on a piece of string causes the knees to grow big.

VILLAGE ETIQUETTE

Travellers venturing well off the beaten path will want to do their utmost to avoid offending the local people, who are usually extremely warm and hospitable. Unfortunately, with the many *fady* prohibitions and beliefs varying from area to area and village to village, it is impossible to know exactly how to behave, although *vazahas* (white foreigners) and other outsiders are exempt from the consequences of infringing a local *fady*.

Sometimes, in very remote areas, Malagasy will react in sheer terror at the sight of a white person. This is probably due to their belief in *Mpakafo* (pronounced 'mpaka<u>foo</u>'), the 'stealer of hearts'. These pale-faced beings are said to wander around at night ripping out people's hearts. For this reason many rural Malagasy will not go out after dark (a problem when you are looking for a guide). The arrival of a pale-faced being in their village is understandably upsetting. In the south-east it is the *mpangalak'aty*, the 'taker of the liver' who is feared.

Villages are governed by the Fokonolona, or People's Assembly. On arrival at a village you should ask for the *Président du Fokontany*. Although traditionally this was the village elder, these days it is more likely to be someone who speaks French — perhaps the school teacher. He will show you where you can sleep (sometimes a hut is kept free for guests, sometimes someone will be moved out for you). You will usually be provided with a meal. Now travellers have penetrated most rural areas, you will be expected to pay. If the *Président* is not available, ask for *Ray amandreny*, an elder.

Philip Thomas, a social anthropologist who has conducted research in the rural south-east, points out several ways that tourists may unwittingly cause offence. 'People should adopt the common courtesy of greeting the Malagasy in their own language. *Salama*, *manahoana* and *veloma* are no more difficult to say than their French equivalents, and to insist on using French displays an ignorance of Madagascar's colonial past.

'*Vazaha* sometimes refuse food and hospitality, putting up tents and cooking their own food. But in offering you a place to sleep and food to eat the Malagasy are showing you the kindness they extend to any visitor or stranger, and to refuse is a rejection of their hospitality and sense of humanity. You may think you are inconveniencing them, and this is true, but they would prefer that than if you keep to yourselves as though you were not people (in the widest sense) like them. It may annoy you that it is virtually impossible to get a moment away from the gaze of the Malagasy, but you are there to look at them and their activities anyway, so why should there not be a mutual exchange? Besides, you are far more fascinating to them than they are to you, for their view of the world is not one shaped by mass education and access to images from around the world supplied by television.

'It is perfectly acceptable to give someone a gift of money for their help.

Gifts of money are not seen by the Malagasy as purchases and they themselves frequently give them. Rather, you give as a sign of your appreciation and respect. But beware of those who may try to take advantage of your position as a foreigner (and you may find these in even the remotest spot), those who play on your lack of knowledge of language and custom, and their perception of you as extremely wealthy (as of course you are by their standards).

'You may well see memorial sites by the side of the road or tombs marked on maps, especially in the south-east. Do *not* think it is OK to visit these or photograph them if no-one is around to ask. Seek out someone, a male elder being best, and ask if you can be allowed to visit the site and under what terms. More often than not your request will be accepted. But what annoys people here is that *vazaha* see something beside the road then trample all over it, photographing it, then carry on with their journey as if they cared nothing for the feelings of those that own the site. To do so shows little respect, as the Malagasy understand it, neither to themselves nor the dead commemorated there.'

Both Henk Beentje and Philip Thomas recommend presenting yourself and your passport to the *Gendarmerie* if you are staying in a small village. Apart from good manners, this could avoid problems for both you and your Malagasy hosts (see page 94).

RESPONSIBLE TOURISM

The impact of foreigners on the Malagasy was noted as long ago as 1669 when a visitor commented that formerly the natives were deeply respectful of white men but were changed 'by the bad examples which the Europeans have had, who glory in the sin of luxury in this country...'.

In 'undeveloped' countries tourism has had profound effects on the inhabitants, some good, some bad. Madagascar seems to me a special case – more than any other country I've visited it inspires a particular devotion and an awareness of its fragility, both environmental and cultural. Wildlife is definitely profiting from the attention given it and the emphasis on ecotourism. For the people, however, the blessings may be very mixed: some able Malagasy have found jobs in the tourist industry, but for some the impact of tourism has meant that whilst their cultural identity has been forced to change some of their dignity and integrity has been lost. Village antagonisms are heightened when one or two people gain the lion's share of tourist revenue and gifts, leading in one case to murder, and hitherto honest folk have lapsed into corruption or thievery.

All readers of this book will want to minimise the harm they do. Often it is simply a question of pausing to think before behaving in a way appropriate only to our own culture.

They do things differently there

I once caught our Malagasy guide scowling at himself in the mirror. When I teased him he said 'As a Malagasy man I smile a lot. I can see that if I want to work with tourists I must learn to frown'. He had learned that the group considered him insufficiently assertive. Tolerance and the fear of causing offence is an integral part of Malagasy social relationships. Not only is showing anger unproductive, it is deeply unsettling to the person at the receiving end who often giggles in response, thus exacerbating the situation. If you are patient, pleasant and keep your temper, your problem will be solved faster.

Avoid being overaffirmative in conversation (you do not have exclusivity of the truth). Make use of 'perhaps' and 'maybe'. Be excessive in your thanks. The Malagasy are very polite; we miss the nuances by not understanding the language. Body language, however, is easier to learn. For instance, 'excuse me, may I come through?' is indicated by a stooping posture and an arm extended forward. Note how often it is used.

Part of responsible tourism is relinquishing some of our normal comforts. Consider this statistic: by the end of the century in Madagascar, fuel wood demand is likely to outstrip supply by two million tonnes a year. Wood and charcoal are the main sources of energy. Do you still feel that hot water is essential in your hotel?

Madagascar's shortcomings can be maddening. Sometimes a little reflection reveals the reasons behind the failure to produce the expected service, but sometimes you just have to tell yourself 'Well, that's the way it is.' After all, you are not going to be able to change Madagascar, but Madagascar may change you.

Photography

Lack of consideration when taking photos is probably the most common example of irresponsible tourist behaviour – one that each of us has been guilty of at some time. It is so easy to take a sneak photo without first establishing contact with the person, so easy to say we'll send a print of the picture and then not get round to it, so easy to stroll into a market or village thinking what a wonderful photo it will make and forgetting that you are there to *experience* it.

The rules are not to take people photos without permission, and to respect an answer of 'no'. Give consideration to the offence caused by photographing the destitute. Be cautious about paying your way to a good photo; often a smile or a joke will work as well, without setting a precedent. People *love* to receive pictures of themselves. If you are travelling on an organised tour your guide is sure to visit that area again so can deliver the prints that you send to him. If you are travelling independently write down the addresses and honour your promise.

Philip Thomas writes: 'A Malagasy, for whom a photograph will be a highly treasured souvenir, as it may be for you, will remember the taking of the photograph and your promise to send them a copy, a lot longer than you might. Their disappointment in those who say one thing and do another is great, and so if you think you might not get it together to send the photograph then do not say that you will.'

A responsible attitude to photography is so much more *fun*! And it results in better pictures. It involves taking some time getting to know the subject of your proposed photo: making a purchase, perhaps, or practising your Malagasy greetings (if the latter doesn't draw hoots of laughter nothing will!). My favourite way is to give my camera to the crowd of onlookers and ask one of *them* to take a picture of me. And then of his/her family. The result may be a little crooked, perhaps even headless, but you will have provided enough entertainment to follow it up with one or two of your own.

Beggars
Whether to give to professional beggars is up to you. I believe that it is wrong to give to the little ragamuffin children that follow you around because they all have access to charities that work with street kids. Far better to give to the charities (see *Tourist aid*). Actually, the same applies to all age-groups. My policy is to give to the elderly and I also single out 'beggar days' when I fill my pockets with small change and give to everyone who looks needy and over school age. And if I make some trickster's day, so be it.

It is important to make up your mind about beggars before you hit the streets so you can avoid standing there looking through a conspicuously fat wallet for a low-denomination bill.

More and more...
Visitors who have spent some time in Madagascar and have befriended a particular family often find themselves in the 'more and more and more' trap. The foreigner begins by expressing appreciation of the friendship and hospitality he or she received by sending a gift to the family. A request for a more expensive gift follows. And another one, until the luckless *vazaha* feels that she is seen as a bottomless cornucopia of goodies. The reaction is a mixture of guilt and resentment.

Understanding the Malagasy view point may help you to come to terms with these requests. You may be considered as part of the extended family, and family members often help support those who are less well-off. You will almost certainly be thought of as fabulously wealthy, so it is worth dispelling this myth by giving some prices for familiar foodstuffs at home – a kilo of rice, for instance, or a mango. Explain that you don't have servants, that you pay so much for rent, and that you have a family of your own that needs your help. Don't be afraid to say 'no' firmly.

Tourist aid

There *are* ways in which you can make a positive contribution to Madagascar. By making a donation to local projects you can help the people without creating new problems by so doing. My favourite is the Streetkids Project, which was started by a couple of English teachers, Jill and Charlie Hadfield. Visiting a charity run by The Sisters of the Good Shepherd in the capital, they could see where a little money could go a long way. The nuns, Irish and Sri Lankan, run – amongst other things – a preparatory school for the very poor. When the children are ready to go on to state school, however, the parents can't afford the £15 a year they must pay for registration, uniform and books, so they were condemned to return to the streets as beggars. The Streetkids Project raises money to continue their education.

Visiting this centre is an intensely moving and inspiring experience. Apart from the school and preschool groups, there is a mother and baby programme involving 260 families where the health and weight of the infant is monitored on a regular basis, a feeding programme, and many other projects. So if you want to help Madagascar by helping the poor, give a donation of money, clothes, medicines, or school supplies to the centre Fihavanana at St Joseph's church in Antananarivo, on the way to Tsimbazaza. The nuns can usually be reached at phone number 299 81 (their house). Ask for Sister Lucy, Sister Anna, or Sister Margaret. The full address is Soeurs du Bon Pasteur, 58 Lalana S. Stephani, Amparibe, Antananarivo 101.

In Britain the Streetkids scheme is administered by Money for Madagascar (see below) so you may prefer to send them your donation.

Although this is the only charity I know personally, there are several others doing equally valuable work. Laura Benson, who spent several weeks researching government, church and private programmes to help the poor was impressed with the Association Akamasoa, run by Père Pedro Opeka, which among other self-help projects provides materials for people to build their own houses. 'I was able to spend a week at the centre at Ambohimahitsy where I could see the change in people's lives. They had gone from digging through the trash for food, to having their own home, a job, and dignity. The centre has nutritional recuperation, a preschool, nursery school, elementary school and a clinic.' Laura adds 'I am convinced now that giving to children directly is only hurting the situation, and that if you really want to help a donation to an organisation such as the Association Akamasoa is the best way. Giving pens, etc can have an even worse effect, especially if you only have one to give. I saw many fights started among children over who got the pen or the empty Coke bottle.'

The World Food Programme assists around 100 NGOs in Madagascar and can advise on their needs. The address is BP 1348 Antananarivo. It is also worth asking your embassy in Antananarivo if they are helping support any charities.

If you prefer an animal project, you could contact the co-ordinator of the Madagascar Fauna Group Project in Tzimbazaza to see how you can help. A donation to the WWF, who are very active in Madagascar, will also help conservation projects.

ORGANISATIONS FOR RESPONSIBLE TOURISM

Tourism Concern   Froebel College, Roehampton Lane, London SW15 5PJ, England.

With the slogan 'putting people back in the picture', Tourism Concern 'promotes tourism that takes account of the rights and interests of those living in the world's tourist areas'. They put pressure on governments or companies which promote harmful tourism, run meetings and conferences, and publish an informative and interesting newsletter.

Center for Responsible Tourism   PO Box 827, San Anselmo, CA 94979, USA. Full title: The North America Coordinating Center for Responsible Tourism (NACCRT). 'Exists to change attitudes and practices of North American travelers, to involve North Americans in the struggle for justice in tourism and to work for tourism practices that are compatible with a sustainable global society.'

CHARITIES ASSISTING MADAGASCAR

Money for Madagascar   29 Queen's Rd, Sketty, Swansea SA2 0SB, Great Britain. A small charitable trust working with rural communities and funding village agricultural projects. One such project, at Betampona, is working to improve the standard of living in a cluster of villages adjoining the rainforest reserve north of Toamasina. Irrigation schemes help the shift from traditional slash-and-burn to permanent agriculture, tree nurseries bring sources of firewood, health care has been improved, and livestock schemes and grain stores improve nutrition and decrease dependence on forest products. Other schemes have included digging (by local people) of irrigation canals in the deeply eroded highlands, the establishment of tree nurseries and the introduction of improved rice cultivation.

Money for Madagascar administers the Street Kids Education Scheme described earlier.

The Sedgwick Trust   Moresdale Hall East, Lambrigg, Kendal, Cumbria LA8 ODH. Administered in England by a former LMS missionary in Madagascar, Dr James Pottinger. Like Money for Madagascar, they work with local organisations at village level to promote self-help projects in health, agriculture and education.

SAF   Both the above charities work with the development organisation of the United Protestant Church of Madagascar. SAF organises and runs a large variety of projects, from emergency relief following natural disasters such as the 1994 cyclone to irrigation, potable water supplies, tree nurseries, small agricultural projects, village pharmacies and so on. They are indispensable for the smooth-running of the British charities.

Finally, if on your return to Britain you want to keep connections with Madagascar, how about joining the **Anglo-Malagasy Society**? The London consulate will give you the current secretary's address.

MALAGASY STAMPS

Like most things Malagasy, their choice of stamp design ranges from the sublime to the ridiculous. In the first category are the beautiful series on the fauna and flora: lemurs, birds, butterflies, orchids. However, their 1991 selection of competitive winter sports such as ski jumping (not a sport in which Madagascar has achieved international standing) was more surprising and we are now on to pedigree dogs. Again surprising since most dogs one sees in Madagascar seem to be made out of discarded string. Never mind, they are mostly very attractive and can be purchased from the Philately department of the main post office, and from street vendors outside the Colbert Hotel.

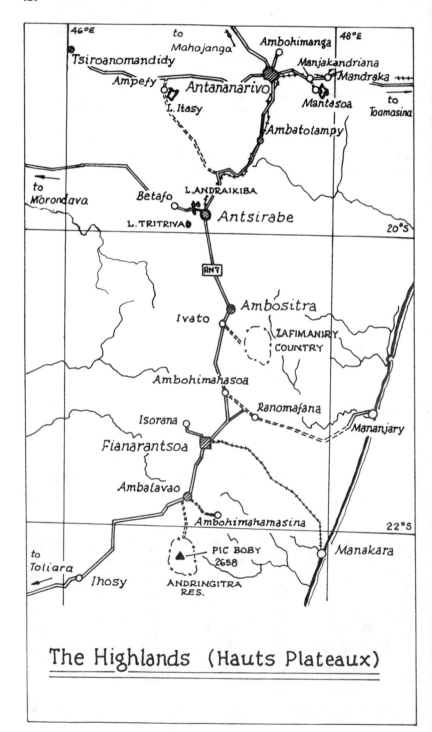

The Highlands (Hauts Plateaux)

Chapter 7

The Highlands

(Hauts Plateaux)

INTRODUCTION

The kingdom of Imerina was born in the highlands. Recorded history of the Merina people (also known as the Hova), who are characterised by their Indonesian appearance and exhumation practices (*famadihana*) begins in the 1400s with a chief called Andriandraviravina. He is widely thought to have started the dynasty that became the most powerful in Madagascar, eventually conquering much of the country.

Key monarchs in the rise of the Merina include Andrianjaka, who conquered a Vazimba town called Analamanga built on a great rock thrusting above the surrounding plains. He renamed it Antananarivo and ordered his palace to be built on its highest point. With its surrounding marshland, ideal for rice production, and the security afforded by its high position, this was the perfect site for a Merina capital city.

In the 18th century there were two centres for the Merina kingdom, Antananarivo and Ambohimanga. The latter became the more important and around 1787 Ramboasalama was proclaimed king of Ambohimanga and took the name of Andrianampoinimerina. The name means 'the prince in the heart of Imerina' which was more than an idle boast: this king was the Malagasy counterpart of the great Peruvian Inca Tupac Yupanqui, expanding his empire as much by skilful organisation as by force, and doing it without the benefit of a written language (history seems to demonstrate that orders in triplicate are not essential to efficiency). By his death in 1810 the central plateau was firmly in control of the Merina and ably administered through a mixture of old customs and new. Each conquered territory was governed by local princes, answerable to the king, and the system of *fokonolona* (village communities) was established. From this firm foundation the new king, Radama I, was able to conquer most of the rest of the island.

The Merina are still the most influential of the Malagasy peoples and dominate the capital. Further south, the highlands are occupied by the Betsileo, who have been heavily influenced by the Merina and also practise *famadihana*. Since the mid 19th century Merina houses have been built of brick or red mud (laterite), often with roofs supported on slender pillars. These typical houses are a feature of the city and its surroundings. Invariably they are of less sturdy construction than the cement tombs that can be seen on the outskirts of town, the dead being considered more important than the living.

There is some splendid scenery on the *Hauts Plateaux*. Route Nationale 7, which runs to Toliara (Tuléar), passes dramatic granite domes and grassy hills, and always the mosaic of paddy fields add colour and pattern to a land journey. These patterns are best appreciated from the air, from where the old defence ditches, *tamboho*, forming circles around villages or estates can be seen. I never tire of staring down as the plane circles before landing at Ivato airport. The aerial view is as exotically different as Madagascar itself.

ANTANANARIVO

History

The city founded by Andrianjaka was called Antananarivo which means 'City of the Thousand', supposedly because a thousand warriors protected it. By the end of the 18th century, Andrianampoinimerina had taken Antananarivo from his rebellious kinsman and moved his base there from Ambohimanga. From that time until the French conquest in 1895 Madagascar's history centred around the royal palace or *rova*, the modest houses built for Andrianjaka and Andrianampoinimerina giving way to the splendid palace designed for Queen Ranavalona I by Jean Laborde and James Cameron. The rock cliffs near the palace became known as Ampamarinana, 'the place of the hurling' as Christian martyrs met their fate at the command of the Queen.

There was no reason for the French to move the capital elsewhere: its pleasant climate made it an agreeable place to live, and plenty of French money and planning went into the city we see today.

Ivato airport
Arriving

The rebuilding and enlarging of Ivato has been completed and the arrivals procedure is now much the same as in other parts of the world. Just to keep travellers on their toes, however, the system is still subject to change. In early 1994 the order of business was this:

1. Forms. An arrivals form is given to you on the plane so you can save time by filling it out in advance. One of the questions is where you spent the last five nights. If you have stopped in a malarial/yellow fever zone your Health Card must show inoculation. The officials may take the card and ask you to collect it the following day from the Institut d'Hygiene Social.

2. Immigration, where your passport is stamped.

3. Douane. A less orderly queue tries to get hold of currency declaration forms (if these are still required). Fill this in accurately (having counted your cash and travellers cheques and made a note of the amounts while on the plane) and have it stamped. Thereafter *always* have it with you when you change money and do not lose it. If you have a video camera or other expensive equipment you may be asked to register it.

4. Final document check, and you descend some stairs to the luggage section. Red-uniformed porters will jostle for your attention but since you will have no francs for the 500fmg-per-bag tip it's best to deal with your own luggage. There are a few trolleys but they tend to come with 'drivers'. Join the queue with the most tourists. Residents are searched thoroughly causing delay. Customs officers are unlikely to give your luggage more than a cursory look.

Leaving

With the renovation of the airport this procedure seems to have become even worse. It can only improve (indeed, recent reports are that it *has* improved, but for international flights be prepared for the following:

1. Try to get to the airport three hours before the flight, with all your Malagasy money spent except for the departure tax of 33,000fmg (or 25,000fmg if you're going to another Indian Ocean destination). Pay this at the kisok marked Adema, on the left of the departure gate, and collect a departure form from a small window on its left.

2. Join the queue and shuffle forward with your bags (if you have heavy luggage you may want to hire a baggage handler to help).

3. When you reach the doorway show your ticket and passport, and pass through to the baggage-check tables. Here your bags may be opened and searched.

4. Proceed to the check-in counter. Any orderly queue will have disintegrated by now as people jostle for priority.

5. Move on to the seat assignment desk (no computer). If late you will now realise why I recommended you come early. It's chaos, with experienced residents (not Malagasy) pushing to the front to get their preferred seats.

6. Police. Show your passport and hand in your currency declaration (having checked that it tallies with your remaining money) and departure form.

7. Security check. X-ray of luggage and body search.

8. Final passport check and you're through into the departure lounge! There are souvenir shops here (hard currency only) and a bar. You'll need it.

Internal flights

The domestic building is separated from the main airport. If you are connecting to an internal flight immediately on arrival in Madagascar, you can pass directly down a linking corridor on the right of the main hall. However, there is no bank in the internal flights building. The domestic airport tax is 3,300fmg. These flights are distinctly no frills. Boarding passes are carefully recycled and there are no seat assignments. Sometimes you have to identify your luggage from a pile on the runway for security reasons.

Lost luggage

Sometimes your luggage doesn't arrive. Most people are on a tight schedule and cannot hang around waiting for the next flight. If you are on an organised tour your guide will handle it, but if on your own it can be a bit of a challenge. For someone else to pick up your luggage you will need to get a proxy form with a signature that is legalised in the town hall. The only alternative is to meet every international flight (assuming it was lost on the way to Madagascar) in the hope that your bag is on it. Unclaimed bags are put under lock and key, and finding *le responsable* may not be easy.

Transport into the city centre (12km)

In the past there was an airport bus service, Air Routes Service, but at the time of writing this is not running. Taxis cost about 15,000fmg. There is a much cheaper local bus (500fmg) if you walk up the road a bit. It stops near some stalls.

Getting *to* the airport is easier. A 12-seater car leaves from the Vasakosy area behind the train station.

Antananarivo today

For many people this is one of the most attractive capitals in the developing world. Antananarivo (popularly known as Tana) has the quality of a child's picture book. Brightly coloured houses are stacked up the hillsides, and there are very few of the modern skyscrapers that deface most capitals. Rice paddies are tended right up to the edge of the city, clothes are laid out on the river bank to dry, and ox-carts rumble along the roads on the outskirts of town. It's all deliciously foreign, and can hardly fail to impress the first-time visitor as he or she comes in from the airport. The good impression is helped by the climate − during the dry season the sun is hot but the air pleasantly cool (the altitude is between 1,245m and 1,469m).

The city is built on two ridges which combine in a V. Down the central valley runs a broad boulevard, Avenue de l'Indépendance (sometimes called by its Malagasy name Fahaleovantena), which terminates at the station. It narrows at the other end to become Avenue du 26 Juin, then dives through a tunnel to reach Lake Anosy and the Hilton Hotel (pedestrians make their way breathlessly up and down flights of stairs). The Avenues Indépendance and 26 Juin are the focal point of the Lower Town, lined with shops, offices, hotels, and crammed with market stalls and lower class bustle, but the 'centre of town' could just as easily refer to the Upper Town where the President's Palace, the Hotel Colbert, the main post office and other assorted offices are located. This is where you will find the most expensive boutiques and the best jewellers' shops.

It is all very confusing, and made worse by streets being unnamed, changing name several times within a few hundred metres, or going by two different names (when reading street names it's worth knowing that *Lalana* means street and *Arabe* avenue). Fortunately you can never really be lost since this is a town for wanderers – you are just seeing a new area. As a rough wandering guide, however, I would recommend that lots of time be spent in the Upper Town – and on the opposite side, above the market – but to avoid the Lower Town where robbery is a danger, distances are long and streets tend to be dreary.

The population of Tana is about two million and growing fast. About 1,500 people survive by scavenging the city's rubbish dumps.

Sightseeing

As if to emphasise how different it is to other capitals, Tana has relatively little in the way of conventional sightseeing. Until recently it had no tourist office, but now the imposing **La Maison du Tourisme de Madagascar** has opened at Place de l'Indépendance. Tel: 325 29. They produce printed lists of hotels, tour operators, car-hire companies, etc. No doubt they will add to the information available as they become established, so are worth a visit. Open 09.30 - 11.30, 15.30 - 17.30.

The Queen's Palace (Palais de la Reine, or *Rova*)

Standing high above the city, this miscellany of mausoleums and palaces dominates the skyline (especially when viewed from Lake Anosy or the Hilton Hotel). It is well worth a visit of several hours, being a fascinating look at Malagasy history before colonisation (read the history section in this book before you visit!) and serving as a reminder of the level of sophistication reached by the ruling Merina in the 19th century.

The energetic can walk there – it's a breathtaking (in both senses of the word) climb which takes about half an hour from the Hotel Colbert, but is well worth it for the views and scenes en route. Start at Lalana Ratsimilaho and when in doubt take the uphill road. The entrance to the *Rova* is topped by a very European-looking eagle; King Radama I had his stronghold here guarded by elite troops known as the Eagles. The Queen's Palace, originally built in wood by Jean Laborde at the request of Queen Ranavalona I, is enclosed in a stone structure, designed by James Cameron in 1873 during the reign of Queen Ranavalona II. Laborde's building is perfectly in harmony with Madagascar, Cameron's would be more in keeping with Edinburgh.

On entering the compound you will see on the left what appears to be two attractive wooden chalets. These are *tranomanara*, sacred houses, over

THE MARTYR MEMORIAL CHURCHES

By Dr G W Milledge

My grandfather, James Sibree, a civil engineer from Hull, was appointed by the London Missionary Society in 1863 to build four memorial churches to commemorate the Malagasy Christians put to death by order of Queen Ranavalona I during the period 1837 to her death in 1861. The sites, mainly within easy walking distance of the palace, were associated with the execution or imprisonment of the martyrs. Mr William Ellis of the London Mission had noted that the sites were suitable for church building, thought of the memorial churches and petitioned King Radama II for the sites to be reserved. This was granted. He also petitioned the mission board who agreed to raise funds in England.

Mention should be made of the difficulties and delays in starting to build large stone churches; quarry men, masons, carpenters all had to be trained. Stone was readily available but other materials were difficult to obtain. Workmen often departed for family functions, government work or military service, and work was held up for weeks. As the spire of Ambatonakangar rose to heights unknown in Malagasy buildings wives of his workmen pleaded with James Sibree not to ask their husbands to go up to such dangerous heights.

Ambatonakangar is situated at the meeting of five roads in an area given on the map as Ambohidahy. The first church in Madagascar was on this site: a low, dark, mud brick building in which Christians were imprisoned, often in chains before, in many cases, being led out to execution. The first printing press was also on this site and the first Malagasy bibles were printed here. The present church, opened in 1867, follows the Early English style, with 'Norman' arches. It was the first stone building in Madagascar.

Ambohipotsy is on a commanding site at the southern end of the ridge beyond the Queen's Palace. Its slender spire can be seen for miles around the surrounding plain. On this site the first martyr, a young woman called Rasalama, was speared to death in 1837. Later 11 other Christians suffered the same fate.

Faravohitra Church is on the northern side of the city ridge, built where four Christians of the nobility were burnt to death on March 28 1849. Though not as fine a site as Ambohipotsy, it also commands good views.

Ampamarinana Church is a short way below the Palace on the west side of the ridge on the summit of the 'The Place of the Hurling' from where prisoners were thrown to their death. 14 Christians were killed here on the same day in 1849.

So the four churches stand on historic sites as a memorial to those brave martyrs for their faith, and witness to the interest and concern of Christians in Britain for their fellows in Madagascar.

Dr Milledge travelled to Madagascar at the age of 88 to visit the place where he was born. Throughout the trip he was honoured as a descendent of one of Madagascar's major benefactors: perhaps the greatest writer the island has inspired.

the Tomb of the Queens, where the remains of four queens are interred, and the Tomb of the Kings which houses three kings. Their bodies lie seven metres below the ground. Nearby is one of Jean Laborde's palaces, a wooden building known as Tranovola, or Palais d'Argent, because silver nails were originally used in its construction. It contains portraits of the monarchs as well as James Hastie, Radama I's adviser, Sir Robert Farquhar, governor of Mauritius, and a fascinating early photo of Jean Laborde.

The reconstruction of Andrianampoinimerina's little palm-thatched house is interesting. The King's bed is high on a platform in the north-east corner, opposite a much wider shelf on which slept 11 of his 12 wives. The lucky 12th spent one week in the royal bed, no doubt in acts of procreation. A tall column rises to the roof by the king's bed. We are told that on hearing the approach of a stranger, his highness would scramble up this pillar (there are tiny handholds) and if the visitor was welcome he would inform whichever wife was tending the cooking pots beneath the pillar by dropping a pebble on her head. Or so we are told. The king's sedan chair, borne by eight men, is here, and an accompanying litter for his luggage. He travelled widely in his kingdom, exhorting the peasants to greater labours by replacing their worn out agricultural tools.

Queen Rasoherina's palace, Manampisoa was built in 1866 as a two storey building by William Poole, the British missionary-architect. The missionary influence on the monarchy is very evident here, and many of the exhibits are labelled in English. These include an interesting collection of objects donated by the descendants of Dr John Wilson, a Quaker missionary from 1877. An inscription, in English, describes his work.

The main palace, Manjakamiadana ('Where it is pleasant to reign'), was closed for many years but now the ground floor is open. It contains a large number of exhibits, mainly beds and palanquins. Other floors are still under restoration.

In the royal compound (which is in need of a good clean-up) is a church in the Wren-classical style built in stone for Ranavalona II by William Poole (see Box for other Martyr Memorial Churches).

The *rova* is open weekdays 10.00 to 12.00, 14.00 to 17.00, Saturdays 14.00 to 17.00, Sundays 9.00 to 12.00, 14.00 to 1700. Closed Mondays. Entry fee: 6,000fmg. You are not permitted to take photos within the compound.

Near the palace is the imposing and newly restored Prime Minister's Palace. At present it is not open to the public.

Tsimbazaza

This comprises a museum (natural history and ethnology), botanical garden and zoo exhibiting — with a few exceptions — only Malagasy species.

Tsimbazaza (pronounced Tsimba<u>zaz</u>) is the centre for the Madagascar

Fauna Group, an international consortium of zoos and univerities working together to help conserve Madagascar's wildlife. An excellent educational programme for visiting school children has been established, captive breeding is successful, and a nocturnal animal house is being discussed. The animals are reasonably well-housed and new cages are being built. There is a good collection of lemurs, including golden bamboo lemur (see page 158) and four aye-ayes. Arrangements may be made to visit the aye-ayes after dark when they are active, for a donation of 10,000fmg per person. Please note, however, that the keepers have found this such a nice little money-earner that some are willing to wake the poor creatures during the day for payment. Please resist this temptation.

The excellent vivarium has a well-displayed collection of reptiles and small mammals.

The botanical garden is spacious and well laid out, and provides a sanctuary for numerous birds including a huge colony of egrets. There are also some reproduction Sakalava graves. It is the museum, however, that attracts the most interest for its selection of skeletons of now extinct animals, including several species of giant lemur and the famous 'elephant bird' or *aepyornis* which may only have become extinct after the arrival of the first Europeans. It is displayed next to the skeleton of an ostrich, so its massive size can be appreciated. Another room displays stuffed animals, but the efforts of the taxidermist have left little to likeness and a lot to the imagination. It's worth taking a close look at the aye-aye, however, to study its remarkable hands. The museum has recently redesigned its ethnological section which is now excellent.

Tsimbazaza is open every day except Mondays, from 10.00 to 17.00. A leaflet is available in English. The fee is 5,000fmg plus a 2,000fmg photography charge (10,000fmg for video). Postal address: BP 4096. Tel: 311 49. There is a souvenir shop with an excellent selection of good-quality T-shirts and postcards. Profits from admission fees and the shop go towards supporting the zoo and its education department.

The park is about 4km from the city centre. There are buses from Avenue de l'Indépendance (no 15), but it is easier to take a taxi there and bus back.

Cemetery

On the recommendation of reader Leone Badenhorst I am including this despite anxious visions of camera-toting tourists trampling on people's sensibilities as well as their tombs. Do show respect. 'Apart from the large variety of interesting tombs (Malagasy, French and Chinese – even a couple of English), some with extraordinary decorations and trimmings, this provides a peaceful break with superb views of the city.' (L.B.). Ask the taxi-driver for Cimetiere Anjanahary. He should charge around 2,500fmg.

Zoma (market)

Zoma means Friday and this is the day when the whole of Avenue de l'Indépendance erupts into a rash of white umbrellas. The market runs the length of the street and up the hillsides, filling every available space with an amazing variety of goods. There are stands selling nothing but bottles, or spare parts, or years-old French magazines; there are men who repair watches, or umbrellas or bicycles; there are flowers and fruit and animals (including cats) and herbal medicines and charms; and there are plenty of handicrafts although the artisans now have their own market (see below). This description by the missionary James Sibree, over 100 years ago, shows how little the market has changed:

> All the chief roads are thronged with people bringing in their goods for sale... and the hum of voices can be heard from a considerable distance. Here everything that is grown or manufactured in the interior province can be procured, and in no place can a better idea of the productions of the country or of the handicrafts skill of the Malagasy be obtained than in this great zoma market... it is certainly one of the most interesting sights in Tananarive.

The *zoma* is notorious for thieves. It is safest to bring only a small amount of money in a money-belt or neck pouch. Enticingly bulging pockets will be slashed. Keep an eye on your camera (but don't leave it behind – the market is very photogenic).

Although the *zoma* proper is on Fridays, there is always a market in Tana, always some white umbrellas shading fruit and vegetables opposite the stairs leading to the Upper Town, and some handicraft stalls down each side of the avenue towards the station.

Shopping for handicrafts and other items

The Marché Artisanal, shows the enormous range and quality of Malagasy handicrafts. Most noteworthy is the embroidery and basketry, wood-carving, minerals, leatherwork (stiff cowhide, not soft leather) and the unique Antaimoro paper embedded with pressed flowers. The market is held in the Andravoahangy region of town. This is to the right of the station (as you face it) north-east on Lalana Me Albertini. It is quite a walk, so take a taxi. Open 10.00 - 17.00.

If you prefer a shop but don't want to pay hotel shop prices, it's worth going to Galerie Le Bivouac, Antsofinondry – on the road to Ambohimanga – which sells beautiful painted silk items as well as other handicrafts of a high quality. Tel: 429 50. Nearby is Atelier Jacarandas which specialises in batik.

Nearer the centre of town, though still a taxi journey away, is Lisy Art Gallery on the Route de Mausolée opposite the Cercle Mess de la Police, and near the Hotel Panorama. Tel: 277 33.

Alan Hickling (Tel: 400 79) sells hand-painted T-shirts of Malagasy wild life and other good quality handicrafts (see advertisement on page 109).

At the Centre Fihavanana (see page 117) you can buy beautiful embroidery and greetings cards made by the very poor, and you will have the opportunity to see the admirable work done by the Sisters of the Good Shepherd. Guaranteed to warm the most resilient of hearts. Phone Sister Lucy on 299 81.

Other locally-produced goodies are chocolate (excellent, especially the dark chocolate) and wine. Also locally produced is the line of herbal beauty products made from Malagasy plants under the brand name Phytoline; they seem only to be available from the Hilton shop or in the airport departure lounge.

Where to stay
Category A

Hilton Hotel   Near Lake Anosy. Tel: 260 60. One of Tana's skyscrapers (as you'd expect), very comfortable with good meals. Its advantages are the offices and shops (including Madagascar Air Tours) in the building and the swimming pool. In the pleasantly hot sun of the dry season this is a real bonus. It is some way from the centre of town (although the walk in is enjoyable). 1110FF double, 920FF single.

Hotel de Palais   (Palace Hotel). A very smart new hotel at the lower end of the Avenue de l'Indépendance. Tel: 256 63. No restaurant, but enormous studio apartments with kitchens. 630FF double, 595FF single, 950FF apartment.

Hotel Colbert   Lalana Printsy Ratsimamanga. Tel: 202 02. Very French, usually full, my choice of the posh Tana hotels for its good location in the Upper Town, nice atmosphere and excellent food. 600FF per room.

Radama Hotel   22 Ave Grandidier, Isoraka (near the Colbert). Tel: 319 27. Fax: 353 23. A very nice small (14 rooms) new hotel (1992) with excellent food. Impractical for groups because there is no parking for tour buses, but ideal for business people (there is a conference room). No lift (elevator). From 500FF double, 425FF single.

Hotel de France   Avenue de l'Indépendance. Ask for an inside room – 59, 60, 61, among others. 500FF double, 475FF single.

Hotel Panorama   Route d'Andrainarivo, on the eastern side of town. Tel: 409 65. This large (86 rooms) hotel opened in 1991 and has deteriorated with spectacular speed; in 1993 it represented the worst value in town. Mould and cockroaches for 500FF double, 475FF single. Perhaps it will improve.

Category B

Le Relais des Pistards   Lalana Fernand Kasanga (same road as Tsimbazaza), about 1km beyond the zoo. Bungalows owned by Florent and Jocelyne Colney who can organise tours for their guests. 50,000fmg double, 35,000fmg single, including dinner and breakfast. Recommended.

Hotel Taj   Near Kianja 19 May 1946 square. Tel: 303 40. New. 48,000fmg double, 45,000fmg single.

Jean Laborde Hotel   3 Rue de Russie, Isoraka. Tel: 330 45. A new hotel near Ave de l'Indépendance. 6 rooms from 35,000 - 48,000fmg.

Central Hotel   7 Rue Rajohnson (continuation of Indira Gandhi). Tel 227 94. Friendly, clean, spacious; en-suite hot showers. From 40,000fmg (communal bathroom) to 54,000fmg (with bathroom and WC). Recommended.

Hotel Mellis   Lalana Indira Gandhi. Tel: 234 25. Once the most popular *vazaha* hotel, but losing favour because of unreliable hot water, among other things. From 25,000fmg to 50,000fmg for a room with a bath.

Auberge du Cheval Blanc   Near Ivato airport. Convenient when you have a late arrival and early departure the following morning. Friendly; food mediocre. 22,000fmg single, 25,000fmg double; breakfast 3,500fmg, meals 10,000fmg.

J&V Guest House   Tel: 454 18. Also near the airport and currently better value than the Cheval Blanc. Small, intimate, and beautifully furnished. Free transport to the airport. 30,000 - 37,500fmg double, 25,000 - 32,500fmg single, including breakfast.

Guest House Le Karthala   48 Lalana Andriandafotsy (near the Adventist church, Mandrosoa, 100m from the *zoma*). Tel 248 45 or 298 30. Mrs Rafalimanana speaks good English. 30,000 - 35,000fmg, including breakfast. Peaceful. Recommended.

Hotel Anjary   Lalana Razafimahandry and Dr Ranaivo. Tel: 244 09. Clean, large, secure, friendly. Hot water. From 20,000fmg double. Recommended.

Saka Manga   Rue A. Ratianarivo, near the Central. Tel: 35 809. 10 rooms and one apartment for 16,000fmg - 20,000fmg with hot shower. French run, very pleasant but almost always full. Excellent French restaurant. To book a room in advance write to them at Lot IBK 7B1S, Ampasamadinika, Antananarivo 101.

Hotel Le Lac   Behoririka (to the right of the train station, near a small lake). Clean and reasonable. 30,000fmg double. Good food. Recommended.

L'Etape Hotel   5 minutes walk from Tsimbazaza. Some English spoken. Clean, helpful. 18,000 - 20,000fmg.

Hotel Select   Ave de l'Indépendance. 25,000fmg.

Hotel Valiha   11, Ave Grandidier, past the Radama Hotel. One of the few budget hotels in the Upper Town. Clean, and now has hot water so earns its 'B' rating. Communal bathroom. 25,000fmg double, 20,000fmg single. Good value.

Category C

Hotel Nishate   Lalana Razafimahandry. From 15,000fmg with hot water and toilet in room.

Hotel Lambert   Through the *zoma* and towards the top of the steps on the Ambondrona side of town. Basic, clean, convenient; very good value and popular (but be prepared to climb a lot of stairs!). 12,500 - 20,000fmg

Bi-ke Eddy   Rue Rabezavana. Friendly, basic, central. Room 9 is the only one with private shower and bidet. 15,000fmg.

Where to eat

Note: the first class restaurants expect a reasonable standard of dress.

All the big hotels, Colbert, Hilton, France, serve good food. Most consider the **Colbert** to be the best. The 'all you can eat' Sunday buffet here costs 27,500fmg and is excellent value. There are two restaurants at the Colbert; the Taverne is the smartest and imposes a dress-code on its diners. Phone 202 02 for reservations. Bring your French dictionary – menus are not translated. The **Hilton** does a whole series of buffets – each lunch-time there is a 'businessman's buffet' with a 'gourmet buffet' on Sundays. For an evening blow-out try the Chinese buffet (Sundays) or Malagasy (Thursdays). The pizzas at the **Hotel de France** are highly recommended.

New restaurants are opening all the time in Tana, and some are superb. My find for 1993 was the Regency, but Le Pavé continues to draw high praise.

Le Regency   15, Rue Ramelina, Ambatonakanga. Tel: 210 13. French owned and run with flair and elegance. Lovely atmosphere and super food.

Le Pavé   Route des Hydrocarbures. One of the best restaurants in town. Very good service, nice atmosphere, live entertainment. 'Christian and Helen (who speak fluent English) are super people, friendly and helpful, the Yellow Pages of Tana.' (H. Steyn). Phone 330 82 for reservations and take a taxi there.

Le Restaurant   65, Rue Emile Ranarivelo, Behoririka. Tel: 282 67. A lovely colonial house with a terrace overlooking superb gardens. Good and reasonably-priced food. Highly recommended.

Relais Normand   Arabe Rainibetsimisaraka (two blocks from the station). Tel: 207 88. Economically priced and very good French food. Recommended.

La Jonquille   7 Rue Rabezavana, Soarano. Tel 206 37. Good, imaginative menu. Especially recommended for seafood.

Restaurant Jasmin   8 Lalana Paul-Dussac (tel: 342 96). Good Chinese food.

La Pradelle   Ambatoroka (south-east of the city). Tel 326 51. English spoken, Malagasy and European food, very highly recommended by readers and residents. Go there for lunch for the superb view of the Queen's palace on the ridge opposite.

Restaurant Grand Orient   4 Kianja Ambiky, near the station. Tel: 202 88. Good food and fun – a pianist plays requests.

Au Bol Pekinois   An excellent Chinese restaurant five minutes by taxi from the station.

Souimanga   Near the Hotel Etape and Tsimbazaza so popular with zoo personnel. Good value and good ambiance.

Kashmir   5-7 Rue Dr Ranaivo (opposite Anjary Hotel). Muslim, very good and reasonably priced food.

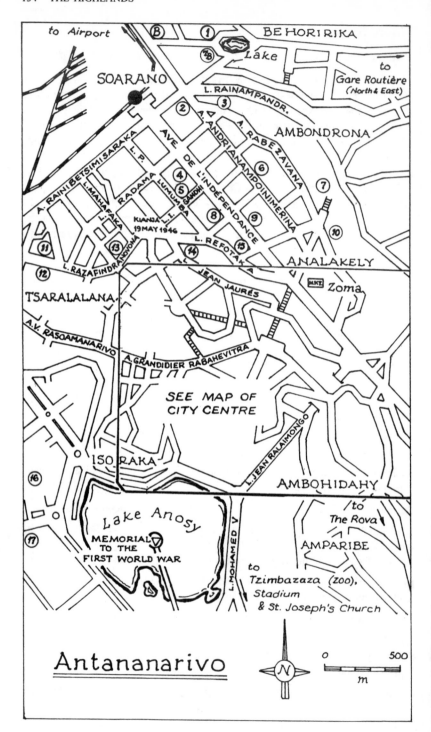

Antananarivo

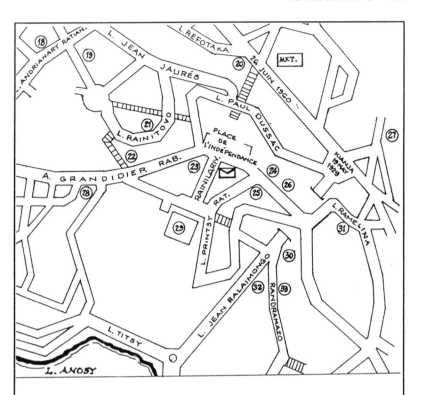

1. HOTEL LE LAC
2. RESTAURANT GRAND ORIENT
3. REST. JONQILLE
4. HOTEL DE PALAIS
5. HOTEL MELLIS
6. INSTITUT D'HYGIENE SOCIAL
7. HOTEL LAMBERT
8. HOTEL DE FRANCE
9. AIR MAD.
10. BE-KE EDDY HOTEL
11. HOTEL ANJARY
12. REST. KASHMIR
13. HOTEL NISHATE

14. FRENCH EMBASSY
15. HOTEL SELECT
16. HILTON HOTEL
17. MINISTRY OF THE INTERIOR (VISAS)
18. HOTEL-REST. SAKA MANGA
19. CENTRAL HOTEL
20. HOTEL GLACIER
21. U.S. EMBASSY
22. RADAMA HOTEL
23. PRISUNIC SUPERMARKET

24. OPTICAM (PHOTOS)
25. HOTEL COLBERT
26. AEROFLOT
27. LE KARTHALA GUEST HOUSE
28. HOTEL VALIHA
29. PRESIDENT'S PALACE
30. ALLIANCE FRANCAISE
31. RESTAURANT LE REGENCY
32. AMERICAN CULTURAL CENTRE
33. ANGAP

Antananarivo - Centre

Shalimar   5 Rue Mahafaka, Tsaralalana (two blocks from the station). Tel: 260 70. Good curries, and a selection of vegetarian dishes. Inexpensive.

Le Buffet   Place de l'Indépendance (at the top of the steps). This fast food restaurant is ideal for lunch, with pleasant outdoor tables. Ideal for people watching.

La Palmeraie   Out of town on the road to Antsirabe (Andoharanofotsy). Tel 460 42. Delicious food eaten in an elegant garden (or indoors). A popular Sunday lunch place for Malagasy and well worth the taxi ride.

There is a growing number of snack bars on Ave de l'Indépendance: **Tropique** (good pastries and icecream), **Honey** (very good for breakfast and icecream), **Solimar** for tamarind juice, and **le Croissanterie** near the *zoma* for fresh fruit juice. Also **Bouffe Rapide** and **La Potinerie** (near Air Mad.) The **Glacier Hotel** bar is the best for people-watching and for *zoma* zombies (the hotel itself is now so bad it is off my list).

Croissant d'Or, Lalana Indira Gandhi, serves great breakfasts and is open at 7.30 all week and 8.00 on Sundays. Everyone raves about it.

In the Upper Town both the **Pattisserie Suisse** (Lanana Rabehevitra) and the **Pattisserie Colbert** do good pastries and teas.

Do it yourself meals can be purchased anywhere. Yoghurt is a particularly good buy and is available even in small towns.

Entertainment

Traditional Malagasy music has become internationally famous in the last few years (see Box on page 110). Look out for authentic performancees in restaurants and bars. But for a truly Malagasy experience try to find a performance of *hira gasy* (see Box on page 95) or keep an eye out for a poster announcing any entertainment which will allow you to join a Malagasy audience (see Box on page 227).

Nightlife

With the austere days of Marxism gone, quite a few discos and nightclubs have opened. **Caveau**, **Kaleidoscope** and **Indra** are nightclubs. Located in Faravohitra (Lalana Andrianahifotsy) on the slope above the market, is **Cocktails et Reves**, which has a darts board for homesick Brits. The most popular nightspot is **Piano Bar Acapulco**, near Place d'Indépendance (14, Rue Ratsimilaho; tel: 232 25).

Safety

Sadly, violent robbery has become quite common in Tana. You are advised to leave your valuables in the hotel (preferably in a safe deposit) and to carry as little as possible. Do not walk around after dark, particularly on the Avenue de l'Indépendance, and be vigilant at all times. If you must carry valuables, such as a camera, it may be safest in a plastic bag.

Be careful when taking a taxi. Thieves sometimes grab handbags through the open window.

One of my regular Mad correspondents who lives in Reunion so visits frequently, has found a very neat solution that helps the local people. She hired a young boy to be her bodyguard. He carried her purchases and kept an eye out for thieves.

Transport

Trains run east to Tamatave and south to Antsirabe from the station at the end of Avenue de l'Indépendance.

Buses (local) are usually crowded and need some skill to use because of the confusing number of district names. You can buy a bus map from FTM (see *Maps*). **Taxis** are plentiful and overcharge *vazahas* outrageously. No meters, so bargain hard. 2,000fmg is about right for a city destination. You can often arrange a good rate for an excursion out of town.

The *gare routières* for **taxi-brousse** and **taxi-be** vehicles are on the outskirts of the city at the appropriate road junctions: Gare du Ouest, Anosibe (Lalana Pastora Rahajason on the far side of Lac Anosy) serving the south and west; Gare du Nord, at Lalana Doktor Raphael Raboto in the north-east of the city, serving the north and the east. Taxi drivers know where these places are.

Vehicle hire
Full details on hiring a **car** are given in Chapter 6. If you are dealing with a Tana travel agent they will also be able to arrange car hire. Recommended car-hire firms are Locaut (tel: 219 81), Rasseta (tel: 257 70), Aventour (tel: 317 61/217 78). Eurorent (tel: 297 66). A full list is available from the Maison du Tourisme. **Mountain bikes** may be hired from Madagascar Outdoor Sports, tel: 351 85/400 79, or Madagascar Wheels, tel: 335 47. There are reports that these places have gone out of business so phone before making plans. Bikes are available from other cities, however.

Miscellaneous
Maps
A large selection of maps can be bought at the Institut National de Géodésie et Cartographie (its long Malagasy name is shortened to FTM), Lalana Dama-Ntsoha RJB, Ambanidia (tel: 229 35). Hours 8.30 to 12.00, 14.00 to 18.00. They do a series of 12 maps, scale 1:500,000 covering each region of Madagascar. These are most inviting, but sadly no longer completely accurate, especially in their concept of a village, which may turn out to be one hut which fell down a generation ago. There are also excellent maps of Nosy Be and Ste Marie. The staff are extremely pleasant and helpful. The more popular maps can be bought in bookshops.

Bookshops
The best bookshop is Librairie de Madagascar, near the Hotel de France on Ave de l'Indépendance. Another, Tout pour l'Ecole, on the left side of Rue de Nice, has a good selection of maps and town plans.

ANGAP
Permits for the national parks and reserves are best purchased here. Although they may usually be bought at the park/reserve itself, this practice lends itself to corruption which ANGAP is trying hard to stamp out.

The entrance to the ANGAP office is on Lalana Razafindratandra Randramazo, opposite the American Cultural Center. Hours 8.00 - 12.00, 14.00 - 16.00. Tel: 319 94.

World Wide Fund for Nature
The WWF address in Tana is BP 4373; tel: (2) 25541.

Visa extension
A two month extension can be obtained overnight from the Ministry of Interior near the Hilton Hotel (see map).

Air Madagascar
Ave de l'Indépendance. Hours: 7.30 - 11.00; 14.30 - 17.00. Be there when it opens to avoid the crush.

Bank and emergency funds
The BTM bank next to Prisunic will let you draw up to US$200 a day on American Express or Mastercard. Banking hours: 8.00 - 11.00, 14.00 - 16.30. Closed on Saturdays. The American Express office is in the Hilton Hotel.

Post Office
The main post office is opposite the Hotel Colbert. There is a separate philately section where you can buy attractive stamps.

Women's hairdresser
The expatriate's favourite is Richard Coiffure, 15 Rue Patrice Lumumba. Tel: 226 50.

Medical Clinic (private)
MM 24 X 24, Mpitsabo Mikambana, Route de l'Université, Tel: 235 55. Inexpensive and very good.

Church services
Anglican (contact tel: 262 68); Cathedral St Laurent, Ambohimanoro; 9.00 service each Sunday. Roman Catholic (tel: 278 30); three churches have services in Malagasy, and three in French. Phone for details.

Golf course
There is a good golf course, the Club de Golf de Rova at Ambohidratrimo, 20km from town on the road to Mahajanga. It is open to visitors except at the weekend. The fee is 10,000fmg plus 10,000fmg for a set of clubs. Good meals are served at the club house and the Wednesday buffet is particularly recommended.

Horse racing
1994 saw the introduction of thoroughbred horses into Madagasscar and the enterprise, run by a Malagasy/South African group, will result in racing becoming a new sport here. Meetings will be held on Sundays at Bevalala, 10km from Tana on the road to Antsirabe.

Embassies
British Embassy. (Ambassador Peter Smith). Immeuble Ny Havana, Cité des 67 Ha, Antananarivo (BP 167). Tel: 277 49/273 70.

American Embassy. (Ambassador Dennis Barrett). Antsahavola (BP 620). Tel: 200 89/212 57.

South African Embassy. Max Cameron. Lot IIJ 169 Ivandry (BP 4417). Tel: 424 94.

Italian Embassy. (Ambassador Francesco Sciortino). Rue Pasteur Rabary, Ankadivato (BP 16). Tel: 212 17.

French Embassy. (Ambassador Gilles d'Humière). Rue Jean Jaures (BP 204). Tel: 237 00/200 08.

German Embassy. (Ambassador Günter Held). Rte Circulaire (BP 516). Tel: 238 02.

EXCURSIONS

EAST OF ANTANANARIVO
Ambohimanga

Lying 21km north-east of Antananarivo, Ambohimanga (pronounced Ambooimanga), meaning the 'blue hill', was for a long time forbidden to Europeans. From here began the line of kings and queens who were to unite Madagascar into one country, and it was here that they returned for rest and relaxation among the tree-covered slopes of this hill-top village. These days tourists find the same tranquility and spirit of reverence and it is highly recommended as an easy day's trip.

Ambohimanga has seven gates, though several are all but lost among the thick vegetation. One of the most spectacular gates, through which you enter the village, has an enormous stone disc which was formerly rolled in front of the gateway each night. Above the gateway is a thatched-roof sentry post. Inside the village the centre-piece is the wooden house of the great king Andrianampoinimerina (1787-1810). The simple one-roomed house is interesting for the insight it gives into everyday (royal) life of that era. There is a display of cooking utensils (and the stones that surrounded the cooking fire), and weapons, and the two beds (as in the Tana *rova* with the top one for the king and the lower for one of his wives). The roof is supported by a ten metre rosewood pole.

Andrianampoinimerina's son, Radama, with British help, went a long way to achieving his father's ambition to expand his kingdom to the sea. After Radama came a number of queens and they built themselves elegant summer houses next to Andrianampoinimerina's simple royal house. Outside influence is strongly evident here, especially British, and you can see several gifts sent to the monarchs by Queen Victoria.

Ambohimanga is reached on a good road by private taxi or bus/taxi-brousse from the Gare du Nord. The latter takes about 30 minutes and costs 500fmg. At present there is no entrance fee although you will need to tip the guide. Bring a picnic or eat at the small restaurant (Chez Ossy) nearby.

Lake Mantasoa

Some 70km east of Antananarivo is Mantasoa (pronounced Mantasoo) where in the 19th century Madagascar had its first taste of industrialisation. Indeed, historians now claim that industrial output was greater then than it ever was during the colonial period. It was thanks to Jean Laborde that a whole range of industries was started including an iron foundry which enabled Madagascar to become more or less self-sufficient in swords, guns

THE TWO-MAN INDUSTRIAL REVOLUTION

Technology was introduced to Madagascar by two remarkable Europeans, James Cameron, a Scot, and Jean Laborde, a Frenchman.

James Cameron arrived in Madagascar in 1826 during the country's 'British' phase when the London Missionary Society (LMS) had attempted to set up local craftsmen to produce goods in wood, metal, leather and cotton. Cameron was only 26 when he came to Madagascar, but was already skilled as a carpenter and weaver, with wide knowledge of other subjects which he was later to put to use in his adopted land: physics, chemistry, mathematics, architecture and astronomy. Cameron seemed able to turn his hand to almost anything mechanical. Among his achievements were the successful installation and running of Madagascar's first printing press (by studying the manual – the printer sent out with the press had died with unseemly haste), a reservoir (now Lac Anosy) and aqueduct, and the production of bricks.

Cameron's success in making soap from local materials ensured his royal favour after King Radama died and the xenophobic Queen Ranavalona came to power. But when Christian practice and teaching were forbidden in 1835 Cameron left with the other missionaries and went to work in South Africa.

He returned in 1863 when the missionaries were once more welcome in Madagascar, to oversee the building of stone churches, a hospital, and the stone exterior to the *Rova* or Queen's palace in Antananarivo.

Jean Laborde was even more of a 'renaissance man'. The son of a blacksmith, Laborde was shipwrecked off the east coast of Madagascar in 1831. Queen Ranavalona, no doubt pleased to find a less godly European, asked him to manufacture muskets and gun-powder, and he soon filled the gap left by the departure of Cameron and the other artisan-missionaries. Laborde's initiative and inventiveness were amazing: in a huge industrial complex built by forced labour, he produced munitions and arms, bricks and tiles, pottery, glass and porcelain, silk, soap, candles, cement, dyes, sugar, rum ... in fact just about everything a thriving country in the nineteenth century needed. He ran a farm which experimented with suitable crops and animals, and a country estate for the Merina royalty and aristocracy to enjoy such novelties as firework displays. And he built the original Queen's palace in wood (in 1839), which was later enclosed in stone by Cameron.

So successful was Laborde in making Madagascar self-sufficient, that foreign trade was discontinued and foreigners – with the exception of Laborde – expelled. He remained in the Queen's favour until 1857 when he was expelled because of involvement in a plot to replace the Queen by her son. The 1,200 workmen who had laboured without pay in the foundries of Mantasoa, rose up and destroyed everything – tools, machinery and buildings. The factories were never rebuilt, and Madagascar's Industrial Revolution came to an abrupt end.

He returned in 1861 and became French consul, dying in 1878. A dispute over his inheritance was one of the pretexts used by the French to justify the 1883-85 war.

and gunpowder, thereby increasing the power of the central government. Jean Laborde was soon highly influential at court and he built a country residence for the queen at Mantasoa. Sadly most of the remains of the buildings have disappeared, drowned to make a reservoir. This extraordinary Frenchman is buried in the cemetery outside the village, along with 12 French soldiers; an imposing mausoleum surrounded by mature trees.

Mantasoa can be reached by taking a train to Manjakandriana and then a taxi or a taxi-brousse for the last 15km, or a taxi-brousse all the way from Tana.

Where to stay/eat

One of the fanciest hotels in Madagascar is located here, Domaine de l'Ermitage (BP 16, Manjakandriana; tel: 05). Rates 545FF single, 315FF double. Lunch/dinner 60,000fmg. Under the same ownership as the restaurant Le Pavé.

Motel le Chalet. BP 12, Mantasoa. Tel: 20. Run by Madame Verbillot, a Swiss lady (now in her 80s). Five bungalows and superb food. Camping is usually permitted in the grounds.

Mandraka

If you take the train towards Tamatave, the station beyond Manjakandriana is Mandraka. Situated opposite the hydro-electric power plant, just west of Anjiro, is the **Nature Farm** run by one of Madagascar's leading naturalists, André Peyrieras. It is a 6km walk from the station or, if you are travelling by vehicle, you can be dropped off at the entrance. The main purpose of the centre is the breeding (for export) of comet moths and various butterflies. There is also a growing collection of insects, reptiles (including many different chameleons and uroplatus) and frogs. These are also for export although, sadly, no breeding seems to be taking place. A herpetologist notes: 'Tourists should realise that keeping a large number of chameleons in confined spaces is very stressful for the animals, hence the fantastic display of colours.'

Visitors pay 10,000fmg to see and photograph this very comprehensive collection, and may also be asked to take a guide for 5,000fmg. Make sure you bring fast film and a close-up lens to make the most of this unique opportunity to get pictures of species seldom seen in the wild.

If prearranged you can eat an excellent lunch at the farm. To arrange a visit contact M. Peyrieras at BP 6218, Antananarivo 101, tel: 321 01, or through a travel agent.

WEST OF ANTANANARIVO

Lake Itasy

Off the road to Tsiroanomandidy (access town Analavory) this lake and its surrounding area is particularly beautiful and is easily reached by taxi-brousse. The nearby village of **Ampefy** has accommodation: the Kavitaha, with very good food, and the humble Bungalows Administratifs. A better bet is the Village Touristique between the lakes: spacious but basic bungalows for 3,300fmg.

It is a 8km walk to Îlot de la Vierge on Lac Itasy. West of the road are the Chutes de la Lily (waterfalls). 'It pays here to climb a hill — any hill — to get an overview of the lakes and volcanic countryside.' (H. Snippe).

The adventurous can walk or bike south to RN7. 'One of the highlights of my trip. I had not realised it would be as scenic.' (John Kupiek).

Tsiroanomandidy

Lying about 200km to the west of Tana, on a (mostly) surfaced road (4 hours), this town is worth visiting for its huge cattle market, held on Wednesdays and Thursdays. There is one fairly good hotel ('clean, food OK, and sometimes even hot water in the — only — bathroom.'). Tsiroanomandidy is linked to Maintirano and Mahajanga by Twin Otter, and also Morondava. See Chapter 11.

NORTHWEST OF ANTANANARIVO

The forest of Ambohetantely

The name means 'Where honey is found' and is pronounced 'Ambweeton<u>tel</u>'. This is the last remnant of natural forest in the province of Ankazobe and there are hopes that it will shortly become a protected area. This report is by Dr Graham Noble and Sandra Baron of South Africa.

'It takes about 2½ hours to get to the forest which lies 150km northwest of Tana off the road to Mahajunga. The access village is Ararazana. The forest is 10km from the road and you do not see a tree until you reach the site. Estimates of its size vary from 1,400 to 3,000 hectares. It is surrounded by a barrier of burnt trees, but as you go two metres into the forest the leaf-litter is already 10 - 15cm deep. There is a network of paths through the forest. The University of Antananarivo has a right to a part of it as a study site and refer to that section as the Botanical Garden. The forestry director is very keen to receive tourists into the area for day walks and will also organise provisions for overnight stays. Good birding and lots of orchids.'

Check with ANGAP on the current status of the forest, and make a further visit to the Department des Eaux et Forêts in Ankazobe, 106km from Tana. Because of a problem with bandits in the area, you are advised to check the the Eaux et Forêts people about where to stay/camp.

'Madagascar only requires the advent of railways and roads to make it one of the most prosperous commercial countries of the world'.
Capt E W Dawson, Madagascar: its Capabilities and Resources, *1895*

THE ROAD SOUTH (RN7)

The drive down the improved Route Nacional 7 is becoming increasingly popular. It provides an excellent overview of the *Hauts Plateaux* and Merina and Betsileo culture, as well as spectacular scenery.

About 15km from the city centre, look out for a huge, white replica of the *rova* across the paddy fields on the right. This was ex-president Ratsiraka's palace, funded by North Korea.

Ambatolampy

This small town lies some two hours from Tana and makes a convenient lunch stop. The Albanian-owned Hotel au Rendezvous des Pecheurs serves fantastic food (8,000fmg) and has clean, reasonably priced rooms with hot water.

About 15 minutes beyond Ambatolampy are some fine painted Merina tombs (on both sides of the road, the most accessible on the right).

RICE

The Malagasy have an almost mystical attachment to rice. King Andrianampoinimerina declared: 'Rice and I are one' and loyalty to the Merina king was symbolised by industry in the rice paddies.

Today the Betsileo are masters of rice cultivation, and their neat terraces are a distinctive part of the scenery of the central highlands. However, rice is grown throughout the island, either in irrigated paddies or as 'hill rice' watered by the rain. Rice production is labour-intensive. First the ground must be prepared for the seeds. Often this is done by chasing zebu cattle round and round to break the clods and soften it – a muddy, sticky job, but evidently great fun for the boys who do it. Seeds are germinated in a small plot and replanted in the irrigated paddies when half-grown. In October and November you will see groups of women bent over in knee-deep water, performing this back-breaking work.

The Malagasy eat rice three times a day, the annual consumption being 135kg per person (about a pound of rice per day!). Rice marketing was nationalised in 1976, but this resulted in such a dramatic decline in the amount of rice reaching the open market that restrictions were lifted in 1984. Madagascar was once an exporter of rice; now half a million tons are imported each year. Most small farmers grow rice only for their own consumption but are forced to sell part of their crop for instant cash. Richer families in the community store this grain and sell it back at a profit later. To solve this small-scale exploitation, village co-operatives have been set up to buy rice and sell it back to the farmer at an agreed price, or at a profit to outsiders if any is left over.

ANTSIRABE

Antsirabe lies 169km south of Antananarivo at 1,500m. It was founded in 1872 by Norwegian missionaries attracted by the cool climate and the healing properties of the thermal springs. The name means 'the place of much salt'.

This is an elegant city, and with its top class hotels and interesting excursions, merits a stay of a few days. A broad avenue links the handsome station with the amazing Hotel des Thermes; at the station end is a monolith depicting Madagascar's 18 tribes.

Antsirabe is the agricultural and industrial centre of Madagascar, but don't worry, there are no Dark Satanic Mills here, it's mainly cotton goods, cigarettes, and − most important for the tourist − Three Horses Beer. You can smell the Star Brewery as you enter the town.

This is the *pousse-pousse* capital of Madagascar. There are hundreds, perhaps thousands of them. The drivers are insistent that you avail yourself of a ride, and why not? But be very firm about the price. Now that tourists come to Antsirabe in some numbers, the drivers have found they can make 1,000fmg just for posing for pictures. To actually have to run somewhere, towing a large *vazaha*, for the same price must seem very unfair.

Saturday is market day. This is held on the far side of the lake (Asabotsy) and resembles Antananarivo's *zoma* in miniature but with an even greater cross-section of activities.

Antsirabe is famous for its gemstones. The master stone-cutter of the town is said to be Monsieur Joseph. His studio is hard to find but someone will show you.

It is worth paying a visit to the thermal baths (*Thermes*) although at the time of writing they are only open on Mondays. There is a wonderfully hot swimming pool full of laughing brown faces that laugh even harder at the sight of a foreigner. But it's friendly laughter. You can also take a private bath here (but there's a 20 minute limit) and have a massage.

On a promontory overlooking the baths stands the Hotel des Thermes: an amazing building both in size and architectural style. There is nothing else like it in Madagascar − it would not be out of place along the French Riviera and is set in equally elegant gardens (see *Where to stay*).

If you are travelling from May to September you will need a sweater in the evening. It really does get quite cold.

Getting there

The more interesting way is by train from Antananarivo. The journey takes anything from four to ten (!) hours, and there are three trains a week, leaving at 06.30 from Tana or Antsirabe. The fare is 4,400fmg (second class only). Don't lean out of the window, you might lose your head!

Antsirabe is also served by buses and taxi-brousses.

Where to stay
Category A
Hotel des Thermes   BP 72; tel: 497 62 or 487 61; fax 492 02. The interior does not match the exterior glamour, but there is a cosy bar and good food is served in the restaurant (55FF). In the warmer months the large garden and swimming pool makes this a very pleasant place to relax. Room prices: 1 to 2 persons, single 371FF, double 221FF.

Villa Nirina   BP 245, 110 Antsirabe; tel: 485 97 or 486 69. Owned by Mrs Zanoa Rasanjison, who speaks fluent English as well as French and German, this private home has been cited as the best accommodation in Madagascar by a couple of readers. The villa has four very modern bedrooms with private bath and Mrs Rasanjison's home cooking, which is excellent. It is just across the road from Diamant Restaurant. She and her husband also rent cars with drivers. Advance booking essential.

Villa Salemako   BP 14, 110 Antsirabe; tel: 481 14. Another extraordinary private home with five rooms for visitors, run by Charles and Rosette Rakotonarivo. Beautiful garden, furniture and ambiance. Rooms cost 25,000fmg and a meal 9,000fmg. The house is on the left just before the Y in the road on the approach to town. Look for the Malagasy motif on the chimney. Best to write or phone before you arrive.

Category B
Hotel Morano   A new hotel (1993) adjacent to the taxi-brousse station towards the south of the city. Double rooms at 15,000 - 25,000fmg all with hot shower and WC. Good, economically priced food. Recommended.

Hotel Baobab   Clean and friendly, with hot water in some rooms. Room with shower 15,000fmg. There are cheaper rooms without hot water (and the *thermes* are only minutes away).

Hotel Soafitel   Tel: 480 55. Four categories of rooms, all with hot water, from 23,800fmg. Rates include breakfast. Bicycles for hire.

Hotel Trianon   Tel: 488 81. Very reasonably priced, spacious, clean and comfortable, with hot water. 10,000 - 15,000fmg. Good food.

Category C
Hotel Coin d'Or   Just off Ave de l'Indépendance in the centre of town. Clean but basic rooms for 10,000 - 15,000fmg.

Hotel Niavo   A family-run hotel with a garden on the far side of the lake. Popular, good food, but rather run-down. 10,000 - 15,000fmg.

Hotel Fo Kri Fa   Rooms from 8,000 - 10,000fmg.

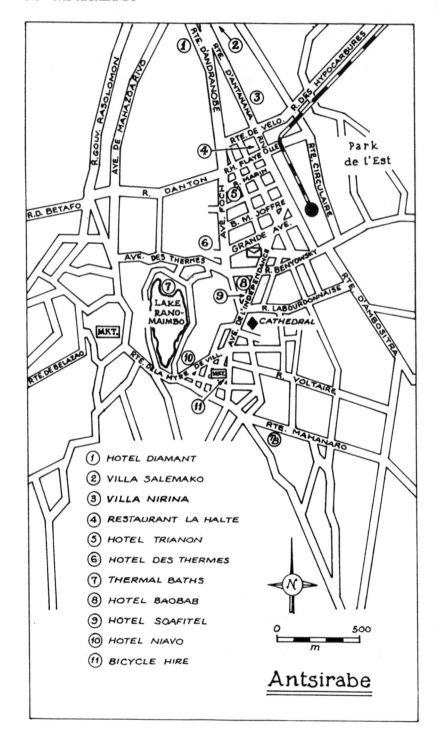

1 HOTEL DIAMANT
2 VILLA SALEMAKO
3 VILLA NIRINA
4 RESTAURANT LA HALTE
5 HOTEL TRIANON
6 HOTEL DES THERMES
7 THERMAL BATHS
8 HOTEL BAOBAB
9 HOTEL SOAFITEL
10 HOTEL NIAVO
11 BICYCLE HIRE

Antsirabe

Where to eat

Restaurant à la Halte   Tel: 489 94. Universally praised for the quality of the food at reasonable prices.

If you want to buy a picnic there are several good supermarkets with a wide range of cheese and salami.

The cafe next to Soafitel is recommended for breakfast.

Wheels and hoofs

In the first street (south) behind the daily market is a **bicycle hire** shop. Good mountain bikes are available for about 20,000fmg per day. Bikes can also be hired from Soafitel. **Horses** may be hired near the Hotel des Thermes, the stables being near Parc d'Est.

Excursions
Lake Tritriva

There are actually two crater lakes, but the first, Lake Andrakiba is unimpressive.

Tritriva is spectacular. The name comes from *tritry* – the Malagasy word for the ridge on the back of a chameleon (!) and *iva*, deep. And this emerald green crater lake is indeed deep – 80 metres, some say. It is reached by continuing past Lake Andraikiba for 12km on a rough, steep road past small villages of waving kids. Apart from the sheer beauty of the place (the best light for photography is in the morning), there are all sorts of interesting features. The water level *rises* in the dry season and debris thrown into the lake has reappeared down in the valley, supporting the theory of underground water channels.

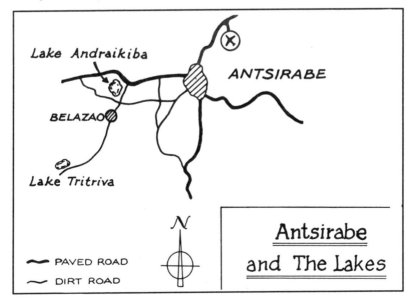

Look across the lake and you'll see two thorn trees growing on a ledge above the water with intertwined branches. Legend says that these are two lovers, forbidden to marry by their parents, who drowned themselves in Tritriva. When the branches are cut, so they say, blood oozes out.

The local people have not been slow to realise the financial potential of groups of *vazahas* coralled at the top of a hill. Don't think you will be alone at the lake.

You can get to Tritriva by taxi (45 mins each way) or by bus to Lake Andraikiba and then walk. The most enjoyable way is to rent a bike and make it a day trip. If you are self-sufficient you can stay in the village of Belazao, midway between the two lakes (no hotel) or camp at the lake.

Betafo

About 22km west of Antsirabe by a tarmac road that goes as far as Morondava, lies Betafo, a town with typical Highlands red-brick churches and houses. Dotted among the houses are *vatolahy*, standing stones erected to commemorate warrior chieftains. These are inscribed and decorated.

Monday is market day. There is no hotel in Betafo, but you should be able to find a room by asking around.

At one end of the town is the crater lake Tatamarina. From there it is a walk of about 3km to the Antafofo waterfalls among beautiful views of ricefields and volcanic hills. You will need to find someone to show you the way. 'It's very inviting for a swim but they told me there are ghosts in the pool under the falls. If you go swimming they will pull at your legs and pull you to the bottom.' (Luc Selleslagh)

On the outskirts of Betafo there are hot springs. It costs 300fmg for a hot bath with no time limit.

CONTINUING SOUTH ON RN7

A taxi-brousse from Antsirabe to Ambositra, the next town of any consequence, costs about 3,500fmg.

Leaving Antsirabe you continue to pass through typical Highland scenery of rice paddies and low hills. About 45 minutes beyond the town you'll cross a river and pass one of the nicest rural markets I've seen. There are strange fruit and vegetables, lots of peanuts, and fascinating grey balls that turn out to be soap made from the fat from zebu humps. At the back of the market is a makeshift barber-shop, and behind the men with the scissors are rolling green hills.

In about 2½ hours you reach Ambositra (pronounced 'Amboostr') the centre of Madagascar's wood carving industry.

Ambositra

Wood carving is taken seriously here – even the houses have ornately carved wooden balconies and shutters. There is an abundant choice of carved figures and marquetry, in several shops, and the quality is improving although there are occasional lapses into pseudo-Africana. In the last edition I complained that I've yet to see a carved lemur. I've now seen some but sadly the carver obviously has yet to see a lemur...

For carvings of people, however, one artist stands out. 'Jean' carves exquisite scenes from Malagasy life, many in a fine-grained, creamy wood known as *fanazava*. Jean has now opened a shop as well as his studio (which is open to visitors). The place is not hard to find. Look for the signs 'Société Jean et Frère'.

The best place to choose from a large assortment of good quality carvings is at the 'Arts Zafimaniry', a co-operative run by a French Catholic mission and housed in their monastery. This splendid complex of buildings is well worth a visit for its location and views, and is reached from the south side of town, up the hill towards the Grand Hotel, opposite the huge Catholic church. The shop is open from 7.30 - 11.15, and 2.15 - 5.30.

Where to stay/eat

Grand Hotel   Recently renovated, this is still not grand but it is charming and comfortable and serves good lunches with lots of vegetables (at least when pre-arranged).

Hotel Violette   has opened an annexe. The old Violette is up the hill and to the left. Old and atmospheric and charging 8,500 - 10,000fmg for a room. There are girlie posters on the walls, one of which has a unique embellishment (so I'm told)... The new Violette is on the south side of town about 200m past the Grand Hotel. Friendly, good restaurant. Rooms are 12,000 - 18,000fmg.

Hotel Baby   Near the southern taxi-brousse station. Friendly. 8,000fmg.

Hotel/Restaurant Tanamasoandro   '10,000fmg for a nice room with a huge double bed.' An extra attraction is that it is near a sign advertising the 'Artiste/peintre Mr Forceplay'.

Beyond the old Violette is a new eatery, the **Restaurant Tourisme Malagasy**. A reader also recommends **Hotely ny Tanamasoandro**: 'good, cheap, complete with punk waiter.'

Zafimaniry villages

The Zafimaniry people follow a traditional way of life in the forests south-east of Ambositra. This is not an area which should be attempted without an experienced guide, however. The danger is not so much in getting lost, but the detrimental effects uncontrolled tourism has already had on the villagers nearest the road.

If you decide to go it alone, you should at least know that taxi-brousses only make the journey to Antoetra, the nearest Zafimaniry village to the road on market days, Saturdays and Tuesdays. On other days, if you can't afford a taxi, you are stuck with a 23km hike from Ivato on RN7.

There *is* a way of seeing the real Zafimaniry. Jill and Charlie Hadfield (who worked in Madagascar for two years and started the 'Street Kids Scheme' – see page 117) went with a French-Malagasy couple who live in Tana and who run small, intimate treks to the Zafimaniry villages.

Dany is a teacher of history and incredibly knowledgeable about Malagasy culture, and Sahondra adds her own Malagasy insights. Three porters were organised, and we set off up a hill along a narrow path... At the next village of Ifasina... all the children were standing shrieking at us as we plodded the last few yards. The houses are completely wood-built, with bamboo roofs; the older ones usually have a foundation of stone, the newer ones are on short wooden stilts. The main feature of the Zafimaniry culture is its wood carving – shutters, doors and posts of all the houses are carved in geometric designs of circles and swirls, sophisticated details which contrast with the utter simplicity of the people's living conditions. The Zafimaniry, according to Dany, originated from a group of Merina who left the north some 150 years ago in order to escape conscriptive or forced labour. In many ways their life style must reflect that of the Merina early last century when the first British and French arrived in Antananarivo. Each house was built on the same plan: the front door is in the south-west corner facing the last rays of daylight. You step over a high sill into the south part of the house, where the square pit fireplace, with a tripod of three cooking stones, is located and along the south wall are stacked all the basic equipment – pots, cutlery, axes, baskets. Most of the family are sitting on the floor round the fire, pushing the logs further in as they burn. The house is choking with smoke and it takes some minutes to take in any detail at all, especially as in this case the five little windows and door are blocked by a crowd of young and not so young villagers gaping at the *vazahas* as we unpack our rucksacks... As guests we were offered floor space in the northern half of the house, where there is usually a raised bed in the north-east corner, and often hanging in that corner a crucifix or religious image (the north-east corner is for the ancestors)... Soon it is bedtime. From the wall a big roll of bed mats is taken down and spread on the floor for us (after the meal mats have been swept and rolled up from beneath our feet). The bed mats have a slightly more intricate weave at the head, and we were told not to put our feet on them. By 8.30 the chicks and hens have been pushed into their box at the south end, everyone is curled up in their cloaks, the doors barred, the candles blown out, and we are snoring in a warm huddle of six in our sleeping bags... until the cockcrow at 3.30, three feet from our heads, and *inside* the house! ... In one house I woke to feel maize beetles crawling in my beard, and after four nights Jill had a total of 75 flea-bites!

It was cold in the mornings and you had to get up quickly in the predawn to find a quiet corner behind a rock to do your 'petits besoins' or 'grands besoins' before all the kids woke up and started following you everywhere. For breakfast we had a supply of increasingly stale bread, and jam, but sometimes we would be offered treats like more maize porridge, or boiled taro roots with

Making Antaimoro paper, Ambalavao. (John R. Jones)

Malagasy saw-mill (Johan Hermans)   *Sorting vanilla in Antalaha (John R. Jones)*

Antananarivo

Part of the upper town, Antananarivo.

Horse-drawn bus.

Early morning in the rice paddies (Johan Hermans)

Fianarantsoa.

Ravenala (traveller's tree) south of Ambalavao.

honey, or honey mixed with rice.

The second day involved a long and very muddy tramp on a switchback path that led up and down and over a succession of steep rainforest-covered hills. We staggered sweatily in the thick, moist heat up the hills and along the crests and descended to squelch muddily through streams and bogs in the valley. Rounding a corner we came across a scene of incredible devastation. The whole hillside in front of us was covered in burnt and smouldering stumps of trees [for slash and burn agriculture]. Across the valley men could be seen laying waste to yet another hillside. Our five hour walk had taken us through the last piece of primary forest remaining in Zafimaniry country.

The remaining three days took us across bare, granite hills, grassland and secondary scrub... We stayed the night at Ranomena, in a beautiful and much more elaborate house with two storeys and carved wooden doves on the eaves and roof ridge... During the next few days we experienced a beekeeper's hut where we saw all the tools used for apiculture (the Zafimaniry keep bees in a hollow tree trunk and dig the honey out with a long-handled knife), a completely deserted village with the whole community at church, several precarious log bridges, several hours walking along bare granite-topped mountain crests... and at the end of the trek some beautifully cultivated rice terraces. These were the first we had seen here and on enquiry we learned that the villagers had been taught to terrace by one Père Coureau, a Jesuit priest. This was not the first time we had heard his name: in one village he had built a school and in another the children, not trusting the postal service, asked us to give the photos we had taken to Père Coureau, assuming we would know him since, like us, he came from the Outside World. We went to see the reverend father and found a bright-eyed, white-haired old man with a firm handshake and a springy energetic stride – I couldn't keep up with him. We gave him money to buy blackboards for the schools we had seen on the way and Dany wanted to donate footballs. 'No', the priest said firmly 'they only get footballs when they have replanted a thousand trees.'

Daniel and Sahondra enjoy taking small groups (4 - 5 people) into Zafimaniry country, and this is undoubtedly the way to do it. Daniel – Dany – (the French half) has lived in Madagascar since 1965, they both speak English, and they can also offer accommodation in Tana. Write to them at BP 4313, Antananarivo; tel: 442 67.

Treks to Zafimaniry are also organised by Jim, of the Tsara guest house in Fianarantsoa.

SOUTH FROM AMBOSITRA ON RN7

From Ambositra, the scenery becomes increasingly spectacular. You now pass remnants of the western limit of the rainforest (being systematically destroyed). The road runs up and down steep hills, past neat Betsileo rice paddies interspersed with eucalyptus and pine groves. The steepest climb comes about two hours after Ambositra, when the vehicle labours up an

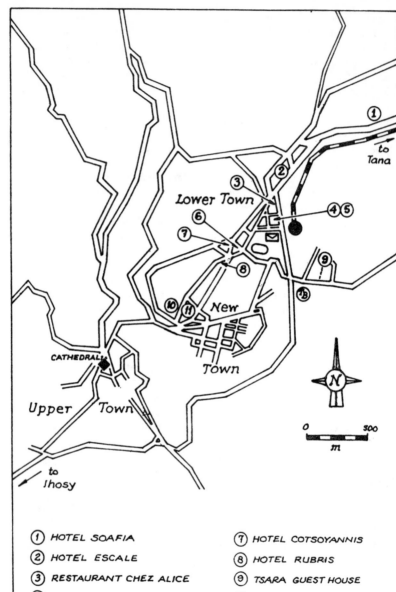

to
Tana

Lower Town

New

Town

CATHEDRAL

Upper   Town

to
Ihosy

0   500
m

N

① HOTEL SOAFIA

② HOTEL ESCALE

③ RESTAURANT CHEZ ALICE

④ AIR MADAGASCAR

⑤ REST./HOTEL CHEZ PAPILLON

⑥ PANDA RESTAURANT

⑦ HOTEL COTSOYANNIS

⑧ HOTEL RUBRIS

⑨ TSARA GUEST HOUSE

⑩ HOTEL MADAGASCAR

⑪ HOTEL RELAIS
          DE BETSILEO

Fianarantsoa

endlessly curving road, through thick forests of introduced pine, and reaches the top where stalls selling oranges or baskets provide an excuse for a break. Then it's down through more forest, on a very poor stretch of road, to Ambohimahasoa. Leaving Ambohimahasoa you pass more forests, then open country, rice paddies and houses as you begin the approach to Fianarantsoa.

FIANARANTSOA

The name means 'Place of good learning'. Fianarantsoa (Fianar for short) was founded in 1830 as the administrative capital of Betsileo. It is one of the more attractive Malagasy towns, built on a hill like a small scale Antananarivo.

There is a dramatic contrast between the charming Upper Town and the unutterably dreary Lower Town. Travellers making only a brief stop tend to see only the Lower Town, dominated by a huge concrete stadium and the stink of urine, and are not impressed. The Upper Town, with its narrow winding streets and plethora of churches should be visited for the wonderful views, especially in the early morning when the mist is curling up from the valley. It's quite a way up: take bus no 3 or a taxi, and walk back.

There is an excellent photographic shop next to the Sofia Hotel. Worth knowing if you have camera problems or need unusual camera batteries or gadgets. They also sell beautiful photos of Madagascar scenes.

Getting there

Taxi-brousse from Ambositra costs about 6,000fmg. Following a report in the last edition of unhelpful/dishonest touts and drivers at the Fianar taxi-brousse station I am happy to report that several readers have written in with nothing but praise for the people who helped find, and squeeze them into, a vehicle. The company KOFIAM, which runs between Fianar and Tana with a lunch stop in Ambositra has been recommended. Price 15,000fmg. One seat per passenger.

In addition to access by road there are several flights a week from Tana by Piper or Twin Otter aircraft. A new airport is being built to take larger planes.

Where to stay
Category A

Hotel Soafia   Tel: 503 53. 'Looks like a cross between Disneyworld, a Chinese temple and a gigantic doll's house!' (J. Hadfield). There are 50 rooms and a good restaurant. 35,000 - 50,000fmg.

Hotel Moderne/Papillon   Tel: 500 03. Near the station. Comfortable. Hot water. Only a limited number of rooms. 25,400 - 30,000fmg.

Hotel Rubis   Overlooks the football ground near the Panda restaurant. Swimming pool and tennis court. Double room with hot shower and WC. 20,000fmg. Three beds, 30,000fmg. Some rooms have a balcony. Friendly and clean. Good Malagasy meals.

Category B

Tsara Guest House   BP 1373, tel: 502 06. This is the most popular *vazaha* place in Madagascar and is universally praised by readers. The secret of its success is Jim, the multilingual and hugely hospitable Malagasy man who runs it with his Swiss wife Natalie. The meals, eaten communally around a large table, are excellent (6,700fmg), there is a large lounge with a log fire, and Jim can organise excursions to nearby places of interest as well as a five day trek.

The guest house is conveniently located a few hundred metres up the hill near the taxi-brousse depot, and Jim has somehow maintained the price at a very reasonable 15,000fmg for a 2 bunk room, 20,000fmg for 4 bunks with bathroom (high season rates). Everything is kept spotlessly clean. There is a quiet garden with a beautiful view.

Success breeds envy. If someone tells you at the taxi-brousse station that the Tsara is closed, you are advised not to believe him.

Hotel Relais du Betsileo   Tel: 508 23. In the upper town, 25,000fmg. Friendly, but poor value for money.

Category C

Hotel Madagascar   7,200fmg for a large double room and uncomfortable bed. Separate bathroom and WC.

Hotel Cotsoyannis   Tel: 514 86. This hotel has had its ups and downs but it may be heading for an up (I've had reports varying from 'Very good value' to 'Ghastly'). 15,000fmg.

Hotel Escale   7,000fmg. Also, near the station, Ideal Hotel.

Where to eat

Chez Papillon   Tel: 500 03. Many people feel its reputation as the best restaurant in Madagascar is overrated, but the majority still praise the quality and wide choice of dishes, and the service, though snooty, is second to none. A meal for two with wine costs around 75,000fmg. Breakfast (5,000fmg) is highly recommended.

Le Panda   Across the street from the Hotel Cotsoyannis. Chinese. Inexpensive. Good.

Resto Blue   Very good, inexpensive food. Friendly.

Chez Alice Pizzeria   A block away from the Papillon. Clean. pleasant, inexpensive.

Tiki dairy shop. Across from the train station. Great yoghurt and cheese. Excellent bread is available from the bakery to the left of the Soafia Hotel.

Train to Manakara

The train leaves for Manakara on Tuesdays, Thursdays, Saturdays and Sundays, returning on the other days (but it manages to run both ways on Sundays. It leaves at 7.00, takes 6-8 hours, and costs 8,800fmg first class (yes, there is still a first class) and 5,800fmg second class. The ticket office opens at 6.00. For more information on the trip see Chapter 9.

Escorted tours

Stella Ravelomanantsoa can arrange transport and organise tours. He (sic) escorts tourists to nearby places of interest including Ambalavao and the Shambavy tea estate, and is very attentive. He can be found at the 'Regional Tourist Office', near the Papillon, opposite Lombardo. Tel: 50667. The daily fee is 15,000fmg.

Excursions
Wine tasting

The Famoriana estate (Domaine Côtes de Famoriana) is one of the largest and best known wine producers in Madagascar. The other large wine estate, Domaine Côtes d'Isandra, has gone bankrupt, but smaller ones such as Maromby flourish. The vineyards are open to visitors. Famoriana is about 35km north-west of Fiana, beyond the small town of Isorana.

Tea estate

The Sahambavy Tea Estate is situated on one side of a very pretty valley beside Lake Sahambavy, 25km by road from Fianar, or by rail to the Sahambavy station on the way to Manakara. Although tea-growing was encouraged in Madagascar in pre-Colonial times, this is a relatively new estate and is now managed by a Dutch company, HVA, and run by a Scot. The company employs 700 people and 75% of the tea produced must by law be exported.

Visitors are welcome at the estate which is a beautiful place for picnics. Camping is not encouraged because of the danger from cattle rustlers. The place is closed at weekends.

RANOMAFANA

Ranomafana itself is little more than a hotel and the thermal baths, set by a river in the lush greenness of the eastern rain forest. The name Ranomafana means 'hot water' and it was the waters, not the lemurs, which drew visitors in the colonial days and financed the building of the elegant-looking Hotel Station Thermale de Ranomafana.

These days the baths are often ignored by visitors anxious to visit the national park which was created in 1991. This fragment of high-altitude rain forest first came to world attention with the discovery of the golden bamboo lemur in 1986 and for a hitherto unprotected area it is particularly rich in wildlife.

I love visiting Ranomafana! First you have the marvellous drive down, with the dry highland vegetation giving way to greenery and flowers. Then there are the views of the tumbling waters of the Namorona river, and the relief when the hillsides become that lovely unbroken, knobbly green of virgin forest and you know you are near the reserve. Hidden in these trees are 12 species of lemur: diademed (Milne-Edwards) sifaka, red-bellied lemur, red-fronted lemur, ruffed lemur and three species of bamboo lemur.

THE GOLDEN BAMBOO LEMUR AND OTHER HAPALEMURS

The story of the golden bamboo lemur (*Hapalemur aureus*) goes back to 1972 when the extremely rare *Hapalemur simus* was sighted by André Peyrieras in the south-east after a gap of several decades.

In the 1980s this lemur apparently turned up in the forest near Ranomafana, where it was seen by a local French school teacher, so in 1986 two primatologists arrived to study it. They were Patricia Wright, from Duke University, North Carolina, and Bernard Meier of Germany. Both thought they were observing *Hapalemur simus* until it was observed that two dissimilar groups of lemurs were sharing the same habitat but feeding on different plants. Meier then realised that these could be two distinct species: *Hapalemur aureus* are smaller and browner than *Hapalemur simus* and were later found to have other differences which put them firmly in the category of a new species: their brachial scent gland is in a different position and, to clinch the matter, the golden bamboo lemur has more chromosomes. So a 'new' lemur had arrived. They are now breeding sucessfully at Tsimbazaza zoo and are protected in Ranomafana.

The different English names given to the Hapalemur genus are confusing. They are called bamboo lemurs, and also gentle lemurs, as well as the more straight forward hapalemur. The various names of the three species are: *Hapalemur griseus*, lesser hapalemur, grey gentle lemur, grey bamboo lemur; *Hapalemur simus*, greater hapalemur, broad-nosed gentle lemur, greater bamboo lemur; *Hapalemur aureus*, golden bamboo lemur (no doubt gentle and Hapa- names will follow!).

At night you can add mouse lemur, avahi, lepilemur, fat-tailed dwarf lemur, and even aye-aye. Then there are the birds: 96 species with 36 endemic. And the reptiles. And the butterflies and other insects. Even if you saw no wildlife, there is enough variety in the vegetation and scenery, and enough pleasure in walking the well-constructed trails, to make a visit worthwhile. And – I nearly forgot – in the warm summer months you can swim in the cold, clear water of the Namorona while a malachite kingfisher darts overhead.

I must think of some negative things... the trails are steep and arduous: this is not a suitable park for those who have difficulty in walking. Accommodation is (so far) basic and often full, so you have to camp. It often rains in the rain forest... Oh, and there are leeches.

The national park and local communities

Because the national park was recently created, not inherited from previous administrations, it has been possible to put nearly 50 years of experience to full use. In the colonial days reserves and parks were established against the will of the people who lived nearby; they were simply told that they were now excluded from their traditional hunting grounds. Not surprisingly, poaching became the norm and wildlife was resented not valued. In Ranomafana, the villagers have been fully involved in the project and are material beneficiaries. A notice by the little museum states the aims of the park: 'To integrate rainforest conservation with sustainable development in and around Ranomafana.' The park is being financed by USAID, and the understanding is that for the park to succeed the communities who have lost the use of the forest must be helped.

Initially Patricia Wright and her colleagues set into motion basic requirements to give tourism a chance of success in Ranomafana:

- Hired a US advisor in charge of eco-tourism and conservation.
- Run training courses for nature guides. Successful trainees receive a T-shirt and boots.
- Established a museum and tourist shop.

The park now employs 100 people. In the three years since it was created the programme has developed to include the following:

- A conservation committee in every village which adjoins the park.
- Promoted alternative agricultural programmes including honey production (using bee-boxes rather than felling large trees to reach the wild honey) and raising chickens and rabbits.
- Instigated crayfish farming. The six endemic species that were found in the park had become threatened. These are now being raised in ponds outside the park. An early problem of poaching has been neatly solved by planting reeds. These prevent poachers casting their nets and provides materials for mat-making.

• Initiated reafforestation to *tavy* (slash and burn) areas. Fast-growing endemic species are used and vegetables grown underneath them. Vegetable gardens are created in areas no longer suitable for rice.
• Water management: small dams and irrigation canals.
• The education team has built six schools. A mobile education team goes round these to teach conservation. The health team is active in all communities and has established a birth-control programme.
• Fuel-efficient stoves are being made locally, and there is a thriving women's co-operative to produce handicrafts to sell in the museum shop.

An impressive list to bear in mind next time you find yourself asking 'What are they *doing* about this?' The project is thoroughly supported by President Zafy who spent two hours in the museum in 1993. His wife is honorary president of the project. Change comes slowly in Madagascar, but the will is there at all levels.

Visiting the national park

You need a permit (standard fee of 20,000fmg) which is obtainable from the national park office near the hotel. You are not allowed into the park without a guide. Most only speak French, but they know the animals' names in English. More work needs to be done to ensure that the guides do not try to get extra money out of tourists (the project personnel are aware of this problem) and that they are skilled at their job. Some guides are very good; Fidi, in particular, is highly recommended. The established

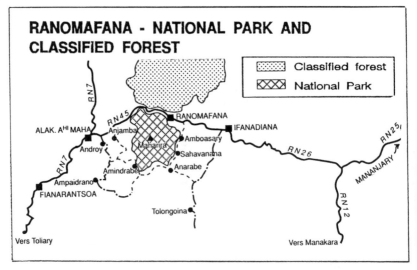

Map reproduced from *Madagascar: Revue de la conservation et des aires protégées* by kind permission of the WWF, Switzerland.

fee for a guide (1994) is 10,000fmg for four hours and 20,000fmg for one full day. Any change in the fees should be posted at the entrance to the park. There are loopholes: you employ one guide and find other 'helpers' coming along who want the same payment. Clarify in advance exactly what you are paying for. You may always add a small tip on top of the standard fee if you feel your guide has been exceptional (and please write to me with his/her name for recommendation in the next edition).

Guides urge you to visit the park after dark to see the nocturnal animals. I am not convinced that this is worth it if you are not camping in the forest or taking a late afternoon tour. The way is steep and rough, and risky in the dark. You will see mouse lemurs (which turn out obligingly to eat bananas) and the civet, *Fossa fossana* or falanouc.

There are standard routes in the forest, mostly lasting a few hours. Your guide will assume that it is lemurs you have come to see, so unless you stress that you are interested in other aspects such as botany, he will tend to concentrate on mammals and birds. You are most likely to see brown lemurs – or to be more specific – red-fronted lemurs (*Eulemur fulvus rufus*) and perhaps the red-bellied lemur, *Lemur rubiventer*. The golden bamboo lemur is less easily seen. If you are camping in the park, however, your guide can take you to the troop. The most memorable of the easily found lemurs is the diademed sifaka, *Propithecus diadema edwardsi*, more correctly known as Milne-Edward's sifaka. Unlike the more familiar sifaka which is largely white, this subspecies is dark brown with cream-coloured sides. They wear snazzy coloured collars, much to the annoyance of tourists who want to take photos. These are radio collars and the colour identifies the troop. You should remember that these rare animals are being extensively studied. Be careful not to let your enthusiasm impede a researcher's work.

A delightful, if strenuous, walk is along the river to Cascade Riana. Allow at least two hours for the round trip plus time to swim in the pool at the base of the falls.

The entrance to the park is some 6km west of the hotel, on the main road. Without your own transport this added 12km makes it a tiring day, although you can often get a lift.

Another trail system has been built on flatter ground at Vohiparara, near the boundary of the park 12km west of Ranomafana on the main road. It only takes about three hours to do all the trails here with a guide.

Getting there

In your own transport the journey is about three hours from Fianar and four hours from Ambositra. There are two roads leading there – an all weather but pot-holed road from Fianar and a deeply rutted dry-season road from north of Fianar off the RN7 (convenient for those coming from Antsirabe).

A taxi-brousse or *baché* (SONATRA is the best company) from Fianar should cost around 5,000fmg, but desperate *vazahas* often end up paying nearly twice as much. It takes about five hours.

Coming from Manakara or Mananjary you should be at the taxi-brousse station as early as possible in the morning. The charge from Manakara seems to be 10,000fmg.

When leaving Ranomafana you are safer to get a taxi-brousse to Fianar, rather than hope to get one going north to Antsirabe. These supposedly run only on Wednesdays and Saturdays.

Where to stay/eat

At the time of writing this is a real problem. The 'good' hotel is so bad and so poorly managed that comfort-seeking visitors should consider giving Ranomafana a miss. It is not practical to consider doing it as a day trip from Fianar. No doubt good accommodation will appear in due course – everyone recognises the need – but until this happens you will have to grin and bear it.

Station Thermal de Ranomafana   BP 13, tel: 1 (!). Rooms at present cost 15,000fmg. The beds are uncomfortable, and there are only smelly, communal toilets. No hot water. The food varies. I have always had good meals there, but I seem to have been lucky.

Hotely Ravenala   Up the road from the Thermal towards the park entrance. 8,000fmg. Adequate. No restaurant.

Hotelin Kavana   This restaurant serves inexpensive, good food.

Camping

Tents can be hired at the park entrance. At present there is one campsite at Belle Vue on a hill in the park with, as the name suggests, a marvellous view over the forest and some charming furry visitors: ring-tailed mongoose (*Galidia elegans*) during the day and mouse-lemurs and the civet-like *Fossa fossana* at night. There is only room for three or four tents here and water must be carried up. By the time you read this another campsite is likely to have opened at a new site by the river with space for four tents. Both these are in the national park so you must be accompanied by a guide (although he/she does not have to stay the night there). Outside the park you can camp by the river near the thermal baths: a very pleasant spot.

Thermal baths

These are close to the hotel: turn left out of the door, down the steps and follow the path. It only costs 50fmg for a wonderful warm swimming pool or a hot shower or bath. Hours are 7.00 - 12.00, 14.00 - 17.00. Closed Fridays.

Museum/gift shop

Part of the Ranomafana National Park Project to improve visitor understanding. The museum is still being added to, but there is now quite a comprehensive collection labelled in English and Malagasy. The gift shop sells handicrafts made locally; the proceeds all go to the people.

CONTINUING SOUTH ON RN7

Coming from Fianar the landscape is a fine blend of vineyards and terraced rice paddies (the Betsileo are acknowledged masters of rice cultivation) then after 20km a giant rock formation seems almost to hold the road in its grasp. Its name is, appropriately, Tanan'Andriamanitra, or 'Hand of God'. From here to Ihosy is arguably the finest mountain scenery in Madagascar. Reader Bishop Brock who cycled the route writes: 'Those three days were the most rewarding of my career as a bicyle tourist. I pity people who only pass through that magnificent landscape jammed inside a taxi-brousse.'

It is worth noting that taxi-brousses from the north continue south in the afternoon. This may the best time to get a place if you're pushed for time.

Ambalavao

56km south-west of Fianarantsoa is my favourite town, Ambalavao. RN7 does not pass through the attractive part of town, and I strongly urge people to stop here for a few hours. 'Nowhere in Madagascar have I seen a town so resembling a medieval European village as here. Although the main street was not narrow, the wooden balconies with their handsomely carved railings leaned into the street, giving them that look of a fairy-tale book tilt. The roofs were tiled, and, lending that final touch of authenticity, pails of water were emptied onto people passing too near the gutter.' (Tim Cross)

This is where the famous Malagasy 'Antaimoro' paper is made. This 'papyrus' paper impregnated with dried flowers is sold throughout the island as wall-hangings and lampshades. The people in this area are Betsileo, but paper-making in the area copies the coastal Antaimoro tradition which goes back to the Muslim immigrants who wrote verses from the Koran on this paper. This Arabic script was the only form of writing known in Madagascar before the LMS developed a written Malagasy language nearly five hundred years later using the roman alphabet.

Antaimoro paper is traditionally made from the bark of the *avoha* tree from the eastern forests, but sisal paste is now sometimes used. After the bark is pounded and softened in water it is smoothed onto linen trays to dry in the sun. While still tacky, dried flowers are pressed into it and brushed over with a thin solution of the liquid bark to hold the flowers in place. The open air 'factory' (more flowerbeds than buildings) where all this happens is to the left of the town (signposted) and is well worth a visit. It is fascinating to see the step by step process, and you get a good tour (in French with a smattering of English) from the manager. A shop sells the finished product at reasonable prices (although rolls of Antaimoro paper do not survive the average taxi-brousse trip).

Another attraction is the market which is held on Wednesdays. Or maybe Thursdays. Jill and Charlie Hadfield visited the cattle market (reached by walking off the road to the right of the taxi-brousse stop).

This area of Madagascar is notorious for cattle-rustling: from Ambositra down to Tuléar is bandit country and for the Bara tribe cattle rustling is a test of manhood... What seems to have started out as a sporting activity is now a very dangerous pastime. From time to time the government makes a half-hearted attempt to put a stop to *dahalo* but it's doomed to failure. Most of the gendarmerie are in the pay of the bandits...

So we were very interested in the goings on at the cattle market which takes place on top of a hill, with a circular view for miles and miles of bare, rolling countryside, with flame trees and the granite-topped mountains in the distance. We got there early and for the next hour or so could see herds of zebu being driven in from all directions – some come from as far as Tuléar, two days' drive away. Betsileo farmers, wearing straw hats and with their blankets draped like ponchos, stood and chatted or strolled round eyeing up the cattle, leather-jacketed smoothies strutted round importantly, prodding zebu with their sticks or pulling their tails. Calculations were done on pocket calculators. We priced a couple of animals ourselves out of interest. A fine-looking bull was 300,000fmg and a calf 100,000fmg.

Getting there/away

Although Ambalavao is on RN7, southward bound travellers may prefer to make it an excursion from Fianarantsoa, since vehicles heading to Ihosy and beyond will have filled up with passengers in Fianar. The taxi-brousse from Fianar should cost around 2,000fmg.

Where to stay

Stop Hotel. 5 double rooms with communal WC and washing facilities. Basic but adequate. They expect you to eat at least one meal a day in the restaurant and to order it in advance.

CONTINUING SOUTH ON RN7

The scenery beyond Ambalavao is marvellous. Huge granite domes of rock dominate the grassy plains. The most striking one, with twin rock towers, is called Varavarana Ny Atsimo, the 'Door to the South' by the pass of the same name. Beyond is the 'Bonnet de l'Évêque' (Bishop's Hat), and a huge lump of granite shaped like an upturned boat, with its side gouged out into an amphitheatre; streams run into the lush vegetation at its foot.

You will notice that not only the scenery but the villages are different. These Bara houses are solidly constructed out of red earth (no elegant Merina pillars here) with small windows. Bunches of corn are often suspended from the roof to dry in the sun. Shortly after Ambalavao you start to see your first Bara tombs — some painted with scenes from the life of the deceased.

The next town of importance is Ihosy, described in Chapter 8.

Andringitra and Pic Boby

South of Ambalavao lies the Andringitra massif, crowned by Madagascar's second highest mountain, Pic Boby (2,658 m). The area constitutes Réserve Naturelle Intégrale de l'Andringitra, which is one of the WWF's 'priority pilot zones'. Concerned as much with the communities surrounding the reserve as the protected area itself, the aim is to look at sustainable development which may include ecotourism. At present, being a Strict Nature Reserve, visitors are not allowed here. If you have a special interest in this area you should contact the WWF or ANGAP for latest details.

A proposal is to make part of the reserve into a national park. If this happens visitors will be able see the endemic fauna and flora, ranging from aloe and pachypodium in lower, rocky areas to cloud forest, with a correspondingly large number of fauna species especially amphibians.

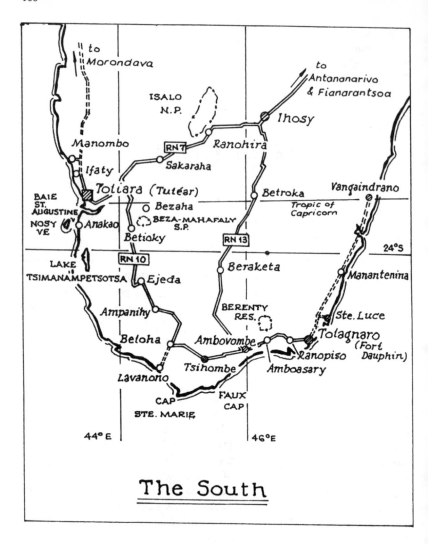

The South

EGG-VENTURE

In 1993 three children playing in sand-hills near a beach in Western Australia dug up a fossilised egg which appears to be that of Madagascar's *aepyornis* or elephant bird. How it got there is a mystery. Gondwanaland broke up before the evolution of birds, but this egg could have floated across the Indian Ocean. Or... your guess is as good as any.

Chapter 8

The South

INTRODUCTION

This is the most exotic and the most famous part of Madagascar, the region of 'spiny forest' or 'spiny desert' where weird cactus-like trees wave their thorny fingers in the sky, where pieces of 'elephant bird' shell may still be found, and where the Mahafaly tribe erect their intriguing and often entertaining *aloalo* stelae above the graves. Here also is the country's most popular nature reserve (Berenty), and one of the country's loveliest beaches (Libanona). No wonder Tolagnaro (Fort Dauphin) features on almost all tour itineraries.

Europeans have been coming to this area for a long time. Perhaps the earliest were a group of 600 shipwrecked Portuguese sailors in 1527. Later, when sailors were deliberately landing in Madagascar during the days of the spice trade in the 16th and 17th centuries, St Augustine's Bay, south of the modern town of Toliara (Tuléar), became a favoured destination. They came for reprovisioning – Dutch and British – trading silver and beads for meat and fruit. One Englishman, Walter Hamond, was so overcome with the delights of Madagascar and the Malagasy, 'the happiest people in the world', that fired by his enthusiasm the British attempted to establish a colony at St Augustine's Bay. It was not a success. The original 140 settlers were soon whittled down to 60 through disease and murder by the local tribesmen who became less happy when they found their favourite beads were not available for trade and that these *vazahas* showed no sign of going away. The colonists left in 1646. Fifty years later St Augustine was a haven for pirates.

The most important tribes in the south are the Vezo-Sakalava (and its offshoot the Masikoro), Mahafaly, Antanosy and Antandroy, occupying areas along the coast and into the hinterland, and the Bara in the centre. These southern Malagasy are tough, dark-skinned people, with African features, accustomed to the hardship of living in a region where rain seldom falls and finding water and grazing for their large herds of zebu is a constant challenge. In contrast to the highland people, who go in for second burial and whose tombs are the collective homes of ancestors, those in the south commemorate the recently dead. There is more opportunity to be remembered as an individual here, and a Mahafaly man who has lived eventfully, and died rich, will have the highlights of his life perpetuated in the form of wooden carvings (*aloalo*) or colourful paintings adorning his tomb. Formerly the *aloalo* were of more spiritual significance, but just as we, in our culture, have tended to bring an element of humour and realism into religion, so have the Malagasy. As John Mack says (in *Island of Ancestors*) 'Aloalo have become obituary announcements when formerly they were notices of rebirth.'

Antandroy tombs may be equally colourful, if less entertaining. They are large and rectangular (the more important the person the bigger his tomb) and, like the Mahafaly, topped with zebu skulls left over from the funeral feast. A very rich man may have over 100 skulls on his grave. They usually have 'male and female' standing stones (or, in modern tombs, cement towers) at each side. Modern tombs may be brightly painted with geometric patterns on the sides. The Antanosy have upright stones, cement obelisks, or beautifully carved wooden memorials. These, however, are not over the graves themselves. This sacred and secret place will be elsewhere.

The spiny forest: an identification guide

The spiny forest (more correctly called 'thorn thicket') is typified by thorny, water-retaining trees and shrubs which are unique to Madagascar. They exist in a bewildering variety, but it adds interest to one's visit to be able to identify a few species.

First, the ones that look like cacti. There are four genera of didiereacea, but non-botanists are most interested in two: *alluaudia* and *didierea*. Some broad ground rules will help you tell the two apart. Look at the stems. In alluaudia the spines and leaves are arranged in spirals, in didierea they are in groups. There are five species of alluaudia: *A. ascendens* (tall, finger-like, with long thorns and short, heart-shaped leaves), *A. procera* (fewer and shorter thorns, long leaves arranged in spirals, and − in the spring − a clump of flowers at the end of each branch; the 'trunks' are woody and used for fencing and charcoal). Somewhat similar is *A. komosa* (tree-like branches, thick, oblong leaves), *A. dumosa* (no leaves and short, stubby thorns) and *A. humbertia* (shrub-like with long thorns and heart-shaped leaves).

There are four species of didierea. Two that are easily identified are *D. trollii*, with anti-social branches trailing on the ground providing an impenetrable barrier, and *D. madagascariensis*, which has the classic, many-fingered silhouette, and long, narrow leaves.

Now you've finished with the cactus-like jobs you can go on to the *euphorbiaceae*, of which there are five families. Among the easily-recognisable are *E. stenoclada*, which has thick, green branches filled with latex, *E. oconclada* with long, droopy 'branches' like strings of sausages, *E. fiha*, similar but with peeling bark, and *E. enterophora*, tree-shaped with many green 'fingers'. Still on the quest for knowledge? Then turn your attention to the numerous Pachypodium species. The name means 'elephant foot' and apart from the ones that really do resemble an elephant's foot crowned with yellow or pink flowers, there are a couple of taller species you may see in gardens which are particularly striking: *P. lamerii* is shaped like a slim bottle, very spiny, and has a burst of leaves at the top, and *P. geayi*, which is more like a standard bottle and topped with branches and white flowers. If your curiosity is still unsatiated, find Roger at Fort Dauphin/Berenty from whom I learned all this!

Getting around

Road travel in the south can be a challenging affair, but roads *are* being improved, and RN7 to Toliara (Tuléar) is now mostly paved. Apart from this and the road between Tolagnaro (Fort Dauphin) and Ambovombe, the 'roads' that link other important towns are terrible, so most people prefer to fly. In addition to the regular flights to the main towns of Tolagnaro and Toliara there are occasional small planes to Ampanihy, Bekily, and Betioky as well as Ihosy. Check the current schedule with Air Mad.

IHOSY

Pronounced 'Ee-oosh', this small town is the capital of the war-like Bara people, who resisted Merina rule and were never really subdued until French colonial times. Cattle rustling is a time-honoured custom in this region — a Bara does not achieve manhood until he has stolen a few of his neighbour's cows (see also page 23). This is a medium-sized town which has, among other things, a BTM bank.

Ihosy is about five hours from Fianar by taxi-brousse, and lies at the junction for Toliara and Tolagnaro. The road to the former is good, to the latter, bad. A road also runs from Ihosy to Farafangana, on the east coast. This was once notorious for bandits, but I am told that the danger is lessened now the road has been improved so I expect it to become a popular route for overlanders. However, given its former reputation you should seek local advice.

Where to stay/eat

Zaha Motel   Tel: 83. 20,000-23,500fmg. Pleasant, comfortable bungalows, cold water.

There is also the poor-value **Hotel Relais-Bara**, 18,000fmg, no hot water but a nice atmosphere. A better bet may be the **Hotel Ravaka**. For meals there is a nice little square of open-sided *hotelys* serving quite good Malagasy food. The Hotely Dasimo is recommended for its excellent *tsaramasy* (rice with beans and pork).

PROTECTED AREAS & SITES OF BIOLOGICAL INTEREST IN THE SOUTH-WEST

Map reproduced from *Madagascar: Revue de la conservation et des aires protégées* by kind permission of the WWF, Switzerland.

FROM IHOSY TO TOLAGNARO (FORT DAUPHIN)

RN13 is in very poor condition. Adventurous travellers will enjoy the consequent lack of tourist development but don't underestimate the time it takes to travel even short distances. The cost of a taxi-brousse all the way is about 28,000fmg.

The first town is **Betroka**, a friendly little place with a basic hotel and restaurant, Des Bons Amis, about 15,000fmg with a loo-shed outside. If you don't want to eat in the hotel there are plenty of *hotelys*. Next comes **Beraketa** which has the even more down-to-earth Herilaza Hotel. This seems to be the last accommodation (except in private houses) before Ambovombe and the paved road to Fort Dauphin.

FROM IHOSY TO TOLIARA (TULÉAR)

After leaving Ihosy, RN7 takes you for two hours across the Horombe Plateau, grasslands dotted with termite hills and telegraph poles, each with its waiting kestrel. As you approach Ranohira, *Medemia* palms enliven the monotonous scenery. Henk Beentje of Kew Gardens writes: 'The palms are properly called *Bismarckia*, but the French didn't like the most common palm in one of their colonies to be called after a German so changed the name, quite illegally according to the Code of Botanical Nomenclature!'

Ranohira

This town lies 97km south of Ihosy and adjacent to Isalo National Park, so is the base for those visiting the park. A taxi-brousse from Ihosy will cost around 5,000fmg.

Where to stay
Category A

La Reine   This new hotel is not in Ranohira but further south, on the edge of the park. It has been thoughtfully designed to blend as much as possible into the surrounding landscape. Solveig Nepstad writes: 'The hotel is impressive by any standards; marble floors, high ceilings, a huge fireplace...' A twin-bedded room with bathroom costs 350FF. The hotel is solar-heated, although in the hot season cooling is more important. Fans are being installed.

Category C

Hotel Berny   15,000fmg; no running water but very friendly, and now has 12 double rooms. If you are driving your own vehicle there is safe parking here. 'Someone always stays up to meet the taxi-brousse which can arrive any time between 11pm and morning. Around 1.30am is usual. They leave one light on which is very welcoming.' (Basia Filzek)

Hotel les Joyeux Lemuriens   12,500fmg. The most popular hotel in Ranohira. Readers are full of praise for the hotel, the food, and its managers, Aujustin and Myriam Jaofera, although many express regret that they keep two unhappy tied-up lemurs.

Chez R Thomas   Clean, new, windowless rooms. Good value.

ISALO NATIONAL PARK

The combination of sandstone rocks (cut by deep canyons and eroded into weird shapes), rare endemic plants and dry weather (between June and August rain is almost unknown), makes this park particularly rewarding. For botanists there is *Pachypodium rosulatum* – a bulbous rock-clinging plant – and a native species of aloe, *Aloe isaloensis*, and for lemur-lovers there are sifakas, brown lemurs and ring-tails. 'Isalo is fantastic! It is not just the abstract sculpturing and colours of the eroded terrain or the sweeping panoramas which so impressed, but also the absolute and enveloping silence. No birds, insects or other animals, no wind, no rumbling of distant traffic and no other people.' (Peter Walbran). 'It's not just the curious sense of isolation… it's the sheer timelessness of it all, the fixed, almost pre-historical feel. Gazing from the top of cliffs over the valley I would have been genuinely unsurprised to have suddenly seen a line of hunter-gatherers in skins making its way across the bottom.' (G Simpson).

Tourists who do not wish to hike (and this should not be undertaken lightly – it is *very* hot and rugged) can still enjoy the sandstone formations from the road and visit an idyllic palm-shaded grotto. The track leading to this oasis is about 5km south of Ranohira, on the left just before a 'milestone' ('Tulear 230km'). There are *Pachypodium rosulatum* nearby, a waterfall and a pool. Being so accessible this beautiful spot is beginning to be trashed. You can help by not leaving rubbish, and how about clearing up a bit as well?

The most popular hiking excursion is to *La Piscine Naturelle*, a natural swimming pool, and the *Canyon des Singes*, usually done in three days. The first day to the campsite at the swimming pool is only two or three hours, then five or six hours the next day to the canyon. This is the place to see lemurs, and in the upper part of the canyon are pools and waterfalls. It is then a three-hour walk back to Ranohira. 'The Piscine Naturelle is the essential Isalo. It appears to have been taken right out of the book of Genesis. The crystal clear water is a wonderful sight after all that walking and the swim makes the toil worthwhile.' (Will Pepper). If you don't want to camp you can take a day trip to the Piscine.

It is worth spending several days in the park; two is really the minimum for proper enjoyment. Sleeping mats and tents can usually be hired in Ranohira (but the cost is high: 10,000fmg). A guide is not essential for experienced well-equipped travellers/hikers. The path to the main attractions is well-trodden and clear.

The less visited parts of the park are even more rewarding. Bishop Brock took a five-day hike. 'The forest of Sakamolia... is one of the most beautiful places I have ever camped in, perhaps not in absolute beauty but in contrasts. In the middle of the dry, grassy plain, surrounded on two sides by massive rock walls, a small crystal-clear river runs over a clean, sandy bottom supporting a 20 metre wide luxuriant green-belt. Paradise!'

Facilities in Isalo have not kept up with its increasing popularity, and popular camping places are starting to get trashed (under every stone lurks some toilet paper). ANGAP have plans to establish designated camping areas with latrines.

Warnings

Hiking Isalo is very hot work; bring a minimum of equipment (but remember it gets very cold at night from May to August) or hire porters. Bring plenty of drinking water, even in the rainy season. There have been reports of robberies from tents. This is a serious problem since it is impossible to protect yourself or your possessions. Discuss the matter with your guide and suggest he/she stays to guard the tent if camping in popular places.

Permit and guides

For an excursion in the park you will need a permit. This can be obtained in Ranohira from the hotels. Please be sure to pay the full amount (20,000fmg) and get a receipt.

Unfortunately there is not yet any printed information to help tourists understand the park's unique geological and botanical features. Guides mostly know the way but that is all. Many are reluctant to take visitors to more remote parts of the park. They charge from 9,000 to 15,000fmg per day. Porters charge about 7,500fmg. Some of the younger guides may speak poor French which can lead to misunderstandings. Make sure you are in full agreement over the price and whether the guide will be responsible for carrying his own food and water (usually you provide food). If you are pleased with your guide write him/her a recommendation. Some guides recommended by readers: Zozoly, Tsamara (the latter highly recommended for his professionalism and knowledge about the more remote areas of the park), Fidel and Jean. I would be pleased to add to this list.

Getting there and away

Getting to Ranohira is usually no problem: about two hours from Ihosy by taxi-brousse, 5,000fmg. If leaving from Toliara note that the taxi-brousses and buses depart early in the morning; best to book your seat the night before. Leaving Ranohira can be a major problem. Most people wait many hours – sometimes days – and pay double the normal fare when they do find transport.

If time is short it's worth considering hiring a car and driver in Toliara.

CONTINUING SOUTH

Continuing south, the rugged mountains give way to grasslands. Some very charming Antanosy villages give added interest, and there are some tombs with *aloalo* near the road. As you get closer to Toliara you'll see your first baobabs and pass through a cotton-growing region. Look out for the enormous nests of hammerkop birds in roadside trees.

Near the village of Sakaraha is Zombitsi Forest which is popular with birders. See *Excursions*. Tombs on the approach to Toliara are also described under that heading.

Although most of the road is paved there are still some quite long, sandy stretches.

ZEBU CATTLE

There are 80 words in the Malagasy language to describe the physical attributes of zebu, in particular the colour, horns and hump. The best specimens are reserved as sacrifices to the ancestors so herds tend to be composed of cows or old bulls. There is little husbandry; the animals are left to fend for themselves, watched over by little boys. Cattle-rustling is rife, and the murder of these small cowherds is not uncommon.

To the rural Malagasy a herd of zebu is as symbolic of prosperity as is a new car in our culture. It is important that this wealth is visible, so cattle are rarely slaughtered except for ritual purposes. Government aid programmes must take this into account; for instance improved rice yields will indirectly lead to more environmental degradation by providing more money to buy more zebu.

The French colonial government thought they had an answer: they introduced a tax on each animal. However, local politicians were quick to point out that since Malagasy women had always been exempt from taxation, the same rule should apply to cows!

TOLIARA/TOLIARY (TULÉAR)

The pronunciation of the French, Tuléar, and the Malagasy is the same: 'Toolee-ar'. Toliara's history is centred on St Augustine's Bay, described at the beginning of this chapter, although the name of the town is thought to derive from an encounter with one of those early sailors who asked a local inhabitant where he might moor his boat. The Malagasy replied: *Toly eroa*, 'Mooring down there'. The town itself is relatively modern – 1895 – and designed by an uninspired French architect. His tree-planting was more successfully aesthetic, and the shady tamarind trees, *kily*, give welcome respite from the blazing sun.

There are two good reasons to visit Toliara: the rich marine life with excellent snorkelling and diving, and the Mahafaly and Bara tombs (see *Excursions*).

The beaches north and south of the town have fine white sand and are protected by an extensive coral reef. However, this is too far from shore to swim out to – a *pirogue* (for hire at the beach hotels) is necessary. Toliara itself, regrettably, has no beach, just mangroves and mud flats.

At present Toliara's reefs are not protected, but the WWF recognises the importance of these in developing ecotourism in the area and a conservation programme is under way, centred at the University of Toliara. The goal of the project is 'To ensure that the coral reefs and coastal zone are effectively conserved through the establishment of a multiple-use marine park and sustainable economic development.'

Certainly there is potential for marine ecotourism. Those who spend some time snorkelling or diving here are rarely disappointed (although some widely travelled visitors report it to be 'nothing special'). Hilana Steyn, who had an enforced stay in Ifaty when the yacht she was on hit the reef and sank, wrote: 'As often as possible I went diving, taking a *pirogue* and a local with me. My total wonderment at the sheer beauty and excitement of each dive was only paralleled and bettered by the next dive. Never have I seen so many, such beautiful, and such an incredible variety of fish, coral, colours and other marine life... I have dived in the Seychelles, Turkey, Malawi and Nosy Be, but these reefs off Ifaty are precious and superior.'

Sightseeing

Toliara has more 'official' sightseeing than most Malagasy towns. Some are worth the trip, others are not.

In town the most interesting place to visit is the small **museum** of the Sakalava and Mahafaly culture on Boulevard Philibert Tsiranana. The entry fee is 1,000fmg. The exhibits are labelled in Malagasy and French, and include some Sakalava erotic tomb sculptures.

The **market** is lively, interesting, and easy to reach by *pousse-pousse* (bargain hard and have the agreed money ready. Change will not be given).

The most spectacular **tombs** within easy reach of the town are those of the Masikoro, a sub-division of the Sakalava. This small tribe is probably of African origin, and there is speculation that the name comes from *mashokora* which, in parts of Tanzania, means scrub forest. The tombs are off RN7 about one hour from Toliara, and are clearly visible on the left as you approach the town. They are painted with scenes from the distinguished military life of the deceased. Another tomb on the outskirts of town, beyond the university, is **King Baba's Tomb**. This is set in a grove of Didierea trees and is interesting more for the somewhat bizarre funerary objects (an urn and a huge, cracked bell) displayed there and its spiritual significance to the local people (you may only approach barefoot) than any aesthetic value. This King Baba, who seems to have died about 100 years ago, was presumably a descendant of one of the Masikoro Kings of Baba mentioned in British naval accounts of the 18th century. These kings used to trade with English ships calling at St Augustine's Bay and gave their family and courtiers English names such as the Prince of Wales and the Duke of Cumberland.

On the way to King Baba's Tomb you may visit a little fenced-off park of **banyan trees**, all descending from one 'parent'. This is known as 'the sacred grove' and in theory would be a place for peaceful contemplation, but the hordes of tourist-aware children are a deterrent.

Getting there/back
Road   Readers of *Muddling through in Madagascar* by Dervla Murphy will be amazed at the beautiful condition of most of Route Nationale 7. Only short stretches remain unpaved and quite comfortable vehicles make the journey from Tana. There are even buses. If you are going the full distance non-stop, try to get a guaranteed seat in a bus and avoid the one in the middle – uncomfortable. A 'luxury Mercedes' leaves Tana on Tuesdays, and returns on Saturdays at 7.00 (but check times and days). Fare around 19,000fmg.

Air   There are flights four days a week, 885FF/US$150, and also a Twin Otter service. Flights are often fully booked, and in the high season the Air Mad office in Toliara is full of desperate *vazahas* trying to get back to Tana. To compound the problems the office is only open from 15.00 to 17.00 (at least in the hot season). Remember you must pay in hard currency. If you can pay in cash your chances of getting on may be better. It's always worth going to the airport, whatever they say in the office.

Car hire
Solveig Nepstad recommends Joshua Calixte (Tel: 427 47). The cost was 200,000fmg per day for a 4WD vehicle. Another possibility is Edgar's Car Tour, Villa Ashik, Andranomena; tel: 423 19.

Warnings

In the cool season (May to October) the nights in Toliara are very cold. The cheaper hotels rarely supply enough blankets.

And in the hot season (November to April) everything closes for midday siesta between 13.00 and 15.00.

Where to stay

IN TOWN

Category A

Hotel Plazza   BP 362. Tel: 427 66. Central, facing the ocean (or – to be more accurate – the mud flats). Hot water, air-conditioned. Good food. English spoken. 182FF double.

Hotel Capricorne   BP 158. Tel: 414 95. 336FF for a double room, 308FF single. About 2km from the town centre (Betania) on RN7. Considered the best of the Toliara hotels. It has a lovely garden, and is well run with excellent food and air conditioning.

Category B

Chez Alain   One of the most popular *vazaha* hotels (bungalows) in Madagascar. Well run, friendly, good food. 15,000 - 20,000fmg. No hot water. Mountain bikes available for hire.

Hotel Sud   Place de la République. 22,000fmg for a double room with a basin, shower, WC and hot water. Very good value.

Category C

Chez Micheline   Rue no 18, Anketa. Tel: 415 86. Micheline is a warm, friendly woman beloved by the *vazahas* who have written recommending this new hotel. Very good value at 7,500 - 12,500fmg with excellent food. 5 minutes' walk (north) from the centre of town, near the *gare routière* for Ifaty.

Hotel Central   About 15,000fmg and the only hotel in the centre of town. Noisy.

Le Corail   Bungalows near the restaurant Etoile de Mer. Clean but very hot during the day (or cold at night, depending on the season) because of the tin roof. Good restaurant.

La Pirogue   About 15,000fmg. Very noisy and food reportedly poor.

Hotel Voamio   Similar price. Very primitive bungalows and – again – noisy (this is one of Toliara's main nightclubs), but friendly.

BEACH ACCOMMODATION OUT OF TOWN

To the north

In Ifaty, 26km north of Toliara (but an awful road, so it can take over three hours) are three sets of beach bungalows. Ifaty is reached by taxi-brousse (frequent) heading for Manombo.

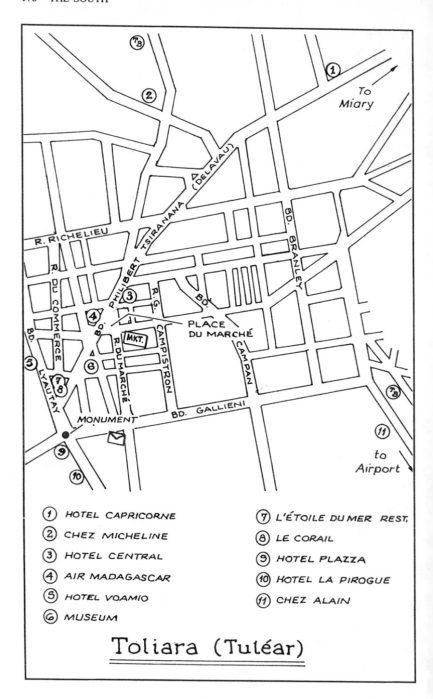

1   HOTEL CAPRICORNE
2   CHEZ MICHELINE
3   HOTEL CENTRAL
4   AIR MADAGASCAR
5   HOTEL VOAMIO
6   MUSEUM

7   L'ÉTOILE DU MER REST.
8   LE CORAIL
9   HOTEL PLAZZA
10 HOTEL LA PIROGUE
11 CHEZ ALAIN

Toliara (Tuléar)

Mora Mora   BP 41. Tel: 410 16. Rumoured to be closed, so make enquiries. If operating it is the longest-established of Toliara's beach resorts, and the least expensive, offering the same facilities as the other Ifaty resorts.

Dunes Hotel   BP 285. Tel: 428 85. A few kilometres south of Mora Mora, this is a set of concrete bungalows with two adjoining bedrooms. 62 rooms in all. Good restaurant (menu 12,500fmg), tennis court. 340FF per bungalow. Transport from Toliara 30,000fmg round trip. Recommended for watersports.

Hotel Lekana Vezo   10 bungalows. 300FF per bungalow. One hour's walk south of the Dunes Hotel. 'Peter DeSwart, the manager, goes out of his way to make your stay enjoyable, and Vincent the chef will prepare (at your request) calamari, octopus, crayfish...' (Hilana Steyn). The Club Nautique is run very professionally by Denis Guillaumot, with a wide variety of activities available, although snorkelling and scuba diving are favourites.

Bamboo Club   BP 47. Tel: 427 17. Five minutes' walk north of Mora Mora. French run, 16 bungalows priced from 17,000fmg to 24,000fmg. A good diving club. For bookings and latest prices enquire at the Bamboo shop opposite the Hotel Central in town.

If you are on a tight budget there are several alternative eateries in Ifaty. Local people will approach you with their suggestions.

To the south

The Mangrove   20km south of Tulear, and 8km from the main road. Run by the owner of Chez Alain. 'There is a stunning natural swimming pool – cool, fresh water flows from the mountain into the pool and a layer of warm salt water flows on top of it from the sea. It costs 18,000 to 22,000fmg a night for a charming, small thatched-roof bungalow with a bathroom (cold water). It is very basic and primitive, but beautiful.' (Solveig Nepstad). Diving lessons including a *baptême* (first dive) plus excursion to Nosy Ve can be arranged here.

Safari Vezo   (Bivouac d'Anakao) BP 427. Tel: 413 81. This unpretentious set of beach bungalows near Anakao costs between 33,000 and 45,000fmg per person full board. The two-hour pirogue journey is 40,000fmg return. Book in advance.

Where to eat (in town)

An excellent meal (seafood) can be had in an unpretentious wooden building on the seafront, the **Etoile de Mer**, between the Plazza Hotel and the Voamio. Nearby is the **Club Za Za** (good fish) and **Corail**, both recommended. According to expatriates, the best food in town is at Chez Alain, located on the road to the airport, and Chez Micheline.

Two good places for snacks are the rival **Salons des Thé** near the Hotel Central. They are in a constant battle to pull customers.

Nightlife
'The Za Za Club has a following across the world. You have not been to Tuléar unless you have been to Za Za!' (Hilana Steyn).

Medical clinic
The clinique Saint-Luc is run by Dr Noel Rakotomavo who speaks excellent English. The profits from his paying beds go towards providing free treatment for the poor. Tel: (9) 421 76.

Excursions from Toliara
Madagascar Airtours has an office in the grounds of the Plazza Hotel and runs some good tours, as do many of the hotels.

St Augustine (Anakao) and Nosy Ve
Accessible by *vedette* or *pirogue*, this historically important spot is also a very pleasant beach resort (Anakao). St Augustine was the haunt of pirates and was mentioned by Daniel Defoe in *The King of Pirates*.

Off shore is the island of Nosy Ve. The first landing there was by a Dutchman in 1595, and it was officially taken over by the French in 1888 before their conquest of the mainland. This is a lovely little island offering fabulous snorkelling and of particular interest to ornithologists because there is a breeding colony of red-tailed tropic birds. It would be possible to camp on Nosy Ve if you can bring enough drinking water with you.

To reach Anakao you need either to take the package offered by Safari Vezo (see page 000) or – if you are truly adventurous – organise your own pirogue from the fishermen that gather with their pirogues near Rue Marius Jalep, 400m south of the Plazza Hotel. 'We agreed on a price of 18,000fmg which was a lot cheaper for me, and for the two fishermen a lot more than they get when fishing. We left at 2 o'clock in the morning when there was almost no wind. The fishermen said it would take almost three hours... in reality it took nine hours.' (Luc Selleslagh).

The beggars in Anakao are some of the most persistent in Madagascar – the result of tourist 'generosity' in the past.

Zombitse and Vohibasia Forests
Near Sakaraha, off RN7, these forests are scheduled to become protected areas under Madagascar's Environmental Action Plan with a low-involvement programme based on community paticipation. The forests are an important example of a boundary zone between the Western and Southern Domains of vegetation and so have a high level of biodiversity. Zombitse is a rewarding place for birding, with the chance to glimpse one of Madagascar's rarest endemics, Appert's greenbul, which is confined to this forest. Many other species may be seen. The forests are about three hours from Toliara.

Betioky and Mahafaly tombs

The first 70km are on a paved road, then it's a very dusty 70km or so on dirt road. The trip takes about five hours by private vehicle, six to nine hours by taxi- or truck-brousse (4,000fmg). It is worth the effort for the chance to see the Mahafaly tombs for which the area is famous. Painted tombs deteriorate quite quickly while new ones are built, so it is probably pointless to give specific details here. Just rely on your guide's knowledge or keep your eyes peeled. You should see both rectangular, painted tombs and the carved stelaes, *aloalo*. Look out for the funeral/tomb 'invoice' which is often painted proudly on the side of the tombs. It is astounding to us westerners how much money may be spent on these memorials.

In Betioky there is the basic but friendly Hotel Mahafaly, 7,000fmg. Meals are also available.

Beza-Mahafaly Special Reserve

This reserve is the model for the WWF's integrated conservation and development efforts. It was established at the request of local people who volunteered to give up using part of the forest. In return they have been helped with a variety of social and agricultural projects, for example by the provision of a school and the building of irrigation canals.

The government has designated the reserve as its number one priority from ten sites in the Environmental Action Plan. Agroforestry is being developed under the guidance of Tana's School of Agronomy and the Direction des Eaux et Forêts, and many research projects take place there. The goal has always been to integrate conservation and rural development projects around the reserve, and to support the sustainable use of natural resources.

The reserve protects two distinct types of forest: spiny forest and gallery (riverine) forest. In this it mirrors Berenty, but there the comparison ends. Tourism is not discouraged, and there are plans for better facilities and information, but at present the Malagasy locals and researchers come first. This is an enormously rewarding place for the serious naturalist or the seriously interested. 'This was one of our best experiences with lemurs in the entire country. The reserve has a lot of ringtails and sifakas, and some of the best spiny forest we saw. It makes an ideal two-day trip from Tuléar, the drive taking about five hours.' (David Bonderman.) 'Our guide spoke only Malagasy. He was, however, not only extremely enthusiastic but also adept at spotting the nocturnal lemurs.' (Gavin & Val Thomson).

Beza-Mahafaly is 30km from Betioky. To get there you need a 4WD vehicle (it is very difficult to reach by public transport, and the roads are often too bad for saloon cars), a bicycle, or a strong pair of legs. The indefatigable John Kupiec walked from Betioky, despite warnings of bandits. 'Many times I was warned not to go somewhere alone. Whenever I did, I always found them to be the safest, most peaceful areas, including the walk to and from Beza Mahafaly.'

There is no accommodation, but a space for tents costs 5,000fmg per night, and evening meals (3,000fmg) are available (but it would be wise to bring emergency rations to be on the safe side). Permits can be purchased at the reserve. Guides cost 3,000fmg for a two hour excursion and speak only Malagasy. If you want to go out with a guide all day you will need to negotiate the price.

NORTH TO MOROMBE AND MORONDAVA

A good sandy track runs from the Mora Mora (Ifaty) road head. A taxi-brousse to Morombe leaves in the mornings, takes about 11 hours, and costs around 8,000fmg. If you want to continue to Morondava, there is a choice of sea (by pirogue, risky) or road. A vehicle known as the 'Bon Bon Caramel' leaves Toliara at 6.00 on Thursdays, spending the night at Manja (good food and bungalows) and arriving in Morondava Friday evening. For a full description of this glorious Mercedes truck and its crew see Chapter 11, *Morondava*.

Galidia elegans

'BIG LEAVES'

Wherever there is still water in Madagascar, you see enormous 'elephant ear' type plants growing in the water near the banks. This is *Typhonodorum* or *viha* in Malagasy. Like so many plants it is utilised in various ways. The roots are eaten (after much preparation, since they are poisonous), the trunks are used for making mats and the leaves for roofs. The leaves also make a perfect umbrella.

The smaller, cultivated plant which also has large leaves, is taro (*Colocasia esculenta*). Here the whole plant is eaten — root, stem and leaves.

THE ROAD TO TOLAGNARO (FORT DAUPHIN)

The price for a taxi-brousse from Toliara to Tolagnaro is about 35,000fmg. The trip usually takes three days. The fastest public vehicle is the Besalara truck, a Mercedes; the slowest is the Bienvenue. It's a shame to pass straight through such an exciting area, however. Much more interesting is to rent a vehicle and driver, or to do the trip by a combination of walking and whatever transport comes along. Luc Selleslagh took this option and provided the information that follows.

20km south of Betioky is the small village of **Ambatry**. The Mahafaly tombs near here are particularly interesting. Next comes **Ejeda**, about 2½ hours from Betioky on a reasonable dirt road. In the dry season you can watch the activity on the dry river bed. Holes are dug to reach the water: upstream for drinking, midstream for washing, and downstream for clothes. The hotel here costs 3,000fmg. 'Good value for money: almost no value but also almost no money.' About 10km south of Ejeda are a few big Mahafaly tombs, one with over 50 zebu horns. Look for them on the right, on a hill.

Ejeda to Ampanihy takes about five hours by truck on a very bad, rocky road.

Ampanihy

The name means 'the place of bats'. For a while it was the place of the mohair goats, but now that industry has collapsed it's just a town on the road south. But it's worth a couple of days. Luc saw (in December) wonderful sunsets every night, and recommends a visit to the WWF nursery for endemic plants. It's near the Protestant church. Walk 2km south to some good Mahafaly tombs. Expect to be found by the *lycée*'s English teacher, Andrianasolo Kotomantsoa, who loves to practise his English on native speakers. He would be happy to receive any books or magazines you have finished with.

Where to stay/eat

Motel Relais d'Ampanihy 25,000fmg provides a touch of luxury in the desert. No hot water. Wonderful food. The owner, Luc Vital, can organise excursions to the forest adjoining the River Menarandra (lemurs), and to see baobabs and Mahafaly tombs.

Hotel Tahio About 300m from the big market. New, very friendly, 7,500fmg. Good, reasonably priced meals. Showers. Highly recommended.

After Ampanihy you enter Antandroy country and will understand why they are called 'People of the thorns'. The road deteriorates (if you thought that possible) as you make your way to **Tranaroa** (about five hours). There's an interesting Antandroy tomb here crowned by an aeroplane which moves in the wind. Another five hours and you approach Beloha on an improving road (much favoured by tortoises, which thrive in the area since it is *fady* to eat them) and with tombs all around.

Beloha has a basic hotel, rather overpriced at 10,000fmg. To raise flagging spirits there is a bar, Les Trois Frères, which serves ice-cold drinks. Luc recommends a visit to the new Catholic church with its beautiful stained glass, made by a local craftsman. Near Beloha is a good area of spiny forest.

Between Beloha and **Tsihombe** is the most interesting stretch of the entire journey. There are baobabs, tortoises (sadly it is not *fady* for the local Antanosy to eat them) and some wonderful tombs. 'On one occasion it was like arriving at a journey-fair. A tomb with a life-size taxi-brousse, one with a big aeroplane, and another with an ocean steamer! There are also people to ask for money to see these attractions.' These tombs are about 33km before Tsihombe.

'If "be" means "big" then "Tsihom" must mean "cockroach"!' Luc describes his night with an army of huge, hissing cockroaches (actually one of my favourite Malagasy creatures, but I appreciate that I am in a minority), a generously proportioned spider and a scorpion. 'This was not a hotel room but a terrarium!' The hotel, fortunately, has no name.

After Tsihombe the road improves and from Ambovombe it is tarred for its home run to Tolagnaro.

Ambovombe

With the end in sight, most travellers prefer to push on to Tolgnaro, but there are several hotels in Ambovombe: the **Relais des Androy** (10,000fmg for a two-bed room, no running water; good food) and the **Hotel des Voyageurs**, both on the main street, and another across the road from the taxi-brousse station. Ambovombe has a good Monday market.

Amboasary

About 30km from Ambovombe is the village that marks the turn-off to Berenty. There is now simple accommodation here (it looks like a local initiative, so deserves support). The **Hotel-Restaurant Mandrare** is just after the village and is a series of Antanosy-style huts. You need your own sleeping bag, etc, but food is provided.

The **Hotel Bon Coin** is on the way to Lake Anony (see page 198). There is also a restaurant here.

Faux Cap and Cap Ste Marie

If you are in a four-wheel drive vehicle, or are a good hiker, you should consider taking a side trip west to the southernmost point of Madagascar.

Faux Cap is a lonely, beautiful spot, with wild breakers, enormous shifting sand-dunes, and a chance to find fragments of *aepyornis* eggs. Luc Selleslagh walked the 30km from Tsihombe and was accommodated by the very friendly Président du Fokontany and his wife. There is a small shop in the village and little else.

Cap Ste Marie is an equally spectacular place with high sandstone cliffs and dwarf plants resembling a rock garden. It is also possible to get here without a vehicle. Andrew Cooke writes: 'I suppose the highlight for me was taking a taxi-brousse to Beloha and then taking a *chavette* to Lavanono (on the coast) and then walking to Cap Ste Marie (the distance is 30km which took us two days). All the way we met great hospitality. Water is in very short supply.' Note that since Cap Ste Marie is a reserve, a permit must be purchased, and this should be arranged in Tana. Visitors arriving without a permit have been turned away.

This is a great area to see humpbacked whales; between September and November they can be observed quite close to shore with their calves.

MINING IN THE SOUTH: THE DILEMMA

The dry south of Madagascar has large deposits of titanium dioxide. Among other things this mineral is used as a base for paint. The Canadian company, Qit-Fer (owned by RTZ) wants to start mining for this mineral; their plan is for the mine to be active for 40 or 50 years. It would be the largest such venture in Madagascar and would involve the building of a US$260 million factory and port facility, with a further US$90 required to create new harbours.

The project would bring 500 new jobs to a severely depressed area of the country. Jobs would create prosperity which would reduce the pressure on the environment through *tavy* and the felling of trees for charcoal. It would mean clearing 6,000 hectares of coastal littoral forest with its endemic flora and fauna.

At present an environmental impact study is under way, but it seems likely that the project will be inaugurated in 1998.

TOLAGNARO/TAOLAÑARO (FORT DAUPHIN)
History
The remains of two forts can still be seen in or near this town on the extreme southeast tip of Madagascar: Fort Flacourt, built in 1643, and one that dates from 1504, so the oldest building in the country, which was erected by shipwrecked Portuguese sailors. This ill-fated group of 80 reluctant colonists stayed about fifteen years before falling foul of the local tribes. The survivors of the massacre fled to the surrounding countryside where disease and hostile natives finished them off.

1642 saw a French expedition, organised by the Société Française de l'Orient and led by Sieur Pronis with instructions to 'found colonies and commerce in Madagascar and to take possession of it in the name of His Most Christian Majesty'. An early settlement at the Bay of Sainte Luce was soon abandoned in favour of a healthier peninsula to the south, and a fort was built and named after the Dauphin (later Louis XIV) in 1643. At first the Antanosy were quite keen on the commerce part of the deal but were less enthusiastic about losing their land. The heavily defended fort only survived by use of force and with many casualties from both sides. The French finally abandoned the place in 1674, but their 30 year occupation formed one of the foundations of the later claim to the island as a French colony. During this period the first published work on Madagascar was written by Pronis's successor, Etienne de Flacourt. His *Histoire de la Grande Île de Madagascar* brought the island's amazing flora and fauna to the attention of European naturalists, and is still used as a valuable historical source book.

Tolagnaro/Fort Dauphin today
The town itself is unattractive, but it is the most beautifully located of all tourist destinations in Madagascar. Built on a small peninsula, the town is bordered on three sides by beaches and breakers and backed by high green mountains which dwindle into spiny forest to the west. More geared to tourism than any other Malagasy mainland town, Fort Dauphin offers a variety of exceptionally interesting excursions (Berenty, the spiny forest, the Portuguese Fort, the Bay of Sainte Luce) and some fine beaches.

Note: after my earlier conscientious use of the Malagasy 'Tolagnaro', I'm reverting to 'Fort Dauphin' because that is still the name most people connected with tourism use, so it is, perhaps, less confusing to the reader.

Warning
Fort Dauphin is buffeted by almost continuous strong winds in September and much of October.

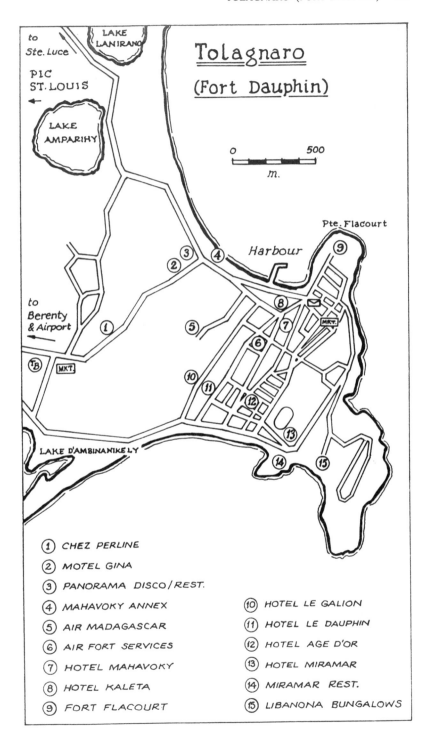

Tolagnaro (Fort Dauphin)

to Ste. Luce

PIC ST. LOUIS

LAKE LANIRANO

LAKE AMPARIHY

0   500
m.

Pte. Flacourt

Harbour

to Berenty & Airport

LAKE D'AMBINANIKELY

① CHEZ PERLINE

② MOTEL GINA

③ PANORAMA DISCO / REST.

④ MAHAVOKY ANNEX

⑤ AIR MADAGASCAR

⑥ AIR FORT SERVICES

⑦ HOTEL MAHAVOKY

⑧ HOTEL KALETA

⑨ FORT FLACOURT

⑩ HOTEL LE GALION

⑪ HOTEL LE DAUPHIN

⑫ HOTEL AGE D'OR

⑬ HOTEL MIRAMAR

⑭ MIRAMAR REST.

⑮ LIBANONA BUNGALOWS

Getting there

Road   The overland route from Tana is reportedly best done with the company SONATRA which operates from the taxi-brousse station on the far side of Lake Anosy. They use 'Tata' buses and go via Ihosy, Betroka and Ambovombe. You should book your seat as far in advance as possible. The fare is around 45,000fmg. From Ihosy it's 35,000fmg.

Air   There are flights to Fort Dauphin four days a week (check the latest Air Mad schedule) for 885FF/US$150. Sit on the right for the best views of Fort Dauphin's mountains and bays. Flights are usually heavily booked. The airport has recently been spruced up and is now quite efficient.

Where to stay

Most of Fort Dauphin belongs to M Jean de Heaulme, the owner of Berenty reserve. His hotels are the Dauphin, the Galion, and the Miramar. You are expected to stay in one of these if you want to visit Berenty, but it is not compulsory.

Category A

Hotels Dauphin and **Galion**   PO Box 54. Tel: 210 48. The Dauphin is the main hotel and Galion its annexe. Meals (excellent) are taken in the Dauphin which has a lovely garden with a crocodile pool. There is now just one croc, destined for a transfer to the botanical garden. Her name is Caroline. She may seem boringly inactive but note this report from a European reader: 'My friend had her hand slightly put on the mesh-wire of the pool, one crocodile being asleep three metres from her, when this "asleep" beast rushed on her like an arrow and bit two fingers of her hand off!'.

Prices are 308FF single and 336FF double. The manager, Saymoi, is very friendly and helpful and speaks good English.

Hotel Miramar   The most beautifully situated hotel and best restaurant in Fort Dauphin. On a promontory overlooking Libanona beach, which is excellent for swimming, sunbathing and tide-pooling. There is a limited number of rooms costing the same as the Dauphin, through which bookings must be made. The restaurant is about 50 metres from the hotel itself, with a superb view overlooking Libanona beach; a rough walk in the dark (bring a torch).

Libanona Beach   BP 70. Tel: 213 78). Its location vies with the Miramar as the best in Fort Dauphin, but the bungalows vary in quality.

Other guesthouses are springing up in the beach area.

Hotel Kaleta   Tel: 212 87 or 213 97. Under the same management as Libanona Beach (both are government-owned), so the same BP number. A 32-room hotel in the centre of town offering a good alternative for those looking for comfort and lemurs but unable to afford the De Heaulme/Berenty prices. Run by a husband and wife team, Armand and Janette Rivert.

Category B

Motel Gina   Six pleasant thatched bungalows located on the outskirts of town. 24,000fmg. Good restaurant.

Hotel Casino   A little further out of town and similar in quality to the Gina.

Category C

Hotel Mahavoky   Town centre opposite the Catholic cathedral. 12,000fmg. Occupies an old missionary school, which gives added interest, and is recommended by everyone for its helpful, English-speaking manager and excellent restaurant. Consequently it is often full.

Maison Age d'Or   Readers' praise has been heaped on this little two-room establishment and its hugely hospitable host, M Hasimboto, known universally as M Maison Age d'Or. He and his family speak only French, but if you can communicate in this language you will learn a great deal about Madagascar. The two rooms cost 7,500 and 10,000fmg.

Where to eat

In Fort Dauphin eating is taken seriously. All the Category A hotels serve very good food with an emphasis on 'fruits de mer'. **Gina's**, part of the hotel of the same name, is said by some to serve the best food in town. Favourites with expatriates are the **Mahavoky Annex**, across from the BTM bank. 'An excellent little restaurant. The name means "to make satisfied with food!"' and **Chez Perline**: 'A great small resto near the markets. Wonderful food but expect to wait at least an hour to get it! **Chez Anita** serves delicious *Sambos* and zebu brochettes, while providing entertainment with a television that alternates between French-dubbed action movies and Malagasy pop-stars singing favourite tunes. The sound and picture quality is so bad it's impossible to know what's going on, but everyone sits glued to the tube anyway!' (Raoul Mulder). There are other small restaurants in the market area, some of which serve great food. Making your own discoveries is part of the fun.

Other recommendations include the **Panorama** (renowned for its disco; see *Nightlife*) and the **Belle Azur** which is very cheap but some way out of town near the airport. Also on the road to the airport is **Relax Mini Resto**, which has a good selection of meals at very reasonable prices. 'An excellent place to stop for a rest on your return from climbing Pic St Louis.'

Nightlife

'The Panorama disco is an institution for locals. Open every night except Mondays, this is rated by everyone who has been there as Madagascar's best disco. Much of its appeal is in its location, perched on the edge of the bay. When you get too hot and sweaty from dancing you can take a stroll outside to cool off in the ocean breeze and watch the waves roll in. Especially great at full moon.' (R. Mulder)

Excursions

Air Fort Services is a tour operator which hires out bicycles, vehicles (from cars to buses), and even small planes, as well as offering a variety of tours. They are located on Ave Gallieni. Postal address: BP 159. Tel: 212 34 or 212 64; fax: 212 24 or 261 9. The rate for renting a 4WD vehicle is 50,000fmg plus 500fmg per kilometre.

EXCURSIONS AROUND TOWN

Apart from its lively market, Fort Dauphin offers a choice of beach and mountain.

The beach is **Libanona**, with excellent swimming and superb tidepools. Admirers of the weird and wonderful can spend many hours poking around at low tide. The pools to the right of the beach seem the best. Look out for a bizarre, frilly nudibranch or sea-hare, anemones, and other extraordinary invertebrates. There is another beach below the Hotel Dauphin, but this is dirty (turdy) and there have been muggings here.

Pic Louis, the mountain that dominates the town, is quite an easy climb up a good path and offers nice views. The trail starts opposite SIFOR, the sisal factory about 3km along the road to Lanirano. Alternatively you can take a taxi to the RC mission near the airport; the trail goes up past the statue of the Virgin Mary. Allow at least a half day to get up there and back — or better still take a picnic. It is a strenuous climb in the midday sun. If you're unsure about doing it on your own several hotels/tour operators run trips up there.

Another arm of the De Heaulme empire is the **Botanical Gardens** situated about 16km out of town towards St Luce.

FURTHER AFIELD

Apart from Berenty, which is described later, there are numerous places to visit in this beautiful part of Madagascar. If you haven't a car you will probably need to join an organised trip. Many hotels run excursions and Air Fort Services go to most places.

Portuguese Fort (Île aux Portuguais)

The tour to the old fort, built in 1504, involves a *pirogue* ride up the river Vinanibe, about 6km from Fort Dauphin, and then a short walk to the sturdy-looking stone fortress (the walls are one metre thick) set in zebu-grazed parkland.

Baie Sainte Luce

About 65km north-east of Fort Dauphin is the beautiful and historically interesting Ste Luce Bay where the French colonists of 1638 first landed. This tour is universally praised by all who've done it.

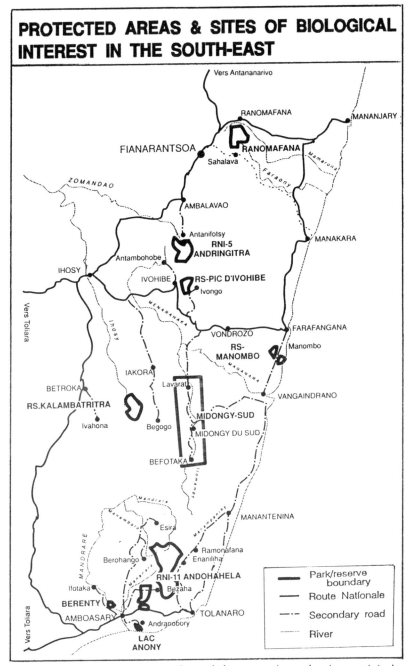

PROTECTED AREAS & SITES OF BIOLOGICAL INTEREST IN THE SOUTH-EAST

Map reproduced from *Madagascar: Revue de la conservation et des aires protégées* by kind permission of the WWF, Switzerland.

Lokaro

Another popular excursion which begins at Lake Lanirano, just north of Fort Dauphin, then passes through various waterways. The trip culminates in a 1½ hour walk to the final destination, a beach resort. The cost is about 50,000fmg including meals.

SISAL

This crop was introduced to Madagascar in the inter-war years, with the first exports taking place in 1922 when 42 tons were sent to France. By 1938 2,537 tons were exported and 3,500 hectares of sisal were planted in the Tuléar and Fort Dauphin region. By 1950 production reached 3,080 tons. In 1952 a synthetic substitute was developed in the US and the market dropped. The French government stepped in with subsidies and bought 10,000 tons.

The Tuléar plantations were closed in 1958 leaving only the De Heaulme plantations. In 1960 these covered 16,000 hectares, and by 1993 30,000 hectares of endemic spiny forest had been cleared to make way for the crop.

BERENTY RESERVE

This is the key destination of most package tours and I've never known a visitor who hasn't loved Berenty (well, there was one...). The combination of tame lemurs, comfortable accommodation and the tranquillity of the forest trails makes this *the* Madagascar memory for many people. The danger is that Berenty is already becoming overcrowded, and too many groups bring problems. Fortunately there is only a limited amount of accommodation, so if you can arrange to spend a night or two you can still have the reserve to yourself in the magic hours of dawn and dusk.

Visits to the reserve must be organised through the Hotel Dauphin and are quite expensive: 65,000fmg per person for transport, and 168FF per person for the night in bungalows. Meals are 10,000fmg.

If your local guide is Roger you are lucky; he is very professional and informative.

The route to Berenty

The reserve lies some 80km to the west of Fort Dauphin, amid a vast sisal plantation, and the drive there is part of the experience. For the first half of the journey the skyline is composed of rugged green mountains often backed by menacing grey clouds or obscured by rain. Travellers' trees (*ravenala*) dot the landscape, and near Ranopiso is a grove of the very rare three-cornered palm, *Neodypsis decary*. To see an example close to, wait until you arrive in Berenty where there is one near the entrance gate.

The first stop is to visit some pitcher plants – *Nepenthes madagascariensis* – whose nearest relatives are in Asia. The yellow 'flowers' (actually modified leaves) lure insects into their sticky depths where they are digested, probably for their nitrogen content.

The next (optional) stop before reaching the spiny forest is at an Antanosy 'tomb' (actually the dead are buried elsewhere) known as the tomb of Ranonda. It was carved by the renowned sculptor Fiasia. The artistry of this unpainted wooden memorial is of a very high standard although the carvings are deteriorating in the frequently wet weather. There's a girl carrying the Christian emblems of bible and cross, someone losing a leg to a crocodile, and the most famous piece, a boatload of people who are said to have died in a *pirogue* accident. On the far side there used to be a charming herd of zebu, portrayed with unusual liveliness (a cow turns her head to lick her suckling calf). In 1990 the cow and her calf were ripped away by thieves. To add to the poignancy, a row of cattle skulls indicate the zebu that had to be sacrificed to counteract this sacrilege. One hopes the revenge of the Ancestors was terrible.

The very reasonable response by the villagers to this desecration has been to fence the tombs and charge tourists an admission fee of 20,000fmg.

In the area are other memorials, but without carvings. These cenotaphs commemorate those buried in a communal tomb or where the body could not be recovered, and look like clusters of missiles lurking in the forest.

Shortly after Ranopiso there is a dramatic change in the scenery: within a few kilometres the hills flatten and disappear, the clouds clear, and the bizarre fingers of Didierea and Alluaudia appear on the skyline interspersed with the bulky trunks of baobabs. You are entering the spiny forest, making the transition from the Eastern Domain to the Southern Domain. If you are on a Berenty tour your guide will identify some of the flora; if on your own turn to page 168.

The exhilaration of driving through the spiny forest is dampened by the sight of all the charcoal sellers waiting by their sacks of ex-Alluaudia. These marvellous trees are being cut down at an alarming rate by people who have no other means of survival. While condemning the practice give uneasy thought to the fact that your sumptuous meals in Berenty will be cooked on stoves fuelled with locally-produced charcoal.

Amboasary (for accommodation see page 184) is the last town before the bridge across the River Mandrare and the turn off to Berenty. The rutted red road takes you past acres of sisal and some lonely-looking baobabs, to the entrance of the reserve.

The reserve

The name means 'big eel' but Berenty is famous for its population of ringtailed lemurs and sifakas. Henri de Heaulme and now his son Jean have made this one of the best protected and studied 260 hectares of forest in Madagascar. Although in the arid south, its location along the River Mandrare ensures a well-watered habitat (gallery or riverine forest) for the large variety of animals that live there. In previous years the forest itself was threatened by the rampant spread of the cactus-like 'rubber vine', *Cissus quadrangularis*, but this is being vigorously tackled.

The following species of lemur are sure to be seen: brown lemur, ringtailed lemur and sifaka. The lemurs here are well used to people and the ringtails will jump on your shoulders to eat proffered bananas. *Lemur catta* have an air of swaggering arrogance, are as at home on the ground as in trees, and are highly photogenic with their black and white markings and waving striped tails. These fluffy tails play an important part in communication and act as benign weapons against neighbouring troops which might have designs on their territory. Ringtailed lemurs indulge in 'stink fights' when they scent their tails with the musk secreted from wrist and anal glands and wave them in the neighbours' faces; that is usually enough to make a potential intruder retreat. They also rub their anal glands on the trunks of trees and score the bark with their wrist-spur to scent-mark their territory. There are approximately 350 ringtailed lemurs in Berenty, and the population has stayed remarkably stable considering that only about a quarter of the babies survive to adulthood. The females which, like most lemurs, are dominant over the males, are receptive to mating for only a week or so in April/May, so there is plenty of competition amongst the males for this once a year treat. The young are born in September and at first cling to their mother's belly, later climbing on to her back and riding jockey-style. Ringtails eat flowers, fruit and insects.

Attractive though the ringtails are, no lemur can compete with the sifaka for soft-toy cuddliness, with their creamy white fur, brown cap, and black face. Sifaka belong to the same sub-family of lemur as the indri (seen in Périnet). The species here is *Propithecus verreauxi verreauxi* and there are about 300 of them in the reserve. Unlike the ringtails, they rarely come down to the ground but when they do the length of their legs in comparison to their short arms necessitates a comical form of locomotion: they stand upright and jump with their feet together like competitors in a sack race. The best places to see them do this is on the trail to the left at the river and across the road near the aeroplane hangar near the restaurant/museum. Sifaka troop boundaries do not change, so your guide will know where to find the animals. The young are born in July. Like the ringtails, sifaka make a speciality of sunbathing – spreading their arms to the morning rays from the top of their trees. They feed primarily on leaves and tamarind fruit so are not interested in tourist-proffered bananas.

The brown lemurs of Berenty were introduced from the west and are now well established and almost as tame as the ringtails. Recent studies have concluded that all the Berenty brown lemurs are hybrids of *Lemur fulvus rufus* and *Lemur fulvus collaris*. They are now called *Eulemur fulvus*. The number has risen from eight in 1974 to 146 in 1993. In contrast with other lemurs, the brown lemurs are not female dominant. Their diet consists mainly of tamarind leaves.

There are other lemurs which, being nocturnal, are harder to see although the lepilemur can be observed peering out of its hollow tree nest during the day. Mouse lemurs may be glimpsed in the beam of a torch/flashlight, especially in the area of spiny forest near the reserve, a popular destination for night walks.

Apart from lemurs there are other striking mammals. Fruit bats or flying foxes live in noisy groups on 'bat trees' in one part of the forest; with their wingspan of over a metre they are an impressive sight.

Bird-watching is rewarding in Berenty, and even better in Bealoka ('Place of much shade') beyond the sisal factory. Nearly 100 species have been recorded. You are likely to see several families unique to Madagascar, including the hook-billed vanga, and two handsome species of couas – the crested coua and the giant coua with its dramatic blue face-markings. The latter likes to nest in the tops of acacia trees. The cuckoo-like coucal is common, as are grey-headed love-birds and the beautiful paradise flycatcher with its long tail feathers (a subspecies of the genus that occurs in East Africa). These birds come in two colour phases: chestnut brown and white. Two-thirds of the Berenty paradise flycatchers are white. Look out for the nest which is built 3 to 4 feet from the ground.

If you visit from mid-October to May you will see a variety of migrant

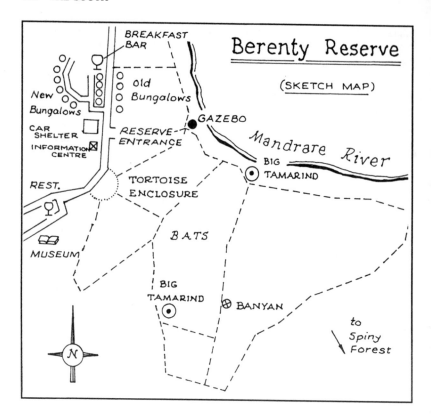

birds from south-east Africa: broad-billed roller, dwarf cuckoo and lots of waders (sanderlings, greenshank, sandpiper, white-throated plover).

The joy of Berenty is the selection of broad forest trails that allow safe wandering on your own, including nocturnal jaunts (remember, many creatures are only active at night and are easy to spot with a torch/flashight; also moths' and spiders' eyes shine red, and all sorts of other arthropods and reptiles can be easily seen. By getting up at dawn you can do your best bird-watching, see the sifakas opening their arms to the sun, and enjoy the coolness of the forest before going in to breakfast.

Berenty has been welcoming tourists longer than any other place in Madagascar, and all who fall in love with it will want to do what they can to preserve it and its inhabitants. Helen Crowley, the reserve manager, has reduced the amount of banana feeding to the area around the bungalows and restaurants, to allow more natural lemur behaviour in the forest. Alison Jolly (who has done long-term studies on the lemurs and the effects of banana feeding) suggests that visitors limit themselves to two bananas per person. Voluntary restraints of this sort will avoid a 'Galapagisation' of Berenty, where strict rules will have to be imposed on tourists to protect the wildlife.

Under Helen's energetic management, Berenty has become instructive as well as enjoyable. An Information Centre has recently opened and there is a library available for students. A museum of Antandroy culture helps us to know the human inhabitants of the region as well as the animals.

Excursions from Berenty include an area (within the reserve) of spiny forest, and a visit to the sisal factory, which sounds boring but is, in fact, fascinating.

Although you are free to explore the reserve on your own, a tour with the excellent English-speaking guides, Andreas or Hambafehy, will greatly increase your knowledge and understanding.

Commonly seen species
* = endemic

Birds
Little egret (black form) (*Egretta garzetta dimorpha*)
Night heron (*Nycticorax nycticorax*)
Purple heron (*Ardea purpurea Madagascariensis*)
White-faced whistling duck (*Dendrocygna viduata*)
Madagascar turtle dove* (*Streptopelia picturata*)
Helmeted guinea-fowl (*Numida mitrata*)
Yellow-billed kite (*Milvus migrans*)
Madagascar kestrel* (*Falco newtoni*)
Madagascar harrier hawk* (*Polyboroides radiatus*)
Madagascar buzzard* (*Buteo brachypterus*)
Madagascar Scops owl* (*Otus rutilus*)
Lesser Vasa parrot* (*Coracopsis nigra*)
Greater Vasa parrot (*Coracopsis vasa*)
Madagascar coucal (* − but also breeds on Aldabra) (*Centropus toulou*)
Giant coua* (*Coua gigas*)
Crested coua* (*Coua cristata*)
Hooked-billed vanga* (*Vanga curvirostrus*)
Madagascar crested drongo* (*Dicrurus forficatus*)
Madagascar Magpie robin* (*Copsychus albospecularis*)
Madagascar paradise flycatcher* (*Terpsiphone mutata*)
Souimanga sunbird* (*Nectarinia souimanga*)
Madagascar bulbul* (*Hypsipetes madagascariensis*)
Broad-billed roller (*Eurystomus glaucurus*)
Madagascar cuckoo shrike* (*Coracina cinerea*)
Grey-headed love bird* (*Agapornis cana*)
Madagascar white eye* (*Zosterops maderaspatana*)
Pied crow (*Corvus albus*)

Mammals
Ringtailed lemur (*Lemur catta*)
Brown lemur (*Eulemur fulvus*)
White sifaka (*Propithecus verreauxi verreauxi*)
Lepilemur (*Lepilemur leucopus*)
Mouse lemur (*Microcebus murinus*)
Flying fox (*Pteropus rufus*)

Reptiles
Chameleo ousteleti
Chameleo vericocus
Chameleo lateralis
Three-eyed lizard (*Chalarodon madagascariensis*)
Spiny-tailed iguana (*Opluros curvieri*)
Land boa (*Acrantophis madagascariensis*
Tree boa (*Sanzinia madagascariensis*)

Kaleta Park (Amboasary-Sud)
The management of the Kaleta, Libanona and Gina hotels have gone into competition with Berenty by starting their own lemur reserve, just south of the Berenty turn off. This is considerably cheaper than its rival, and most (but not all) visitors speak highly of it. For the specialist naturalist it cannot compare to Berenty because it is degraded forest (ie not in its natural state) and has been browsed by domestic animals, so you are unlikely to see the rarer small creatures. That said, however, the average Berenty visitor is mainly interested in lemurs, which can be seen here in abundance, so a visit to Amboasary can be equally rewarding.

The reserve is run by Rolande Laha, who for many years worked in Berenty and makes guests feel really special; it is geared to independent travellers rather than groups, and for day trips. Camping is allowed but costs 10,000fmg per person with no facilities. The cost for a day's visit is 50,000fmg which includes lunch and a visit to a sisal factory.

One of the attractions here is the sifakas which are more approachable than in Berenty and even accept food from visitors. Whether this is a Good Thing I'm not sure, but it is certainly a marvellous experience.

The usual Berenty extras along the road to Ambovombe – tombs and pitcher plants – are also visited.

Lac Anony
About 12km south of Amboasary is a brackish lagoon, Lac Anony. There are flamingoes here and a large number of other wading birds in a lunar landscape. There is a village, Antsovelo, and accommodation and food are available.

Andohahela

At present this is a Strict Nature Reserve, and so closed to tourists. Plans are afoot, however, to reclassify parts of the reserve as a National Park, thus allowing visitors access to one of Madagascar's most diverse and exciting regions.

The reserve spans rain forest and spiny forest, and thus is of major importance and interest. A third component is a the east/west transition forest which is the last place the triangulated palm (*Neodypsis decaryi*) can be found. These three distinct zones make Andohahela unique in its biodiversity.

At the time of writing ecological monitoring is underway (financed by USAID and two American foundations) before a decision about if or when reclassification can take place. It is widely recognised that tourist revenue will do much to help this economically depressed region, and access to this wonderful reserve will certainly make for happy tourist-naturalists! For an update contact ANGAP in Antananarivo.

'When this island was first inhabited the ground was all cleared by means of fire. It would, however, have been prudent to leave rows of trees here and there at certain distances. Those rains, which in warm countries are so necessary to render the earth fertile, seldom fall on ground after it has been cleared; for it is the forests that attract the clouds and draw moisture from them... cultivation without measure, and without method, has sometimes done much more hurt than good'.
Abbe Rochon, A Voyage to Madagascar and the East Indies, *1792*

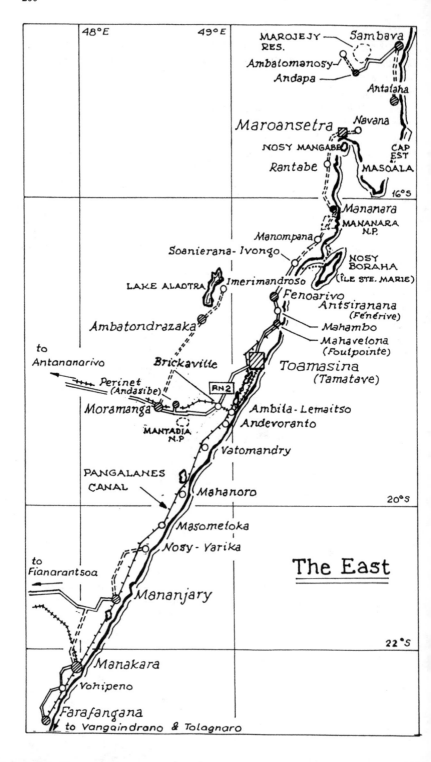

Chapter 9

The East

INTRODUCTION

Punished by its weather (rain, cyclones), the east coast is notoriously challenging to travellers. In July 1816 James Hastie wrote in his diary: 'If this is the good season for travelling this country, I assert it is impossible to proceed in the bad'. With this in mind you should avoid the wettest months of February to March, and remember that June to August can be very damp as well. The driest months are September to November, with December to January worth the risk. April and May are fairly safe apart from the possibility of cyclones.

The east coast has another problem: sharks (see Box, page 208). So although there are beautiful beaches, swimming is only safe in protected areas. Despite this, there is plenty to draw the adventurous traveller. Much of Madagascar's unique flora and fauna is concentrated in the eastern rainforests and any serious naturalist will want to pay a visit. So should others for the rugged mountain scenery with rivers tumbling down to the Indian Ocean, the friendly people, abundant fruit and seafood, and the lovely island of Nosy Boraha (Sainte Marie).

The chief products are coffee, vanilla, bananas, coconuts and cloves.

This region has an interesting history dominated by European pirates and slave traders. While powerful kingdoms were being forged in other parts of the country, the east coast remained divided among numerous small clans. It was not until the 18th century that one ruler, Ratsimilaho, unified the region. The half-caste son of Thomas White, an English pirate, and briefly educated in Britain, Ratsimilaho responded to the attempt by Chief Ramanano to take over all the east coast ports. His successful revolt was furthered by his judiciously marrying an important princess; by his death in 1754 he ruled an area stretching from the Masoala Peninsula to Mananjary.

The result of this liaison of various tribes was the Betsimisaraka, now the second largest ethnic group in Madagascar. Some (in the area of Maroantsetra) practise second burial, although with less ritual than the Merina and Betsileo.

Getting around

Although the map shows roads of some sort running almost the full length of the east coast, this is deceptive. Rain and cyclones regularly destroy bridges so it is impossible to know in advance whether a selected route will be usable, even in the 'dry' season. The rain-saturated forests drain into the Indian Ocean in numerous rivers, many of which can only be crossed by ferry. And there is not enough traffic to ensure a regular service. For those with limited time, therefore, the only practical way to get to the less accessible towns is by air: there are regular planes to Nosy Boraha (Île Sainte Marie), and usually flights between Toamasina (Tamatave) and Antsiranana (Diego Suarez). There are flights several days a week from Toamasina to Maroantsetra, Antalaha and Mananara, and to Sambava.

For the truly adventurous it *is* possible to work your way down (or up) the coast providing you have plenty of time and are not afraid of walking.

TOAMASINA (TAMATAVE)

History

As in all the east coast ports, Toamasina (pronounced 'Tourmasin') began as a pirate community. In the late 18th century its harbour attracted the French, who already had a foothold in Île Sainte Marie, and Napoleon I sent his agent Sylvain Roux to establish a trading post there. In 1811, Sir Robert Farquhar, governor of the newly British island of Mauritius, sent a small naval squadron to take the port of Toamasina. This was not simply an extension of the usual British/French antagonism, but an effort to stamp out slavery at its source, Madagascar being the main supplier to the Indian Ocean. The slave trade had been abolished by the British Parliament in 1807. The attack was successful, Sylvain Roux was exiled, and a small British garrison remained. During subsequent years, trade between Mauritius and Madagascar built Toamasina into a major port. In 1845, after a royal edict subjecting European traders to the harsh Malagasy laws, French and British warships bombarded Toamasina, but a landing was repelled leaving 20 dead. During the 1883-85 war the French occupied Toamasina but Malagasy troops successfully defended the fort of Farafaty just outside the town.

Theories on the origin of the name Toamasina vary, but one is that King Radama I tasted the sea-water here and remarked 'Toa masina' – It's salty.

Toamasina (Tamatave) today

Following cyclone Geralda, which struck on February 2 1994 with winds of 230mph, there is today not much left of Toamasina. It was the worst cyclone since 1927 and destroyed more than 360,000 buildings. However, the people of this port are used to rebuilding their city, and that's what they are doing. By the time you read this things should be back to normal. Most of my information is pre-cyclone.

Before Geralda, Toamasina had an agreeable look of shabby elegance with some fine palm-lined boulevards and once-impressive colonial houses. There was always a good variety of bars, snackbars and restaurants, and I would expect them to be the first to open their doors.

Getting there

Road. Poor Madagascar! The new road linking the capital to the country's main port has been in the process of improvement for 20 years. First the Chinese completed their version in 1985. This deteriorated almost immediately and a highly competent Swedish company was brought in and by 1993 RN2 was the best — and most heavily used — road in the country.

BY TRAIN TO THE EAST COAST

The train from Antananarivo to Tamatave is considered to be one of the great railway journeys of the world. Between 1901 and 1913, 3000 Chinese coolies provided by the government of Indo-China laboured to complete the line. The mortality rate was 23 per cent. 240 Indian workers were also involved in the scheme. When even more workmen were needed, the colonial government imposed a 'labour tax' which required each Malagasy male living near the route to work for 40 days on the project.

For 375 km the railway runs through tunnels, over viaducts, and on the edge of cliffs overlooking tumbling rivers. After a dawn start from Tana, the train goes south, circling the city before heading east through typical scenery of the *Hauts Plateaux* — paddy fields, villages, and rocky outcrops (if you sit on the right you'll have the best views). Then, after Manjakandriana, comes a welcome area of forest before the train climbs up to the Angavo massif, gateway to the east. Here it reaches its highest point just before Anjiro, where the railway makes a complete loop, running under itself, before starting the descent. The scenery gradually changes, from the transition zone of bamboo, to what is left of the evergreen rainforest. Look out for the large river Mangoro which you cross soon after Ambohibary. Moramanga is reached in four hours, and Périnet (Andasibe) in another half hour. Here the train takes a lunch break (20 to 30 mins), to allow the first class passengers to dine at the Hotel Buffet de la Gare (see page 193). After Périnet the railway leaves the road (RN2) which it has hugged since Tana, and strikes out on its own following the river Sahatandra (Vohitra). Sit on the left for this leg of the journey; the views are spectacular. This is the stretch with tunnels and bridges every kilometre or so — an impressive feat of engineering. Passing through the remnants of the rainforest, you don't need an experienced eye to see the ravages of slash-and-burn agriculture.

Shortly before dusk (if it is winter) the train stops at Vohibinany (Brickaville), then passes through groves of traveller's trees before heading north to its destination. The map shows the tracks running right along the edge of the sea, up the narrow ribbon of land isolated by the Pangalanes lakes and canal, but the view is obscured first by dense brush and then (in winter) by darkness. The arrival in Tamatave, after a journey of twelve hours, comes as a relief.

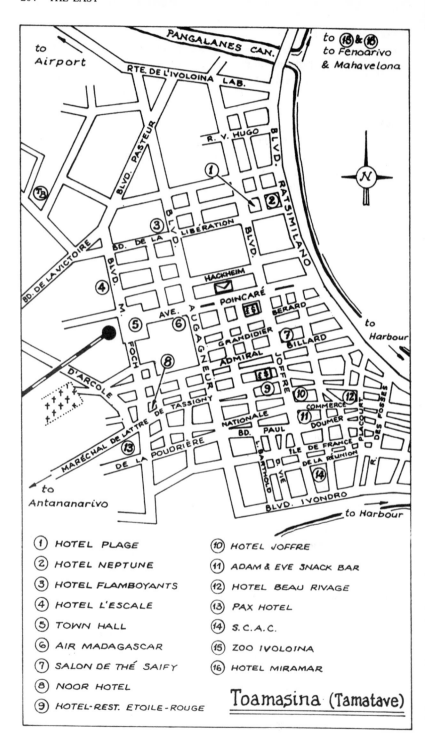

1. HOTEL PLAGE
2. HOTEL NEPTUNE
3. HOTEL FLAMBOYANTS
4. HOTEL L'ESCALE
5. TOWN HALL
6. AIR MADAGASCAR
7. SALON DE THÉ SAIFY
8. NOOR HOTEL
9. HOTEL-REST. ETOILE-ROUGE
10. HOTEL JOFFRE
11. ADAM & EVE SNACK BAR
12. HOTEL BEAU RIVAGE
13. PAX HOTEL
14. S.C.A.C.
15. ZOO IVOLOINA
16. HOTEL MIRAMAR

Toamasina (Tamatave)

It will take many months to repair cycone Geralda's damage (a traveller in April 1994 counted over 300 landslips) but the road is too important to be neglected. By the time you read this it is likely to be the best way of reaching Toamasina.

The fastest and most comfortable transport is the Fitato Bus which even has a video! The ticket office in Toamasina is about 2km beyond the taxi-brousse station. Reserve your seat one day in advance. A comfortable minibus service is run by Sodiat, whose depot in Tana is in Behoririka, near the lake. Buses leave Tana at 08.00 on Mondays, Wednesdays and Fridays, and Toamasina at the same hour on the other days (there is no Sunday service); 40,000fmg. Otherwise there are plenty of taxi-brousses which leave throughout the day; the journey takes from six to eight hours. It's best just to go along to the taxi-brousse departure point in the east of the city.

Air. There are daily flights between Tana and Toamasina for 350FF/US$60.

Train. This used to be the most popular way for tourists. The service had deteriorated long before the cyclone, however. During the political upheavals of 1991/2 the line was repeatedly sabotaged, and the management seemed to lose heart. First class carriages were removed, and the service reduced to three times a week. The line was cut by landslides in the cyclone, but should be back in operation by the time you read this and I suspect that the new tourist-aware government will try to bring back this attraction to something resembling its former glory. Information should be available at the station in Tana.

When functioning the ride takes 12 hours (twice as long as the bus) but passes through beautiful scenery. The train makes a lunch stop at the Buffet de la Gare at Andasibe, but this is too rushed. Better to bring a picnic or purchase snacks from station vendors; bring plenty of small change. The train arrives late in Toamasina so it's a good idea to pre-book a hotel for the first night.

Where to stay
Category A

Neptune   35 Boulevard Ratsimilaho (on the seafront). Tel: 322 26. Fax: 324 26. The poshest hotel in town. 442FF double. Swimming pool, excellent food, good bar. Proprietor: M. Norblin.

Noor Hotel   Tel: 338 45. At intersection of Blvd Mal. Foch and Rue de Mal. de Lattre de Tassigny (north side). About 300FF (air-conditioned), 200FF (with fan). No restaurant.

Hotel Joffre   Boulevard Joffre. Tel: 323 90. An atmospheric old hotel with all facilities, rooms in the 250FF range.

Hotel les Flamboyants   Av. de la Libération. Tel: 323 50. Air-conditioned room with WC and shower: About 250FF.

Hotel Miramar   Tel: 328 70. This beautiful new seaside hotel with swimming pool was destroyed in the cyclone, but is expected to be rebuilt.

Category B

Pax Hotel   7 Rue de la Pondriere (about 800m from the station, turn right on leaving the station and head down Blvd Foch. The hotel is down a small street on the right). Tel: 329 76. Double room with shower 15,000fmg, room with 2 beds 17,000fmg.

Hotel Etoile-Rouge   13 Rue de Lattre de Tassigny. Tel: 322 90. About 17,000fmg for a room with twin beds. Recommended.

Category C

Hotel Plage   Boulevard de la Libération (round the corner from the Neptune). 25,000fmg, with shower, 15,000fmg without. Very noisy at times (night club downstairs) but quite clean and comfortable.

Hotel Beau Rivage   (better known by the name of its restaurant, La Paillotte). Rue de Commerce (near the Adam and Eve Snack Bar). 12 rooms. Noisy (all-night disco) but good value. About 15,000fmg.

Hotel L'Escale   Near the station, 15,000fmg. Outside shower and WC.

Hotel Capucine   Near the station (off Blvd Poincare, opposite the Hotel de Ville). Clean, friendly. Outside bathroom. 15,000fmg.

Where to eat

The Hotel **Neptune** has the best restaurant; especially recommended is its all-you-can-eat Sunday buffet (lunch). The **Joffre** and **Flamboyants** are almost as good.

Restaurant Fortuna   Popular Chinese restaurant near the Joffre Hotel (11 Rue de la Batterie. Tel: 338 28). Open lunchtime and 18.00 to 21.30. Opposite is the Restaurant **La Pacific**, also Chinese, said to be cheaper and better than the Fortuna.

Queens Club   (round the corner from the Hotel Plage). Recommended.

Salon de Thé Saify   (near Hotel Joffre). Excellent selection of cakes and snacks.

Adam & Eve Snack Bar   13 Rue Nationale. Tel: 334 56 (near Hotel Joffre). 'Best cuppa in Madagascar'.

Patisserie du Coeur   'This excellent Chinese-run cafe next to the taxi-brousse station is a good place to wait until the price for a taxi-be is bargained down.' (R. Wade).

JAWS

Sharks are a real danger to swimmers in unprotected bays on the east coast, where an average of 12 people a year die in this way. Shark associated deaths seem particularly high in Toamasina – everyone has a gruesome story. Often the victims were in quite shallow water and one tourist died of his injuries after an attack when he was wading.

So however inviting the water, only swim in areas protected by a coral reef or artificial shark barrier. Ask local advice – the French for shark is *requin* and in Malagasy *Antsantsa*.

Here's a further alarming piece of information. In 1993, 90 people died after eating the meat from one shark. The source of the poison has not been discovered.

Car and bicycle hire

Aventour has an office here: Rue Bir Hakeim. Tel: 322 43.

A bike hire service has opened behind the Hotel Joffre (you may have to ask around to find it). About 5,000fmg per half day, 7,000fmg full day.

Excursions from Toamasina

Zoo Ivoloina

This began life in 1898 as a rather grand Botanical Garden, but is now an animal rehabilitation centre and zoo, funded mainly by Duke University (North Carolina) and restored with great dedication by Charles Welch and Andrea Katz. Other donors are the Madagascar Fauna Group and Wildlife Preservation Trust International. Radiated tortoises and lemurs live in ample enclosures, and there is also an education pavilion and a library. The black and white ruffed lemurs (*Varecia variegata variegata*) are unique in Madagascar in that they were brought here from America (where they were born) to form the nucleus of a population that will eventually be returned to the wild. There are plans to breed other highly endangered lemur species such as diademed sifaka. A troop of wild brown lemurs are frequent visitors.

The zoo is 12km north of town (just right for a bike ride) and is the strongest reason to go to Toamasina. It is open daily 9.00 to 17.00; entrance fee is 3,500fmg. There are picnic tables near the entrance and refreshments are available at a kiosk next to the lake (on which you can take a pirogue trip for 5,000fmg).

If you don't want to bike it, take a taxi-brousse to Antsampanana. The turn off to the zoo is on the left, just before the Ivoloina River, from where it's a pleasant 2km walk.

Mahavelona (Foulpointe)

The road north is usually in good condition – although Geralda will have taken its toll – and a taxi or bus ride at least as far as Mahavelona is recommended. This can be done in a day, but for those with more time there are some good beach bungalows in Mahavelona.

Before reaching the town you will pass the very smart **Manda Beach** hotel (modern, double room 480FF) and the smaller, **Au Gentil Pêcheur** next door. Both offer bungalows, safe swimming, and the Gentil Pêcheur is known for its excellent food.

It is an interesting drive. You will pass cinnamon trees, palms, bananas, tropical fruit trees such as lychee, breadfruit, mangoes, and perhaps the vine that produces pepper. There should also be clove bushes. About 30km from Toamasina, on the left, you will see some open-sided sheds with corrugated iron roofs. These are Betsimisaraka grave sites: not, as sometimes stated, 'canoe burials' but the exposed part of wooden coffins containing several bodies (which are buried underground). In this area the Betsimisaraka do not practise second burial.

Mahavelona itself is unremarkable, but nearby is an interesting old circular fortress with mighty walls made from an iron-hard mixture of sand, shells and eggs. There are some old British cannons marked GR. This fortress was built in the early 19th century by the Merina governor of the town, Rafaralahy, shortly after the Merina conquest of the east coast. There may be a charge to visit the fortress.

THE ROUTE NORTH

Mahambo

A beach resort with safe swimming and some beach chalets. The best is **Le Dola**, Spanish run, with good food, mosquito nets, and endless beaches. And alternative is **Le Récif**. Beware of sandfleas on the beach.

Fenoarivo Atsinanana (Fénérive)

This is the former capital of the Betsimisaraka empire. There are several basic hotels.

Soanierana-Ivongo

There are some *hotelys* and basic hotels. **Hotel Zanatany** is a friendly, family-owned place.

There is now a reliable boat service to Île Ste Marie, which will no doubt bring more visitors to this little town. For details see page 237.

Continuing north

The tarmac ends at Soanierana-Ivongo and the condition of the road north is notoriously unreliable. As fast as bridges are repaired they wash away again. You may have a fairly smooth taxi-brousse ride with ferries taking you across the rivers, or you may end up walking for hours and wading rivers or finding a pirogue to take you across. You should get local advice before setting out, especially if you have a lot of luggage to carry or are on a tight schedule.

Manompana

For many years this town, pronounced 'Manompe', has been a departure point for Nosy Boraha/Ste Marie and in the past the friendly hotel (5,000fmg) was often taken over by *vazahas*. Now with the more reliable Soanierana Ivongo boat offering competition, Manompe is likely to slide back to its previous sleepy state.

If conditions are right, you can continue north by taxi-brousse to Mananara.

Mananara

Mananara, 185km north of Soanierana-Ivongo at the entrance to the Bay of Antongil, is the only place in Madagascar where one can be pretty much assured of seeing an aye-aye in the wild, on Aye-Aye Island (otherwise known as Roger's Island).

To visit the island you must stay **Chez Roger** in bungalows with running water and shower. Good and plentiful Chinese and Malagasy food. A room Chez Roger is 10,000fmg, meals 7,000fmg, and the excursion to Aye-Aye Island is 25,000fmg per person. 'Well worth it, although we were expecting a pristine island and Roger's Island is far from it. Sharing it with the aye-ayes are the warden and his family, dogs, chickens, pigs and a pet lemur. But seeing an aye-aye is almost guaranteed. On the night we visited we saw a mother and her baby. The warden was very entertaining and obviously very fond of, and proud of, his aye-ayes. It was a wonderful experience.' (R. Harris & G. Jackson).

An alternative hotel is the Chinese-run **Hotel Aye-Aye**, near the airport. 15,000fmg per night. Remember, though, that Aye-Aye Island is owned by Roger so to go there you must patronise his hotel.

Mananara to Maroantsetra

The intrepid Luc Stelleslagh set out in a small boat: 'On the way the sea got rougher and rougher, the waves twice as high as the boat... I thought we were going to end between the sharks. The five other passengers were all sick. I was too afraid about what was going to happen to be sick. Finally the captain decided to return!' After that Luc set out on foot. The bridges across the rivers sounded almost as dangerous but at least he was master of his fate. After two days and one lift he reached **Rantobe** from where there is at least a vehicle a day heading for Maroantsetra. Luc warns that even in ideal conditions it takes at least eight hours to go the 110km. The mind boggles at what this journey will be like now Geralda has done her bit. Possibly, however, it will force the building of new bridges. The Malagasy have embraced the saying 'If it ain't broke, don't fix it.' They just have a different idea of what constitutes broke. Luc writes: 'A good example of how the Malagasy maintain their roads comes before Rantobe. A huge tree fell over the road. Instead of cutting the log in two they made a big big hole under the tree in the road!'

MAROANTSETRA

Despite its awful weather, dodgy air-service and lack of a first class hotel this is a sought-after destination for naturalists and wildlife enthusiasts because of the nearby island reserve of Nosy Mangabe (aye-ayes, ruffed lemurs, plus uroplatus and other exciting fauna) and the Masoala Peninsula with its pristine rain forest.

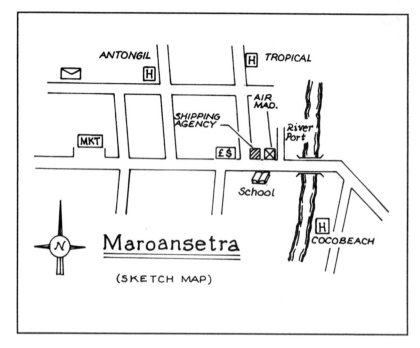

Maroantsetra is a sizable town with plenty of well-stocked shops if you want to get trekking supplies.

Weather

This is the rainiest place in Madagascar (you'd know that without reading the record books) and it's worth giving some thought to the best months to visit. Avoid March to August, when the constant wind and rain can make jungle trekking a miserable experience. September to December are the best months; January and February are possible but there is the danger of cyclones.

Getting there and away

Most people will fly. Consequently flights tend to be booked for months ahead. Check latest schedules/availability with Air Mad. The airport is 8km from town.

Real Travellers wouldn't dream of flying when there's the option of a leech-infested trail to Antalaha (see page 214) or the shark-infested sea to Mananara or Île Ste Marie (see page 237).

Where to stay/eat

Motel Coco Beach   BP 1, Maroantsetra. Tel: 18. Bungalows on the outskirts of town. Those with a cold-water shower and a WC cost 17,500fmg, but there are cheaper ones without a WC. Meals in the spacious dining room are 6,000fmg.

Permits for Nosy Mangabe can be bought from the very helpful manager, Fidel, who can also arrange boat hire from Ramil (Pierre Ramilison). One attraction of Coco Beach is the striped tenrecs running about in the garden at night.

Hotel Vatsi   New bungalows and small restaurant. Recommended.

Le Tropical   Three bungalows, good food. 10,000fmg.

Hotel Antongil   A budget hotel under the same management as the Coco Beach. Smelly WCs and the ever-present *ampela* (prostitutes) in the street outside might put you off but it's perfectly adequate.

Excursions
Andranofotsy and Navana
A very worthwhile tour is a pirogue trip up the Andranofotsy river to the village of the same name. The vegetation and riverlife viewed on the way is fascinating, and the unspoilt (so far) village, with its inquisitive inhabitants, is peaceful and endearing.

Equally worthwhile is a visit to Navana. Follow the coast east along a beach backed by thickets, through waterways clogged with flowering water-hyacinth and past plenty of forest. You need to cross a lot of water on a pirogue, a regular local service. It takes an hour through little canals and costs very little. There is a hotel in Navana. You can also get there by boat from Maroantsetra.

Nosy Mangabe
To visit the island you must have a permit. These are available from the Motel Coco Beach, as is boat hire information. The cargo boat that goes to Ste Marie usually stops at Nosy Mangabe and may be a cheaper option. All boats leave early in the morning when the Bay of Antogil is calm. It takes 45 minutes to Nosy Mangabe.

Don't forget to bring sunscreen and drinking water.

There is a camping place on the island with a natural cold shower – a waterfall. Aye-ayes are secretive and nocturnal but are becoming somewhat habituated so are more often seen these days. Anyway, there is a wealth of other creatures: ruffed lemurs (two species), brown lemurs, bright red frogs, and reptiles such as the marvellous leaf-tailed lizard, *Uroplatus fimbriatus*, chameleons, and snakes. The warden of the island will give you a guided tour and also take you to see aye-aye at night. 'The closeness with which we were able to observe these fascinating creatures made this the high point of the whole trip.' (Derry Edwards).

Nosy Mangabe is also an extraordinarily beautiful island, with sandy coves (no swimming, alas, because of sharks) and a hill (a very hard, slippery climb) topped by a lighthouse with lovely views.

The Masoala Peninsula

The peninsula (pronounced 'Mash<u>wahl</u>') is one of the largest and most diverse areas of virgin rainforest in Madagascar, and probably harbours the greatest number of unclassified species. Its importance to naturalists was recognised by the French who gave it reserve status in 1927, but sadly it was degazetted in 1964. Now the WWF are hoping it will regain protected status as a National Park which would allow ecotourism. Progress has been made in this protracted procedure.

Meanwhile energetic nature-enthusiasts can have a taste of the peninsula in an area being studied by naturalists from the Missouri Botanical Gardens and the Peregrine Fund. The access village is **Ambanizana** which can only be reached by boat (2½ hours from Maroantsetra). The boat costs 140,000fmg for a round trip (returning the next day) and the one owned by Ramil carries about 15 people. It is arranged through the Coco Beach Hotel. A larger boat (20 passengers) owned by Eric may also be available.

Put your gear in plastic bags to protect it from rain, and bring sunscreen to protect yourself from sunburn.

Near Ambanizana is The Modeste Settlement. Georges and Malene Modeste take care of the research centre and any tourists who turn up. They allocate camping space (at present you must bring your own tent but huts may be available in the future), Malene is an excellent cook and Georges an expert guide. The charges are 10,000fmg for camping and 5,000fmg for meals. Guides should receive 12,000fmg for the long, arduous trails. If Georges is not available, Hanitra Raharisoa and Pierre Ramilson know the trails and can identify some of the creatures.

You need to be fit and seriously interested in the natural world to do these hikes – the lower semi-cultivated slopes are very hot, and where it is cooler and wetter there are leeches – but they are infinitely rewarding, especially for birdwatchers. Species recorded here include helmet and Bernier's vanga, red-breasted coua and scaly groundroller. There is also a good chance of seeing red ruffed lemurs. 'We descended the mountain just before dusk. It was for me unquestionably the most incredible part of Madagascar I have experienced. I kept thinking "This is how Madagascar *should* be" because there are still 600,000 hectares of pristine, undisturbed rain-forest left... But Maroantsetra has several timber yards and foreign companies are extracting the trees.' (Derek Schuurman)

There are snorkelling possibilities around the coral reefs off Masoala but *never* go into the water without checking on safe areas with your guide; the Bay of Antogil is notorious for sharks.

Walking from Maroantsetra to Antalaha

Luc Selleslagh walked (of course) across the Masoala Peninsula. It took him five days to cover the 152km. Normally this trip is done with a guide but Luc points out this is not really necessary. The path is well used by Malagasy and if you become confused just wait for someone to come.

Abandon any idea of keeping your feet dry. A tent is useful in emergencies (and a mosquito net, or at least mosquito coils, is essential) but there are houses you can stay in and meals will be cooked for you for a reasonable charge. The villagers may expect presents. They may also expect medicines. Be cautious of introducing – or perpetuating – expectations here.

You should have the relevant FTM map. If you don't manage to buy this in Tana there is one in the Hotel Coco Beach which you can trace.

There are alternatives to the shortest route detailed below. One trail goes from Ampokafo to Ambohitralalana (Cap Est), the most easterly point of Madagascar. This goes through untouched forests and villages are few and far between. A guide is advised. It may be easier to walk *from* Ambohitralalana; see below.

Day 1. Maroantsetra to Mahalenana. Mahalenana is the village beyond Navana, described under *Excursions*. A pleasant 5km walk.

Day 2. Mahalenana to Ankovona. The track climbs into the mountains and there are rivers to cross.

Day 3. Ankovona to Ampokafo. A long trek to Ampokafo which marks the halfway point. Very hilly and very beautiful, with lots of streams and orchids. The village has a small shop.

Day 4. Ampokafo to Analampontsy. Less wild, but still orchids along the way. Most villages en route have shops.

Day 5. Analampontsy to Antalaha. You emerge onto the road at the village of Marfinar, about 30km from Antalaha. From here you can get a taxi-brousse to Antalaha.

Antalaha

A prosperous, vanilla-financed town with large houses and broad boulevards. The European-run **Hotel du Centre** (about 10,000fmg) is comfortable with good meals. **Hotel La Plage** has bungalows for about the same price. More upmarket is the **Hotel Ocean**, about 15,000 - 20,000fmg for bungalows. No restaurant, but Le Bamboo has been recommended.

The road to Sambava is fairly good, about three hours by taxi-brousse.

There's a boat from Antalaha to Île Sainte Marie (see page 237).

Excursions

Antalaha provides access to the Masoala Peninsula. In addition to the walk to Maroantsetra described on page 000, the adventurous can head for **Cap Est**, the most easterly point in Madagascar. Hotel Le Club in Sambava does the trip as an excursion, but it is possible on your own providing you are equipped for walking and camping. The village at the cape is **Ambohitralanana**, reached by a rough track (occasional vehicles). Here you can find a pirogue to take you further south to Ampanavoana. From here back to Ambohitralanana is a two day trek through rain-forest via the village of Ratsianarana. Alternatively from Ambohitralanana you can head due west and end up at Ampokafo from where you walk to Maroantsetra.

VANILLA IN MADAGASCAR
by Clare and Johan Hermans

Vanilla, the cured fruit of a Mexican orchid, is the major foreign currency earner for Madagascar: together with Reunion and the Comoros they grow 80% of the world's crop. Its cultivation in Madagascar is centred along the hot and wet eastern coastal region, the main production centres being the towns of Andapa, Antalaha and Sambava.

The climbing plants are normally grown supported on 1.5m high moisture-retaining spongy trunks and under ideal conditions it takes three years for the vanilla plants to mature. When the plants bloom, during the drier months, the vines are checked on alternate days for open flowers to hand-pollinate. The pod of the vanilla plant then takes nine months to develop to full maturity; each 15cm to 20cm pod will contain tens of thousands of tiny seeds.

The pods are taken to a vanilla processing plant, where the curing takes place. They are first blanched in a huge submerged cauldron of boiling water for twenty seconds, then the pods are sun-dried for about five months, initially in full sun, later under a shelter.

After maturing, the pods are sorted by size; the workers sit in front of a large rack with 'pigeonholes' for the different lengths. They are then thrown into the appropriate box with a quick flick of the wrist and the bundles of sorted pods, approximately 30 to a bunch, are tied with raffia. They are checked for quality by sniffing and bending before being packed into wooden crates. 90% of the product goes to the USA for use in the ice cream industry. Stacks of crates are piled high filling almost the whole town with the heady aroma of vanilla. Some processing plants can be visited; a good bet is the Lopat Vanilla Factory in Sambava where Sambava Voyages can organise guided tours.

The vanilla used in cultivation in Madagascar is called Vanilla planifolia which originates from Mexico. It was brought to Madagascar by the French once the secret of hand pollination had been discovered – the flower does not have a natural pollinator in its foreign home. The culinary and pharmaceutical use of vanilla dates back to pre-Aztec times when it was used as a drink or as one of the ingredients of a lotion against fatigue for those holding public office. Similarly a native Malagasy vanilla stem can be found for sale in the Zoma in Tana as a male invigorator.

Four different species of vanilla orchid occur naturally in Madagascar; most are totally leafless, one species can be seen on the roadside between Sambava and Antahala resembling lengths of red-green tubing festooned over the scrub, another is to be found in the unlikely habitat of spiny forest near Berenty in the south. Most of the native species contain sap that burns the skin and their fruits do not contain enough vanillin to make cultivation economic.

Isalo National Park (Johan Hermans)

Didiera stem

Pitcher plant near Tolagnaro (Steven Garren)

Pirogue

Petite Cascade, Montagne d'Ambre National Park.

Fish drying in the sun, Nosy Komba

On the beach, Lokobe

Baobabs near Morondava. (John R. Jones)

SAMBAVA

The centre of the vanilla and coconut growing region, and an important area for cloves and coffee production. Sambava can also be a base for exploring the eastern rain forest. There's plenty to do here and some excellent hotels. Excursions can be made on your own or with Sambava-Voyages or the Hotel Le Club.

'Sambava was one of our best memories: a sublime bay; to the south some beautiful and deserted beaches; to the north lovely countryside with high mountains on the horizon. At the end of the world, but no worse for that!' (P. Weber & L. Durand)

Getting there/away

Sambava has quite good air-connections with Toamasina and Antsiranana, and is accessible by road from Vohemar (7 hours, 5,000fmg).

Where to stay/eat

Category A

Hotel Carrefour   Situated by the beach, with all mod cons (hot water). Great food. Around 25,000fmg per room.

Hotel Centre Ville   (Hotel Le Club). BP 33. Large rooms with fans or air-conditioning, from 25,000 to 35,000fmg.

Hotel Le Club   (bungalows). Near the sea. Swimming pool. 2-person bungalows for 38,000fmg. Bungalow de luxe 50,000fmg.

Hotel Le Club offers a choice of 13 tours, including trekking, and transfer to and from the airport. Hiring a 4WD with driver costs 95,000fmg per day; mountain bikes for 20,000fmg, guides available.

Category B

Orchidea Beach   BP 86. Tel: 128. Very pleasant bungalows overlooking the ocean. Cold water. 15,000fmg. Good value and recommended. Run by an Italian, M. Filossi (who speaks excellent English) and his daughter who are great favourites with travellers. 'An air of gentle decrepitude, but highly agreeable.' (Henk Beetje)

Nouvel Hotel   6,000 - 15,000fmg. Recommended for its good food.

Category C

Hotel Pacifique   3 rooms at about 10,000fmg. Bungalows at around 18,000fmg.

There are other small hotels in this category.

Excursions

The nearby **River Bemarivo** has plenty of possibilities. Boats go to the village of Amboahangibe to transport coffee. You may be fortunate enough

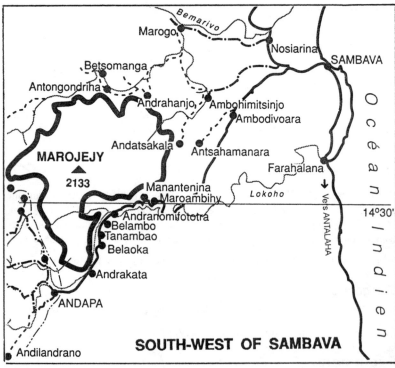

Map reproduced from *Madagascar: Revue de la conservation et des aires protégées* by kind permission of the WWF, Switzerland.

to get a lift, or arrange your own pirogue.

There is a very beautiful lake and fishing village about 9km south of the airport.

Derry Edwards recommends a two day trip along the **Lokoho River** organised by Herman, who can be contacted at the Orchidea Beach hotel. 'After a taxi-brousse journey to Ambinanynantsahabe we walked for a couple of hours seeing vanilla, cloves, jackfruit, papaya, ylang-ylang, coffee, banana and several chameleons. We then took a pirogue for several hours to the village of Marojala, where Herman's grandparents gave us dinner and put us up for the night – a wonderful experience. After breakfast we again took to the river for the long trip to Farahalana. From there we took a taxi-brousse back to Sambava. Herman speaks good French and passable English.'

A very efficient travel agency, Sambava-Voyages (BP 28a. Tel: 110) will look after your hotel bookings and airport transfers and offers a large choice of excursions including river and hiking trips which sound ideal for those wishing to get off the beaten track but not quite ready to go it alone. The Manageress is Mme Seramila who speaks some English.

Marojejy and Anjanaharibe-Sud Reserves

The two reserves are not yet open to visitors but part of the WWF's plans for the future include low-impact ecotourism in part of Marojejy. It will be a treat: the slopes of the massif are covered with vegetation which varies according to altitude, producing great biodiversity. 17 amphibians and 22 species of reptile have been recorded here. The 23 species of mammal include the very rare sub-species of diademed sifaka, *Propithecus diadema candidus*, which is pure white.

Anjanaharibe-Sud is 20km south-west of Marojejy and is lower and more gentle. It is an outstanding example of lowland and mid-altitude forest.

The reserves typify the environmental problems facing Madagascar and how the destruction of vital forests is affecting crop production, thus creating further poverty and more need to clear forests for subsistence farming. Because of the high rainfall of the area (more than 3,000mm in parts of Marojejy) this is the country's most productive area for growing irrigated rice. The Lokoho River, which rises in Anjanaharibe-Sud, is the *only* source of water for the largest irrigated rice producer in the country. Deforestation has already affected the river water which is laden with silt and threatening to clog the irrigation pumps, forcing their closure. Slash-and-burn cultivation is eating into the forests on Marojejy's steep slopes where crops can only be grown for a couple of years before the soil washes away and a new area is cut.

The WWF has opened an office in Andapa and is seeking solutions to the problem. It will not be easy.

Andapa

The relative prosperity of the area is shown by the rather good road to this town in the heart of the rice-growing area (2½ hours by taxi-brousse) which is backed by spectacular hills. A new road is being built linking Andapa with Beamalona, near Anjanaharibe-Sud.

Where to stay/eat

Hotel Vatosoa   Excellent food. The Chinese owner, Mr Tam-Yock, has built some bungalows on a hillside 15 minutes drive above the town. Lovely setting but you need your own transport.

WEST OF TOAMASINA (TAMATAVE)

Andasibe (Périnet)

A visit to Madagascar's most accessible Special Reserve, Périnet-Analamazoatra, is a must for anyone interested in the flora and fauna of the eastern rainforest (moist montane forest at this altitude: 930 - 1,049m). This small reserve (810 hectares) protects the largest of the lemur family, *Indri indri*. Standing about three feet high, with barely visible tails, black and white markings and surprised teddy-bear faces, the indri looks more like a gone-wrong panda than a lemur. The long back legs are immensely powerful, and an indri can propel itself backwards 30 feet, execute a turn in mid-air, and land face-forward to gaze down benevolently at its observers. And you will be an observer: most people see indris in Périnet, and if they don't see them they hear them. For it is their voice that makes this lemur extra special: whilst other lemurs grunt or swear, the indri sings. It is an eerie, wailing sound somewhere between the song of a whale and a police-siren, and it carries for up to two miles as troops call to each other across the forest. The indris are fairly punctual with their song: if you are in the reserve between one to two hours after daybreak and shortly before dusk you should hear them. There's no point in looking for indri at other times; they spend much of the day dozing in the tops of trees. Indri live in small family groups of up to five animals, and give birth in June. At the last count there were 280 indris in Périnet.

In Malagasy the indri is called *babakoto*. There are various legends connected with the indri, and explaining the esteem with which the local people hold them (it is *fady* to kill an indri). One that links the indri with the origin of man (thus supporting modern evolutionary thought) is described on page 00, and another popular legend tells of a man who climbed a forest tree to gather wild honey, and was severely stung by the bees. Losing his hold, he fell, but was caught by a huge indri which carried him on its back to safety.

There are nine species of lemur altogether in Périnet, (including aye-aye) although you will not see them all. Most likely you will find the troop of grey bamboo lemurs (*Hapalemur griseus*) which are diurnal and sometimes feed on the bamboo near the warden's house, and perhaps a sleeping avahi, curled up in the fork of a tree. It is worth going on a nocturnal lemur hunt (the guides are experts at this) to look for mouse lemurs, and the greater dwarf lemur (*Cheirogaleus major*) which hibernates during the cold season.

Lemurs are only a few of the creatures to be found in Périnet. There are tenrecs, beautiful and varied insects and spiders, and lots of reptiles. One of Madagascar's biggest chameleons lives here: *Chameleon parsonii*, which is bright green, about two feet long and has twin horns at the end of its snout, and the smallest, *Chameleon nasutus*. The guides keep a selection of chameleons near the entrance for tourists to photograph. Boas are quite common and placid.

This is a good place for bird watching. Near the warden's house there are flowering trees of a species much favoured by the Madagascar green sunbird (*Cinnyris notatus*) which has an iridescent green head and throat, and sucks nectar like the New World hummingbirds. There are also cuckoo-like blue couas, cuckoo-rollers, blue pigeons, paradise flycatchers, two species of falcon (Newton falcon and Madagascar falcon), two species of black vasa parrot, and many others.

Botanists will not be disappointed. In French colonial days an orchid garden was started by the lily pond to the right of the road to the reserve, and a variety of species flourishes here although most flower in the warm wet season.

Leeches can be an unpleasant aspect of Périnet if you've pushed through vegetation and it's been raining recently. Tuck your trousers into your socks and carry salt; this usually dislodges the creatures before they get dug in. A lighted cigarette or petrol does the same trick. Malagasy leeches are very small − not African Queen proportions − but the anti-coagulant they inject when they bite means you bleed dramatically.

Permits and guides

Get your permit from ANGAP in Tana.

Though not compulsory, a guide is advisable and the guides here are the best in Madagascar. Maurice, Lala, Eugene and Nirina are recommended but there are other rising stars. The fee is now set at 5,000fmg for two hours, and the Association des Guides Andasibe (AGA) ensures that standards are maintained.

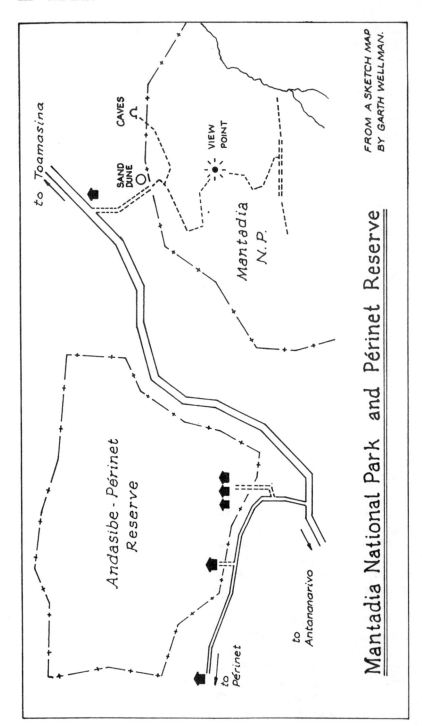

to Toamasina

CAVES

SAND DUNE

VIEW POINT

Mantadia N.P.

Andasibe - Périnet Reserve

to Antananarivo

to Périnet

FROM A SKETCH MAP BY GARTH WELLMAN.

Mantadia National Park and Périnet Reserve

Mantadia National Park

This is a newly created national park 7km from Périnet with the same wildlife including indri. To reach it walk back to RN2 and turn left towards Toamasina. Look out for the entrance to the park: a wooden gazebo and a gate.

There is a campsite here, and an 8km trail leading to the top of one of the forested hills with a stunning view. You will need a guide.

Getting there/back

When running, the train from Tana to Andasibe leaves at 06.00 three days a week and costs about 6,500fmg (2nd class); Toamasina to Andasibe leaves 06.00 and costs a little more; it takes about six hours. The train leaves Andasibe for Toamasina at 11.00 and for Tana at approximately the same time.

Taxi-brousses are much faster and those used on this route tend to be quite comfortable. You will pay less from Tana if you take a taxi-brousse to Moramanga (a regular stop) and a local taxi-be to the Andasibe turnoff from RN2.

Where to stay/eat

Hotel Buffet de la Gare   Until 1993 this was the only place to stay in Andasibe, and its list of distinguished guests ranged from Prince Philip, Gerald Durrell and David Attenborough to humble backpackers. Intriguingly, it is a typical Category C hotel, with saggy beds, a non-functioning loo, and a certain amount of non-endemic wildlife in the bedrooms. A great social leveller. In addition to the hotel, which was built in 1938, there are newish bungalows which are more comfortable. Some have adjoining bathrooms, others sort-of-adjoining.

The hotel has its devotees. It is run by Monsieur Joseph with an old world courtesy, and the dining room is truly elegant – fresh flowers on the tables and a marvellous rosewood bar. Most people like the food.

There are eight rooms costing 22,000fmg, and seven chalet-bungalows for 30,000fmg.

In construction, and probably ready by the time you read this are six new bungalows with three beds, fireplaces and hot water. Expected price: 55,000fmg per bungalow. Situated a hundred metres or so up the road towards the reserve, you are here surrounded by wildlife including, if you're lucky, lemurs.

Maison des Orchidées   A new wooden hotel right in the village of Andasibe. Comfortable, Malagasy-run, hot water. 18,000fmg per night. Very good food. Highly recommended by all who have stayed there.

Also in the village is the **Italian mission** with six beds for 10,000fmg per person with communal shower and WC. Clean, pleasant and basic.

Hotel Feon' Ny Ala   The name means 'Nose of the forest'. There are six new bungalows (14,000fmg for shared outside bathroom/WC, 22,000fmg with adjoining bathroom) and a flat, grassy area for camping (7,000fmg). No electricity as yet. The

Chinese owners, M and Mme Sum Chuk Lan are very helpful and eager to please, and the food is ample and excellent. This well-recommended place is on the right side of the road that runs from RN2 to Andasibe. You are close enough to the reserve to hear the indri call.

An alternative is to **camp** at Maromizaha, about 7km from Andasibe in the direction of Toamasina, off RN2. The track leading to Maromizaha is on the right, about 4km from the Andasibe turning.

Moramanga

This formerly sleepy town gained a new lease of life with the completion of the Chinese road (there is a memorial here to the Chinese workers) and the absence of comfortable hotels in Andasibe. Even though the latter is no longer true it is still a popular lunch stop on the way to Andasibe by vehicle.

Where to stay/eat

Grand Hotel   Tel: 620 16. From 18,000fmg single to 35,000fmg for a two person bungalow. Helpful, friendly, hot water. Popular with Périnet-bound travellers.

Emeraude   Tel: 621 57. About 18,000fmg double. Hot showers. Good value.

Basic hotels include the **Restau-Hotel Maitso an'Ala**, the **Hotel Fivami** and **Hotel au Poisson**. All cost less than 10,000fmg.

The Chinese restaurant **Guangzou** serves excellent food and is popular with groups so reservations may be necessary in the high season. Tel: 04 62089. Almost as popular is the **Au Coq d'Or**. Tel: 62045.

Panda restaurant is fast, good, and inexpensive.

Mandraka (butterfly farm)

Described in Chapter 7 (Highlands).

Marovoay

This is the first stop on the railway line north towards Lake Alaotra, and the name means 'Many Crocodiles'. Appropriately, a commercial crocodile farm has been started here which is open to visitors. There are over a thousand *Crocodylus niloticus*, some over two and a half metres in length, living in semi-wild conditions. The best season to visit is January, when the eggs are hatching. Write to: Reptel Madagascar, 50 Ave Grandidier, BP 563, Isoraka, Antananarivo. Tel: 348 86. Fax: 206 48.

Lake Alaotra

This is the largest lake in Madagascar and looks wonderful on the map: one imagines it surrounded by overhanging forest. Sadly, forest has made way for rice, and this is one of the most abused and degraded areas in Madagascar. Deforestation has silted up the lake so that its maximum dry-season depth is only 60cm. Introduction of exotic fish has done further damage. The area has been designated a Site of Special Biological Interest by the WWF because of its endemic waterfowl, although it is too late to save the Alaotra grebe (*Tachybaptus rufolavatus*) which is now extinct. The Madagascar pochard, (*Aythya innotata*) may have gone the same way. Lemurs are faring better. Some Aloatran grey bamboo lemur, *Hapalemur griseus alaotrensis*, are breeding happily in their new home at Jersey Zoo (having been brought there by Gerald Durrell) although whether there will be any habitat to release their descendants into is debatable.

Getting there/back

A spur of the railway runs from Moramanga, leaving at 09.40 (but check time) costing around 10,500fmg second class to Ambatondrazaka, near the south-east side of Lake Alaotra. It arrives at 19.15. The return train from Ambatondrazaka leaves at 05.00 (check time) connecting with the train to Toamasina.

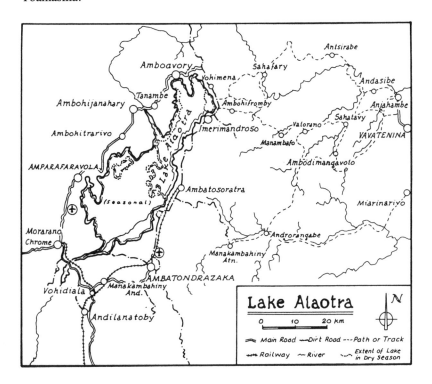

The dirt road from Moramanga is being improved, bridges are being built, and it may soon be the easiest way to reach the lake.

Ambatondrazaka
The main town of the area, and a good centre for excursions.

Where to sleep/eat
Hotel Voahirana. BP 65, Côte Postale 503. 16,500fmg, including a nice breakfast. Quite a walk from the station. Next door is the restaurant **Cantonnais**; very good value.

Hotel Max. Near the station. 14 rooms, 15,000 - 20,000fmg. The restaurant **Fanantenana** is next door.

Imerimandroso
A small town near the lake; half an hour's walk to the south is a village from where you can take a pirogue.

There is one basic hotel, the **Bellevue**.

Note. There are no hotels in Ambatosoatra, midway up the east side of Lake Alaotra.

Excursions
Probably the best reason to come to Lake Alaotra is to meet the guide Jean-Baptiste Randrianomanana and join him for one of his excursions. 'He speaks excellent English, studied sociology and philosophy and is extremely knowledgeable about all aspects of Madagascar. His wife is a geographer. He will take you on a tour of the lake which involves a taxi drive to a traditional village on the shores of the lake, a night with a local family at Imerimandroso, a pirogue crossing the lake to another village called Vohitsara to meet the medicine man and the school teacher, etc, and a taxi-ride back to Ambatondrazaka. He charges a minimum of 40,000fmg per day and gives a proportion to the villagers who form part of his tour.' (J & R McFarlaine) This is both an excellent opportunity to support local enterprise and to learn about Madagascar from an insider.

Jean-Baptiste may be able to invite you to a *famadihana* and can guide you along the Smuggler's Path to the coast — a four or five day hike. He meets the train and keeps an eye out for *vazahas* or he can be contacted through the Hotel Voahirana.

"There are fewer and fewer forests, the rivers are drying up, the wild creatures are becoming extinct, the climate is ruined, and every day the earth is growing poorer and more hideous... I realise that the climate is to some extent in my power, and that if, in a thousand years man is to be happy, I too shall have had some small hand in it. When I plant a birch tree and see it growing green and swaying in the wind, my soul is filled with pride ..."
Anton Chekhov, Uncle Vanya, 1899

THE MAGIC SHOW

By Chris Ballance

We saw a poster in Manakara for a Magic Show so bought tickets. The magician was quite good in a relaxed way. The audience were brilliant. About 120 people in a dingy youth centre hall without lights. He began with a couple of simple disappearing tricks that drew rounds of applause. It was the lesser tricks that were applauded; the better ones left the audience too spell-bound to think of clapping. His magic wand was a flute-sized rod which he empowered by touching a plastic skull with a red robe hanging from it. He used few other props – two or three magic boxes, a few packs of cards and a glass. He filled this with flour, wrapped it in a 'magicked' newspaper and turned it into a glass of bon-bons which he threw into the audience. From this moment the audience were his, body and soul. There was no 'willing suspension of disbelief'. These people had eaten the proof of his powers.

He repeated the trick later, turning coffee powder into cigarettes. He put one of the cigarettes into a guillotine and cut it. Then he put a volunteer boy's finger into the guillotine. Another boy had to hold a hat to catch the finger. Down came the guillotine, the hand was hidden in the hat and then magicked better. As the boy left the stage he was mobbed. All we could see was a heap of every child in the audience. Suddenly a finger shot up from the centre of the heap, triumphantly showing everyone it was attached to its hand. And when the conjurer got a girl in the audience to lay an egg, everyone – but *everyone* – had to see it, touch it, and marvel at it.

The show ended with a draw in which names were put into a hat (we prayed we wouldn't win). There were prizes of 1,000, 5,000 and 10,000fmg notes. Each winner was given the note to put into an envelope which was put into a magic box, magicked, and then given back. We suspected they got a message to the effect of 'You've been had'. The girl next to me goggled – that's the only word – at the sight of the money. 'Cinq mille francs!' she kept repeating over and over in an ecstasy of hope. The sight of the 10,000fmg note shut her up entirely.

Next day we changed £40 to last us for three days. We received 138,000fmg. The obscenity of international finance, beside that girl, shamed us.

'France, Spain, Italy and the Indie... *must be ransackt to make sauce for our meat; while we impoverish the land, air and water to enrich our private table... Besides, these happy people have no need of any foreign commodity, nature having sufficiently supplied their necessities wherewith they remain contented. But it is we that are in want, and are compelled like famished wolves to range the world about for our living, to the hazards of both our souls and bodies, the one by the corruption of the air, the other by the corruption of religion'.*
Walter Hamond, A Paradox Prooving that the Inhabitants of ... Madagascar ... are the Happiest People in the World, *Walter Hamond, 1640*

SOUTH OF TOAMASINA (TAMATAVE)

Pangalanes

This series of lakes was linked by artificial canals in French Colonial times for commercial use, a quiet inland water being preferable to an often stormy sea. Over the years the canals became choked with vegetation and no longer passable, but attempts are now being made to rehabilitate them and re-establish the unbroken waterway which stretched from Toamasina to Vangaindrano.

It is possible to travel stretches of the canal yourself on barges carrying cargoes of bananas, coffee, etc. There are no sharks, so swimming is safe. Bird and people-watching is also rewarding.

Where to stay/eat

There are four sets of beach-bungalows near the train station of Andranokoditra, one stop after Ambila Lemaitso (60 km south of Toamasina). Some were damaged in the cyclone but are being rebuilt.

Hotel des Pangalanes   Also reached by motor pirogue from Toamasina (four people minimum 300,000fmg). Bookings: BP 112, Toamasina; Tel: 334 03 or 321 77. Seven 2-person bungalows, 450FF including all meals. Excursions.

Bush House   Book through Boogie Pilgrim, 40 Ave de L'Indépendance, Tana. Tel: 331 85 or 204 54. 380FF with all meals. German run, reportedly very comfortable and in a beautiful situation. Only five rooms so a pleasant family atmosphere.

'There is a small private reserve a 30 minute stroll away along the beach. Well worth the 5,000fmg entrance fee. The best part was walking along a quiet path, watching the butterflies, and hearing and seeing the lemurs calling in the trees.' (Hilana Steyn)

Les Everglades Near Ambila Lemaitso, on Lac Rasoabe. Tel: 442 97 in Tana for further information and bookings. French run. In a wonderful setting but erratic food supplies and rather basic. 15,000 - 20,000fmg. Excursions on the Pangalanes.

Antafana Between the ocean and Pangalanes. 2-person bungalows for 20,000 - 40,000fmg, excellent meals (10,000fmg) and excursions. Highly recommended by reader Apolline Bucaille. Reservations in Tana: BP 121, through the agency MTB, 20 Rue Ratsimilaho (near the Colbert); tel: 223 64.

If you've failed to make a booking, it's worth getting off the train at Andranokoditra in the hopes that someone from one of the hotels is meeting the train. Failing that, the first two places can be reached independently by taking a pirogue from behind the station, and then walking along a clear track, 15 minutes to the Pangalanes and 45 mins to Bush House. Obviously, though, it is more convenient for everyone if you make a reservation.

If you forget to get off the train at Andranokoditra do not despair: there is a small hotel at Ambila Lemaitso. Very run down in 1992 so perhaps flattened in 1994. Or perhaps rebuilt. It is called the **Hotel Malaky** (15,000fmg).

Continuing south

You can travel down the coast as far as Mahanoro (occasional transport) and can sometimes find a pirogue to take you to Nosy Varika and Mananjary, which is linked by road to Fianarantsoa. This is adventurous stuff, and not for those with limited time. Helena Drysdale writes: 'We travelled from Tamatave to Mananjary over two weeks. Generally people assured us it was impossible, that there were no roads, that all the bridges were down in the cyclone, and the ferries were *en panne* (that familiar phrase). But with luck and ingenuity we made it. One taxi-brousse per week from Tamatave to Mahanoro (2 days), otherwise river boats available at Tamatave's river port for hitching (we went on boats travelling south to a graphite mine in Vatomandry – a very uncomfortable three days).

'In **Vatomandry** we stayed in the Hotel Fotsy; thatched bungalows (12,000fmg). Good food here and some Chinese restaurants in town.

'From there to **Mahanoro**, one day by taxi-brousse, two by boat. Hotel Pangalanes, full of ladies of the night and noisy revellers but a nice atmosphere. Boat from Mahanoro to **Masomelika** one day; very simple hotel but friendly people (I asked for the toilet and was pointed to a bucket. This was the shower – the toilet was in the bushes). From Masomelika to **Nosy Varika** took half a day hitchhiking. There's a relatively expensive Chinese hotel here. Then on to Mananjary, one night by boat.' (Helena describes this journey in her book *Dancing with the Dead*. See *Bibliography*.)

Mananjary

A very nice small town accessible by good road and taxi-brousse (lovely scenery) from Ranomafana, and famous for its circumcision ceremony which takes place every seven years. The next one will be in the year 2000.

There is a long beach with terrific breakers (dangerous swimming – and there are sharks) and the Pangalanes Canal, and all the attractions of people-watching. 'The men go out early (4am) in a tremendous surf and row or sail back into the river. Shrimps are sold to wholesalers. Other fish (some very pretty ones) are eaten. Some fishermen's *fady*: Wives are not allowed to look at another man until 12pm or something will happen to the husband at sea; a man who eats pork cannot go to sea.' (C & J Hermans)

Where to stay/eat

Jardin de la Mer   10 bungalows (28,000fmg single, 33,000fmg double) and 7 rooms in annexe, 24,000fmg. Super food, friendly, English-speaking Belgian/Malagasy owners. Recommended.

Motel Enterprise Touristique du L'Est   (the previous name of Solimotel was more alluring). Blvd Maritime. 18,500fmg to 23,500fmg. Good, but rather expensive food.

Hotel aux Bons Amis   5,000 - 8,000fmg. Another basic hotel is the **Nirintsoa**, on the main street.

The road between Mananjary and Manakara is surfaced, and travel between the two towns takes only four hours.

Manakara

The old part of town is recommended by Andrea Jarman. 'The *allée des filaos* running between ex-colonial buildings and the ocean makes the waterfront a very attractive part of town. The beach, with its crashing waves, is the favourite place for gymnasts and martial arts enthusiasts to train. The new town and station are across the river bridge and of no interest. Pousse-pousses provide the best local transport.'

You should not swim here because of dangerous currents and sharks.

Where to stay/eat

Two hotels under the same ownership (Alex Andriamifidy and his wife) are **Hotel Sidi**, and **Hotel Eden Sidi** situated 13km north of Manakara on the coast. BP 80, Ambinagny. Tel: 212 02/212 03. Sidi rooms cost from 17,000fmg to 40,000fmg, and Eden Sidi bungalows from 38,000fmg to 40,000fmg.

Parthenay Club   Tel: 211 60. Really a posh tennis club for the locals, with a swimming pool, but also some bungalows. A bit south of the Hotel Manakara. Bungalows with two double beds 15,000fmg per night, one double bed 8,000fmg per night. No regular restaurant but you can order food in advance.

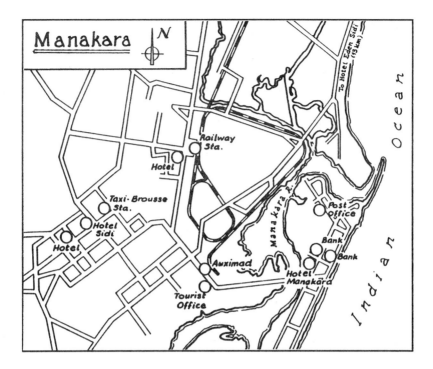

Hotel Manakara A friendly, once-pretty hotel popular with travellers (and ants), in town but near the ocean. 10,000fmg per room, 18,000fmg with hot water. 'The hotel waiter approached us over breakfast. "Excuse me. You had a small bottle of beer yesterday evening and I'm afraid we charged you for a large one. Here is your change." Can you imagine that happening in Britain?' (Chris Ballance)

From Mananjary or Manakara there's a weekly Twin Otter to Tolagnaro; from Manakara there is the train to Fianar, or you can continue south by taxi-brousse.

Fianarantsoa to Manakara by train
Not as popular as the Tana-Toamasina train, this is nevertheless a spectacular railway trip. 'We preferred this to the Tamatave line. There's much more of a sense of weaving through uncharted jungle. And the waterfalls! And the wonderful stations! Some simply a sign with a path leading from it, and one person and his bag and two well-wishers.' (Chris Ballance). At the time of writing the train is not running due to damage by cyclone Geralda, but it can be expected to resume its normal schedule. It leaves Tuesdays, Thursdays, Saturdays and Sundays at 07.00 and takes about seven hours to reach Manakara. Second class is (was) 5,800fmg. Breakdowns and delays are common. For the best views sit on the left hand side. The train returns from Manakara at 06.45.

Vohipeno

About 45km south of Manakara, this small town is the centre of the Antaimoro tribe who came from Arabia about 600 years ago, bringing the first script to Madagascar. Their Islamic history is shown by their clothing (turban and fez, as well as Arab-style robes). They are the inheritors of the 'great writings' *sorabe*, written in Malagasy but in Arabic script. *Sorabe* continue to be written, still in Arabic, still on 'Antaimoro paper'. The scribes who practise this art are known as *katibo* and the writing and their knowledge of it gives them a special power. The writing itself ranges from accounts of historical events to astrology, and the books are considered sacred.

Farafangana

Accessible by taxi-brousse from Manakara (3,500fmg), this is a pleasant and comfortable town to hang around in for a while.

Where to stay/eat

Hotel Les Cocotiers   A new up-market hotel near the post office. Rooms are said to be 25,000fmg.

Hotel Les Tulipes Rouges   Rooms for 9,000 to 14,000fmg and all called after different shades of red! Clean, good food and safe parking.

There are several small *hotelys* with rooms for as little as 3,000fmg. For snacks the **Salon de Thé Dahlia** is recommended.

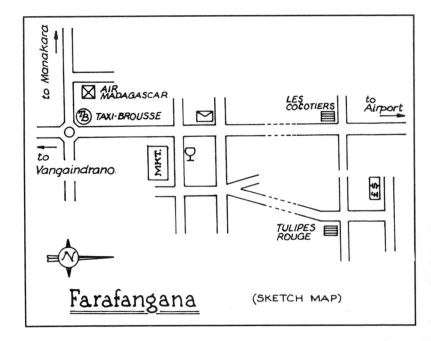

Farafangana   (SKETCH MAP)

CONTINUING SOUTH OR WEST

The road from Farafangana to Ihosy has recently been improved, allowing a Highlands/East Coast circuit of great interest. Those with time, a 4WD vehicle or mountain bike, or a light backpack and lots of energy, can continue south. The following notes are from two readers who travelled the area in 1992. Conditions are likely to have got better, rather than worse.

Vangaindrano

'It has the feel of a frontier town and the bridge which cross the Manañara river just before you get there is only about ten years old. There is a BTM bank and three basic hotels, the Ny Antsika (a yellow-fronted shop, with the best rooms of the three), and the Finaritra and Camelia, the latter two near the taxi-brousse station.'

Vangaindrano is the end of the road for most people, but you can continue further: 'There is a road southwest to **Midongy Atsimo** (no regular TB service, occasional bashie) which is maintained reasonably well because of a new coffee project. Muddy in places. 4WD advisable but not essential. 95km, 5-6 hours, with one excellent ferry. Food on the road in La Rose du Sud in **Ranomena**, oodles of *couleur locale*. No hotel in Midongy, but we rented a nice house with three beds, outside toilet, and tub of water for

4,000fmg. All this, plus meals, was obtained from the Epicerie on the Befotaka road (south end of town). The road to **Befotaka** (40km) was impassable most of the time, very skiddy, but has some very good forest at 20-25km south of Midongy.'

'Maps show that you can follow the gloriously named RN12 to Fort Dauphin. Only those prepared to suffer some privations should attempt to do this. Transport in the area is erratic and unpredictable, the roads are very bad. Be prepared to travel over rickety bridges in overladen lorries, walk long distances, and cross rivers in what may appear to be very unstable dug-out canoes (without a counter-balance). Of the latter the secret is to get your centre of gravity as low as possible, so for *vazaha* this invariably means kneeling down in the bottom of the canoe and remaining still. It is also advisable to remove footwear for a crossing. You may only fear losing your luggage if the canoe capsizes, but remember that most people here cannot swim well and that luggage is not what they fear losing, but their lives.'

THE DRONGO

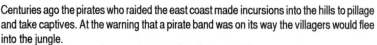

One of the most recognisable birds in Madagascar is the drongo. Unmistakable in silhouette, with its deeply forked tail and silly crest, it is ubiquitous and fearless, and is said to be an excellent mimic. For the villagers near Maroantsetra it is *fady* to kill a drongo. Here's why:

Centuries ago the pirates who raided the east coast made incursions into the hills to pillage and take captives. At the warning that a pirate band was on its way the villagers would flee into the jungle.

One day in Ambinanitelo word came that a pirate band was approaching. The people scattered, but the women with young children could not keep up with the others and hid in a thicket. Just as the pirates were passing them a baby wailed. The pirates spun around and approached the source of the cry. They heard the baby again, but this time the cry came from the top of a tree. It was a drongo. Believing themselves duped by a bird, the pirates gave up and returned to their boats. And the drongo has been honoured in this valley ever since.

NOSY BORAHA (ÎLE SAINTE MARIE)
History
The origin of the Malagasy name is obscure. It either means Island of Abraham or Island of Ibrahim, with probable reference to an early Semitic culture. Most people still call it Île Sainte Marie, the name given by European sailors when the island became the major hide-out of pirates in the Indian Ocean. From the 1680s to around 1720 these pirates dominated the seas around Africa. There was a Welshman – David Williams, Englishmen – Thomas White, John Every, William Kidd, and an American – Thomas Tew, among a Madagascar pirate population which in its heyday numbered nearly one thousand.

Later a Frenchman, Jean-Onésime Filet ('La Bigorne') was shipwrecked on Ste Marie while escaping the wrath of a jealous husband in Réunion. La Bigorne turned his amorous attentions with remarkable success to Princess Bety, the daughter of King Ratsimilaho. On their marriage the happy couple received Nosy Boraha as a gift from the king, and the island was in turn presented to the mother country by La Bigorne (or rather, put under the protection of France by Princess Bety). Thus France gained its first piece of Madagascar in 1750.

Île Sainte Marie today
Here is a cliché of a tropical island with endless deserted beaches overhung by coconut palms, bays protected from sharks by coral reefs, hills covered with luxuriant vegetation, and a relative absence of unsightly tourist development – although this is changing fast. Most travellers, however, still love it.

Ste Marie unfortunately – or perhaps fortunately, given the dangers of overdevelopment – has a far less settled weather pattern than its more sophisticated island rival, Nosy Be. Cyclones strike regularly and you can expect several days of rain and wind all year round, but interspersed with calm sunny weather. The best months for a visit seem to be June and mid-August to November, although a reader tells me she twice had perfect weather in January.

The only real town is Ambodifototra (pronounced 'Amboodifotootr'). Other small villages comprise bamboo and palm huts.

Getting there and back
In the past this has always been a problem: flights were overbooked and boats so uncomfortable and unreliable that only the bravest travellers used them. This seems to have changed. As I go to press there is news of a new boat service from Soanierana Ivongo which sounds ideal although I have as yet no first hand reports.

Ambodialafana

COCOTERAIE ROBERT

Ambatoroa

Tsirakalanana

Anivorano

Forêt d'Ambohidena

Ankirihiry

Sahasifotra

LA CRIQUE

Forêt de Kalalao

ATAFANA

Lonkintsy

Forêt d'Ampanihy

ORANGE

Anafiafy

Maromandia

DRAKKAR

Ambodifototra

BUNGALOWS ORCHIDÉE

ILOT MADAME

BAIE DES FORBANS

Mahavelo

Pirate's Cemetery

LA BALEINE

Ambodiforaha

Ankoalamare

LAKANA

Ambondrona

SOANAMBO

STANY'S

CHEZ VAVATE

CHEZ NAPOLEON

ÎLE AUX NATTES

N

0   5
km

Nosy Boraha (Île Sainte Marie)

By boat

Ferry   Two launches are making the trip from Soanierana Ivongo, leaving daily, weather permitting. The trip takes 1½ hours, leaves at 12.00 and costs 40,000fmg one way, 70,000fmg round trip. It returns from Ste Marie at 08.00. Reservations are made on the spot. There are also pirogues from Soanierana Ivongo, described later.

For exquisite discomfort try the *Rapiko*, which leaves Toamasina on Wednesdays at 20.00 and takes 10 hours. The fare is 40,000fmg, and tickets are available from SCAC (see map). It returns the following day (Thursday) also at 20.00. Tickets are available in advance from Roso's, next to Le Barachois Salon de Thé in Ambodifototra. 'This trip should carry a health warning! By the time we arrived the below deck area was packed, so we staked our position on deck with about 12 other *vazaha*. Within five minutes of leaving port the boat was pitching and rolling to an alarming degree... many people succumbed to sea sickness, and if you fell asleep you rolled across the deck. The only hope was to wedge yourself between your rucksack and someone else. An hour into the journey the heavens opened and so it continued until dawn... Even after three days on the island our things were still damp. The *Rapiko* is forever etched on my memory!' (Emma Webb). The *Rapiko* may continue from Ste Marie to Mananara. Check with SCAC.

Erratic ferries run from Manompana, on the mainland 25km away. Manompana is not always accessible from the south – it depends on the state of bridges and ferries crossing the several rivers up the east coast. The *Vedette Alize* costs around 15,000fmg and takes four hours. Its departure time is determined by the weather and tides, but is generally pre-dawn. 'Plenty of flying fish, dolphins which attempted to surf in the bow waves, bonito and lots of very visible plankton particularly a luminescent blue variety.' (W Pepper)

Cargo boat   Cargo boats run from Maroantsetra via Nosy Mangabe, taking 22 hours (including a wait of six hours at Nosy Mangabe for the tide to change). The cost is 30,000fmg. The crossing can be cold, wet, and rough. There are also cargo boats from Antalaha, which take even longer, but some have bunk beds.

Pirogue   Rick Partridge sent this report: 'We took a taxi-brousse from Tamatave to Soanierana Ivongo. Next morning we negotiated 5,000fmg per person to travel by dug-out canoe along the inland waters for about 15km to a small ferry-point village where there are bungalows. Then next morning we had to walk at least 15km to the headland (*pointe*), where there is a village called Andangazana, from where we took a larger dug-out sailing boat to Île Ste Marie. The crossing cost 10,000fmg and took 1½ hours. An unmissable experience! Arriving at Bon Coin on Ste Marie made us feel like Christopher Columbus.' The walk is the tough part, but there is talk of a 4WD vehicle to take passengers to Andangazana.

Plane

Air Madagascar flies to Ste Marie most days (check the latest schedule). It costs 485FF/US$83 from Tana but you can fly more cheaply from Toamasina. All flights are heavily booked, especially in July and August, and you should make your reservations well in advance. Reconfirm your return flight at the Air Mad office in the north part of Ambodifototra. The office is closed when the personnel are needed at the airport because a flight is coming in, but there is a cafe next door in which you can wait. However adamant the Air Mad people are that the flight is full, it is worth going stand-by.

There are no taxis on the island, but one truck serves as hotel transport. Some hotels have their own vehicles and meet the incoming planes. Check with the 'courtesy vehicles' if there is room at their hotel before climbing aboard.

Where to stay

Category A

Soanambo   BP 20. Tel: 40. Manageress: Agnes Fayd'Herbe. 3km from airport, 10km from Ambodifototra. The most expensive hotel on the island. 316FF per bunglow. Breakfast about 30FF, other meals 75FF. Very comfortable with many facilities – ping pong, volley ball, swimming pool, hot water, bicycles, 'pedalos' (pedal boats) for hire, plus sailing, wind-surfing and deep sea diving at the nearby Centre Nautique.

Bungalows Orchidée   Tel: 54. Located 3km south of Ambodifototra, and trying hard to outsmart Soanambo. They put out a charming brochure explaining that the 'granit wall-tile has some refreshing virtue' and praising the lacquered pork they serve at dinner. They add, rather obliquely: 'As the beach is 3 meters only away from bungalows tourists may, not only have sunburn, but also, watch families of whales...' Single 225FF; double 300FF. 10 bungalows, 4 double rooms. Hot water, air-conditioning, water sports, excursions. Bookings may be made in Tana, tel: 237 62/270 15; fax: 269 86. Also in Toamasina, tel: 333 51/337 66.

La Cocoteraie Robert   In the extreme north of the island, described by one who knows as 'the most beautiful beach in the world', and has recently added 40 more bungalows. Transport from the airport costs 35,000, but a boat goes there from Soanambo (it's run by the same French family). It even has its own airstrip. 320FF double, 264 single. Meals 55FF.

Category B

La Crique   BP 1. Deservedly the most popular of all hotels, in one of the prettiest locations, a kilometre north of Lonkintsy, with a wonderful ambience and good food. A three course meal costs 18,000fmg. Bungalows with all facilities, 40,000fmg. More simple ones are 25,000fmg. Often full, so try to book ahead. Transport to/from the airport costs 15,000fmg, and there is a regular minibus to town.

Atafana   About 4km south of La Crique, run by the Noel family. Described as having the best location, on a private bay with good food.

Chez Vavate   6 rooms/bungalows, 16,000fmg. 11,000fmg for an three-course meal. On first appearance an unprepossessing collection of local huts built on a ridge overlooking the airstrip. Don't be taken in by first impressions, the food here is wonderful (and the *punch coco* ensures that you spend your evenings in a convivial haze) and the relaxed family atmosphere makes this a very popular place with young travellers. The only catch is you must walk 1½km from the airport. There is no road, and the 'courtesy vehicle' is a man with a wheelbarrow! If you miss him take the wide grassy track which runs parallel to the airstrip then veers to the left up a steep hill, but be warned – if Chez Vavate is full you will have missed the vehicles going to the other places.

Lakana   Six simple but very comfortable wooden bungalows, 5km from the airport, and including four perched along the jetty. Bed, breakfast and one meal per day cost 28,000fmg. Mountain bikes for hire (20,000fmg per day).

Category C

Hotel La Baleine   Owned by Albert Lanton this set of bungalows is receiving rave reviews. It is one of only three hotels on the island that are Malagasy-owned. With the proceeds of the hotel Albert sponsors a youth football club and other local projects. There are 8 rustic bungalows with mosquito nets and the minimum of furniture, about 7km from the airport. Communal bathroom with cold water. 10,000 - 15,000fmg per bungalow and 7,000fmg for dinner. 'The chef, Mama Sua, cooks up a storm. Best food I had in Madagascar. There is no menu but they tell you what is coming and will cater for you if you don't like the choice of the day. They make you feel like you are in a family home.' (Derek Schuurman). 'The food is absolutely superb! I spent 10 days here and never had rice cooked the same way twice.' (Luc Selleslagh). The only negative point is that the beach is not particularly nice here... but who cares?

Hotel Drakkar   1km north of Ambodifototra. Simple bamboo bungalows with cold shower 10,000fmg. The main building is an old colonial house with lovely decor and a sitting/dining room on the water's edge. Excellent food.

Stany's Bungalows   About 10km south of Ambodifototra, 20 minutes up the road from the airport. Adequate bungalows. Nice view looking out to sea. Bush showers and toilet. Very helpful and friendly owner.

Hotel Zinnia   In Ambodifototra. Clean, pleasant bungalows.

La Falafa   This restaurant in Ambodifototra (good food) also has a few inexpensive rooms.

Hotel Orange   Approx 10km north of Ambodifototra. Inexpensive bungalows, good reasonably priced food and excellent coco punch.

ACCOMMODATION ON ÎLE AUX NATTES

Chez Napoleon   Napoleon was a charismatic character who 'ruled' − in various guises − this little island south of Ste Marie and enjoyed entertaining *vazahas*. He died in 1986, but his name lives on. There are bungalows with hot water and a restaurant where his famous *poulet au coco* is still served to appreciative diners, even if taped pop music has replaced the sound of wind in the palm trees, and a meal with beer now costs 29,000fmg.

There are other groups of bungalows in the north end of the island, ranging from 10,000 to 25,000fmg.
    A pirogue to Île Aux Nattes should cost about 1,000fmg.

Where to eat in Ambodifototra

Restaurant **La Jardine** serves good, inexpensive food. Recommended for breakfast. Home-made hot croissants with hot chocolate, and friendly people. **The Hotel Antsara** is recommended for its set dinner for 12,000fmg.

Excursions around Ste Marie

The choice is yours. There are very few cars on the island, and you can walk or bike anywhere. At low tide you can walk as far as you want along beaches, or cross the island from west to east. There are plenty of paths although you may be pestered by children.

Bike rides

Bikes can be hired from many of the hotels but are cheaper (8,000fmg as against 25,000fmg) at Ambodifototra. You can see quite a lot of the island this way, but don't reckon on covering much ground − the roads are very rough.
    If you are staying at Ambodifototra you will have time to explore the north of the island, which is more dramatic scenically than the south. There is quite a good stretch of tarred road between the town and La Crique.
    You can hire motorbikes opposite the Hotel Soanambo and mopeds are also available in Ambodifototra.

Pirates' Cemetery

This can only be visited at low tide since there are several tidal creeks to be crossed. Just before the bay bridge to the town (when coming from the south) is a track leading to the cemetery, 20 minutes away. Children will guide you (whether you want them to or not). This is quite an impressive place, with grave stones dating from the 1830s, one with a classic skull and cross bones carved on it. There is now a 1,000fmg charge to visit the cemetery.

Town cemetery

As a change from the rather touristy Pirates Cemetery, try the graveyard about 6km north of Ambodifototra, at Bety Plage on the right side of the road.

Whale-watching

September seems to be the best time to see humpbacked whales; you can watch them from the beach at La Crique or Atafano, or take a boat excursion (offered by some of the hotels or the Centre Nautique).

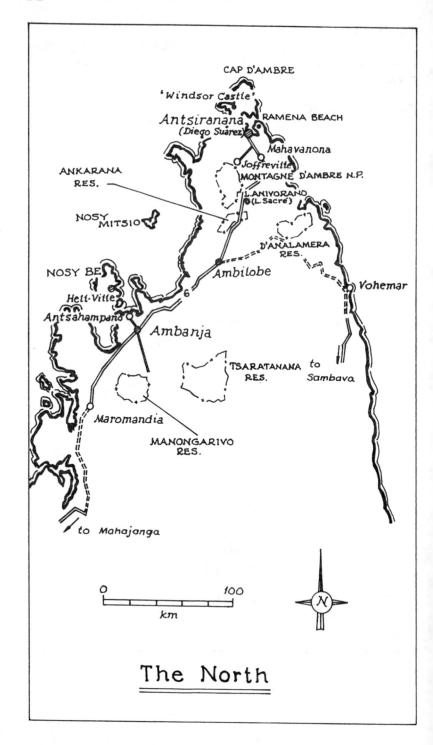

The North

Chapter 10

The North

INTRODUCTION

The northern part of Madagascar is the domain of the Antakarana people. Cut off by rugged mountains, the Antakarana were left to their own devices until the mid-1700s when they were conquered by the Sakalava; they in turn submitted to the Merina king Radama I, aided by his military adviser James Hastie, in 1823.

The north is characterised by its variety. The Tsaratanana massif (which includes Madagascar's highest peak, Maromokofro, 2,876m) brings more rain to the Nosy Be area than is normal on the west coast, and there is a pocket of dry climate around Antsiranana (Diego Suarez) which has seven months of dry weather with 90% of the 900mm of rain falling between December and April. With changes of weather go changes of vegetation and its accompanying fauna, making this region particularly interesting for botanists and other naturalists, as well as holiday makers.

Getting around

Roads in the area are being improved and Antsiranana is losing its isolation. Distances are long, however, so most people prefer to fly.

ANTSIRANANA (DIEGO SUAREZ)

History

Forgivingly named after a Portuguese captain, Diego Suarez, who arrived in 1543 and proceeded to murder and rape the inhabitants and sell them into slavery, this large town has had an eventful history with truth blending with fiction. An often told story, originated by Daniel Defoe, is that pirates in the 17th century founded the Republic of Libertalia here. Not true, say modern historians.

The Malagasy name simply means 'Port' and its strategic importance as a deep-water harbour has long been recognised. The French installed a military base here in 1885, and the town played an important role in the second world war when Madagascar was under the control of the Vichy French. To prevent the island falling into Japanese hands, Britain and the allies captured and occupied Diego Suarez in 1942. There is a British cemetery in the town honouring those killed at this time.

Antsiranana (Diego) today

This is Madagascar's fifth largest town (population 80,000) and of increasing interest to visitors for its diverse attractions. Traditionally rated second in beauty after Rio de Janeiro (presumably by people who had never seen Brazil) the harbour is encircled by hills, with a conical 'sugar loaf' plonked in one of the bays to the east of the town. From the air or the top of Montagne de Français, Antsiranana's superb position can be appreciated but the city itself is in the usual state of decay, though with a particular charm. The port's isolation behind its mountain barrier and its long association with non-Malagasy races has given it an unusually cosmopolitan population and lots of colour: there are Arabs, Creoles (descendants of Europeans), Indians, Chinese, and Comorans.

It's a town you either love or hate; generally speaking, independent travellers love it (good food, beach, atmosphere) whilst groups hate it because of the lack of a good hotel in town and any semblance of efficiency.

The name Joffre seems to be everywhere in and around the town. General Joseph Joffre was the military commander of the town in 1897 and later became Maréchal-de-France. In 1911 he took over the supreme command of the French armies, and was the victor of the battle of the Marne in 1914.

Antsiranana is a pleasant town for wandering; take a look at the amazing, decaying building to the east of Clémenceau Square on Rue Richelieu. This was formerly a French Naval hotel, and has reportedly been bought by an American (or French?) hotel group, to be restored to its original glory. Eventually.

There are several good souvenir shops, mostly selling rather tacky items (we boycotted those selling stuffed turtles or tortoises). The best is Bijouterie Chez Babou, at 10 Rue de Colbert. Also recommended is Chez Bardou, Rue Monsignor Corbel.

Car and bike hire

Droopy and Co (That's the company name not my comment!) at Place Joffre (tel: 8 226 25) has vehicles and drivers for hire for set itineraries to hard-to-reach destinations, and per day. Nearby is a place that hires out bicycles.

Getting there

Flights go from Tana (returning the same day) via Mahajanga on most days; 955FF/US$162. You can also fly via the east coast towns of

Toamasina and Sambava. There are also flights from Nosy Be, Mahajanga, and Vohemar. For the overland route to Sambava or to Nosy Be see page 254.

Where to stay
Category A
Hotel Ramena Nofy BP 239. Tel: 294 15, fax: 261 8 294 13. 18km from town (near Ramena beach) 45 mins from the airport. At last, a top-class hotel! 15 chalets each with modern bathrooms, hot water, pine furniture, mosquito nets; 370FF double, 328FF single. There is a large restaurant with terrace, excellent food and pleasant staff. Deep-sea fishing safaris are run from here by Blue Marine, and mountain bikes are available for hire. This hotel can be booked in Tana through MADERA travel; tel: 29 339.

Hotel de la Poste BP 121. Tel: 214 53. Near Clémenceau Square, overlooking the bay. Once the best hotel in town, it is now so run-down and casually managed that it cannot be recommended. There's an annexe where the air-conditioning and hot water sometimes work and there's a wonderful view. Caged lemurs in the courtyard of the main hotel. Poor value at 30,000fmg.

'Ma Contstance' The owners of the restaurant (see *Where to eat*) have a few comfortable rooms for 13,000fmg. English spoken. Recommended.

Category B
Hotel Paradis du Nord Rue Villaret Joyeuse, across from the market; taxi drivers know it. This is probably the best value in town since everything works – air-conditioning, hot water... The rooms themselves are cell-like (18,000fmg) except for No 1 (30,000fmg) which is marvellously spacious and overlooks the colourful market. There is a pleasant balcony dining room (with good food) a laundry service, and a secure garage if you are driving (you can rent cars from here). The noise from the Saturday night disco could be disturbing but doesn't seem to penetrate the rooms.

Hotel Valiha 41 Rue Colbert. BP 270. Tel: 215-31. Popular, with helpful staff. About 20,000fmg. Some rooms have air-conditioning and hot water – if they're working.

Hotel Fian-tsilaka 13 Bvd Etienne. Tel: 223-48. 25,000 - 30,000fmg. Good restaurant.

Hotel la Rascasse Rue Surcouf, opposite Air Mad. Tel: 223 64. 23,000fmg with air-conditioning, 18,000fmg with fan. Adequate.

Category C
Nouvel Hotel 75, Rue Colbert. Tel: 222 62. Double rooms with all facilities, 15,000fmg, but noisy with an all-night disco. The restaurant is particularly recommended.

Hotel Maymoune 7 Rue Bougainville. 15,000fmg. Recently refurbished and good value; rooms have fan, bidet, shower and sink. Balcony with view onto street. Very helpful owner/manager.

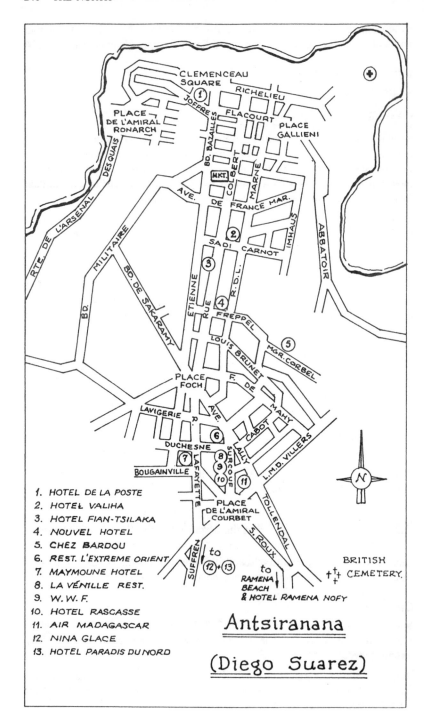

1. HOTEL DE LA POSTE
2. HOTEL VALIHA
3. HOTEL FIAN-TSILAKA
4. NOUVEL HOTEL
5. CHEZ BARDOU
6. REST. L'EXTREME ORIENT
7. MAYMOUNE HOTEL
8. LA VÉNILLE REST.
9. W. W. F.
10. HOTEL RASCASSE
11. AIR MADAGASCAR
12. NINA GLACE
13. HOTEL PARADIS DU NORD

Antsiranana

(Diego Suarez)

Where to eat

La Venilla   This is the best food in town; the restaurant, run by two Malagasy brothers, is up the road from the Hotel Rascasse and next to the WWF office.

Yachy   (pronounced Yahshee) about 100m north of La Venilla (next to the Alliance Francaise) is recommended.

L'Extreme Orient   An inexpensive and popular restaurant near Air Mad.

Snacks and fast food are easy to find. The **Hortensia**, near the post office, does fast food at all times of the day. If your hotel does not serve breakfast, go to the **Boulangerie Amicale**, between the Rascasse and the cinema. Excellent hot rolls and *pain au chocolat*. The **Ninaglace** is recommended for its tasty icecream, yoghurt and fruit juice. **Glace Gourmande** probably serves the best ice-cream in town.

Excursions

NEAR TOWN

The British cemetery

On the outskirts of town on the road that leads to the airport, the British cemetery is on a side road opposite the main Malagasy cemetery and is well-signposted. Here is a sad insight into Anglo-Malagasy history: rows of graves of the British troops killed in the battle for Diego in 1942, and the larger numbers, mainly East African and Indian soldiers serving in the British army, who died from disease during the occupation of the port. Impeccably maintained by the Commonwealth War Graves Commission, this is a peaceful and moving place.

Ramena Beach

This is a lovely sandy beach about 20km from the town centre. Get there by taxi-brousse (5,000fmg) or private taxi. On Sundays there is a bus. It's a beautiful drive around the curve of the bay, with some fine baobabs en route. A restaurant has recently opened near the beach.

Montagne des Français (French Mountain)

The mountain gets its name from the memorial to the French and Malagasy killed during the allied invasion in 1942. Another sad reminder of a war about which the locals can have had little understanding. There are several crosses but the main one was laboriously carried up in 1956 to emulate Jesus's journey to Calvary.

It is a hot but rewarding climb up to this high point with splendid views and some nearby caves. Take a taxi 8km along the coast road towards Ramena beach, to the start of the old road up the mountain. The track winds upwards, with obvious short cuts; the big cross is reached in about an hour. It's best to go very early in the morning (good bird-watching) or in the evening. The mountain supports unusual vegetation: baobabs, aloes, and until recently pachypodium, but these have evidently all been dug up.

FURTHER AFIELD
Windsor Castle and Courriers Bay

A half day drive (4WD) or full day bike excursion takes you to the fantastic rock known as Windsor Castle. This monolith (visible from Antsiranana) is steep-sided and flat-topped, so made a perfect look-out point during times of war. The views from there are superb. It was fortified by the French, occupied by the Vichy forces, and liberated by the British. A ruined staircase still runs to the top (if you can find it). There are some *tsingy* here, and many endemic water-retaining plants including a local species of pachypodium, *Pachypodium windsorii*.

To get there take the road that runs west towards Ampasindava, where you turn right (north) along a rocky road, then left towards Windsor Castle. The road continuing north is the very rough one to Cap d'Ambre. 'I didn't find the track to the top of the rock but left my bike in the bushes and climbed to the top (one hour). Very good views (360°) over Madagascar's most northern area, and indeed an exceptional flora! Take enough drinking water! The last shop is about 25km before reaching Windsor Castle. Also don't forget a puncture repair kit.' (Luc Selleslagh)

Courriers Bay, half an hour beyond Windsor Castle, is an exceptionally fine beach.

Towards Cap d'Ambre

To reach the northerly tip of Madagascar you need a 4WD or motor-bike and nerves of steel. Or a mountain bike and plenty of time. If you can carry enough water this area merits exploration; it is seldom visited and is particularly interesting for its flora.

Lac Antanavo (Lac Sacré)

The sacred lake is about 75km south of Antsiranana, near the small town of Anivorano. It attracts visitors more for its legends than the reality of a not particularly scenic lake and the possibility of seeing a crocodile. The story is that once upon a time Anivorano was situated amid semi-desert and a thirsty traveller arrived at the village and asked for a drink. When his request was refused he warned the villagers that they would soon have more water than they could cope with. No sooner had he left than the earth opened, water gushed out, and the mean-minded villagers and their houses were inundated. The crocodiles which now inhabit the lake are considered to be ancestors (and to wear jewellery belonging to their previous selves. So they say).

On the two occasions I have been there I have seen no crocs (and there are reported to be only three left now), but other travellers have been luckier. The crocodiles are sometimes fed by the villagers, so you may do best to book a tour with Madagascar Airtours or Hotel Ramena Nofy in Antisiranana; they should know when croc feeding day is.

There are two smaller lakes nearby which the locals fish cautiously –

often from the branches of a tree to avoid a surprise crocodile attack.

Personally I feel that Anivorano is not worth a special trip but is an interesting stop if you are coming by road from the south.

MONTAGNE D'AMBRE (AMBER MOUNTAIN) NATIONAL PARK

This is part of the Montagne d'Ambre Reserves Complex which also includes the Special Reserves of Ankarana, Analamera, and Fôret d'Ambre. The project is funded by USAID, the Malagasy government and the WWF and was the first to involve local people in all stages of planning and management. The aims were: conservation, rural development, and education. Ecotourism has been encouraged successfully with good information and facilities now available.

Montagne d'Ambre National Park is a splendid example of upland moist forest. This volcanic massif ranges in altitude from 850m to 1,475m and has its own micro-climate with rainfall equal to the eastern region (see *Weather*). There are tall trees, orchids, unusual birds, an assortment of reptiles, amphibians and insects, and two subspecies of the brown lemur – Sanfords lemur, (*Eulemur fulvus sanfordi*) and crowned lemur (*Eulemur coronatus*). Both are endangered, and this is the most easily accessible place to see them. Sanfords lemur is brown, the males having splendid white/beige ear-tufts and side-whiskers surrounding black faces, whilst the females are of a more uniform colour with no whiskers and a grey face (but note that Sanfords colouring can vary a lot; in Ankarana they are of a uniform colour, and very dark – almost black – females may be seen). Crowned lemurs get their names from the triangle of black between the ears of the male; the rest of the animal is reddish brown, with white belly and face. Female crowned lemurs have a little red tiara across the forehead, grey backs and tails, and the same white belly and face as the male. Young are born from September to November. Ben Freed, who spent two years studying these lemurs and provided the above description, adds: 'A useful way of locating them is to listen. The calls, particularly of the crowned lemur, are quite distinct and loud. It is a short, piercing *Waee*. Sanford's lemur often gives a rasping call that lasts for several seconds.'

The park has, in theory, 30km of paths, but many of these are overgrown. 10km of paths would now be more accurate: they lead to the Petit Lac, the Jardin Botanique, and two waterfalls, Grande Cascade and Petite Cascade. There is also a Sentier Touristique and a beautiful, two day trip to the highest point.

The waterfalls provide the two focal points. If time is short and you want to watch wildlife rather than walk far, go to the Petite Cascade (along the track beyond the old warden's house). Here you'll find an idyllic fern-fringed grotto with waterfalls splashing into a pool and feeding a stream which is visited by malachite kingfishers. In the hot season there is a colony of little bats (I don't know the species) twittering in the overhang to the right of the pool. The area between the building and the waterfall is also the best place to see lemurs. Be quiet, take your time, and please don't leave litter in this marvellous spot.

The more energetic can take the marked track (on the right as you walk up from the park entrance) to the Grande Cascade. Excellent bird watching here, some lovely tree ferns, and finally a steep descent to the foot of the waterfall (only do it when dry – it's slippery and dangerous when wet). On your way back you'll pass a path on the right (left as you go towards the waterfall) marked 'Jardin Botanique'; don't be misled into thinking this will lead you to the rose-garden. It's a tough up-and-down but rewarding walk that eventually joins the main track to the old building.

'I guess my main bit of advice for tourists is not to expect too much – this is *not* Berenty or Nosy Komba. For me the beauty of the place is not that you have lemurs eating out of your hands, nor that you are guaranteed to see lemurs (you are not); the beauty lies in appreciating what fate allows you to see, hear and feel.' (Ben Freed)

Permits and information

Permits and a very good information booklet are available in Antsiranana from the WWF office on Rue Surcouf, opposite Air Mad (the entrance is on a side street). It costs the usual 20,000fmg.

Weather

The rainy season (and cyclone season) is from December through April. The dry season is May through August, but there is a strong wind, *varatraza*, almost every day. The hot season is September through November. In the park this is a very pleasant time, cooler than Antsiranana, some rain, and baby lemurs.

Getting there/staying there

Although the park can be done in one day with Madagascar Airtours, it is really much too nice a place to hurry through. Camping is now permitted in the park and there will eventually be accommodation for visitors.

The road from Antsiranana to Joffreville (about 27km from Antsiranana, and the nearest 'town' to the park) is tarred, and the remaining 7km to the park is kept in in good condition. Taxi-drivers will take you to the barrier. Taxi-brousses run regularly to Joffreville.

Note: the temperature in the park is, on average, 10°F cooler than in Antsiranana, and it is likely to be wet and muddy. There may also be leeches. Do not wear shorts and sandals. Bring rain gear, insect repellent, and a sweater, however hot you are at sea-level.

ANKARANA

108km south of Antsiranana is a small limestone massif, Ankarana. An 'island' of *tsingy* (limestone karst pinnacles) and forest, the massif is penetrated by numerous caves and canyons. Some of the largest caves have collapsed, forming isolated pockets of river-fed forest with their own perfectly protected flora and fauna. The caves and their rivers are also home to crocodiles, some reportedly six metres long.

After a preliminary look in 1981, The Crocodile Caves of Ankarana Expedition, led by Dr Jane Wilson, spent several months in 1986 exploring and studying the area, and their findings excited considerable scientific interest, a TV film and a book by Jane Wilson (see *Bibliography*).

Ankarana is a Special Reserve but until recently had received poor protection. Now it has been included in the WWF's Montagne d'Ambre Reserves Complex and ecotourism is being encouraged.

The main campsite is known as 'Camp des Anglais' (following the Crocodile Cave Expedition). There are three separate areas, so although it tends to get crowded you can usually escape from other travellers. Visitors to your campsite will almost certainly include a troop of crowned lemur (the photo on the cover of this book was taken here) and *Galidia elegans*. The water supply is a good 30 minutes walk away down a slippery slope.

The best *tsingy* is about two hours away, over very rugged terrain. The vegetation is similar to that in the south, with many euphorbias, pachypodium and other succulents. The destination of this hike is Lac Vert, an incredibly beautiful place even if you and your guide are unlikely to be alone there.

Other campsites are Camp des Americains, Camp des Africains, and Camp de Fleur. Camp des Africains is near the caves, five hours walk from Camp des Anglais. There is a total of 97km of mapped cave passages in the massif. Camp de Fleur is about two hours from Camp des Anglais and is a good base for visiting Lac Vert and some of the best *tsingy*.

The pockets of forest in Ankarana are home to a large number of animals including ten species of lemur: crowned lemur, Sanfords lemur, grey bamboo lemur, grey lesser mouse lemur, fat-tailed dwarf lemur, avahi, phaner, lepilemur, diademed sifaka and aye-aye.

Getting there/back

There are two access towns off the main Antsiranana-Ambanja road, Anivorano and Amilobe (see map). Most people approach from the north, turning off at Anivorano and heading for the village of Matsaborimanga. The road is very bad – suitable for 4WD only. Allow five hours from Antsiranana. You can also approach from the south but the road is even worse; be prepared to walk.

You can camp at Matsaborimanga, and there are limited food supplies in the shops. There is a bathing pool, but observe village customs: men and

to Anivorano
Antanamisondrotra

Matsaborimanga

CAMP DES ANGLAIS
CAMP DES AMERICANS
Ω Antsiranandaha

Ω Andetobe

Antsatrabombo

Ambatomena
×Ω

Mahamasina

Lac Vert

Andrafiabe

FIRST CANYON
Andrafiabe
Ω

SECOND CANYON

RN6

Bats Cave
Ω

Anjohimilaitety
Ω

COMORO

BARRIER of MAHAMASINA

to Ambilobe

Diego Suarez

Anivorano

Matsaborimanga

Andrafiabe

Tsingy

Ambataoharana

SUGAR CANE FIELDS

Ambilobe

Schematic of Region

N

Ankarana

Reserve

women bathe at different times. From Matsaborimanga it is still quite a way to the campsite.

Most visitors hike out of the reserve: a very hot 2½ hour walk which brings you onto RN6. The wide track starts at Camp des Anglais and runs east, becoming narrower as it cuts through the reserve, crossing a dry (in the dry season) river bed, and joining another broad track which meets the main road about 18km south of Anivorano. If you have arranged your guide beforehand you can take this route in. Look for the track near a sign '26N' opposite a sign for Ankarana.

What to bring
You'll need strong shoes or boots, a rucksack, food for the duration of your stay, and food for your guide (rice can be bought in Matsaborimanga), water bottle, insect repellent, torch (flashlight) for the caves plus batteries.

Organised tours
Given the difficulty of getting to Ankarana, many people prefer to do it as part of an organised tour. In theory Madagascar Air Tours in Diego can provide this, but so far they have failed to meet the challenge (ie to provide 4WD vehicles, knowledgeable guides, porters for the hike back, etc). A better bet is the Hotel Ramena Nofy or the agency Palma Rosa in Antsiranana and also in Anbanja (where it is cheaper). No doubt there are other agencies that could do an equally good job.

Permit and guides
A permit for Ankarana should be purchased from the WWF in Antsiranana. If you are going straight to Ankarana from Tana check the permit situation with ANGAP.

It would be dangerous to go into the reserve without a guide. Not only do they know the paths and the most interesting areas, but they know where scarce water is to be found. Guides live in Matsaborimanga. Christo works for the WWF and knows the area well. Felix is equally well recommended. Solimo knows the area but speaks no English and only a little French. Try to check your guide's credentials. One unhappy correspondent had seen nothing after a very expensive trip to Ankarana because the 'guide' had not been there before. The guide's fee is 10,000fmg per day.

Thanks to Christina Raymondo, Adrian Deneys, and Clare Hermans for information on Ankarana.

'The baboon grows to an enormous size... at least seven feet high when standing on its hind legs. It is a very savage and untractable animal and its imperfect and hideous resemblance to the human form gives it an horrific appearance'.
Samuel Copland, History of the Island of Madagascar, 1822

THE ROUTE FROM ANTSIRANANA TO SAMBAVA

A French correspondent defines this trip as 'Ambiance "Camel Trophy" garantie'. Not for the faint-hearted or soft-bottomed. You go via Ambilobe on a reasonable road, and then take a terrible road to Vohemar (Iharana). Take any transport that's going; probably a truck. Diego - Ambilobe 6 hours, Ambilobe - Vohemar, 20 hours.

Vohemar (Iharana)

A pleasant town with a reasonable selection of places to stay if you need to recover from travelling. There are regular flights to/from here. The Air Mad office is hard to find; it's tucked away in the Star Breweries yard.

Where to stay/eat

Sol y Mar   'Excellent bungalows in a beautiful setting by the shore with shower and WC (cold water). 25,000fmg. Good, reasonably priced food.'

Poisson d'Or   Around 10,000fmg with a good restaurant.

Etoile d'Or   A good, inexpensive restaurant.

Taxi-brousse on to Sambava (see Chapter 9) takes about 7 hours, 5,000fmg.

THE ROUTE FROM ANTSIRANANA TO AMBANJA AND NOSY BE

This route is popular with travellers heading for Nosy Be but there is plenty to see in the area so it is a shame to rush through. The journey from Antsiranana to Ambanja at present takes about seven hours and costs 10,000fmg by taxi-brousse. The road, however, is being upgraded.

The first place to break your journey is **Ambilobe**. A recommended hotel/restaurant is L'Escargot; there is also the Hotel Golden. Then on to Ambanja, which merits a stay of a few days.

Ambanja
Where to stay/eat

Hotel Patricia   Shared WC, no running water. Popular with travellers. 12,500fmg.

Hotel Palma Rosa   This has a good restaurant, can arrange inexpensive tours to Ankarana and is the Air Mad agent.

Hotel Riviera   Room with a shower and WC, 8,000fmg.

Ankify

This is a beautiful beach 25km south of Ambanja with some newly built bungalows for 25,000fmg.

NOSY BE

History

Nosy Be's charms were recognised as long ago as 1649 when the British colonel, Robert Hunt, wrote: 'I do believe, by God's blessing, that not any part of the world is more advantageous for a plantation, being every way as well for pleasure as well as profit, in my estimation.' Hunt was attempting to set up an English colony on the island, at that time known as Assada, but failed because of hostile natives and disease.

Future immigrants, both accidental and intentional, contributed to Nosy Be's racial variety. Shipwrecked Indians built a magnificent settlement several centuries ago in the south east of the island, where the ruins can still be seen. The crew of a Russian ship that arrived during the Russo-Japanese war of 1904-5 with orders to attack any passing Japanese vessel and were then forgotten, are buried in the Hell-Ville cemetery. Other arrivals were Arabs, Comorans, and — more recently — Europeans flocking to Madagascar's foremost holiday resort.

When King Radama I was completing his wars of conquest, the Boina kings took refuge in Nosy Be. First they sought protection from the Sultan of Zanzibar, and he obliged by sending a warship in 1838, then two years later they requested help from Commander Passot, who landed his ship at Nosy Be. The Frenchman was only too happy to oblige, and asked Admiral de Hell, the governor of Bourbon Island (now La Réunion), to place Nosy Be under the protection of France. The island was formally annexed in 1841.

Getting there/back

By air   There are regular flights from Tana, Mahajanga and Antsiranana; 885FF/US$150 from Tana.

By boat from Mahajanga   Two days and two nights of acute discomfort. See Chapter 11.

By road and ferry   The nearest town of any size is Ambanja. The overland route here is described earlier in this chapter, and in Chapter 11.

Times of boats to Nosy Be are posted on a board in the Hotel Patricia. Taxis leave from outside the Hotel de Ville for Antsahampano, the departure point for the ferry. There are two ferries a day; the sailing times depend on the tide, and the trip takes two hours and costs 2,000fmg. You have the alternative of going by small steam boat (*vedette*). Being smaller, they are less tied to the tides, and also call first at Nosy Komba. However, you are likely to be overcharged (5,000 to 10,000fmg).

If you are taking the ferry back from Nosy Be to Antsahampano, check the board outside the ferry office in Hell-Ville (A M Hassanaly et fils) a few doors up from Air Madagascar.

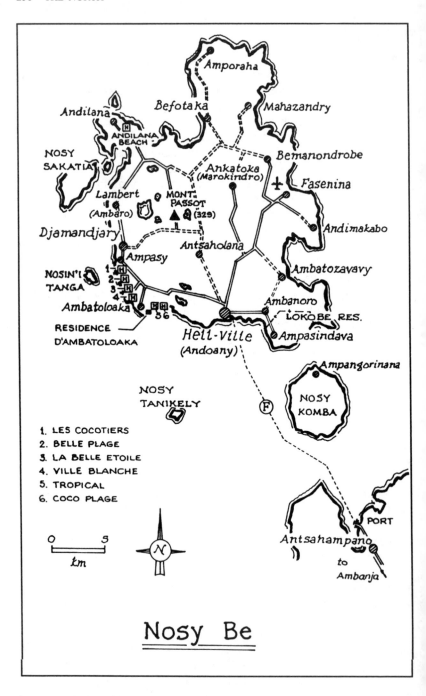

1. LES COCOTIERS
2. BELLE PLAGE
3. LA BELLE ETOILE
4. VILLE BLANCHE
5. TROPICAL
6. COCO PLAGE

Nosy Be

Nosy Be today

The name means 'Big Island' and is usually pronounced 'Nossy Bay' although 'Noos Bay' is nearer the Malagasy pronunciation. This is very much a holiday island, which comes as a bit of a shock after the rest of Madagascar. Those who have become happily accustomed to the unstructured nature of travel in the mainland find Nosy Be unbearably touristy; those who have barely survived the effort breathe a sigh of relief.

Blessed with an almost perfect climate (sunshine with brief showers), fertile and prosperous, with sugar, pepper, and vanilla grown for export, and the heady scent of *ylang-ylang* blossoms giving it the tourist-brochure name of 'Perfumed Isle', this is the place to come for a rest — providing you can afford it. Compared with the rest of Madagascar Nosy Be is *very* expensive.

Most of the easily accessible beaches on Nosy Be have been taken over by hotels, but adventurous visitors can find completely unspoilt places. The FTM map of Nosy Be (scale 1:80,000) which is readily available in Tana is very detailed and marks beaches.

Nosy Be even has some good roads (money from sugar and tourism has helped here). Transport around the island is by taxi-be or private taxi (of which there are plenty). Taxis are much more expensive than on the mainland. Bicycles are the best option.

In a hard-hitting article in the *Madagascar Tribune* entitled 'Has Nosy Be become a brothel?' the author points out that only two hotels in Nosy Be are Malagasy-owned: the Villa Blanche and Andilana Beach. Sex tourism is flourishing, the AIDS statistics are soaring. The article reflected a general uneasiness over the way foreigners are taking over Nosy Be and corrupting the culture/morals of the locals. Whether any action will be taken remains to be seen.

Hell-Ville (Andoany)

The name comes from Admiral de Hell rather than an evocation of the state of the town. Hell-Ville is quite a smart little place, its main street lined with boutiques and tourist shops. There is a market selling fresh fruit and vegetables (which may also be purchased from roadside stalls), and an interesting cemetery neatly arranged according to nationality.

You can stay in Hell-Ville, but only if you're desperate. Then there is the infamous **Hotel de la Mer**, Boulevard du Docteur Manceau, sometimes known as the Hotel de Merde. Tel: 61 353. Its rooms range from quite nice with a view of the sea, to unbelievably squalid. Prices 40,000 - 20,000fmg. There's a great view from the restaurant.

If you're determined to stay in town there are other smaller hotels around.

Where to stay (beach hotels)

There are numerous beach hotels and more going up every year. High season (mid-July to mid-September, and over the Christmas holiday) prices are high. Low season rates are more reasonable.

THE NORTH

Andilana Beach Hotel   Tel: 611 76. Built as a Holiday Inn, it has 117 characterless rooms with air conditioning (hot water erratic, though). Swimming pool, tennis, etc. High season: 930FF double, 635FF single (half board). Low season: 616FF double, 467FF single. Dinner 110FF. A lovely location (though 45 minutes' drive from town) with a choice of two beaches and some snorkelling if you are willing to wade out far enough. Good food and everything the holiday maker could desire. Madagascar Airtours has its office here.

DJAMANDJARY AREA

There is a string of hotels along the beach near this ugly small town. The beach is shielded by coconut palms and pleasant − although some visitors complain that it shelves so gradually you cannot swim easily − and is well-maintained (swept) by each hotel.

Les Cocotiers   BP 191. Tel: 613 14. 16 very pleasant bungalows in full working order. Very good food. High season: 515FF per person (double) and 730FF single half board. Almost half that price low season. Dinner 17,000fmg.

Hotel Palm Beach   This used to be my favourite hotel before it deteriorated into something resembling a brothel. At the time of writing it is closed for complete renovation under new management. Well worth checking out.

Villa Blanche   Tel (in Tana): 228 54. Malagasy owned bungalows just up the beach from Palm Beach. Single with breakfast 215FF, Double 160FF per person. Main meal 'Plat de résistance' with seafood, 80FF. Airport transfer, 50FF. Very pleasant and friendly.

The Villa Blanche brochure is most evocative. Among the delights they offer are 'transfert by car or motor-bat' and an excursion to Nosy Iranja, 'A beautiful island... with its thin and white beaches. And the lunch served by Villa Blanche is also thin and fine.' If you are still undecided they give further encouragement: 'You are not ready to die, but let profi of some this tropical heaven... You surely will be enjoyed by beauties, fragrances and cooking. You'll say, if the Eden existes again, you've seen it.' And to dispel the last shadow of doubt they assure you that they 'agree paying Master-Cad'.

Belle Plage   A new hotel north of Villa Blanche. 204FF per person (double), 291FF single. Meals about 17,000fmg.

La Belle Etoile   North of Villa Blanche offers camping for 2,000fmg and a meal for 5,000fmg. Warmly recommended by a trio of shoestring travellers who rightly point out there is very little for this price in Nosy Be.

AMBATOLOAKA

This is a charming little fishing village with the best options for inexpensive places to stay. Several private houses rent out the odd room, so ask around. The established places are listed below.

Résidence Ambatoloaka   BP 130. Tel: 613 68. 165FF per person (double) and 230FF single, half board. Dinner 17,000fmg. The full range of tours are available here, including Nosy Iranja and a luxury trip to Nosy Komba with lunch at the restaurant La Pazziella when it reopens.

Hotel Tropical   Four new bungalows with more being built. 35,000fmg per bungalow with shower and WC. Breakfast included. Recommended.

Hotel Coco Plage   1km from the Résidence Ambatoloaka (away from town). About 30,000fmg per person with breakfast. Very nice beach bungalows with bathrooms.

There are several **restaurants** at Ambatoloaka, including the **Tonga Soa** and the modest but highly acclaimed **Chez Angeline** which does a superb set meal of sea food and *poulet au coco* for about 10,000fmg. Book it in advance. Competition for Chez Angeline is provided by a Malagasy woman in a food-stall opposite. 'Cooking on an open fire she turns out the best food in the village. We had grilled fish, crab, salad, and rice all for 4,000fmg.'

Excursions

NOSY BE

Mont Passot

The highest point of the island (315m), affording marvellous views of a series of deep-blue crater lakes. These are said to contain crocodiles (though I have never seen one) and to be sacred as the home of the spirits of the Sakalava and Antakarana princes. It is *fady* to fish there, or to smoke, wear trousers or any garment put on over the feet, or a hat, while on the lakes' shores. It is, in any case, difficult to get down to the water since the crater sides are very steep.

There are two roads to Mont Passot: one runs from near the Andilana Beach Hotel, and the other from **Djamandjary**, the island's second biggest town, noted for its cyclone-proof cement igloos and sugar factory (bring your own bottle and rum is cheaper to buy than water). Most people come to Mont Passot to see the sunset, but in the clear air of Nosy Be the sunset is generally less than spectacular, so if you are on foot or bike make a day excursion of it and take a picnic. Souvenir sellers have discovered the joys of having captive *vazahas* waiting for the sun to dip, and have set up tables for their wares. This is not a hill of solitude.

Lokobe

This is one of the most worthwhile trips in Nosy Be. Jean-Robert, an enterprising native of Lokobe, takes you to his little village adjoining the reserve which is only accessible by pirogue. During the course of the day you are served a sumptuous meal by his wife and taken on a tour of the forest where Jean-Robert, who speaks excellent English and is a natural show-man, explains the traditional uses of various plants and points out a variety of animals. His knowledge of and enthusiasm for natural history is excellent and the experience is heightened by the knowledge that these visits benefit the villagers and bring home to them the importance of conserving the wildlife that tourists come to see.

The trip starts at Ambatozavavy, a fishing village of palm thatched huts, a school, and a few pirogues drawn up on the yellow sand. The name of the village means 'Woman stone', a reference to the nearby sacred rock which is said to represent women's genitalia, and to bestow fertility on those who visit it. Depending on the tide you either board your pirogue at the village or walk past mangroves, while Jean-Robert explains their ecology and points out the fiddler crabs and mud-skippers. The pirogues are narrow, somewhat leaky, but very stable with their outriggers. Villagers do the paddling, so you can either sit, feeling like a tourist, or paddle and feel hot and sweaty but involved. It takes about 45 minutes to cross the bay to Ampasipohy (which means 'Short beaches').

After a drink, you are taken on your tour of the forest. The trails are clear (though steep) and the pace slow, but the insects can be ferocious so bring repellent. You are bound to see a lepilemur, *Lepilemur dorsalis*, which, unlike the species in Berenty, spends its day dozing in the fork of a favourite tree rather than in a hole. You should see black lemurs (shyer than those on Nosy Komba) and with luck a boa and chameleons. The chameleons here are the *pardalis* species and in the breeding season (November to May) the male is bright green and the female a pinkish colour. The villagers grow vanilla and peppers, so you will observe the non-destructive combination of crops and forest.

When you arrive back at the village, lunch will be ready: imaginatively cooked local produce served on a banana leaf table cloth. Then you are ready to climb into the pirogue for the trip back.

This excursion costs about 45,000fmg which includes food but *not* drinks. Some groups are charged a 'landing fee'. Clarify these extras with Jean-Robert before you leave and anyway bring lots of small change since the handicrafts sold in the village are of good quality and it's another way the villagers can benefit from your visit. Bring sunscreen, insect repellent, a water bottle, and a plastic bag for your shoes and camera while you are in the boat.

Your hotel will know where to find Jean-Robert.

OTHER ISLANDS

Excursions to nearby — and far-off — islands are part of the Nosy Be experience. There are various boat-owners that offer these trips. Two are

THE BLACK LEMUR
FOREST PROJECT

Lokobe is Nosy Be's only reserve, and as such is closed to tourists. It protects the last fragment of forest on this once lush island, and there is a proposal for it to become a National Park so visitors may get a taste of the forest and its inhabitants.

Since 1991 a small team of enthusiastic conservationists (British and Malagasy) have been studying the black lemurs that live in Lokobe, and working with the nearby villagers whose slash-and-burn agriculture and selective tree felling (for house building and pirogues) threaten the animals' survival. Josephine Andrews, the project coordinator and her Malagasy colleagues have worked tirelessly and sympathetically to get the conservation message across, particularly to school children. The results are very encouraging.

Tourists are invited to visit the project and learn more about the work. Their visits will also benefit the local communities and make them less dependent on agriculture. Two villages next to the reserve, Marodoka and Ambalohonko, will be opened to visitors so their traditions and way of life can be explained by the people themselves. Information sheets on each village are being prepared describing everything of interest, from legends and stories to flora and fauna. Eventually it is hoped to set up an information centre in Hell-Ville so that tourists in search of sea and sand may also learn about the inhabitants of the island, both human and animal.

For more information write in advance of your visit to Josephine Andrews, Bureau de Poste, Hell-Ville, Nosy Be or 53 Priory Way, North Harrow, middlesex HA2 6DQ, England.

HAINTENY

It is through his subjects that the sovereign reigns,
It is the rocks that cause the stream to sing.
It is its feathers that make the chicken large.
The palm-trees are the feet of the water.
The winds are the feet of the fire.
The beloved is the tree of life.

French: Jean-Francois Py, who lives in Ambataloaka (and has rooms to rent), operates two boats, one of which sleeps nine people. His company is called Soleil et Découvertes. Daniel visits hotels looking for passengers for his tours to Nosy Komba and Nosy Tanikely.

If you want to see the Nosy Be archipelago in style there is a 114ft vessel, the *Etranger*, which takes a maximum of eight passengers in luxury staterooms. Watersports equipment is on board, including scuba diving gear. Information from Elite Nautique, PO Box 1700, Durban, 4000 South Africa. Tel: 223 096; fax: 222 591.

Nosy Komba (Nosy Ambariovato)
'Komba' means 'Lemur' (interestingly it is the Swahili word for bush-baby which of course is the African relative of the lemur) and Lemur Island is a 'must' for most visitors to Nosy Be which now includes an increasing number of cruise-ships. Understandably, with several boat-loads of camera-toting tourists arriving every day, the villagers of Nosy Komba seem rather fed up with visitors and even the lemurs have eaten their fill of bananas by noon. Nevertheless, it is a typical Malagasy village and full of charm.

Black lemurs have lived here unmolested for centuries (it had been *fady* to hunt them and they now support the village financially. The ancestor who initiated the *fady* must be pleased with himself). If you want the lemurs-on-your-shoulders experience and can't get to Berenty, you should definitely come here since it's an unforgettable experience to see these engaging animals at such close quarters, and the photo-opportunities are excellent, especially in the spring when they have babies. Only the male *Eulemur macaco* is black; the females, which give birth in September, are chestnut brown with white ear-tufts.

A small fee (1,500fmg) is charged to see the lemurs, and en route to their 'compound' everyone in the village will try to sell you something. Since you are buying direct from the grower/maker, this is the best place to get vanilla and handicrafts (carved pirogues, clay animals, and unusual and attractive 'lace' table-cloths and curtains).

One of the former glories of Nosy Komba, its coral, has sadly completely disappeared (see Box on page 59) so snorkelling is no longer rewarding. The sea and beach near the village is polluted with human waste, but there is a good swimming beach round to the left.

All the hotels do excursions to Nosy Komba which is usually combined with Nosy Tanikely. The price is around 40,000fmg. An excellent lunch is included. A pirogue can be hired to take you there (late afternoon is the best time) for about 10,000fmg.

Staying on Nosy Komba
This is a relaxing place to stay for a few days. The two very simple backpacker hotels have been joined by the more upmarket Floralies. How much this will change the character of the village remains to be seen.

Hotel Floralies   A very nice new, French-owned hotel by the swimming beach (to the right as you land). Bungalows at 200FF including breakfast.

Hotel Lemuriens   Bungalows for 12,000 to 25,000fmg. Run by Martin (German) and Henriette (Malagasy). For bookings write to BP 185, Nosy Be.

Hotel Madio   BP 207. Run with flair by Toto. 5,000fmg.

Nosy Tanikely

Although now much-visited, this is still pretty close to Paradise. Nosy Tanikely is a tiny island inhabited only by the lighthouse keeper and his family (I think... there seem to be quite a lot of them these days!) and mostly unspoiled by tourism. The island is a marine reserve and it is for the snorkelling that most people visit it. And the snorkelling is wonderful. In clear water you can see an amazing variety of marine life – coral, starfish, anemones, every colour and shape of fish, turtles, lobsters... The underwater world is always astonishing; perhaps because we see less of it on television than other natural wonders, or perhaps that there is just so *much* there, so much variety, so much colour, so much weirdness. The Mad Airtours brochure has got it right when it says 'If you are eager for unreal surprises and pleasant emotions, make up your mind now and discover our new world ...'.

With this new world beneath your gaze there is a real danger of forgetting the passing of time and becoming seriously sunburnt. Even the most carefully applied sunblock tends to miss some areas, so wear a T-shirt and shorts.

Don't think you have finished with Nosy Tanikely when you come out of the water; at low tide it is possible to walk right round the island. During your circumambulation you will see (if you go anticlockwise): a broad beach of white sand covered in shells and bleached pieces of coral, a couple of trees full of flying foxes (*Pteropus rufus*), and graceful white tropic birds (*Phaethon lepturus lepturus*) flying in and out of their nests in the high cliffs. At your feet will be rock pools and some scrambling, but nothing too challenging.

Then there is the climb up to the top of the island for the view and perhaps a tour (tip expected) of the antique and beautifully maintained lighthouse.

Nosy Tanikely has lost its 'total paradise' rating given in the first three editions of this book because of the rubbish left by tourists and the boat crews that prepare the sumptuous lunches. If every reader brought a large plastic bag and did their bit to clear it up, the island would once again be spotless. As would be your conscience.

Most hotels arrange trips to Nosy Tanikely, usually combined with Nosy Komba although I think this is a bit rushed. To do justice to Nosy Tanikely you really need a full day. Instead of an organised trip you can hire a pirogue to take you there for about 50,000fmg.

Nosy Mitsio

By Charlotte de la Bedoyère

If you are something of a desert island/snorkelling addict, and have been to Nosy Tanikely, try to visit the archipelago of Nosy Mitsio. This handful of islands lies some 60 - 70km from Nosy Be and about the same distance from the mainland. The largest is La Grande Mitsio, but the one I visited was the uninhabited Tsara Banjina ('Beautiful Beaches'). It is a tiny jewel. The red, grey and black volcanic rocks, rising quite high at its centre, have a mass of lush, green vegetation clinging to them, from full-grown trees to tiny rockery plants. But its real glory are the pure white beaches of coarse sand, along which laps a crystal-clear green/indigo sea. Every rock, however small, sparkles with an abundance of coral and marine life. Turtles and stingrays loll near the beaches.

In a small boat it takes 6 - 8 hours to reach Nosy Mitsio, depending on the winds, so you must reckon on a minimum of 2 - 3 days or you will have no time to experience its peace and purity. Almost any of the major hotels on Nosy Be will organise a trip which costs about 400FF per day per person for a group of 3 - 5, all meals (but no drinks) included.

The long journey is also rewarding. We saw dolphins and fished tuna and carangue. The latter was made into a superb dinner by the crew. I spent the night in a very adequate tent, sleeping on the groundsheet, so if you want something softer than sand, bring it with you.

I kept asking myself how long can this island stay a pure paradise? Already I found plastic bottles and cans, although the rules say you must take these away with you, the island being privately owned. Across the water on La Grande Mitsio one could see the horrifying smoking black patches amid the green, despite the fact that the island is only inhabited by a few fisherfolk. When the ocean was absolutely calm, one could detect a very thin film on the surface. No-one could positively tell me what it was. Some said it was whale excrement! I wish I could believe this rather than the other explanation that it is from the silt-laden rivers that pour into the ocean.

Nosy Iranja

The classic palm-fringed island (actually two islands connected by a sandy causeway) with clear water for swimming and snorkelling. This is a breeding area for sea-turtles. To be worthwhile you need to make this a three day excursion (with tents). Prices are comparable with Mitsio.

THE M/S ASGARI

By Lisa Rose

We arrived in Majunga at 5.00am on a Tuesday. My Malagasy companion started a long series of enquiries about the cargo boat to Nosy Be. Each time the departure time was moved back several hours. We were finally told to be shipside at midnight.

The sight of the rusty little *M/S Asgari* did not inspire much confidence. We joined boxes of cigarettes, sacks of foot-long planks of wood, and several Malagasy families. We had our provisions: bananas, a baguette, two bottles of Eau Vive and a wheel of *La vache qui rit* cheese. We left at 2.00am. I settled down on a potato sack next to the the smokestack and fell miraculously asleep. Two hours after sunrise it became unbearably hot and I took refuge under a borrowed umbrella. At 4pm the engine stopped and some banging started below. After the sun went down and we were still just bobbing on the waves a terrible wind turned the tropics into the arctic. The banging stopped.

Thursday morning the banging started while I fried above and prayed for breeze. At 2.30pm a man covered in black grease emerged to tell me it would be three more hours before they got the engine fixed. At 5.30, as promised, the smokestack sent a beautiful burst of black smoke into the air and we were chugging along again. Spirits soared.

Friday at 2.30am it began to rain on us in the freezing wind. The engine stopped. At 7.00 a man began to radio for help. At 8.30 we received a response: the promise of a rescue boat within a day. Because of our lack of food and dwindling water supply it was hard to look on this as good news. At 10.00pm the rescue boat arrived and those that could afford it jumped across. The rest stayed with the *Asgari*. We got to Nosy Be on Saturday morning at 8.00. After nearly four days on the ocean I had to restrain myself from kissing the solid ground!

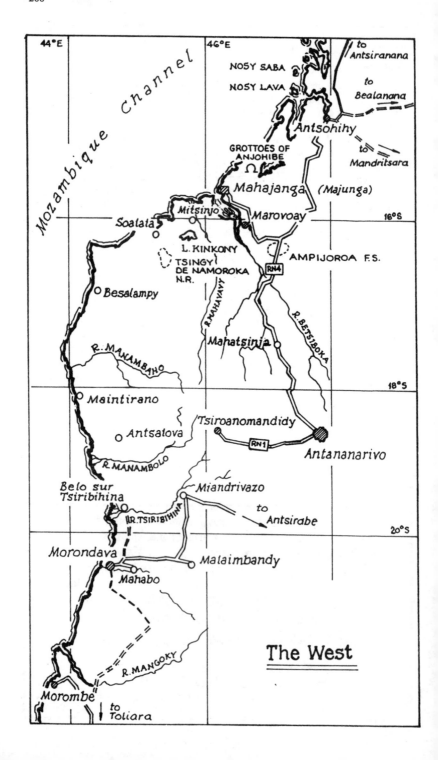

The West

Chapter 11

The West

INTRODUCTION

The west of Madagascar is the home of the Sakalava people. For a while in Malagasy history this was the largest and most powerful tribe, ruled by their own kings and queens. The Sakalava kingdom was founded by the Volamena branch of the Maroserana dynasty which emerged in the south-west during the 16th century. Early in the 17th century a Volamena prince, Andriamisara, reached the Sakalava river and gave its name to his new kingdom. His son, Andriandahifotsy (which means 'white man') succeeded him around 1650 and, with the aid of firearms acquired from European traders, conquered the south-western area from the Onilahy river to the Manambolo river which became known as the Menabe. Later kings conquered first the Boina, the area from the Manambolo to north of present-day Mahajanga, and then the north-west coast as far as Antsiranana.

By the 18th century the Sakalava empire occupied a huge area in the west, but divided into the Menabe in the south and the Boina in the north. The two rulers fell out, unity was abandoned, and in the 19th century the area came under the rule of the Merina. The Sakalava did not take kindly to domination and sporadic guerrilla warfare continued in the Menabe area until French colonial times.

The Sakalava kingdom bore the brunt of the first serious efforts by the French to colonise the island. For some years France had laid claims (based on treaties made with local princes) on parts of the north and north-west, and in 1883 two north-west fortresses were bombarded, followed by Mahajanga. This was the beginning of the end of Madagascar as an independent kingdom.

The modern Sakalava have relatively dark skins. The west of Madagascar received a number of African immigrants from across the Mozambique Channel and their influence shows not only in the racial characteristics of the people, but in their language and customs. There are a number of Bantu words in their dialect, and their belief in *tromba* (possession by spirits) and *dady* (royal relics cult) are of African origin.

The Sakalava do not practise second burial. The quality of their funerary art (in one small area) rivals that of the Mahafaly: birds and naked figures are a feature of Sakalava tombs, the latter frequently in erotic positions. Concepts of sexuality and rebirth are implied here. The female figures are often disproportionately large, perhaps recognising the importance of women in the Sakalava culture.

Sakalava royalty does not require an elaborate tomb since kings are considered to continue their spiritual existence through a medium with healing powers, and in royal relics.

The west offers a dry climate, deciduous vegetation, endless sandy beaches with little danger from sharks — although the sea can be very rough — and fewer tourists than most parts of the country. The lack of roads is one of its attractions; this is the ideal area for mountain bikers or walkers. Adventurous travellers will have no trouble finding a warm welcome in untouristed villages, their own deserted beach and some spectacular landscapes.

Opposite major rivers, the seawater along the west coast is a brick red colour: 'like swimming in soup', as one traveller puts it. This is the laterite washed into the rivers from the eroded hillsides of the highlands and discharged into the sea: Madagascar's bleeding wounds.

Getting around

Going from town to town in the west is even harder than in the east: in much of the area the roads simply aren't there and you must take to the sea. There are regular flights to the large towns and a Twin Otter serves many of the smaller ones.

MAHAJANGA (MAJUNGA)

History

Mahajanga was always a cosmopolitan city. Ideally located for trade with east Africa, Arabia and western Asia, it has been a major commercial port since the 18th century, when the Boina capital was moved here from Marovoay. Mahajanga was founded in 1745. One ruler of the Boina was Queen Ravahiny, a very able monarch, who maintained the unity of the Boina which was threatened by rebellions in both the north and south. It was Mahajanga which provided her with her imported riches and caught the admiration of visiting foreigners. Madagascar was at that time a major supplier of slaves to Arab traders and in return received jewels and rich fabrics. Indian merchants were active then, as today, with a variety of exotic goods. Some of these traders from the east stayed on, the Indians remaining a separate community and running small businesses. More

Indians arrived during colonial times.

In the 1883-85 war Mahajanga was occupied by the French. In 1895 it served as the base for the military expedition to Antananarivo which established a French Protectorate. Shortly thereafter the French set about enlarging Mahajanga and reclaiming swamp-land from the Bombetoka river delta. Much of today's extensive town is on reclaimed land.

Mahajanga today

A hot but breezy town with a large Indian population and enough interesting excursions to make a visit of a few days well worthwhile. Besides, you can eat one of the best meals in Madagascar here (Chez Chabaud)!

The town has two 'centres', the town hall (Hotel de Ville) and statue of Tsiranana (the commercial centre), and the streets near the famous baobab. Some offices, including Air Madagascar, are here. It is quite a long walk between the two – take a pousse-pousse, of which there are many. There are also some smart new buses, and taxis which operate on a fixed tariff.

A wide boulevard follows the sea along the west part of town, terminating at a lighthouse. At its elbow is the Mahajanga baobab, said to be at least 700 years old with a circumference of 14 metres.

Getting there and back

Mahajanga is 560km from Tana by fairly good road. There is a regular airservice.

Road. The most comfortable transport seems to be the Mazda bus run by Transtour. It even has head-rests! Their office in Tana is on the road that leads from the station to the Marché Atisanal. Seats are bookable in advance (14,000fmg).

There are also regular taxi-brousses which leave around 8.00, take 15 to 18 hours and cost around 13,000fmg. It's a lovely trip (at least until it gets dark) taking you through typical *Hauts Plateaux* landscape of craggy, grassy hills, rice paddies, and characteristic Merina houses with steep eaves supported by thin brick or wood pillars.

The taxi-brousse station in Mahajanga is on Ave Philibert Tsiranana.

Air. There is a twice weekly service from Tana to Mahajanga (which goes on to Nosy Be so is likely to be crowded). 550FF/US$94. Flights on other days are by Twin Otter.

Where to stay

Category A

Zaha Motel   Tel: 23 24. At Amborovy beach (not far from the airport, and 8km from Mahajanga). Beach bungalows with air-conditioning but no hot water. A fair amount of wildlife in the rooms. Air-conditioned bungalows 300FF, without air-conditioning 250FF. An air-conditioned room costs 125FF. Meals for 8,000fmg. Excellent swimming and all tourist amenities.

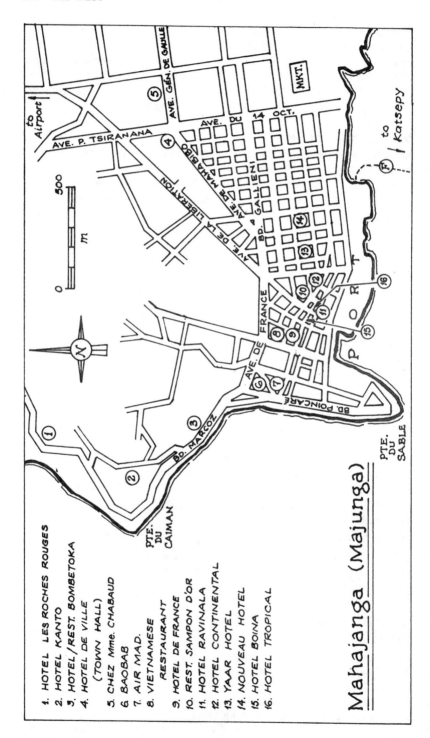

Mahajanga (Majunga)

1. HOTEL LES ROCHES ROUGES
2. HOTEL KANTO
3. HOTEL/REST. BOMBETOKA
4. HOTEL DE VILLE
   (TOWN HALL)
5. CHEZ Mme. CHABAUD
6. BAOBAB
7. AIR MAD.
8. VIETNAMESE
   RESTAURANT
9. HOTEL DE FRANCE
10. REST. SAMPON D'OR
11. HOTEL RAVINALA
12. HOTEL CONTINENTAL
13. YAAR HOTEL
14. NOUVEAU HOTEL
15. HOTEL BOINA
16. HOTEL TROPICAL

Kanto Hotel   Tel: 229 78. Overlooking the sea about 1km north of the town. Good rooms with a lovely view for 25,000fmg; basic rooms for 10,000 to 13,000fmg. Good food. Recommended.

Hotel Les Roches Rouges   Tel: 238 71. Rather sterile newish big hotel, with airconditioning. 174FF double, 157FF single. They are accustomed to providing vehicles and driver for trips to Ampijoroa.

Nouveau Hotel (New Hotel)   Tel: 221 10. Recently upgraded and now very good indeed – probably the best hotel in town. Clean, airconditioned rooms with bathrooms en suite, hot and cold running water, good restaurant, English spoken. 280FF double room with air-conditioning, 230FF double room with fan.

Hotel de France   Rue Maréchal Joffre. Tel: 237 81. 35,000fmg; shower and WC in all rooms plus air-conditioning. You pay an extra 5,000fmg if you want a room with hot water.

Category B

Chez Carron   Bungalows at the 'Village Touristique' on a long windy stretch of beach, 25,000fmg. Good food.

Hotel Voanio   Tel: 238 78. In a quiet part of town; very clean and friendly. Rooms 15,000 to 25,000fmg.

Hotel Ravinala   20,000fmg with toilet, bathroom, and air-conditioning. Very good value. Recommended.

Category C

Hotel Tropical   Near the port. 15,000 to 20,000fmg for nice rooms and a modern bathroom. There are other similarly priced hotels in the same area.

Hotel Boina   25,000fmg with shower, roaches and mosquitoes.

Yaar Hotel   Near the Nouveau. About 10,000fmg.

Hotel des Voyageurs   Near the market. Basic.

Hotel Nassib   12,000fmg.

Chez Chabaud   (see *Katsepy*). Mme Chabaud's daughter runs a basic hotel near the Hotel de Ville. Rooms 9,000 to 12,000fmg. The restaurant opposite is run by another daughter, Christiane, who is a marvellous cook. All the family speaks excellent English.

Where to eat

The **Nouveau Hotel**'s restaurant serves very good, if expensive food. **Le Sampan d'Or**, a Chinese restaurant, is recommended. Round the corner is a wonderful bakery.

   Restaurant Kizmat is highly recommended for curry and samosas. It is Muslim, so does not serve alcohol.

   The **Salon de Thé Saify**, near the cathedral, has good snacks.

Car hire

A car and driver from Transtour (18 Rue de France) costs about 75,000fmg per day. Enquire also at the Nouveau Hotel.

Excursions
Marohogo Forestry Station

Don't go here. Despite its name there is almost no forest here, and the only obvious wildlife are some brown and mongoose lemurs in a tiny cage. More interesting are the Sakalava weaver birds which have colonised an old building, but it's not worth the trip unless substantial improvements are made.

Cirque Rouge

12km from Mahajanga and about 2km from the airport (as the crow flies) is a canyon ending in an amphitheatre of red, beige and lilac-coloured rock eroded into strange shapes – peaks, spires, and castles. The canyon has a broad, sandy bottom decorated with chunks of lilac-coloured clay. It is a beautiful and dramatic spot and, with its stream of fresh water running to the nearby beach, makes an idyllic camping place. The area, Amborovy, is popular with Mahajangans who have holiday beach bungalows there so if you decide to camp you can probably hitch a ride back to town, particularly at weekends. Bring your own food.

As a day trip, a taxi will take you from Mahajanga and back for about 25,000fmg. An alternative is to take bus no 70 in the direction of the airport. The bus leaves from in front of the market near the Hotel de Ville. Ask to get off near the Zaha Motel and walk the final 6km or so. Give yourself at least one hour to look around. Late afternoon is best, when the sun sets the reds and mauves alight.

Anjohibe caves

The *Grottes de Anjohibe* are about 80km north-east of Mahajanga and accessible only by 4WD vehicle. 'Incredible, cathedral-like caves with large, cool, natural pool where you can swim. Many bats, lemurs and birds.' (Derek Schuurman). The guide Alfonse, who can be contacted at the Nouveau Hotel, is recommended.

Katsepy

No visit to Mahajanga is complete without a meal Chez Madame Chabaud. She runs a small beach hotel at Katsepy (pronounced 'Katsep'), a tiny fishing village across the bay from Mahajanga. Trained as a cook in France (Nice) she returned to her home town to practise her art for weekend visitors and now an increasing number of tourists. I've never eaten better in Madagascar, and have had nothing but praise from readers.

Katsepy is 45 minutes' journey by ferry (*avotra*) which runs three times a day at 07.30, 11.30 and 15.30 although departures are influenced by the whim of the captain. It costs 3,000fmg return and takes an hour. Be prepared for a 'wet landing' if you arrive at low tide.

On arrival there are rows of stalls selling basic food and coconut milk if you don't want to splash out at the restaurant, and also souvenirs. Do try to buy something from these local traders who gain little profit from tourist visits. Chez Chabaud is signposted. There are ten simple bungalows, with mosquito nets, shower and WC for 18,000fmg, and three beautifully presented meals a day. The main meal, lunch or dinner, costs about 13,000fmg and a special Sunday lunch may cost a little more.

In between eating you can walk on the miles of deserted beach, watch mud-hoppers (tree-climbing fish!) skipping around the mangroves, and swim in the murky-red sea.

It is best to make a reservation in advance through Mme Chabaud's daughter in Mahajanga.

FROM MAHAJANGA TO NOSY BE BY CARGO BOAT

If you're determined to go to Nosy Be the uncomfortable way, there are occasional cargo boats from Mahajanga. Their office, Ramzana Aly, is at Armement Tawakal, around the corner from the Sampon d'Or restaurant. Boats leave once a week (currently Tuesdays) and in theory take 48 hours. Bring your own food and water, and read Lisa Rose's description (page 265) before making your booking.

FROM MAHAJANGA TO NOSY BE OR ANTSIRANANA BY ROAD

Stretches of the road between Mahajanga and Ambanja, gateway to Nosy Be, are terrible, but funds are available to improve RN6 and the countryside is lovely. If you enjoy suffering you can do the trip non-stop to Antsiranana in three days and two nights. If taken slowly or in your own 4WD vehicle, however, it is a very worthwhile trip. The information below was supplied by Henk Beentje and Marten Mosch, both of whom know the route well, and by Dr Philip Jones.

Marovoay

The first town of any importance after Mahajanga on RN4. Formerly the residence of the Boina kings, the town's name means 'many crocodiles'. When the French attacked the Malagasy forces assembled in Marovoay in 1895, in their successful drive to conquer Madagascar, it is reported that hundreds of crocodiles emerged from the river to devour the dead and dying. Malagasy hunters have since got their revenge, and you would be lucky to see a croc these days.

North on RN6

After Marovoay you pass through the reserve of **Ampijoroa** (see page 277) to meet RN6, the road to Antsiranana. Heading north, on the very bad road, you can spend the night at **Mampikony**. The Hotel Les Cocotiers is adequate. **Port Bergé** (Boriziny) is a pleasant town with a nice hotel costing 8,000 to 12,000fmg. Henk recommends the restaurant Chez Joli Pain, on the big square, with fast service and good food. Try the *tsaramasa henan' kisoa*.

The road improves after Port Bergé and is quite good to Antsohihy.

Antsohihy

Pronounced 'Antsooy' this town was the birthplace of Madagascar's first president, Philibert Tsiranana. It is a good centre for exploration; there is a Solima petrol station here so you can be sure of finding transport. There is also a BTM bank. Like many towns in Madagascar it is built on two levels.

Marten lived for six months at the **Hotel de France** which is run by Housen who is helpful and knowledgable about the area. 5,000fmg with good food.

An alternative is the **Hotel Central**, in the upper town. Double room with basin, shower and bidet but no running water, 15,000fmg.

The restaurant **Baiana** doubles as the Air Mad office. The food is good but service slow.

A taxi-brousse to/from Mahajanga takes 15 hours and costs 12,000fmg.

Excursions from Antsohihy

Antsohihy is situated on a fjord-like arm of the sea which becomes the River Loza. With luck you can find a pirogue here to take you to **Ananalava**, an isolated village accessible only by boat or plane (Twin Otter). There is a hotel here costing about 5,000fmg and an open-air television.

From Ananalava you may be lucky enough to find a sturdy boat to take you to **Nosy Saba** for a few days. I have been here and doubt if any island comes closer to paradise. There is fresh water, a few fishermen's huts (abandoned in the rainy season), coconut palms, a densely-forested section with fruit-bats, coral...

Mandritsara

From Antsohihy a recently-paved road runs south-east to Mandritsara, a small town set in beautiful mountainous scenery. The name means 'Good sleep'. Taxi-brousses leave every morning, passing through **Befandriana** where there is a hotel, the Rose de Chine, for 6,000fmg. In Mandritsara you will find the **Hotel Pattes**, a nice little place with excellent food. Rooms 6,000fmg, meals 3,000fmg. There is a problem with water supply in Mandritsara − it is only available for a short time in the evenings.

There is a Twin Otter service from here.

Bealanana

An alternative road from Antsohihy runs north-east to Bealanana, also served by Air Mad. The road has also been paved recently but does not have regular public transport. However, if you have a vehicle or a mountain bike or don't mind waiting a bit, this is a worthwhile trip. It is quite high, and the temperate climate with ample rainfall allows the cultivation of potatoes and a great variety of fruit. There is no electricity in Bealanana. **Hotel La Crete** has double rooms with basin and shower, but cold water (and remember, this is a cold place). 20,000fmg. Good food. Friendly.

KOMAFIBO run taxi-brousses to Bealanana; four hours, 5,000fmg. The Air Mad office is situated in a convent and is run by a nun!

From Antsohihy to **Ambanja**, on the currently terrible road, takes about seven hours when dry. Forever when wet.

SOUTHWARD TO MITSINJO AND SOALALA

At Katsepy, taxi-brousses sometimes meet the ferry for the onward journey to **Mitsinjo** (and vehicles taking the ferry are almost certainly bound for that town). The journey takes about four hours. 'Mitsinjo is a lovely town with a wide main street, trees with semi-tame sifakas, a general store that has a few rooms available, and Hotely Salama which serves wonderful food and even has a fridge so cold beer! You order your meal in advance, and get a real feast.' (Petra Jenkins).

Not far from Mitsinjo is **Lake Kinkony** (a protected area). Petra reports: 'About once a week in the dry season the fishermen of Lac Kinkony do a supply run to Mitsinjo and you may be able to get a lift. The lake is wonderful. It boasts fish eagles, flamingoes, sacred ibis ... need I say more? It is free from bilharzia but the north-east end is a bit silty for swimming. Cadge a lift by pirogue and you've got paradise! Crocodiles are friendly and don't bother swimmers (!).'

From Mitsinjo you can make your way to **Soalala**. Joanna Durbin, working on the Project Angonoka, reports: 'During the dry season taxi-brousses run fairly regularly from Katsepy, or you can catch a motor vedette from Mahajanga. These go to Soalala to collect prawns, crabs and fish. There is no hotel in Soalala, but you can camp on the beach and the local Hotely serves excellent fish in coconut sauce – *filao voanio*. You should also try the coconut cakes *godrogodro* and *firafira* which are specialities of the region. The APN (Agents pour la Protection de la Nature) based at the Eaux et Forêts office should be able to find you a guide to take you to **Sada**, the most accessible Angonoka tortoise location, which is visible from Soalala on the peninsula on the east side of Baly Bay. It is a long walk and a short sail in a pirogue, or if you are lucky with the wind you can sail all the way. Angonoka are hard to find, especially in the dry season, but there is usually a family of Decken's sifaka, *Propithecus verreauxi deckeni* — the all-white sifaka — living in the village of Antsira, near Sada. They are protected from hunting by a *fady*.

There is an air service (Twin Otter, once a week) out of Soalala, or you can go on to **Besalampy** (which is also served by Air Mad). Then you can continue to make your way down the coast, taking cars, pirogues or whatever transport presents itself. This route is only practical in the dry season and for rugged and self-sufficient travellers. You can fly out of Maintirano, Antsalova or Belo sur Tsiribihina (and other towns — check the Air Mad timetable). Good luck!

PROJECT ANGONOKA

By Joanna Durbin

The Angonoka *Geochelone yniphora* has the dubious distinction of being the rarest tortoise in the world. It is only found in a few small patches of bamboo forest in areas around Baly Bay, near the town of Saolela, 120km south west of Mahajanga. Its most unusual feature is a long upturned projection that extends from the lower shell under the neck, giving it one of its names, the ploughshare tortoise. The projection is used by the males to turn each other over when fighting over the females, and then the victor uses his projection again to turn the female over a few times before mating.

The Angonoka are protected by a *fady* (taboo) and are not eaten by the local Sakalava people, but they are collected as pets. In the past there are stories of boats stopping at Soalala to stock up with Angonoka as provisions for a long voyage. Probably the greatest threat now to the survival of the Angonoka is the destruction of its habitat by uncontrolled bush fires.

Project Angonoka is a programme managed jointly by the Departmént des Eaux et Forêts of the Malagasy Government and Jersey Wildlife Preservation Trust (the conservation organisation created by Gerald Durrell), with support from the World Wide Fund for Nature, which aims to protect the Angonoka from extinction and to promote the protection and sustainable use of the environment in the Soalala region. A captive breeding programme based at Ampijoroa forestry station 100km south east of Mahajanga has had remarkable success since its inception in 1986 and how has 32 young Angonoka. Recommendations are in preparation for the legal protection of remaining patches of Angonoka habitat. Research projects are in progress to find out more about Angonoka distribution and ecology and also to study local people's use of natural resources so the project can be based on local participation from the start. An education and awareness programme about the Angonoka and environmental protection has so far resulted in the gifts of thirteen Angonoka pets to the project by the people of Soalala.

The breeding programme at the forestry station of Ampijoroa can be visited easily (see page 215). The more adventurous might like to make an expedition to the sandy, palm fringed outpost of Soalala which can be reached by air, taxi-brousse from Katsepy (during the dry season from April to October), or by sea in a motorised vedette from Mahajanga, which travel regularly to Soalala to collect prawns, crabs and fish.

SOUTH OF MAHAJANGA
The Forestry Station of Ampijoroa

This is part of the Réserve Naturelle Intégrale d'Ankarafantsika. Ampijoroa (pronounced Ampijeroo) is one of the very few areas of protected western vegetation, and is now under UNEP (United Nations Environmental Programme) control. A lot of research is being done there, so although there is simple accommodation it is reserved for use by students. This is a super reserve, however, so if you have a tent you should plan on camping there, and if tentless go very early in the morning from Mahajanga (the Hotel Les Roches Rouges run a pre-dawn trip for birders, or you can arrange to stay until nightfall) or stop on your way north from Tana.

One of the important projects here is the Angonoka tortoise programme run by Don Reid, a British herpetologist working with the Jersey Wildlife Preservation Trust. A visit to the project is recommended; it is encouraging to see how successful it has been. There are very nice Angonoka T-shirts for sale here.

Wildlife viewing in Ampijoroa is easy and thrilling. Right beside the warden's house is a tree that Coquerel's sifaka, *Propithecus verreauxi coquereli*, use as a dormitory. They are extremely handsome animals with the usual silky white fur but with chestnut-brown arms and thighs. I watched them for about an hour while they slowly woke up, stretched languidly, then spread their arms to take in the warming rays of the morning sun before starting their breakfast of leaves. Other lemurs to be seen in the forest are brown lemurs, *Eulemur fulvus fulvus*, *Eulemur mongoz* (if you're very lucky), and *Lepilemur edwardsi* if the guide shows you its tree. 'Birding was phenomenal. Within minutes we found sicklebill, Chabert's and hookbilled vangas all nesting round the campsite... and then the highlight: whitebreasted mesites which walk just like clockwork toys.' (Derek Schuurman).

Across the road is a lake; popular for bathing (although one can no longer say it is completely safe; the water is now polluted from clothes-washing, there have been cases of Giardia and crocodile attacks). A path runs right round it, providing excellent birding; lots of waterfowl and the very rare fish eagle.

Warnings There are no ablutions facilities at the campsite. Also 'more mozzies here than I have ever seen in my life' (D S) although I had no problem in June. Bring plenty of water. There is a small shop at the village of Andranofasika which sells soft drinks, but no Eau Vive. At some future date it is likely that there will be simple accommodation available in this village so it is worth making enquiries.

Permits and guides

Permits must currently be obtained from the Dept Eaux et Fôrets in Mahajanga, but check first with ANGAP in case the situation has changed.

The best guide is undoubtedly Jackie – highly praised by several readers.

Getting there

Ampijoroa is over 100km south of Mahajanga (about 2½ hours' drive along a good road which splits the reserve in two. It is just north of Andranofasika. A taxi-brousse costs 5,000fmg and leaves very early in the morning – about 05.00. For a small group it is worth hiring a car and driver (about 120,000fmg for 24 hours).

The reserve is on the Tana - Mahajanga road. From Tana there is a taxi-brousse run by KOFMAD which costs 11,000fmg and takes about 16 hours.

Maintirano

This small western port is attractive for people who want to get off the beaten track. As a Department of Tourism brochure puts it: 'Dare to take the quiet risk for an adventure by crossing the bay of Bombetoka and heading south towards Maintirano.' Nothing much happens here, but there is a pleasant though basic hotel and a restaurant which turns out excellent food in a primitive kitchen. The **Laizama Hotel,** which overlooks the sea, is recommended. The best restaurant is on the outskirts of town on the airport road – its name is **Buvette et Repas Mahateatea** and it looks like a garage. Book your meals in advance.

Maintirano is one of the places served by Air Mad (Twin Otter) on its Tana - Mahajanga run.

MORONDAVA .

The Morondava area was the centre of the Sakalava kingdom and their tombs — sadly now desecrated by souvenir hunters — bear witness of their power and creativity.

This was evidently a popular stopping place for sailors in the past and they seemed to have treated the natives generously. In 1833, Captain W F W Owen wrote of Morondava: 'Five boats came alongside and stunned us by vociferating for presents and beseeching us to anchor'.

Today it is a prosperous, rice-growing area and a seaside resort. It is also an excellent centre for visiting the western deciduous forest. Morondava is not on the main 'tourist circuit' and sees few groups, but is becoming popular with independent travellers.

Getting there and back

By road Morondava is 700km from Tana served by a once good road. There are regular taxi-brousses which take about 14 hours (although one reader reports a nightmare 27 hour journey) and cost around 20,000fmg. From Antsirabe the fare is 14,000 to 16,000fmg. The adventurous might like get off at Miandrivazo and continue their journey by river. See also *Travelling between Morondava and Toliara*.

By air There is a regular service from Tana or Toliara, and the Twin Otter calls here after visiting small west coast towns.

Where to stay
Category A
Chez Maggie British-owned and very comfortable 2-storey chalets on the beach. Said to be *the* place to stay in Morondava. 40,000 to 45,000fmg per person double, 173FF single.

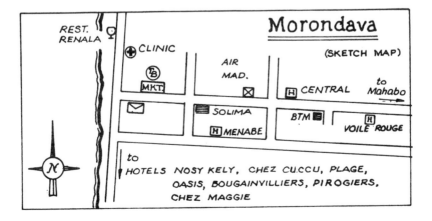

Chez Cuccu   Similar price and comfort to Chez Maggie. Next to Bougainvilliers, Italian owned, good food.

Les Bougainvilliers   BP 78. Tel: 521 63. Beach houses, around 25,000fmg, but with various levels of comfort/price. Lunch/dinner is about 9,000fmg. The waiter Michel organises excursions.

Nosy Kely   BP 22. Tel: 523 19. On the other side of the fence from the Bougainvilliers Annexe are several beach bungalows of varying prices. The most expensive is 52,000fmg for a de luxe beach bungalow, but there are others that are considerably cheaper.

Hotel Les Pirogiers   BP 73. Tel: 526 19. New French-owned (Pierre Boisard) bungalows in Betania (the beach area) past Nosy Kely. Horse-riding and water sports.

Category B

Hotel Central   BP 50. Tel: 523 78. On the main street, newish and recently revovated. 10,000 to 20,000fmg with hot shower and WC. No restaurant but breakfast served (2,000fmg). Said by expatriates to offer the best value in town.

The Oasis   Tel: 521 60. A near-beach hotel (100m from the shore). Bungalows from around 20,000fmg. Mountain bikes available here.

Hotel Menabe   10,000 to 20,000fmg, depending on whether they have hot water. 23 spacious, pleasant rooms, but a church bell next door tolls all night.

Hotel de la Plage   Tel: 520 31. Not on the plage (100m away). 7 rooms, each with basin and communal WC, from 10,500fmg. Pleasant and clean, with a balcony. Run by Muslims so no alcohol. Indian food (set menu).

Category C

La Voile Rouge   (formerly Riviera). On the left side of the main street as you enter town. Rooms range from 10,000 to 15,000fmg. Air-conditioning for the upper price range. Pleasant setting with balcony overlooking main street. Good restaurant serving French food. Main course 5,000 to 8,000fmg.

Kismat   Basic and clean, but rather noisy.

Where to eat
Renala   On the seafront and specialising in seafood.

Nosy Kely/Chez Cuccu Restaurant.

Excursions
Most of the hotels organise excursions. The most popular destinations are the **Avenue of the Baobabs** (a 'must' if you are not taking the road to Belo sur Tsiribihina anyway), Les Baobabs Amoureux (two entwined baobabs) and Sakalava tombs.

The area is famous for its **tombs**, but these are not really worth the effort. Most of the celebrated erotic sculpture has been looted, and the tombs that remain are (understandably) protected by *fady*. 'We went to Belo sur Tsiribihina to visit the royal Sakalava tombs, but we never managed to see them. The guide demanded that we go barefoot, wear no trousers, reach the tombs only in the second part of the afternoon, and then not to enter them. In the end we gave up!' (H Snippe & J Geels)

Mountain bikes are available at some of the hotels (the Oasis has them for 7,500fmg) and are an excellent way to see the Avenue of the Baobabs and other local attractions. Beware of the heat, flies, and thorns on the road.

Belo sur Tsiribihina

Apart from being the town at the end of the river Tsiribihina (see *River trips*), this place has little to offer. The famous Avenue of Baobabs is nearer Morondava and an easy excursion from there. The name means 'where one must not dive', supposedly because of the crocodiles. The warning still holds true – a woman doing her washing was eaten by a croc in 1986.

There is one hotel, the Menabe. The rooms are comfortable and clean (12,500fmg), the restaurant...unusual...and the management friendly.

You have to cross the river by ferry to get to the taxi-brousse station for Morondava.

Reserves north of Morondava

The dry deciduous forests between the rivers Morondava and Tsiribihina are of great biological importance. Many endemic species of flora and fauna are found here; the area is particularly rich in reptiles such as turtles, snakes and a variety of lizards. The fossa, *Crytoprocta ferox*, is common in these forests and seven species of lemur are found, including white sifaka, *Propithicus verreauxi verreauxi*, and the rare fork-marked lemur, *phaner furcifer*. The giant jumping rat, Madagascar's most charming rodent, is unique to this small area.

There are three protected areas between the two rivers: Andranomena, Kirindy, and Analabe. Heading north from Morondava, the first one you come to is **Andranomena**, a Special Reserve. As such it may be visited by tourists but there are no facilities or information. Much more rewarding is **Kirindy**, also known as The Swiss Forest or – more commonly – La Fôret Suisse, which lies north of Andranomena to the right of the road beyond the village of Marofandilia. It is open to visitors (but please don't get in the way of the scientists!) and there are two separate trail areas with numbered trees. You may camp near the research station (but bring water). Permits cost 7,000fmg and are available from the CFPF (Coopération Suisse) headquarters in Morondava. The office is on the outskirts of town – taxi drivers know where it is. Here you can pick up an information sheet to identify the numbered trees. If you are planning to spend any time in the forest the CFPF would prefer you to write to them in advance with your arrival date.

Analabe is a private nature reserve owned by M Jean de Heaulme. For years the plan has been to bring this up to the level of Berenty, but there are, as yet, no facilities for tourists.

Analabe lies 60km north of Morondava, to the west of Kirindy by the village of Beraboka. In addition to forest it contains some mangrove areas as well as marshes and lakes typical of coastal plain.

Tsingy de Bemaraha

The Réserve Naturelle Intégrale du Tsingy de Bemaraha lies north of the River Tsiribihina, and is Madagascar's largest reserve at 152,000ha. As with all Strict Nature Reserves tourist access is forbidden, but an area within the reserve is now open to tourists.

Without a 4WD vehicle access is very difficult, even in the dry season. The nearest town accessible by taxi-brousse from Belo Tsiribihina is Ankilizato (not to be confused with the town of the same name east of Morondava) which is 57km north of Belo. From there you must either walk (porters can be hired) or take an ox-cart the 24km to **Bekopaka**.

The effort is rewarded by the splendid *tsingy* and succulents growing in the crevices, not to mention lemurs and reptiles.

'We made our second visit to the *Tsingy* mid 1993. The area is now controlled by UNESCO. They charge a fee of 10,000fmg for one to two people and 15,000fmg for larger groups irrespective of how long you stay there. They have several different tours. The highlight for us was a trip up the Manambolo River to visit the Vazimba tombs. The *tsingy* forms spectacular cliffs along the river. On arrival at the tombs a ritual had to be performed: I had to ask the ancestors' permission for us to be there, and poured an offering of rum over the bones.' (R Harris & G Jackson)

Accommodation in Bekopaka is in four simple bungalows owned by the Ibraham family for 5,000fmg; breakfast 2,000fmg, meals 4,000fmg.

TRAVELLING BETWEEN MORONDAVA AND TOLIARA

Road   In the dry season, from April to the end of November, the venerable *Bon Bon Caramel*, a 25 year old green Mercedes truck, makes the journey between Morondava and Toliara. It leaves Morondava on Monday at 6.00, arriving Tuesday at about 17.00. The return from Toliara is Thursday at 6.00, arriving Friday evening. The night is spent in Manja (where there are bungalows and good food), or at the river some 80km from there (where you can sleep on the beach). 'It is reasonably well organised. The staff is trained on being stuck. Once *Bon Bon Caramel* was with one wheel at least one metre stuck in mud; they fixed it in 20 minutes!' (Luc Selleslagh)

If this all seems a bit soft and predictable, there is a taxi-brousse which makes the trip on Fridays.

Road-and-sea   You can find road transport between Morondava and Belo Sur Mer, and between Morombe to the Ifaty road-head north of Toliara. The sea stretch in the middle is done by pirogue. John Kupiec took the Friday taxi-brousse as far as the Vezo fishing village of Ankeva Sur Mer, then walked south along the beach for 16km to Belo Sur Mer (there was a pirogue-ferry to cross the river). In Belo John met a pirogue builder called Aime, who speaks English, and who took him to Morombe for 45,000fmg – a rough and rather dangerous trip, made more eventful by rescuing a family whose pirogue had capsized. From Morombe he found a taxi-brousse to Toliara. They leave at 02.00 and 04.00 (I'm afraid!). There may be others. The cost is 9,500fmg. If you don't find a vehicle going all the way, there is a hotely in Befandriana.

Here are some details for the journey when coming from Toliara: 'Taxi-brousse from Mora-Mora roadhead to Morombe, about 12 hours, pirogue/sail from Morombe to Morondava, 40,000 - 60,000fmg for one person excluding food and drink. The trip takes two days and one night. Contact "Serieux" through the Hotel Brillant in Morombe'. (Peter Mainwaring-Burton)

Morombe
Chris Ballance writes 'Morombe clearly died when the French left, but 9,000 souls remain and they spend their time walking up and down the main street, very slowly, shaking hands with each other and discussing the possibility that someone might build a proper road to them someday.'

Despite this, the town seems to be bursting with hotels, as well as having a smart BTM bank so you can pay for them.

Where to stay/eat
Hotel La Croix du Sud   BP 33; tel 56. 8 spacious rooms with bathrooms and hot water; restaurant. About 20,000fmg. Manager: Haidraly Tohora.

Hotel Baobab   14 concrete bungalows with lego-land style red, green and blue tiled roofs, on the shore on the south side of the town. Air-conditioning. Same management as Hotel La Croix du Sud. About 45,000fmg.

Hotel le Dattier   Reed huts for about 12,000fmg, 5 concrete and airless rooms 15,000fmg. No restaurant.

Hotel Mozambic   To the right of La Croix du Sud. 6 double rooms with shower.

Hotel Brillant   On the right of Hotel Dattier, 7 new wooden rooms with a poor restaurant and service.

Hotel Kuweit City   Very comfortable reed huts; best value in town: 4,000fmg.

40km south is Andavadoeka, 'the best beach in Madagascar'. Bungalows **Coco Beach**, under the same management as Hotels Baobab and Croix du Sud, provide excellent accommodation and diving/snorkelling.

Miandrivazo

Said to be the hottest place in Madagascar, with an average temperature of 28°C. The town lies on the banks of the Mahajilo, a tributary of the Tsirihina, and is an important centre for tobacco. 'The name comes from when Radama was waiting for his messenger to return with Rasalimo, the Sakalava princess of Malaimbandy with whom he had fallen in love. He fell into a pensive mood and when asked if he was well replied "Miandry vazo aho" – I am waiting for a wife.' (Raniero Leto).

It's a ten hour journey from Morondava by taxi-brousse, costing about 10,000fmg.

There is no bank in Miandrivaza.

Where to stay/eat

Hotel Chez la Reine Rasalimo   Concrete bungalows on a hill overlooking the river, 35,000fmg. Good restaurant.

Le Relais de Miandrivazo   BP 22. On the main square. 15,000fmg for basic but comfortable room. Reasonable food, good atmosphere.

Hotel Laizama   'A simple but homely hotel – we often found ducks in the shower – with very helpful management. 8,000fmg. We ate at the Buvette Espair in town. Meals must be booked in advance; great value for 2,000 to 3,000fmg for more than we could eat.' (R Harris & G Jackson)

Excursions

David Rasolofoarijaona, who can be found at Le Relais de Miandrivazo, runs a variety of tours.

RIVER TRIPS

The most popular river trip (arranged in Belo Tsiribihina or Miandrivazo) is down (or up) the Mahajilo and Tsirihina rivers. Several tour operators run this, and you can also organise it yourself. Expect to pay about 200,000fmg for a boat carrying up to four people, and add 20,000fmg for food.

We paid a fair price, 220,000fmg for four people (we had our own tent and food). Our paddler/guide was David Rakotovao who knew the river very well and spoke good French (no English) and could identify many of the birds. He can be reached at the Hotel Relais de Miandrivazo. Try to contact him beforehand (BP 22) with approximate arrival dates. The trip took us almost four days but was one of the highlights of our stay. The bird-life is phenomenal on this stretch and we saw many lemurs in the trees on the banks as well as chameleons and snakes. We camped on the beach at night, where it was too hot to use the tent – I simply arranged my mosquito net over my sleeping bag. A mosquito net is absolutely essential for this trip, and you need to bring fresh food and plenty of drinking water from Miandrivazo although of course you can purify or boil the river water. At the end of the wet season the trip changes dramatically: camping on the beach is impossible due to the high river so you walk to the nearest village. The trips are much shorter due to the faster-flowing river. Daniel said he had completed a trip in 2½ days.' (Leone Badenhorst)

If you are looking for something different, adventurous, but are not ready to go it alone, try one of the river trips run by Conrad Hirsh of Nairobi. Conrad takes small, informal groups down the rivers Manambolo (between Ankavandra – west of Tana – and Bekopaka) and Mangoky (between Beroroha – west of Fianar – to Lake Ihotry, which is east of Morombe). For more information write to Conrad Hirsh, Remote River Expeditions, Box 59622, Nairobi, Kenya. Fax: (254 2) 891 307.

THE GLOBETROTTERS CLUB

An international club which aims to share information on adventurous budget travel through monthly meetings and *Globe* magazine. Published every two months, *Globe* offers a wealth of information from reports of members' latest adventures to travel bargains and tips, plus the invaluable 'Mutual Aid' column where members can swap a house, sell a camper, find a travel companion or offer information on unusual places or hospitality to visiting members. London meetings are held monthly (Saturdays) and focus on a particular country or continent with illustrated talks.

Enquiries to: Globetrotters Club, BCM/Roving, London WC1N 3XX.

Bradt Publications
Travel Guides & Maps

——— Sales & Accounts ———
41 Nortoft Road · Chalfont St. Peter · Bucks · SL9 0LA · England Fax/Telephone: 0494 873478
——— Editorial Office: Hilary Bradt ———
Grey House (Flat) · Beeches Drive · Farnham Common · Bucks · SL2 3JU · England Fax/Telephone: 0753 646580

June 1994

Dear Readers

This book is a group effort. If it wasn't for all the wonderful letters I receive correcting, augmenting and updating the guide, I could never bring out new editions with so much fresh information and so many different viewpoints. Apart from the practical aspect, I love hearing from you and travelling vicariously in my favourite country through your descriptions.

I do hope you will write. The guide is updated every two years, so it will not be long before your information can be used.

Letters are welcome in any form (but please print place names – and your name and address – in handwritten ones) and give the dates that you were in Madagascar. If you want to be really helpful you could indicate on the maps the location of hotels and other recommended places. Please put your name at the top of each page in case they become separated.

Best wishes,

Hilay Bradt

Appendices

HISTORICAL CHRONOLOGY

Adapted from 'Madagascar, Island of the Ancestors' with kind permission of the author, John Mack

AD 500   Approximate date for the first significant settlement of the island.

800-900   Dates of the first identifiable village sites in the north of the island. Penetration of the interior begins in the south.

1200   Establishment of Arab settlements. First mosques built.

1500   'Discovery' of Madagascar by the Portuguese Diego Dias. Unsuccessful attempts to establish permanent European bases on the island followed.

1650s   Emergence of Sakalava Kingdoms.

Early 1700s   Eastern Madagascar is increasingly used as a base by pirates.

1716   Fénérive captured by Ratsimilaho. The beginnings of the Betsimisaraka confederacy.

1750   Death of Ratsimilaho.

1780   The future Andrianampoinimerina declared king of Ambohimanga.

1795/6   Andrianampoinimerina established his capital at Antananananarivo.

1810-28   Reign of Radama I, Merina king.

1818   First mission school opened at Tamatave.

1820   First mission school opened at Antananarivo.

1828-61	Reign of Ranavalona I, Merina queen.
1835	Publication of the bible in Malagasy, but profession of the Christian faith declared illegal.
1836	Most Europeans and missionaries leave the island.
1861-1863	Reign of Radama II, Merina king.
1861	Missionaries re-admitted. Freedom of religion proclaimed.
1863-8	Queen Rasoherina succeeds after Radama II assassinated.
1868-83	Reign of Queen Ranavalona II.
1883	Coronation of Queen Ranavalona III.
1883-1885	Franco-Malagasy War.
1895	Establishment of full French protectorate: Madagascar became a full colony the following year.
1897	Ranavalona III exiled first to Réunion and later Algiers. Merina monarchy abolished.
1917	Death of Ranavalona III in exile.
1942	British troops occupy Madagascar.
1947	Nationalist rebellion suppressed with many dead.
1958	Autonomy achieved within the French Community.
1960	Madagascar achieves full independence.
1972	General Ramanantsoa assumes power.
1975	Didier Ratsiraka first elected president.
1991	Demonstrations and strikes. Ratsiraka steps down.
1992	Albert Zafy elected president.
1993	The birth of the Third Republic.

BIBLIOGRAPHY

During the last two years I have completed a bibliography of Madagascar in the *World Bibliographical Series* for Clio Press, Oxford. This is a selection of nearly 400 titles on Madagascar, mainly in English but some in French, with a description and evaluation of each. In the selection below I have mostly picked those that are still in print and my favourites of the classic early works. The Clio bibliography is available by mail order from Bradt Publications. No Madophile should be without his/her own copy!

General — history, the country, the people

Bradt, H, editor. (1988). *Madagascar* (Exotic Lands series). Aston Publications (distributed by Bradt). Madagascar in colour photos.

Brown, M (1994). *A History of Madagascar*. D Tunnacliffe, UK. The most accurate, comprehensive and readable of the histories, brought completely up to date by Britain's foremost expert on the subject.

Covell, M (1987). *Madagascar: Politics, Economics and Society*. Frances Pinter, UK. (*Marxist Regimes* series.) An interesting look at Madagascar's Marxist past.

Crook, S (1990). *Distant Shores: by Traditional Canoe from Asia to Madagascar*. Impact Books, UK. The story of the 4,000 mile Sarimanok Expedition by outrigger canoe across the Indian Ocean from Bali to Madagascar. An interesting account of an eventful and historically important journey.

Drysdale, H (1991). *Dancing with the Dead: a journey through Zanzibar and Madagascar*. Hamish Hamilton, UK. An account of Helena's journeys in search of her trading ancestor. Informative, entertaining and well-written.

Ellis, W (1867). *Madagascar Revisited*. John Murray, UK. The Rev. William Ellis, of the LMS, was one of the most observant and sympathetic of the missionary writers. His books are well worth the search for second-hand copies.

Fox, L (1990). *Hainteny: the traditional poetry of Madagascar*. Associated University Presses, UK and Canada. Over 400 beautifully translated *hainteny* with an excellent introduction to the history and spiritual life of the Merina.

Lanting, F (1991). *Madagascar, a World out of Time*. Robert Hale, UK. A book of stunning, and somewhat surreal photos of the landscape, people and wildlife.

Murphy, D (1985). *Muddling through in Madagascar*. Murray, London. An entertaining account of a journey (by foot and truck) through the highlands and south.

Sibree, J (1896). *Madagascar before the conquest: the island, the country, and the people*. T Fisher Unwin, UK. With William Ellis, Sibree was the main documenter of Madagascar during the days of the London Missionary Society. He wrote many books on the island, all of which are perceptive, informative, and a pleasure to read.

Ethnology
Bloch, M (1986). *From Blessing to Violence*. Cambridge University Press, UK. History and ideology of the circumcision ritual of the Merina people.

Mack, J (1986). *Madagascar: Island of the Ancestors*. British Museum, London. A scholarly and informative account of the ethnography of Madagascar.

Mack, J (1989). *Malagasy Textiles*. Shire Publications, UK.

Powe, E L (1994). *Lore of Madagascar*. Dan Aiki Publications, USA. An immense work – over 700 pages and 260 colour photos – with a price to match: $300. This is the only book to describe in detail, and in a readable form, all 39 ethnic groups in Madagascar.

Sharp, L A (1993). *The possessed and the dispossessed: Spirits, identity and power in a Madagascar migrant town*. University of California Press, USA. Describes the daily life and the phenomenon of possession (tromba) in the town of Ambanja.

Wilson, P J (1993). *Freedom by a hair's breadth*. University of Michigan, USA. An anthropological study of the Tsimihety people, written in a clear style and accessible to the general reader.

Natural history
READILY ACCESSIBLE LITERATURE
Attenborough, D (1961). *Zoo Quest to Madagascar*. Lutterworth, UK. Still one of the best travel books ever written about Madagascar, with, of course, plenty of original wildlife observations. Out of print, but copies can be found.

Durrell, G (1992). *The Aye-aye and I*. HarperCollins, UK. The focal point is the collecting of aye-aye for the Jersey Zoo, written in the inimitable Durrell style with plenty of humour and traveller's tales.

Haltenorth T and Diller, H Trans. by Robert W Hayman (1980). *Field Guide to the Mammals of Africa including Madagascar*. Wm Collins & Son, UK. The illustrations are not accurate enough to be of much use in the field.

Jolly, A (1980). *A World Like Our Own: Man and Nature in Madagascar*. Yale University Press. The first and still the best look at the relationship between the natural history and people of the island. Highly readable.

Jolly, A, Oberle, P, and Albignac, R, Editors (1994). *Madagascar*. Pergamon Press, UK and Canada. This book in 'The Key Environments' series is mainly a translation of the French *Madagascar: Un Sanctuaire de la Nature*. Now a little dated, but nevertheless one of the best overviews of the natural history.

Langrand, O (1990). *Field Guide to the Birds of Madagascar*. Yale University Press, US & UK. A marvellously comprehensive guide to the island's birds and their distribution, behaviour and habitat. 40 colour plates.

Martin, J (1992). *Chameleons*. Facts on File, USA; Blandford, UK. Beautifully illustrated with photos by Art Wolfe; everything a chameleon aficionado could hope for.

Preston-Mafham, K. (1991). *Madagascar: A Natural History*. Facts on File, UK and US. The most enjoyable and useful book on the subject. Illustrated with superb colour photos (coffee-table format) it is as good at identifying strange invertebrates and unusual plants as in describing animal behaviour.

Wilson, J (1990). *Lemurs of the Lost World: Exploring the Forests and Crocodile Caves of Madagascar*. Impact Books, UK. An interesting and informative account of the Ankarana expedition and subsequent travels in Madagascar.

SPECIALIST LITERATURE

Harcourt, C (1990). *Lemurs of Madagascar and the Comoros*. IUCN, Cambridge. A Red Data book with scientific descriptions of all Madagascar's lemurs.

Hillerman, F E, & Holst, A W (1990). *An Introduction to the Cultivated Angraecoid orchids of Madagascar*. Timber Press, USA. The most accessible book covering the orchids of Madagascar, with a good section on climate and other plant life.

Jenkins, M D, editor. (1987). *Madagascar: An Environmental Profile*. IUCN, Gland, Switzerland and Cambridge, U.K. Descriptions of the nature reserves, with check-lists of flora and fauna.

Nicholl, M E & Langrand, O (1989). *Madagascar: Revue de la Conservation et des Aires Protégées*. WWF, Switzerland. Currently available only in French, but an English edition is in preparation. A detailed survey of the reserves studied by the WWF, lists of species, and excellent maps.

Richard-Vindard, G & Battistini, R (editors) (1972). *Biogeography and Ecology of Madagascar*. W Junk, Netherlands. Largely in English including chapters on geology, climate, flora, erosion, rodents and lemurs. Each chapter includes an extensive bibliography.

Tattersall, I (1981). *The Primates of Madagascar*. Columbia UP, US. A comprehensive description of the biology of Madagascar's lemurs.

MAP OF MADAGASCAR

We sell a good map of the country (scale 1:2,000,000). £5.95 from Bradt Publications, 41 Nortoft Road, Chalfont St Peter, Bucks SL9 0LA.

OTHER INDIAN OCEAN GUIDES FROM BRADT

Guide to Mauritius by Royston Ellis.
A complete guide to every aspect of Mauritius and its dependency, Rodrigues.

No Frills Guide to the Comoro Islands by Ian Thorpe.
Four seldom visited islands lying between Madagascar and Africa, rich in natural history and local culture.

AFRICA

Guide to South Africa by Philip Briggs.
Budget travel and bird-watching, walks and game parks, beaches and cities, suggested itineraries.

Guide to Namibia and Botswana by Simon Atkins and Chris McIntyre.
On and off the beaten track in these less-known countries.

Guide to Zimbabwe and Botswana by David Else.
Handy pocket-sized book for budget travellers, full of hard information on where to stay, what to see, and how to get around.

Africa Handbooks: Zaire, Malawi, Senegal, Ivory Coast.
Four pocket-sized guides to the less-visited countries of Africa.

Through Africa: the overlander's guide by Bob Swain and Paula Snyder.
Driving, motorcycling, or mountain-biking throughout the continent. Preparations, routes, campsites, travellers' tales.

Backpacker's Africa — East and Southern by Hilary Bradt.
Hiking and backpacking off the beaten track with an emphasis on natural history. Covers Eritrea, Ethiopia and Sudan, and countries south.

Guide to Zanzibar by David Else.
A detailed guide to the islands of Zanzibar and Pemba.

Guide to Mozambique by Bernhard Skrodzski
The first guide to this former Portuguese colony.

Guide to Tanzania by Philip Briggs
On and off the beaten track in every corner of the country.

Guide to Uganda by Philip Briggs
Includes gorilla viewing in Rwanda and Zaïre.

And then there's the rest of the world...
Send for a catalogue from Bradt Publications, 41 Nortoft Road, Chalfont St Peter, Bucks SL9 0LA, England. Tel/Fax 0494 873478

INDEX